Moving Deserts

Moving Deserts

Interrogating Development and Resilience in the Pastoral Drylands of
Northern Kenya

Greta Semplici

British Library Cataloguing in Publication Data
A catalogue record for this book is available from the British Library

ISBN: 978-1-912186-96-9 PB
        978-1-912186-97-6 Open Access ebook
doi: 10.63308/63891908548751.book

To my mother, who made me brave
To my father, who made me nomad
To Ekitela, who was there with me

Contents

Contents

Acknowledgements

Precious pages, the acknowledgments. This book is the result of five years of direct research and personal involvement and five more years of continued reflection. That is a long time. Time for many encounters, for many stories, adventures, crises, surprises. New friends, new mentors, new families, new homes. Indeed, a long journey. I will not be able to thank everyone who played a crucial role in these years. It is inevitable. But I trust that anyone who held my hand along this journey, offered some comfort, a meal or a glass of wine, a pair of ears, knows how grateful I am, and how much it helped. Now, I'll try to find some words to express my gratitude, hopefully with some laughter, as Turkana herders have taught me, next to what already feels like nostalgia.

A huge thank you goes to my host families during fieldwork, to my adopted mothers and fathers and all the siblings. For all the times you held my hands, showed me around; you taught me so much about life and hope and laughter, and all the practical stuff of life too. For all the times you let me make mistakes while watering livestock, milking goats, chopping firewood or weaving sticks for your huts. For all the times you waited for my slower pace. For all the times you took care of me. For all the times you decided to tell me a story regardless of my not understanding, regardless of the tiredness, regardless of all the differences. From that intention, I learnt, I felt, that we were family. The most special thank you is for you.

I am really grateful to my Ph.D. supervisors whose mentorship and support helped me persevere through all those years. Oliver Bakewell for seemingly never doubting and Naohiko Omata for stepping in as a second supervisor. His attention to detail and earth-grounded approach to my research helped me to remain anchored, to be more careful, and not to abuse metaphors!

There are some people I must then thank upfront because without them this work might not have existed. Matilde. It was 25 April, my favourite day of the year, 2015. I had just substantially changed my research project, and was starting to realise what it implied: following herders in a desert – and, admittedly, I was a little scared. With the most sincere, heartfelt and passionate look, she said: 'oh finally! Some real fieldwork!' I realised it too and humbly agreed. These words remained a mantra throughout. Then I must thank Alberto Salza. For my choice to go to Turkana I can only thank him. He, future mentor, source of inspiration, providing constant support and encouragement and challenging the limits of my imagination; he was right there when constellations turned, and I decided to go back to Kenya for my doctoral study. Master of space-time physics, he located himself in the right place at the right time and pushed me towards Turkana, and also never abandoned me. Thank you. And thank you also Gabriella for hosting and feeding me and having me around your magical house. Ekuri. We found each other in the most unlikely circumstances and you have been of profound, mutual and vital support ever since. Without your friendship, unconditional presence, intellectual stimulus (including disagreements) I would have not been able to bring this project to an end. Inspiration and support also came from the network of pastoralism scholars I met along this long journey; they immediately transmitted a sense of family. In particular, the Commission on Nomadic People (Saverio Krätli, Ariell Ahearn, Dawn Chatty and many others), and the PASTRES family (Michele Nori, Ian Scoones, Linda Pappagallo, Natasha Maru, Giulia Simula, Tahira Shariff, Masresha Taye, Palden Tsering, Ryan Unks).

My greatest appreciation and obligation go to my research assistants (all of them!): Ejore, Lokaale, Erus, Ewal, Ewoton, Jerhemaya, Nehemaya. However complicated our work-relationships were, without your help, careful translation and logistical support, I would have not been able to carry out this work. Thank you for your time, patience, endurance and companionship. Especially, I would like to thank Peter Ewoton who kept on teaching me, being curious about and committed to this study, sending me news and updates, and helping me even past fieldwork. Together, we learnt to be strong while keeping walking.

For all the homes and families I found along this journey. Thank you, Erika, and Naroa for the heart-stopping love and support. Thank you for giving me a home in Nairobi and making me feel part of Doa. I wish to thank the Startup Lion family in Lodwar too. Thank you, Ludwig, Tony, Charlotte, Wilhelm, for accepting me in your house and sharing your daily lives with me, and Jan for not losing track. Whoever knows me, knows how important talking about homes is for me. I learnt the significance and meaning of home through my homes in Oxford. Thank you to Nora and Caitlin for building a magic nest where we could find refuge together after our fieldwork. Thank you for choosing me and waiting for me and always being there. Thank you to Maayan and Almut for making our nest even more a nest, even more a refuge. For making me postpone my departure so many times, because it was so hard to imagine not living with you. For the cowleyflours, the Drink&Draw evenings, Pocahontas, the puzzles, the mattresses and the spiders :) for everything that has 'a life, a spirit, a name', and all the sage! Thank you, to all of you, for being family.

Acknowledgements

I am now struggling to find words to conclude. Thank you Ekitela for having shared surreal parts of this journey, heavy luggage and modest meals with me. For the sense of protection, treasuring presence and care, for having been home.

Finally, to my father and my mother. To both of you, thank you for supporting me and letting me explore and go. For being the bravest parents in the world, my source of inspiration and the greatest love.

List of figures

All photographs by the author

List of figures

List of tables

Acronyms

AGIR	Global Alliance for Resilience Initiative
ALRMP	Arid Lands Resource Management Project
ASALs	Arid and Semi-Arid lands
ASAUK	African Studies Association of the UK
ASP	Arid Land Support Programme
AU	African Union
BMU	Beach Management Units
CIDP	County Integrated Development Plan
DFID	Department for International Development (Gov.UK)
DMP	Drought Monitoring Project
DPIRP	Drought Preparedness Intervention and Recovery Programme
DRM	Disaster Risk Management
DRR	Disaster Risk Reduction
ECHO	European Commission Humanitarian Aid and Civil Protection Office
EDE	Ending Drought Emergency
EU	European Union
FA	Factor analysis
FAO	Food and Agriculture Organization of the United Nations
FAI	Italian Aid Fund
GPS	Global Positioning System
HFA	Hyogo Framework for Action
HoA	Horn of Africa
HSNP	Hunger and Safety Net Programme
IDDRSI	Drought Disaster Resilience Sustainability Initiative
IFAD	International Fund for Agricultural Development
IGAD	Intergovernmental Authority on Development
ILRI	International Livestock Research Institute
IUAES	International Union of Anthropological and Ethnological Studies
IUCN	International Union for Conservation of Nature
KEMFRI	Kenya Marine and Fisheries Research Institute
LAPSET	Lamu Port and Lamu-Southern Sudan-Ethiopia Transport Corridor
LRRD	Linking Relief, Rehabilitation and Development
M&E	Monitoring and Evaluation
MDGs	Millennium Development Goals

Acronyms

NDMA	National Drought Management Authority
NGOs	Non-governmental organisations
NORAD	Norwegian Agency for Development Co-operation
NRT	Northern Rangelands Trust
OCHA	United Nations Office for the Coordination of Humanitarian Affairs
ODI	Overseas Development Institute
ODID	Oxford Department of International Development
OECD	Organisation for Economic Cooperation and Development
SDGs	Sustainable Development Goals
SES	Socio Ecological System
SFDRR	Sendai Framework for Disaster Risk Reduction
SIDA	Swedish International Development Cooperation Agency
SLA	Sustainable Livelihood Approach
SLF	Sustainable Livelihood Framework
SRC	Stockholm Resilience Centre
TRP	Turkana Rehabilitation Project
UN	United Nations
USA	United States of America
UNCOD	United Nation Conference on Desertification
UNDP	United Nations Development Programme
UNESCO	United Nations Educational, Scientific and Cultural Organization
UNICEF	United Nations Children's Fund
UK	United Kingdom
USAID	U.S. Agency for International Development
VSF	Veterinarie Sans Frontieres
WB	World Bank
WFP	World Food programme
WCDRR	World Conference on Disaster Risk Reduction
WFP	World Food Programme

Turkana vocabulary

Abarait	Circular knife
Abor	Temporary satellite camp
Aburo	Herder's staff
Abwo	Front skirt (from livestock hides)
Achoan	The capacity for inventive thought and quick understanding, keen intelligence
Adakae	Sediment or residuals of local brew from fermented sorghum or maize
Adakar	Neighbourhood based on relationship
Adwel	Back skirt (from livestock hides)
Agata	Prayer
Agulu	Clay pot
Aite	Cow
Akaloboch	Wooden spoon
Akamu	Dry season, drought
Akidedet	Butterfat
Akigum	Livestock bleeding practice: small incision close to the nose for shoats and on the neck for cows and camels
Akiit	To be observant
Akilip	To ask for something
Akimad	Healing process though burning
Akimiet	Ghee
Akimookin	To stay still, to be immobile
Akine	Goat (used also generally for small livestock)
Akiporo	Rainy season, especially when corresponding to plenty of grass for livestock
Akireb	To scout
Akiriket	Meat ceremony
Akiring	Meat
Akiru	Rain
Akoloch	Calf teeth
Akoro	Hunger
Akuj	A monotheistic divinity, God
Akurum	Calabash
Akuuta	Wedding
Akutwam	Calabash
Akigum	The practice of puncturing animals to take blood
Akilip	To ask for something
Akwap	Unbounded place
Alagai	Necklace
Alaar	Homestead fences
Alagama	Aluminium ring (for married woman)
Alogita	Age group dances
Amok	Ritual performed to leave 'bad things' behind. For example, after a healing process or to restore the path of tradition when norms have been violated. It is instructed by a local seer
Anaikis nghichan	Going through, adjusting, overcoming problems

Turkana vocabulary

Anok	Kraal, enclosure for livestock for night protection
Aperor	To visit
Apol	Part of the kidney, muscles, and fat cut from the hip of an animal; each clan cuts this part of an animal in different ways during *akiring* (meat ceremony)
Arigan	A composite migration unit
Aruak	Fat from a cow's stomach
Aruba	Belt
Arumrum	Defence cluster
Asapan	Initiation ceremony
Asajait	donkey saddle for transporting belongings
Atap	Ugali, local dough made from maize flour
Ateker	Ethnic group composed of Karamojong, Jie and Dodos of Uganda; Taposa and Jiye of southern Sudan; Nyangatom of Ethiopia; Turkana of Kenya
Atoroth	Wooden container
Atubwa	Wooden bowl
Awi a ng'orot	Home of long ago
Awi	Household
Baraza	Village meeting
Boma	Homestead (Kiswahili)
Ebela (or akeat)	Walking stick for women (depending on her brand/clan)
Ebob	Delicious, (sweet!)
Ebur	Wood container
Echuka	Maasai blanket (derived from Kiswahili)

Edeke	Disease
Edeke a akuj	Disease of God
– a ngikapilak	Diseases of witches
– a Ngi'turkana	Diseases of the Turkana
Edodo	Dry milk
Edonga	Village dances
Egech	Stirring stick
Egolos	Long front-dress made of livestock hides
Ejomu	Livestock hides/ mat made of animal skin
Ekaal	Camel
Ekapilan	Healer, witch
Ekaru	Year
Ekaru a korie	The year of something colourful
– a Red-Cross	The year of the Red Cross
– a wimbi	The year of millet
– adicho a anyang	The year of yellow maize powder with egg yolk
– amuja kimet	The year to eat fat
– ekalakal	The year of sacks
– emuudu	The year when everything finished
Ekebotoonit	Someone who has no animals (used to indicate someone who is poor)
Ekechodon	Temporary lack of animals (used to indicate someone who is poor)
Ekedalan	An employee you hire to help take care of your livestock, someone who does not have livestock
Ekeriau	*Cyperus articulates*
Ekicholong	Stool
Ekilton	Type of edible shrubs
Ekitela	Territorial section *(pl. Ngitela)*

Turkana vocabulary

Ekol	Sleeping hut	*Esebo*	Hunting club
Ekuwom	Wind	*Etaba*	Tobacco (derived from Kiswahili)
Ekude	Headband		
Ekwar	Land	*Ethekon*	*Salvadora persica*, or toothbrush tree
Elado	Whisk made from cow's or camel's tail		
		Ethikiria	Donkeys
Eleu	Long skirt sewed together from multiple hides differently patterned	*Etid*	Spleen
		Etirae	*Prosopis (pl. Natirae)*
		Etio	Gourd
Elepit	Milking can/jar	*Ewoi*	Acacia
Elongait	Someone who has no relatives (used to indicate someone who is poor)	*Ewote*	To migrate with livestock, migration
Eloto	Ritual of asking a woman for marriage	*Fagy* fish	Spoilt fish sold along the lake shores to be used as chicken food
Emachar	Clan, or livestock brand	*Githeri*	Mix of beans and maize (Kiswahili)
Emoit	Enemy – expression used to indicate other pastoral groups who are contending for vegetation resources, water and livestock, as well as white or African foreigners, non-Turkana	*Hoteli*	Restaurants
		Loline	A village that developed along a road
		Longapen	Disease of craziness, described when people start running around naked, jumping on people's huts, and talking nonsense
Emuna	Mixes of wild fruits and animal fat		
Emoru	Mountain or rock	*Lorara*	a name of a month
Emuron	Seer *(pl. ngimurok)*	*Magadi*	Dry salt
Engol	Palm tree	*Mandeleo*	Development (Kiswahili)
Enyath	Fried meat	*Mkeka*	Mat (Kiswahili)
Epeduru	Tamarid tree	*Mzungu*	White foreigner (Kiswahili)
Epocho	Ground maize-flour		
Ere	Broadly translated into 'home-area' (Müller-Dempf 2014); it is often referred by the Turkana as the 'father's land', the 'place where one was born' and the 'place to always return'	*Mwarobaini*	Neem tree (Kiswahili)
		Mzee	Old man, or Head of Household
		Namanang	Lactating animals
		Nakhaabaran	Salty water
		Ng'agario na ngorok	Cows with black and white patches
Erot	Path *(pl. ng'irotin)*	*Ng'abwelin*	Pools of water

Turkana vocabulary

Ng'ageran	Scarification
Ng'akoromwa	Beads
Ng'alup	Soil
Ng'ichok	Seeds
Ng'ichwei	Sacks made of livestock hides
Ng'imeramuk	The clan who wear crocodile sandals
Ng'imor	Age-set stones
Ng'ipian	Evil spirits
Ng'irithai	Age-set leopards
Ng'irupei	Short showers of rain
Ng'iturkana	Turkana people, literally: 'people of the caves'.
Ng'achoto	Dry cow urine-grains
Ng'akile	Milk
Ng'akibuk	Sour milk
Ng'akoromwa	Necklace
Ng'ing'alur	Kidneys
Ng'itit	Acacia pods

Ng'iukoi	Lungs
Ngujit	Chyme
Raiya	An expression which indicates belonging to a livelihood group (herders) but also to a lifestyle, aesthetics, and code of behaviour
Royco	Cube stock
Shamba	Garden (Kiswahili)
Sukuma	Kale (Kiswahili)
Unga	Flour (Kiswahili)
Wazungu	White foreigners (Kiswahili)

Edung, Engomo, Edome, Epat, Ng'akalalio: Some wild fruit.

Lokwan, Lodunge, Lomaru, Titima, El El, Lochoto, Losuban, Lotiak, Lomuk, Lopoo, Lorara, Lolongu: Months from seasonal calendar

Note on data reference and text

The empirical chapters two, three, four and five draw on a combination of field notes, field diaries, recorded conversations and interviews. Verbatim phrases that are included in the main text are enclosed in single quote marks. Longer quotes are separated from the main text in a new, indented, line.

The book is typeset in Adobe Garamond Pro (main text) and *Adobe Garamond Pro Semibold Italic* (unfolding storyline). Headings and captions are in **Gill Sans**.

Acronyms for field data reference

FD	Field Diary
FGD	Focus Group Discussion
FN	Field Note
HH	Household Interview
KI	Key Informant Interview
SSI	Semi Structured Interviews

∼ Thinking like a desert. ∼

Foreword by Alberto Salza

You can always come back, but you can't come back all the way.
Only one thing I did wrong, stayed in Mississippi a day too long.

BOB DYLAN[1]

Butterflies. Two white butterflies. You see them just because of the flicker of wings on a typical Turkanaland visual background: greyish sand. Remember – when acting in a desert, any movement means life. Not necessarily yours, but go and check.

Kneel down. With thumb and index finger, feel the sand's texture. The desert talks, if you listen. These grains of sand are not rounded but slightly sharp. 'Not wind, but water is the stone artisan here', says the dry river bed I'm in. So I start digging with my hands, chasing the butterflies away. And some water gurgles up. Be calm: throw the water away – it's brown and dirty. Wait.

The crypto-ecosystem around Lake Turkana, in northern Kenya, is made out of subterranean rivers and hidden resources: rhizomes, precious stones, nutrients, viruses, parasites, bulbs, fossils, who knows what. But water got to this sand – maybe after some months of crypto-flow – from a faraway place where rain eventually fell, got here just in time to be felt in the air by two humidity-sensitive butterflies. Spotted by a thirsty me.

In this sort of communicating desert, the water-related operational algorithm is: find, dig, throw, wait, repeat the sequence three times to get clean water. Then drink. 'No, you don't', said Lepukei, my life-coach number 2 some fifty years ago (the first ones were a band of G/i San of the Central Kalahari). 'Before, rinse your mouth: most of thirst is on the tongue. Then rinse again. Now drink. Slowly.' This harsh tutor and bush-lore master was a young Turkana man, half herder and half apprentice boat-driver. As a man of both cultures, for about forty years he kept saving my life on many occasions, but I didn't notice most of the time. Stupid of me: now he's dead.

On that butterfly morning I followed his teachings: first rinse twice, then drink. And I walked back to camp. Lepukei was busy packing. His friend Eregai,

---

1.   Robert Zimmerman, 'Mississippi', *Love And Theft*, track 2 (2001).

doi: 10.63308/63891908548751.fore

whose name in Turkana means *Acacia reficiens*,[2] was rounding up goats and sheep. I used to think of him as 'the donkey man' because he spent hours amongst our pack animals, talking with them. Out of kindness, I suppose. In Turkanaland – like everywhere long-range nomadism is the main survival strategy – the borders between species and classes, even between man and animal, are lines of fusion, not fission.[3]

'I found good water. What's up?' asked I (no pun intended: in those days there were no mobile phones or apps). 'This place stinks like old', replied Lepukei. 'Let's get away from here. We stayed a day too long'. I sort of realised that stale smoke, droppings or garbage trigger the nomadic behaviour. It's style, not survival.

Now imagine that you are walking at a 102 steps per minute (dromedaries go at 74, according to my counts in the Sahara)[4] on small, black lava stones over a flat sandy plain, up to the horizon. You have to choose: look down to where you put your 'rubbers' (recycled-tyre sandals), or up to the sky for signs of rain. Stumble. Remove the stones on the pathway, with some respect: minerals move in Turkanaland, displaced by water, wind, gravity or men. In this place, a microscope isn't the best instrument to take a good look around you. So scan 360 degrees. Vary scale. Perception is not passive, something that happens to you or in you: it's movement and interaction, both directed by a pre-structured brain. Perceptual content has an intrinsically perspectival aspect,[5] fundamental in this book, where the imperative to 'see like a herder' is a high pitch mantra.

While enacting perception in Turkanaland, all your six senses are involved in crucial information-gathering and decision-making: sight for clouds and dangers, smell for wild foods, stereo hearing and tuning for wind direction, touch for soil texture, taste for water and grass palatability, proprioception[6] for correctly situating your body in a mobile horizon. You *are* the ecosystem, and you act as its living sensor. This applies to all living organisms and abiotic elements of the desert landscape.

2.　Malcolm Coe and Henk Beentje, *A Field Guide to the Acacias of Kenya*, pp. 116–17 (Oxford: Oxford University Press, 1991).

3.　Edmund Carpenter, Anne Bahnson, Miknhail Bronshtein, Kirill Dneprovsky, Ann Fienup-Riordan, Robert McGhee and Patricia Sutherland, *Upside Down: Arctic Realities*, pp. 16–17 (New Haven: Yale University Press, 2011).

4.　Alberto Salza, 'Le strade del deserto', *Airone* 217 (May 1999): 88.

5.　Alva Noë, *Action in Perception* (Cambridge (Mass.): MIT Press, 2004), pp. 2, 70.

6.　The sense of awareness of our body's position and movement in space, to know where our limbs and body are. See John C. Tuthill and Eiman Azim, 'Proprioception', *Current Biology* **28** (5) (2018): 194–203.

First, take a look at grass, the limiting factor for pastoralists. For them, Turkana included, grass is poly-dimensional and moving. Rhizomes are underground, where grass eats and drinks. Above ground level, grass stems have two volumes: the upper one is for browsers like goats; the inferior layer is for grazers, sheep. Therefore, goats must get to grass before sheep. Forget about camels: they eat leaves from acacias: haven't they got a long neck, like giraffe? Obviously, herders move to pasture where grass is plenty. But it may happen the opposite way. When animals go back to camp after eating their favourite grass, they carry with them grass seeds in their droppings and hair. So, the most palatable grass moves back and forth, colonising the pastoral area.

Second, look after rocks and stones, the underestimated limiting factors regarding access to pasture. While walking, herders use their staffs to remove stony obstacles and open easy and safe pathways for their flocks. Sometimes – in specific places I never managed to receive consonant information about the reason behind the choice – the Turkana pick up some stones and place them on top of a sort of cairn. They always invite me to do the same. Nice practice, going back to prehistory.

Turkanaland is one of the places with the highest chrono-diversity (in analogy with biodiversity) on Earth: from hominins of six million years ago to third millennium remote workers, in continuity. Since the Upper Palaeolithic, throughout the world, rocks had a poietic agency for *Homo sapiens*.[7] By inspiring awe they still can initiate psycho-physical interactions in selecting places for marking territory by means of signs, symbols, paintings, engravings, cult sites, monuments. For instance, in the Turkana Basin, local people refer to some megalithic structures as *Namorutunga* ('people of stone'), attributed to a hypothetical 'ancient tribe'. As I have experienced in many places, from the Saharan Ennedi to the Mexican Wirikuta desert, from the Somali Ogaden plateau to the many rock-art sites I discovered in Turkanaland, the field specific dispositions of rock formations catalyse, mould and scaffold the behaviour of other agents, humans and animals alike.

Therefore, take care of rocks and stones will take care of you. One day I was trying to make a stone tool, striking and chipping to no avail. After a noisy while, Lepukei asked me: 'Why are you disturbing that stone?' He literally meant it. In the Turkana language the word *moru* means 'stone' or 'mountain', in a fractal topologic gradient. But *moru* is also used to describe one of the moieties that

---

7. Shumon T. Hussain, 'The animal within: The triple inheritance of late Pleistocene rock art', in M. Haidle, S. Wolf and M. Porr (eds), *Images, Gestures, Voices, Lives. What Can We Learn from Palaeolithic Art?* (Heidelberg: Heidelberg University Publishing, 2018), p. 8.

divide all Turkana males in *Ngirisae* (leopards) and *Ngimoru* (stones/mountains).[8] So Lepukei, an *emorut* (singular), was identifying himself with the poor stone I was massacring. And, thinking like a stone, he wanted to protect it.[9] Forget about leopards: I never saw one in Turkanaland, but they saw me for sure.

Like these stories, *Moving Deserts* is about a certain number and type of Turkana persons: no Turkana would admit excessive similitude to any other individual, far less to this book's author, a European researcher, and a girl. Like I realised after so many years, all field ethnology you can get from people like the Turkana is what quantum mechanics defines as *ansatz*: an educated guess, to be later verified. But that's a theoretical impossibility: people continuously change in a feedback relationship with their environment, time and events. The Turkana met by any researcher are no longer there and then, for sure.

Notwithstanding all odds and difficulties, this book by Greta Semplici, Ph.D. in International Development, shows that a mental and physical full immersion among the Turkana can bring illumination about some of the most sensitive topics in social and natural sciences of our times: a) Are we a different entity from the environment we live in? b) Are drylands and their intrinsic tendency to non-equilibrium states an option for the future? c) Is nomadic pastoralism viable? In case of disasters, can we consider resilience a survival tool? d) Is it possible to enact the scenario 'looking like a herder'? Let's try to move deserts and be moved by them.

Consider this: drylands, the places the Turkana live in, are bad guys. A desert is a desert, full stop; as a Tuareg told me about the Sahara: 'You can't live in it. You just cross it'. Drylands are tricky: while the desert repels you, drylands lure you in. All in all, there are trees with green leaves (some of them mutated to poisonous thorns), bushes, grass (not all the time or everywhere), animals of all kinds and size, from insects (too many) to elephants (still alive on the eastern Turkana shores in the 1960s), water here and there, a rich crypto-environment (well hidden); and, wow, sometimes it rains.

Drylands have the bad reputation of being a dangerous human terrain, a shatter zone for borderline people (BEWARE OF NOMADS). Taken as a whole organism, drylands reveal an interesting sentiment: while walking in their conditions,

---

8.   Boniface Korobe, 'Dynamics of Turkana socio-political organization and implications on internal and external relations: an analysis of the moiety and age-set aystem', *Journal of African Interdisciplinary Studies* 5 (10) (2021): 22.

9.   For the blurred and variant relationship between humans and the biotic and abiotic elements of an environment, see Eduardo Kohn, *How Forests Think: Toward an Anthropology beyond the Human* (Berkeley and Los Angeles: University of California Press, 2013).

pain is inevitable, but suffering is optional.[10] This comes from their being VUCA: Volatile, Uncertain, Complex, Ambiguous. Consider that, at the end of the twentieth century, a deep survey of the Turkana District (now a County) highlighted an intricate environmental mosaic, with thirty vegetation types and 25 range units.[11] Turkana herders and their livestock, being fully nomadic, could then choose from a menu that went from evergreen forest to woodland, from bushland to grassland, from shrubland to a grass-shrub-bush mix; and from all ecotones in between, to end with a des(s)ert: what ecologists briefly call 'barren', like the Suguta valley and part of Kerio plateau. Ever been on Mars? These are some of the more desolate areas of the Planet, but even there I always met a few Turkana herders with their animals (or vice versa). Most probably, today's modernity and oddities may have changed the situation from a manageable – and helpful, as demonstrated in this book – probabilistic uncertainty[12] to an extreme weirdness,[13] conditions that are going to shape our postnormal future.

A great part of the Turkana, according to the author of this book, are still clinging to their old customs, and indeed it's valuable describing them from within. But they are antifragile,[14] a word I prefer to the buzzing 'resilience' narrative that – although critically – plays a great role throughout Semplici's analysis. When I tried to explain the concept of resilience by crushing a plastic bottle, Eyepan, the most elegant Turkana I travelled with (ostrich feathers and all), looked at the result of my experiment and pronounced: 'Who wants to bounce back? Let's move ahead'. Being antifragile means to jump on occasions, adapt behaviours, exapt errors, evolve.

So the new Turkana follow the communication lines to found ephemeral villages (*lolines*) in order to intercept aid or take refuge from raiders. Like Kalashnikovs – today endemic as a new species of birds – smartphones are ubiquitous, to

---

10. From Haruki Murakami, *What I Talk About When I Talk About Running* (New York: Knopf, 2008).

11. Dennis Helocker, Salim B. Shaabani and Sybella Wilkes (eds), *Range Management Handbook of Kenya Vol II, 9. Turkana District* (Nairobi: Ministry of Agriculture, Livestock Development and Market, 1994), pp. 40–74 and 119–48.

12. David Lindley, *Uncertainty. Einstein, Heisenberg, Bohr, and the Struggle for the Soul of Science* (New York: Doubleday, 2007).

13. Christopher B. Jones, 'When things fall apart: Global weirding, postnormal times, and complexity limits', in L.A. Wilson and C.N. Stevenson (eds), *Building Sustainability Through Environmental Education*, Ch. 7 (Hershey: IGI Global, 2019).

14. Something or somebody that gets stronger when stressed or deformed; see Nassim N. Taleb, *Antifragile: Things That Gain from Disorder* (New York: Random House, 2012).

the point that I propose to change the SES (Social-Ecological System) paradigm to SEDS, adding the digital component. Turkana youth are disintegrating gerontocracy. Elders are living meteo-stations, but inertial: maybe the air is a bit hotter, the wind is coming from the wrong direction, leaves are less nutritious, wild fruit is becoming unavailable, and the rain season is too late, but the elders' thoughts and decisions are still far from global warming risk prevention. On the other hand, if you literally keep on surfing the fourteen million year old continental drift (Lake Turkana is just inside the Great African Rift Valley), and you live off uncertainty,[15] who cares about climate change?

This carelessness towards physical consequences from a negatively acting landscape (impermanent, transitory, and of all kinds according to Dr Semplici and myself: lifescape, bodyscape, desertscape, etc.) leads us to another key topic of *Moving Deserts*: food or, worse, 'no food'. The Turkana live continuously saying *akoro*, 'I'm hungry', no matter if they are or not. That's confusing, I admit, but consider this: it's a way of life, not a gastric condition. On the same wavelength with Semplici, the only way I found to align to this systemic hunger is to show off, and pretend that you're able to stay without food just like any other decent Turkana begging for food.

There are exceptions, though meagre. One day, while passing from the Suguta Valley to the Loriu Plateau, we finished all food: you are not supposed to carry it (such a shame!), but to find it wherever you go. Where zero is the number, none is the total. So, Lepukei and I launched a meticulous search for roots and berries. Wrong season. No herders around and, anyway, they wouldn't sell their animals; for sure not here, at a ten-day forced march to the first place where inedible money would mean a trifle. Then we saw a thin smoke coming from where we left Lekokoine, a very old Turkana who had served as a scout for the British Army. We ran back and found him stirring something inside a pot: two dried-up goat hooves, leftover aeons before. 'Have some soup', said he with grandeur.

I'm a hybrid scientist and a wayfaring alien. I know that, in Turkanaland like everywhere, my only means of survival are relationships. Obviously with people, but also with non-human selves and agents. As far as I know, recent genomics research

---

15. Saverio Krätli and Nikolaus Schareika, "Living *off* uncertainty: The intelligent animal production of drylands pastoralists', *The European Journal of Development Research* 22 (5) (2010): 605–22.

is exploring the possibility that evolution, in human and non-human animals, selects not simple individuals or genes, but systemic relation-webs.[16]

Dr Greta Semplici and I have never been wayfaring together; nor sat around a campfire dreading the sunset because of night's incoming noises and shining eyes; nor drunk raw blood from the same bowl; nor helped each other in piercing a sheep belly to prevent deadly bloating after wet grass eating. Of course, I never wore a rawhide skirt (tanned with brain-fat and urine), but she might not have spent a night watching the sky with a bunch of Turkana cosmic war fans, betting on the probability that a satellite might happily crash against one of the million stars; or tried to remember the results of our last bone densitometry, bouncing in the back of a pick-up while crossing the corrugated roads of Turkanaland. No, but we talked a lot, from the very beginning of her experience among the Turkana, throughout her research (common ground for the above-mentioned disasters), and up to the writing of these *Moving Deserts*.

Most of the time, we've been talking drylandese, a trans-species pidgin[17] that takes into account also the intentionality of non-human entities like grass, hyenas or rocks, a conceptual terrain we don't even have a vocabulary for[18]. Yet.

Hey girl, how does it feel to be like a rolling stone?[19]

Alberto Salza, Stuck in Turin, Italy, May 2025

---

16. Nicholas A. Christakisa and James H. Fowler, 'Friendship and natural selection', *PNAS* **111** suppl. 3 (2014): 10796–801.

17. Kohn, *How Forests Think*, p. 205.

18. Amitav Gosh, *Smoke and Ashes: Opium's Hidden Histories*, Ch. 3 (London: John Murray, 2023).

19. Obvious reference to Bob Dylan's 'Like a Rolling Stone', from *Highway 61 Revisited*, track 1 (1965).

～ Prologue ～

The woods are lovely, dark and deep,
but I have promises to keep,
and miles to go before I sleep.

ROBERT FROST (1923)

Where: from Lokiriama, at the Uganda–Kenya border, to Urum, a village in Loima subcounty.

When: the night of 21 December 2016.

Who: myself, a researcher from Oxford, two assistants (one originally from Loima and one from the shores of lake Turkana), a border patrol officer, a lorry driver, two Turkana boys and a dik-dik.

Why: to reach Urum, in order to continue field research among the Turkana herders.

The girl looks back to Uganda, then south-east; her two assistants slouch under a thorn tree. One is sick, maybe with malaria. The border patrol, at the last checkpoint before entering Uganda, tells her they cannot stay there; the night is approaching, and they do not want to be disturbed by her presence. So, they stop a lorry. The lorry driver is a smuggler of beers (Senators) from Uganda to Kenya. He hates having passengers (let alone a white girl), but he cannot refuse the patrol, and he is going to Kakuma along the same rough road which cuts through Urum. They agree on a fee that she will pay for each passenger. Everybody gets on board. The girl squeezes inside the cabin, between the Ugandan driver and the ill assistant, while the other assistant holds on to the luggage on top of the illicit cargo. Off they go.
They enter the landscape: barren hills, dry riverbeds, sparse thorny bush, deep ravines, scattered lava rocks, stony flats, patches of dried up, half chewed grass. The lorry whips up gusts of dust that stay in the air like whirlwinds. Locals refer to them as ng'ipean *(malevolent spirits). These are the drylands.*
The night falls like the sun had a heart attack. Perceiving the drylands-in-black, the girl is alerted to new senses: ups and downs, bumps, nausea, banging metal/ rocks, hurting body-parts, the intoxicating smell of fuel, temperature variations,

doi: 10.63308/63891908548751.prol

horrible sounds from the battered lorry, maybe a complaint from the assistant or curses from the driver. The sky is pitch black, and the stars are like sharp holes of light. No thirst nor hunger. They have not eaten the whole day and it is impossible to drink with the bumpy movement of the lorry; but who cares in the drylands? The girl starts dozing; it is inevitable. Maybe the driver too, but nobody would notice. A stone hits the metal under her seat and wakes her up. She opens her eyes and sees it: they are passing Urum, full speed. She recognises the blue roof of the primary school. In a mixed English and Swahili, she shouts to the driver to stop, that they have arrived. The driver says he is no taxi. Dark drylands are eating Urum up, fast. The girl leans on the driver and grabs the key from the ignition. The lorry stops, the driver swears, she turns to her left, opens the passenger door, holds and pushes her assistant down the truck, and screams at the second assistant to throw down all their luggage (including: 50 kg of beans, 20 kg of maize, 10 kg of rice, 5 kg of tobacco, 5 kg of sugar, plenty of tea leaves, some empty jerrycans) and to jump down himself; quick! She hears the driver swearing; his door opening and shutting noisily. His first steps.

Total silence. The night suddenly becomes still.

In the cloud of dust thrown up by the sudden stop, two lights appear from the bush. They look like the eyes of an alien moving in a desert storm. No, they are modernised drylands dwellers: two very young Turkana boys with bows and arrows. They hold a dead dik-dik they just hunted. They are stark naked, with headlamps on their forehead.

The Ugandan driver, the two assistants, the young researcher, the two Turkana boys, and it seems even the dead dik-dik, all face a few seconds of incredulity. Also, the two boys blind everybody, slicing the pitch-black night with their headtorch. Then, they all wake up (except the dik-dik). Together with the two assistants, the young girl gathers the luggage, tries to calm the driver, gives him the promised fees for the lift and, as quickly as possible (despite the heavy luggage) starts walking towards the primary school. The two Turkana boys pay no attention to her: they head to the driver.

The girl and the two research assistants walk following the smell of dung (where else?) towards the crowded huts of the village, ghastly lit by the first green light of dawn. Smoke is twirling in the air, metal cattle-bells tinkle and lambs bleat for milk. The last image, turning backwards: the two boys are selling the dik-dik to the Ugandan driver; they shout for more money. Then the morning comes.

An outsider's view as a comment

In the real-life episode narrated above, all actors are outsiders: the research girl is me, a second year doctoral student beginning her fieldwork with the Turkana herders, I had never been in Turkana before and had no previous experience with pastoral cultures; the border patrol, the Ugandan driver, the assistants (educated Turkana youths), even the two young Turkana boys, herders and hunters, naked but with quite a modern torch and a keen sense for business and cash. All characters, in their *alienness*, show flexibility, adaptation, shock absorbance, innovation, recovery and mobility: they are, in other words, resilient.

The resolution of the episode came after the girl suddenly stopped the movement of the lorry; but it was only enabled by the successive micro-movements generated by the trigger-action. Pastoralism is in the background, at dawn: Urum as a lifescape (the locus of livelihoods), with smell, smoke and sounds. The bleating and the bells tell a tale of livestock rearing; Urum as a landscape (an ever-changing dryland, in colour, shape, smell, vegetation); Urum as a bodyscape (the body of the actors in the drylands, and the body of drylands too).

This book tells a story of continuous movement. Mobility on foot, by lorry, inside the mind, over a hidden socio-geography, going from household to household, along dry creeks, plains, mountains and lake shores. To understand movement as a foundational act of resilience, this book unfolds along a journey that takes place after reaching Urum that night of 21 December 2016. It is a book of encounters, negotiations of the self and the other, perceptions of an ever-changing place, constructions and destructions of materials, villages and settlements, and a book about all the lines of movement which thread into a story of mobilities and resilience, drylands and pastoralism, taking place in Turkana County, a desertscape in Kenya.

∼ Introduction ∼

One night, towards the end of my second visit to a village called Kambi Lore, situated in the Turkana central plains, about two hours' drive from the county capital town, Lodwar, I realised I should stop asking direct questions about meanings and definitions of resilience. I had arrived in Turkana, in the northern Kenyan drylands, five months earlier to conduct field research for my doctoral study on the impact of development interventions in the region, especially around the notion of resilience, which was gaining popularity among donors and practitioners. I wanted to see whether the new resilience framework was bringing change in the projects and development practices implemented and also to understand how the local population was making sense of the newly promoted resilience narrative. I wanted to understand from their own perspective what resilience could possibly mean. Armed with a rather open and flexible script of questions for interviews, I took off to meet the Turkana people and ask them about their lives and histories, and vernacular translations of resilience in language, social practice and cultural repertoire. I soon realised that those questions were not providing me with innovative answers. I realised I should instead start living, working, resting, playing and hearing stories as much as my untrained body would allow, there where shade is only found in the shadows of clouds. That night, Enyes, one of my research assistants, was telling me a story from his childhood. He comes from Turkana west, where the plains meet the mountains. He remembered playing with his friends, running and following shadows of clouds. Those who managed to stay protected from sun rays under the clouds' shades the longest were the winners of the game. A game for kids. A game for kids played at times when trees did not have a crown. A game for kids, when there were no bird traps to set. When there was no water to waste. No other games to play but running away from the sun. It must have been a time of drought. While Enyes was telling me this story, I understood that he was speaking of the form of resilience I was researching. It is a story of movement, running bodies and drifting clouds. It is a story of transformation of the harsh reality of a drought into a game. It is a story of attention to the environment and how it constantly changes, moulded by the relationship between humans, animals, rains, wind, river, grains of sand. It is a story of a group of friends supporting each other. And it is a story of games and laughter. This is the everyday form of resilience I hope to portray in this book.

doi: 10.63308/63891908548751.intro

Figure 1. Children running to the well. Lorengelup, Turkana Central. November 2015.

This book is about a pastoral population of the northern drylands of Kenya, a region called Turkana and today inhabited by the *Ngiturkan,* a pastoral offshoot of Easter Nilotic groups formed about 300 years ago. However, through their stories, this book also aims at rescuing drylands and pastoralist communities across the world from the fog of misconceptions that still today trap them, despite increasing recognition of the drylands as functional environments, and pastoralists as stewards of sustainable futures. Drylands and pastoralists, two eco-social underdogs as they continue to be described by mainstream narratives.

The world drylands

The drylands are the frame of this book, as a subject on their own, alive, capricious and ever-changing. It was a surprise to me, back at the beginning of my Ph.D. in 2014, to find out that drylands are the largest landform on earth, covering approximately forty per cent of land surface, including Mediterranean systems, cold deserts in Mongolia and Chile, the hot deserts of the Sahara and the Sahel, high altitude drylands in Iran, Tibet and Afghanistan, the low plains of the Horn of Africa's, and the tundra of the Arctic Circle ecosystems. The general classification of drylands includes hyper-arid, arid and semi-arid zones, defined by an aridity index based on evaporation, transpiration and rainfall. Before I travelled to Turkana for the first time, the human ecologist Alberto Salza shared with me the most precise definition of drylands I have heard: the drylands are lands of the empty bucket. 'If you place a bucket outside on the ground and it never fills up, you are in a dryland!' That is, in the drylands, evaporation exceeds precipitation. Even so, the world drylands are far from being barren lands, as I have learnt thanks to my host families in Turkana who taught me to see the richness of their lived environment. Drylands are complex, rich environments high in biodiversity, hosting a variety of habitats of which extensive rangelands represent the largest part, but also including savannahs, shrublands and woodlands, as well as rapidly expanding urban hubs. Home to three billion people, drylands are found in all continents. Ninety per cent of the world's dryland population is in developing countries, including forty per cent of the African population, 39 per cent of the Asian population, and 38 per cent of the South American population. These populations have made a living in the drylands successfully for thousands of years using ingenious techniques, their livelihood evolving together with the lived environment, shaping dryland landscapes and infusing them with cultural meaning.

But local meanings often escape the sensibility of outsiders, namely those who do not inhabit the drylands. Drylands are places of love and freedom, but also fear and terror, misery and poverty, strain and hardship. Mostly, drylands, to the eyes of outsiders and increasingly also to the eyes of the colonised local populations, are wastelands, unproductive, ruined, awaiting development to fulfil their potential. This way of thinking dates back to Anglo-European and western imperialism and is unfortunately very present even today. I was initially utterly alarmed when, in summer 2024, on a course on Mediterranean pastoral systems held by some major research institutes and established scholars, we were offered an image of the drylands as inhospitable lands, places of difficult living and little value unless development occurs. I could not understand why, despite many years of scientific revaluation of the drylands, they were still portrayed with such negative contention. One of the professors on the course, explained it to me very simply: 'because we are not mainstream'. Confronted with the reality of the bubble in which I was trained as researcher during my doctoral years, I realised that we are still far from recognising the value drylands hold and the respect they deserve, and in turn I found the motivation to finish writing this book. There are many scholars fighting for a different narrative of the drylands in the hope of informing more adequate policy making. I wish to align with their work in protecting the drylands that taught me so much about co-existence among human beings, domesticated and wild animals, and the environment; lightness, against a culture of accumulation and consumerism; endurance, by being open minded about adversity and strategic about assistance so as not to turn it into dependency; and mostly laughter. The Turkana people have a very distinct sense of irony, which I hope the readers will be able to trace in this book, through the jokes and entertainments I often report with their own words nested in the main text. I believe irony and laughter offer important lessons for us all in facing contemporary challenges that force us to re-imagine a more sustainable future.

In a recent volume titled *Drylands Facing Change: Interventions, Investments and Identities*, editors Angela Kronenburg García et al. warn us about the pervasive reach of dryland narratives that hold long terms consequences and shape identities (2023). These narratives reproduce ideas of drylands as 'lacking in some ways': unproductive, fragile and with scant resources, remote and peripheral to urban hubs and cities that serve as vantage point for analysis and intervention (Krätli 2013: 1). The wasteland narrative, on the one hand, links to a discourse of *terra nullius* blind to the very existence of drylands' populations and the resources actually present in the drylands; on the other hand it weaves into an environmental crisis narrative, which delegitimises local institutions and knowledge. In reconciling these narratives, Behnke and Mortimore in the edited volume *The End of Desertification?* shed light on the dissonance between policy and science (2016). Policymaking is based on a 'development narrative': a clear storyline, with bold implications and urgent funding required (Swift 1996). In the drylands, the development narrative draws on a story of desertification. Despite there being no agreed definition of desertification or standardised measures, Angela Davies in her book *Arid Lands: History, Power, Knowledge* reports that up to seventy per cent of global arid and semiarid lands are claimed to be suffering from varying degrees of desertification (2016). The story of desertification is one that portrays drylands as barren and deforested, in Angela's words: 'aberrations that need to be repaired and improved' (2016: 24). It is a story of exploitation of pristine environments because of human greed and self-interest through overgrazing, overcultivation, uprooting of plant species, deforestation. And it calls for external interventions by means of technical solutions and expert consultancies to prevent and reverse deterioration. This is a longstanding sentiment. Since Aubreville coined the expression 'desertification' (1949), and since the first United Nation Conference on Desertification (UNCOD) in 1977, following a severe multi-year drought in the Sahel (1968-1973), drylands are fundamentally presented as a waste of land-space.

> It is the implied grandeur and emptiness of the natural landscape that distinguishes deserts from subtler environments. Their vastness and sense of uniqueness are matched by climatic extremes and lives carved out of natural limitations. We are drawn by absence rather than plenitude, endurance over comfort, unpredictability over the familiar, as deserts touch the limits of survival for man and all living things. (Mol and Sternberg 2012).

These words open an edited volume about arid landforms and livelihoods, and well represent outsiders' views towards deserts, namely those of outsiders, people who do not make a living in the drylands. These views are somehow implicit in the etymology of the word desert itself. It originates from the Egyptian *tesert*, a place left behind (El-Baz 1988); from the Latin *deserere*, to abandon; and *desertum*, wasteland. From its etymology, not only does a 'sense of absence' emerge but also the idea that deserts used to be better places which have now become abandoned. In this context, pastoral populations, the main inhabitants of drylands, have long been considered responsible for the progressive degradation of their environments, because of their limited knowledge and irrational behaviour. Early ethnographers tried to contrast this argument by presenting dryland pastoral populations in a romantic balance with their ecosystem (Evans-Pritchard 1940; Jacobs 1965; Spencer 1965). However, these attempts were strongly countered by the rising colonial preoccupation with the creeping of the Sahara, largely attributed to the exploitative behaviour of pastoral populations (Bovill 1921; Stebbing 1935). During colonial administrations, interests in the peripheral drylands were largely skewed towards the commercial value of livestock production, which implied large fencing schemes, coercive settlement of nomadic pastoralists, and introduction of livestock taxes, as well as towards the geopolitical use of borderlands as buffer zones for military purposes. Most of these interventions have had the consequence of curtailing livestock mobility, which is a critical tool in the highly variable environments that constitute the drylands.

The concept of drylands, as we know it today, is rooted in the increasing debate about desertification that followed the Sahelian droughts at the end of the 1970s, the first major environmental issue to be recognised as occurring on a global scale, and to receive media attention. At the time, ecology theory, developed in relatively stable and temperate ecosystems, was describing ecosystems dynamics as centred around notions of equilibrium based on a vegetation cycle towards a

Introduction

Figure 2. The drylands. Turkana central plains. November 2015.

Figure 3. The flock. Turkana central plains. November 2015.

climax point, an ideal state of ecosystem stability to be safeguarded. Taken and transported over the analysis of drylands ecological dynamics, equilibrium assumptions fed into views of drylands populations as environmental destroyers causing observed desertification, mostly by over-stocking and over-grazing. Thus, romantic accounts of pastoral lives in balance with their environments were successively changed into the portrait of pastoralism as a source of disturbance contributing to the encroachment of deserts. Backward and disruptive, pastoral lifeways were understood as merely surviving through hardship, moving irrationally and being prone to war. As a mere background, drylands were pictured as non-places, void of life, awaiting developments. In these years, pastoral development policies received their first international attention. Imbued with classical ecology theory and equilibrium thinking, these were largely skewed towards the search for ecosystem stability, reduction of uncertainty and control of pastoral behaviour. Interventions aimed at reversing land degradation through afforestation, destocking measures and grazing taxes. Other interventions aimed at the improvement of livestock commercial production, registration of people for administrative purposes and restriction of movement and traditional pastoral practices, including: controlled stocking based on stock-rates per unit area; introduction of mechanised irrigation and high-yielding crops; imposition of private forms of land tenure, fencing and control of key resources (such as water boreholes); establishment of protected areas for wildlife conservation; large-scale assistance through fixed term interventions to improve national economies (roads, market infrastructure, slaughter houses, railway, mechanised boreholes, dipping facilities); introduction of new economic resources to promote alternative livelihoods (agriculture, fisheries, wage employment); provision of famine-relief in the form of paupers' camps and sedentarisation programmes. It goes without saying, that most of these interventions have largely proven unsuccessful, at best. Worse is that these interventions have in many cases contributed to the same degradation claimed to be occurring in the first place, as a result of policies based on the ideas that deserts are without value and that desertification is caused primarily by traditional uses of land by local populations. As well argued by Angela Davis, with detailed evidence, the world drylands are today facing salinisation from overirrigation, inappropriate reforestation in which a great many of the trees have died or turned into carpets of invasive species, extension of agriculture into marginal lands, and failed range improvement schemes (2016: 28). She shows how over the few contemporary cases of serious dryland degradation, the vast majority are found in places with strong political economic forces shaping development, such as capitalist expansion, authoritarian rule and developmentalist states. Some scholars went as far as referring to 'policy-induced desertification' (Hogg 1987).

Scientific evidence on the state of dryland degradation has debunked narratives of desertification. The observed regreening of the Sahara (Olsson, Eklundh and Ardö 2005) has allowed for a different understanding of the behaviour of drylands in terms of long-term fluctuations. Most deserts expand and contract in relation to rainfall more than any other single factor and have done so for millions of years. For example, Angela Davis writes that, during the planet's great ice ages, deserts were many times expanded because much water was locked up in ice sheets, allowing less precipitation (2016: 37). The natural resource base of drylands is now understood as dispersed, variable and available only seasonally. Although average rain level seems to be a variable of self-evident significance, and indeed it is an important element of dryland ecology (the bucket law), Saverio Krätli, scholar and advocate for pastoral livelihoods, warns us that average measures are of little value in contexts of high variability such as the drylands (2016). Instead, an array of other components has gained recognition as important for the study of drylands, including soil type, terrain topography, moisture and plant palatability. Research also shows that most degradation occurs in humid areas (78 per cent), whereas only 22 per cent is in drylands (Krätli 2015). And current stress found in drylands is no longer attributed to the fragility of the landscape or to the misbehaviour of its inhabitants; rather, it is believed to emerge from intensification and commercialisation processes that inevitably lead to long-term resource degradation. Renewed scientific understandings of drylands thus contradict the orthodox paradigm of dryland desertification and many of its underlying assumptions. Some of these changes have been incorporated in an emerging paradigm, defined by Mortimore as the 'resilience paradigm' (Mortimore 2016), drawing from ecological theories about 'instability but persistence' that emerged in the late 1970s in a study of complex ecosystems led by Holling Crawford Stanely (1973). As the new resilience thinking was rising in ecology theory, concepts such as carrying capacity and vegetation climax corresponding to a state of equilibrium could no longer be used to describe the behaviour of dryland ecosystems. Strong fluctuations in dryland ecologies were instead observed regardless of density-related processes, indicating that an equilibrium point was hardly to be found and maintained (Behnke and Scoones 1992; Ellis and Swift 1988; Sandford 1983; Scoones 1995a; Westoby, Walker and Noy-Meir

Figure 4. Ugandan escarpment. Loima. January 2017.

1989). Various alternative models have since been proposed[20] around the concept of non-equilibrium and merging in a 'new rangeland paradigm' (Behnke, Scoones and Kerven 1993; Niamir-Fuller 1999; Sandford 1983; Scoones 1995a). Thus, perspectives towards drylands changed and local production strategies (pastoralism), which in equilibrium models appeared as chaotic, irrational or disruptive, now made sense in terms of land use based on herd flexibility, diversity and mobility and were considered opportunistic and adaptive to a variable environment (Chatty 1972; Roe, Huntsinger and Labnow 1998; Westoby et al. 1989).

During the last twenty years, these shifts have gained policy attention. Following a period that Ian Scoones called one of 'pastoral crisis', largely because of the failure of previous interventions in drylands, continued land degradation and subsequent withdrawal of donors (1995b), renewed interest towards drylands grew in policymaking circles, mainly following concerns about climate change and the urge to 'build resilient communities' to withstand extreme weather events.

---

20. Westoby, Walker and Noy-Meir 1989 for state and transition models; Roe, Huntsinger and Labnow 1998 for reliability models; Ellis and Swift 1988 for persistency models; NRC 1994 for rangeland health; Oba, Stenseth and Lusigi 2000 for climate-plant-herbivory interaction model, among others.

Introduction

National governments and the international community scaled up their presence in drylands (especially in Africa) calling for a paradigm shift in the approach to dryland development: building resilience.[21] Even so, notwithstanding evolutions in ecology and pastoralism scholarship, new narratives remain mostly enclosed within academic circles, with few exceptions; and the new resilience language promoted within the development sector in drylands ends up reiterating old myths, as I argued with Tom Campbell in an article for the journal *Climate and Development* (2023). The language adopted in the humanitarian and development sphere is, in fact, still one of fragility, coping and scarcity, while pastoralism remains largely characterised in these depictions by 'narratives of deficit' (Krätli et al. 2015; Krätli and Schareika 2010), struggling through a difficult environment. Legal frameworks continue to deny customary rights (Abbink et al. 2014), as most governments still see pastoral land as empty, degraded, unproductive and in need of development. Climate change narratives, reinforcing old views of desertifica-

---

21. See, for example, Global Alliance for Action for Drought Resilience and Growth; the Drought Disaster Resilience Sustainability Initiative (IDDRSI); the Global Alliance for Resilience Initiative (AGIR); Resilient Pastoralism: towards Sustainable Futures in Rangelands; the Regional Enhanced Livelihoods in Pastoral Areas; the 'Building Resilience in Africa Drylands' initiative, Resilience and Economic Growth in Arid Lands (REGAL), Resilient Arid Lands Partnership for Integrated Development (RAPID), Strengthening Adaptation and Resilience to Climate Change (StARCK+), Supporting Horn of Africa Resilience (SHAREa), among others. In a recent review of drought management approaches in the Horn of Africa, Mohamed and colleagues (2025: 7) estimate ECHO and DEVCO resilience funding commitments for the Horn of Africa and the Sahel between 2007 and 2015 to be about five billion Euros, while the European Union Trust Fund for Africa (EUTFA) has invested close to 1.1 billion euros in the Horn of Africa across 131 projects, between 2015 and 2020, with an objective of 'strengthening community resilience'. Across these interventions, the EU aims to provide institutional support for elementary service provisions, bolster early warning systems, mainstream drought preparedness into development planning, and coordinate national disaster and drought contingency funds. Additionally, USAID has been operationalising its resilience activities through the Horn of Africa Resilience Network (HoRN), with the goals of 'strengthening resilience, ending extreme poverty, and promoting regional collaboration'. HoRN works at the intersection of arid regions of the greater Horn of Africa to bolster cross-border coordination and encourage resilience learning among the partners through the 5-year USAID-led Resilience Learning Activities (RLA), focusing on capacity development among regional, national and local institutions in East Africa and the Horn. Through RLA, USAID has established the Partners for Resilience and Economic Growth (PREG) in Northern Kenya, bringing together development, humanitarian and government actors to enhance resilience and economic growth. Between 2013 and 2024, PREG invested $400 million in strengthening partner coordination through layering and sequencing activities, learning and information sharing, promoting the livestock value chain and improving governance.

Figure 5. Koomyo. Loima. December 2016.

tion, are short-sighted, ignoring the long-term expansion/contraction of drylands (Ellis 1995; Scoones 2018), and reiterate control-oriented measures (destocking, green-belts, forest planting) and engineering solutions rather than working with the structural variability of drylands (Behnke and Mortimore 2016). One of the emerging arguments supporting these approaches is that pastoralists are vulnerable. Having been irrational, then disruptive, then adaptive agents, pastoralists are now largely considered 'vulnerable' to recurrent shocks. And drylands remain framed as poor, remote and degraded, with few and scant resources for the subsistence of dryland people. New resilience narratives in drylands portray pastoralism in the context of climate change and mass disasters as no longer viable and pastoralist areas as in need of transformation to avoid future human catastrophes (Catley 2017). Thus, most policies are once more geared towards agricultural development, urbanisation, settlement and promotion of alternative livelihoods; so that 'over the long run structural transformation of the economy may generate opportunities for new livelihood activities that are less vulnerable to the impacts of droughts and other shocks' (Cervigni and Morris 2016: 4). The same goal of transforming herders into something else has been reiterated since colonial days, time and again. No longer (necessarily) because pastoralists are *irrational* or *disruptive*, rather because they are *vulnerable* to their own environment.

Figure 6. Returning to the kraal. Loima. December 2016.

More recently, drylands also are increasingly framed as new frontiers, where the notion of frontier refers to a 'space of opportunity' (Imamura 2015: 96), of untouched resources that are free and available, at the disposal of external investors. In this framing, we can situate mega-infrastructure projects in Africa and Central Asia developed to improve connectivity, increase agricultural production, generate energy or to *green* landscapes. Conservation is also a new green-grabbing frontier. And of course, there are extractive industries, as reviewed by Tsering and Unks in a comparative book chapter about China and Kenya land governance institutions:

> In pastoral China and Kenya, increased exploration and competition for natural resources, notably land requisition, commercialization and preservation of land, and increasing focus on wildlife conservation, green energy, carbon sequestration and mining, have frequently resulted in pastoralists losing their rights and ability to access rangeland and resources on the ground (2024: 190).

As García and colleagues conclude, the general picture that emerges is that dryland populations are progressively losing access to and control of land and resources and that their commons are shrinking (2023: 9). While the majority of arid lands ecologists contends that 'there is insufficient scientific evidence of largescale permanent desertification' (Herrmann and Hutchinson 2006), the desertification narrative itself persists, highlighting the political nature of these debates. Herrmann and Hutchinson contend that 'we have a nonequilibrium world that is saddled with an overriding equilibrium mindset and policies that reflect it'. Decades of objections have only partially scraped the *development story*, which was reaffirmed in the Millennium Development Goals (MDGs) and even more recently in the Sustainable Development Goals (SDGs) with Goal 15:

> By 2030, combat desertification, restore degraded land and soil, including land affected by desertification, drought and floods, and strive to achieve a land degradation-neutral world.

It therefore appears that the renewed resilience narrative is not yet sufficient to change dominant attitudes towards drylands; or perhaps it is yet to be faithful to the contexts in which it is applied. Another narrative of drylands is still needed, one which Stafford Smith defined as 'uncomfortable' (2016) as it contests years of inappropriate interventions and billions of dollars spent uselessly. This should be based on an 'alternative science' built from within and not from above drylands, starting from the knowledge and perceptions of the people of the desert. It is still too common to believe that pastoralists should be settled, trees planted, agriculture promoted to the detriment of the environment and local peoples. At the same time the sustainability of pastoral systems is increasingly recognised as making excellent use of stochastic environments, with minimal if any degradation, certainly if allowed to operate according to their own logic. Pastoral systems are also proven to be more resilient and less vulnerable to climate variability and drought, being best suited to dealing with the uncertainties and variabilities of dryland environments, thanks to the flexibility and adaptability of their practices, once again if allowed to operate according to their own logic. This leads me to take some extra space in this introduction for some concise reflections about pastoralism, mainly for readers who are not necessarily familiar with the practices and principles that bring together pastoral communities across the world.

Some notes on pastoralism

Pastoralism is the most widespread land use worldwide. Between 200 and 600 million people, depending on definitions, live raising domesticated animals and practising livestock rearing. A report for the German International Cooperation Society (GIZ) estimates that in Africa alone pastoralism supports the livelihoods of about 100 million people (Krätli et al. 2022). Pastoral studies have historically been dominated by anthropologists, in response to initial colonial interests in large herds and use of extensive grazing in rangelands. Several monographs were published, like *The Nuer*, resulting from the commission by the British ruled government to Evans-Pritchard to study the political structure, social organisation and ecological conditions of a Nilotic ethnic group that occupies the wide Savannah plains of Sudan (1940). Another important early African monograph on pastoral societies, *Savannah Nomads*, was written by Derrick J. Stenning, providing historical, social and ecological accounts for the formation and evolution of a community of pastoral Fulani, the Woodaabe of Bornu Emirate, in northeastern Nigeria (1959). In Asia, Owen Lattimore is remembered for his writings on the steppe environments of Inner Asia and the nomadic pastoral tribes inhabiting them. *Inner Asian Frontiers of China*, for example, first published in 1940, was one of the first books to critically examine the rise of nomadism on the steppes and the interactions between nomads and settled peoples. In the Arabian Peninsula, but also in North Africa, Ibn Khaldun, fourteenth-century Arab historian and sociologist, extensively discusses the Bedouin societies as a cornerstone of his broader theory on the rise and fall of civilisation – born in the simplicity and solidarity of tribal life, maturing through conquest and urbanisation, and eventually declining due to luxury and disunity. While undoubtedly important testimony, these studies are infused with romantic stereotypes and tended to ignore the complexity of pastoral livelihoods, reflecting dominant views of pastoralists as 'brave, independent, fierce men, freely moving with their herd' (Dyson-Hudson and Dyson-Hudson 1980: 15). Increasing research funds, which followed the Sahelian droughts in the 1970s, made a new set of pastoral studies possible about a wide range of pastoral societies across the world, and each decade has since seen a new collected work on pastoralism, progressively rejecting the boundedness and stability of local systems, to recognise instead the enormous variability, heterogeneity and flexibility which characterise pastoral livelihoods. Recent definitions tend to recognise that 'the term "pastoralism" represents a large spectrum of realities' (Krätli and Schareika 2010: 606).

As scholarship on pastoralism evolved, it critically engaged with recurrent myths about pastoralism found among policymakers and development or humanitarian agents. For example, a recurrent myth, as highlighted by Dawn Chatty in an edited volume on nomadic societies in the middle east and north Africa at the doors of the twenty-first century, is that pastoralists are a 'throw-back to a past era' (2006: 1), or lazy and engaging in irrational economic practices. Other myths state that pastoralists are violent, warlike and lawless, as described by Rada Dyson-

Figure 7. In the homestead. Loima. December 2016.

Hudson and Neville Dyson-Hudson (1980) and more recently by Nick McDonnel in his book *The Civilization of Perpetual Movement: Nomads in the Modern World* (2016). It is also believed that, disconnected from global, or even national, economies, pastoralists need to settle to benefit from service delivery and more generally *modernise*. These myths have yet to be overcome. Despite the contemporary acknowledgment of the sustainability and knowledge base of pastoral systems across the world, the plethora of funding available for *innovation in pastoral systems* to my understanding paraphrases ideas of backwardness and necessity of modernisation. The *terrorist identity* ascribed to many drylands has also contributed to the labelling of pastoralists as combatants for militia groups, reiterating images of violent, warlike and lawless people. The rise of international events around pastoralism, and especially transhumance, featured as folklore, echoes views of absence inscribed in the rhetoric of *terra nullia*, void of people, at best a memorable past but certainly fading today. The reality is that marginalisation of pastoralists corners them, giving them only a very limited political weight and mostly limited capacity to manage natural resources sustainably, forcing them to adopt strategies that can have the countereffect of weakening their livelihood. The resulting deterioration turns against them through accusations of triggering unsustainability and insecurity, even if it

Figure 8. Herding Camels. Lorengelup, Turkana Central. January 2016.

is the external triggers that drive them to such situations, of which they are main victims. In a vicious circle, they see their capacity to manage landscapes limited, with shrub encroachment or land degradation eroding their economic base further and putting them in an even shakier position.

It is about time to recognise the value pastoralists across the world hold, through their important contributions to the lived environment, society and culture. The starting point is to see pastoralism, as defined by Saverio Krätli, as a specialisation to take advantage of the variability of rangeland environments, where key resources such as nutrients and water for livestock can be relied on in the form of unpredictable and short-lived concentrations more than in uniform and stable distributions (Krätli 2015; see also FAO 2021). The term *specialisation* highlights expertise, knowledge and qualified experience. That is, it takes a lifetime to become a good herder, to manage herds and access resources, with care and intimate knowledge of the territory. No policy can come from outside without the involvement of local communities who are the best placed to know what is most needed. *To take advantage*, turns framings of pastoral strategies as *coping strategies* on their heads to highlight instead opportunism, rationality and situatedness. *Variability* is key in understanding pastoral livelihoods worldwide. Variability (of the socio-ecological environment) is embedded in operational processes and institutional arrangements so that these can be rapidly adapted to short-notice changes in the external conditions. These include, for example, strategic mobility, namely the possibility to move animals at the right time towards the right place, in this way keeping livestock on a diet that is higher in nutritional value than the average value of the range with no or minimal use of external energy-intensive inputs; access to a variety of species, so as to take advantage of their specific qualities ; and institutional flexibility that generally embraces inclusionary principles and a combination of individual and collective decision-making approaches, for example concerning the managing of resources through negotiation, complementarity and integration over exclusivity, competition and separation (communal land-tenure systems or the seasonal patterns of crop-livestock integration, with specialist farmers and specialist pastoralists using the same space in different ways at different times of the year) (Krätli et al. 2022: 9). It is important to pass the message that these basic principles of pastoral practices are not exclusive to the pastoral systems in the drylands. In fact they sit at the core of pastoral systems across the world, and reward them with comparative advantage with respect to other production systems in marginal lands, whether the high mountains of Central Asia and Latin America; or the dry savannahs of Africa, the Middle East and South Asia; the mountains, hills and plains in Europe; or the Arctic tundra – namely in those socio-ecological systems that work under laws of variability and non-equilibrium. Relying on pockets of relatively wetter rangeland and farmland to survive during the dry season, and in times of droughts, these systems produce substantial economic value by making use of the vast expanses of rangelands not suited for crop production. There is no escaping the necessity of rethinking the ways in which we have grabbed and fragmented rangelands, rigidised resource use and management, and curtailed the possibility for pastoralists to move, including how we have shaped mindsets. When I confront colleagues who study pastoralism in Europe about the need to incentivise pastoral mobility, if only to reduce economic and energy costs of stabled feeding, the most *critical* response I often obtain is that 'it is unimaginable today to ask livestock farmers to move with their animals' or even to guide livestock through grazing when extensive pastoralism is practised. It follows that most research and investment in this field are today oriented towards virtual fencing, remote sensing and herd control, technologies to automatise animal feeding, all measures that go in the direction of separating herders from their animals to spare time, but at what cost in terms of knowledge creation and transmission, generational renewal and presence in the territory? And what about the limits we pose to our own imagination?

Figure 9. At the well. Lorengelup, Turkana central. December 2015.

Thanks to the specific forms of livelihood specialisation, pastoralism can bring a number of benefits, starting with its impacts on the environment. Thompson and colleagues support an ecological base for sustainable livestock, based on the argument that herbivores are a natural constituent of the world's ecosystems and have played a key role in the last several million years (2023). As the numbers of wild herbivores or megafauna have greatly decreased, the maintenance of such roles depends on the practice of adequate livestock management (Manzano, Pardo et al. 2023). Many now recognise the role of pastoral practices for the conservation of the world's biodiversity. Several reports sponsored by relevant international organisations show how livestock create and maintain mosaic landscapes, connecting ecosystems by transporting seeds, restoring soil fertility through manure and reducing risk of fires by feeding on long grass; and how trampling and grazing can improve the water-holding capacity of grasslands. Pastoralism creates habitats without which other species could not survive and prevents the spread of invasive species, sustaining botanical diversity to a high degree (Manzano and Salguero 2018). In addition, new research has also countered arguments against livestock production as a major greenhouse gas emitter. Not only do these arguments fail to make qualitative distinctions between intensive and extensive livestock production systems but they also ignore that pastoral systems mimic natural carbon cycles, replacing natural methane emissions from wild herbivores rather than adding to them. If pastoralism were to be removed, the forms of land use that would fill the same ecological niche would either release soil carbon or maintain emission rates similar to those of pastoralist systems (Manzano, Del Prado and Pardo 2023; Manzano and White 2019). Worse would be if the same freed ecological niche were taken instead by mechanised fossil-fuel based production systems. In other words, the capacity of pastoral systems to produce in the absence of significant fossil fuel inputs, actually makes them an important livelihood and food system option for a decarbonised world (Krätli, Huelsebusch et al. 2013). What is more, rangelands are one of the largest carbon sinks on the planet with a large potential to reduce emissions globally. These ecosystems co-evolved with the presence of herbivores, which can play a crucial role in the restoration of landscapes, demonstrating their relevance as a tool for the United Nations Decade on Ecosystem Restoration (2021–2030). Benefits derived from pastoralism are not only limited to the environment but also to society more broadly. Pastoralism, as a food production system, contributes immensely to the food security of millions of people. It produces a vast range of foods and services for humans, from inputs that are largely inedible for humans, converting grass to meat, milk and derivatives, while meeting the rising demands for sustainable and healthy food that supports social and cultural values. As these systems make only negligible use of cereals as feed, and of external inputs based on fossil fuels, they are amongst the most efficient in the world in sustainably producing human-edible proteins (FAO 2021). Stewards of sustainable futures, pastoralists also play a crucial role as custodians of rangelands, potentially being key informants for the observations of changes at a localised level with grounded evidence, and pastoralism is an important resource to fight the depopulation of rural and mountain areas that is one the greatest contemporary challenges, while protecting immaterial heritage and cultural landscapes in all countries where it persists (Bindi 2022).

I have had the privilege of being hosted by pastoral families in many countries of the world, sharing long grazing days under various weather conditions, searching out the best grass, being attentive to the signs of predators, attending the needs of livestock, nurturing the weak, checking if they all returned to the kraal in the evening and otherwise venturing into unknown marches following their footprints when some animals were lost. I learnt how skilled pastoralists across the world are, what attuned knowledge they preserve, adapt and transmit, and the care that nests in their hands and eyes, attentive and vigilant. I owe them so much and take the opportunity of this book to thank them all, who taught me to recognise that precise instant where nature and culture meet and overlap, as an instant of new energy and hopes.

Turkana County and the arid north

Figure 10. Dust and thorns. Lorengelup, Turkana Central. November 2016.

Among all pastoral people, this book focuses on the Turkana herders, who make a living in the homonymous Turkana County in the arid and semi-arid lands of northern Kenya. Turkana County is one of the 47 Kenyan counties and lies wholly in the eastern branch of the Rift Valley. A place made of thorns and dust, Turkana is known to be *the cradle of humankind*, and also one of the poorest and harshest environments in the world. Certainly, this image is reproduced when one travels to Turkana for the first time. Covering an area of 77,000 square kilometres, including water bodies, it is the most north-westerly county in Kenya, bordered by Uganda to the west, South Sudan and Ethiopia to the north and north-east, and Lake Turkana to the east. Neighbouring counties in Kenya are Marsabit County to the east, on the opposite shores of the lake, Samburu County to the south-east, Baringo and West Pokot County to the south. Past the Eldoret and Kitale highlands that are largely shaped for agricultural purposes, vast semi-desert plains open. In a birds-eye view, sitting next to the window of a small aircraft, the Turkana land is creased. Like wrinkles, dry creeks cut through flat golden plains. A few huts blend in with the land, scattered in the expanse. Hot air trembles outside the window when landing at the small airport in Lodwar, now serving several low-cost flights a day. The other way to reach Lodwar, Turkana's capital, is by road, a much longer and exhausting journey. Buses leave Nairobi early in the morning and reach Kitale by night. At sunrise, buses and pick-ups resume travel through rough roads unfolding from the Marich Pass, at the border of West Pokot and Turkana Counties, into the Turkana plains. The landscape, coursing in front of the traveller's eyes, blurs at the horizon where desert plains meet a white sky. It is only in walking through this apparently dull land that a different view emerges. In this way, the complexity and richness of Turkana landscape comes to life, as it appears to the eyes of herders.

Barren places like Turkana are classified as Arid and Semi-Arid Land (ASAL) (Pratt and Gwynne 1977), subject to extreme climatic variability and uncertainty, and commonly defined as 'drought-driven systems' (Ellis and Swift 1988). Though most of the county consists of low plains, it nonetheless shows a varied landscape. In the North, mountain ranges and escarpments mark the borders with South Sudan and Ethiopia, while hills and plains spread wide in the South. Valleys are carved by seasonal rivers and dry-creeks and by two major perennial rivers (Turkwel and Kerio). Lake Turkana, a *jade sea* and the biggest desert lake in the world, lies long, like a teardrop, in the east of the county. Fishing is a major activity around the lake shores, which have always been a site of refuge during times of hunger for the otherwise dominantly pastoral population. Despite such varied landscape, Turkana is mostly known for its remoteness, ecological instability and scarcity of resources, and frequently described as inhospitable and unforgiving. The following quotes mirror each other, even though they come from different historical periods and are extrapolated from different discourses: colonial officers exploring the resisting province at the turn of the twentieth century; ecologists and anthropologists studying dryland ecosystems and livelihoods at the turn of the twenty-first century; and, most recently, development organisations in support of pastoral populations. Even so, they all reproduce a similar sense of desolation, desperation, and resistance.

Hostile natives of exceptional size, strength, warlike, treacherous and enterprising (British Major Herbert H. Austin 1902, cited in Hatcher 2014).

This one-time cradle of humanity is now a harsh and inhospitable environment where drought and famine are all too common (McCabe and Ellis 1987: 33).

Introduction

One of the most desolate inhabited places of the continent and an area of absolute need (NGO Burnabi Blue Foundation, cited in Müller-Dempf 2014a).

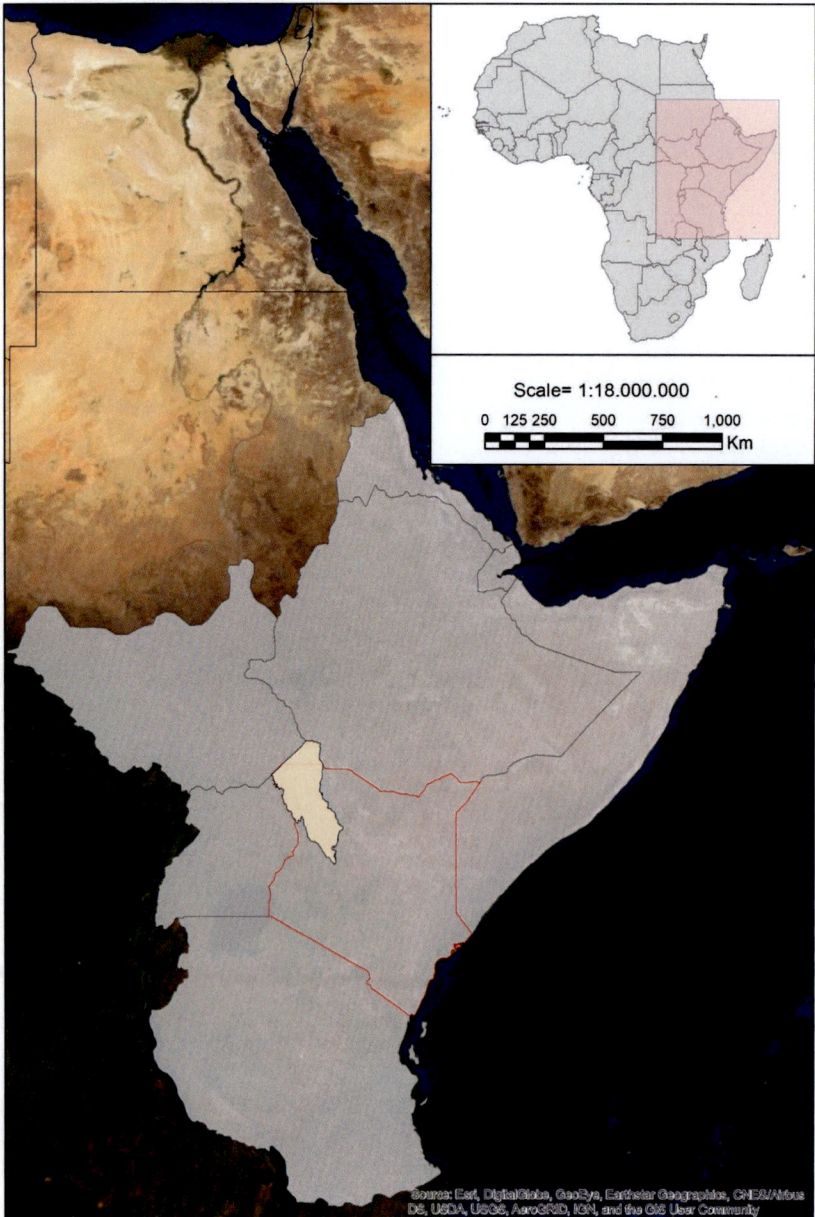

Figure 11. Turkana

Turkana people are 'hostile' and 'warlike', in the eyes of colonial patrols sent to defeat them; in the eyes of researchers studying survival strategies; and in the eyes of humanitarian agents fighting poverty. The most common element in the various narratives about the Turkana is the harshness, scarcity and remoteness of the space they inhabit. Turkana is seen as a place where a constant battle takes place. Theatre of perennial catastrophes (recurrent droughts, land degradation, water scarcity, famines, conflicts), it is a place where one inevitably asks how life is possible. Nonetheless, there are signs of human presence in the region since four to five million years ago, evidence not only of the possibility of life but also of its evolution. Hominid evolution in the Turkana area was triggered by the Rift Valley orogenesis, that opened, about six million years ago, a new niche to a number of species with bipedal locomotion (Genus *Australopithecus* and *Homo*). The climatic trend was from forest to savanna to drylands (where moving long distances on two legs became an advantage), in a progressive *desertisation* of abiotic origin (distinct from desertification, which is of human origin), showing the potential advantages of dryland occupation by humans (Little and Leslie 1999: 25). People inhabiting Turkana today are locally known as *Ngiturkan*, which literally means 'people of the caves' (McCabe 2004: 47). Part of Eastern Nilotic groups, the Turkana emerged as a separate ethnic group about 300 years ago, as an offshoot of a larger linguistic family known as *Ateker*.[22] At the beginning of the eighteenth century, they moved down the Karamoja escarpment, now bordering Kenya and Uganda, and ventured into the Tarach-Valley, in what is today north-west Turkana. Here they probably came into contact with previous occupants of the land, such as Kor and Siger peoples (Lamphear 1988). Intermarriages, population growth and ecological pressure pushed further territorial expansion south-east. Moving down, they started destroying, displacing or assimilating other pastoral groups on the vast plains west of Lake Turkana (Dyson-Hudson and Dyson-Hudson 1999: 28). By the mid-nineteenth century they emerged as a major power in the north-western region of the country (Awuondo 1990: 28).

Soon after, however, Turkana became an area contested by various powers, especially caught between the Ethiopian Empire, under King Menelik's expansionistic plans, and the British colonial administration. British patrols managed to suppress Ethiopian attempts to colonise the region by 1918, but then had to face a longer and bloodier resistance by the N*giturkan*. The Turkana were remem-

---

22. Composed of the Karamojong, Jie and Dodos of Uganda; the Taposa and Jiye of southern Sudan; the Nyangatom of Ethiopia; the Turkana of Kenya.

bered by British officers as the finest fighting men in east Africa, organising and maintaining the longest opposition to colonial domination remembered in African history. The British responded to the Turkana's resistance by increasing punitive patrols, imposing hut-taxes payable with livestock, disarming, institutionalising the role of chiefs and eliminating pastoral expertise (seers, medicine-men, elders, and war leaders). British efforts to conquer Turkana were brutal and bloody despite their minimal interests in the region. Because of limited expectations of profitable returns from investment in the region, when finally, in 1926, civil administration was introduced, Turkana was in fact confined and classified as a *closed district*. Roadblocks prevented access to the district and outsiders were largely denied permission to cross Turkana, including missionaries who were only allowed into Turkana after independence. As a result, when Kenya achieved independence in 1963, there were only two primary schools, few dispensaries and barely any roads in the northern province.

The initial impetus for *development* can nonetheless be traced back to those years of early colonial administration, through, for example, the imposition of a new hierarchy of headsmen and chiefs and a progressive capitalistic penetration of an urban elite (Awuondo 1990; Broch-Due and Sanders 1999; Hogg 1982). Indeed, the landscape had already begun to transform quite dramatically. Before colonisation, there were hardly any settlements, except some small fishing villages along the shores of Lake Turkana and Somali trading centres in South Turkana (Rodgers 2018). Nomadic pastoralism was the dominant and most suited livelihood strategy, given the climatic and geographic conditions of the Turkana basin. The composite profile of the landscape, with increasing precipitation, woodland covers and grasslands following increasing elevation gradients, allowed for mosaic patterns of mobility between the outer mountainous ridges, the vast central plains and lake shores. In addition, livestock husbandry was commonly integrated with various forms of wild food gathering and hunting, as well as fishing in the waters of Lake Turkana. With colonisation, administrative centres started being built as well as livestock markets and towns, such as Lodwar, the capital town founded in 1920 and set up as the heart of the British administration (CIDP 2013– 2017). In addition, investments carried out by British settlers, even though limited, such as road construction, needed local labour, which was compensated with in-kind payments, consequently creating new forms of jobs and contributing to further diversification of the pastoral economy and the general landscape of the basin. This trend advanced at a faster speed after independence, despite the same policy of

Turkana County and the arid north

Source: Turkana County Integrated Development Plan 2023–2027

Figure 12. Map of Turkana Administrative Units

containment having been perpetuated, with investments largely directed towards the high-lands, so-called *high-potential areas*, and road-blocks maintained until 1973 (Little and Leslie 1999). Nevertheless, by the 1980s, the number of roads, missions, towns, trading centres and shops had increased sharply, together with an urban population involved in activities other than herding.

Most recently there emerged a vibrant class of politicians, entrepreneurs and investors who, especially since the new Constitution in 2010, are strongly shaping the socio-ecological and economic landscape of the county. Turkana today shows a complex administrative profile organised around 7 sub-counties, 17 divisions, 56 locations, and 156 sub-locations (Table 1).

Table 1. Turkana administrative profile

Sub-county	Division	Location	Sub-location
Turkana South	3	6	17
Turkana East	2	9	20
Turkana North	3	11	31
Kibish	1	3	7
Turkana West	3	12	34
Turkana Central	3	8	21
Loima	2	7	26
Total	*17*	*56*	*156*

Data source: Ministry of Interior and National Coordination, Turkana County

Despite the auspicious socio-economic growth that all these investments may be bringing to the county, there is also the danger of new forms of social differentiation, marginalisation and further polarisation between interior rural lands and the new urban hubs that are spreading across the county. Certainly, those who promote these interventions are rarely familiar with the Turkana people, their livelihoods, challenges and ways of responding. Moreover, a *crisis discourse* prevails, as narratives of harshness, remoteness, and insecurity remain dominant, largely anchored to a long history of development and humanitarian interventions. The first famine camps were opened in the 1920s, in response to heavy human losses, reduction of livestock and ecological collapse caused by the war between the British and the Turkana (Awuondo 1990), marking the beginning of over ninety years of humanitarian and development interventions. During this process, famine camps came to be increasingly criticised for many reasons, including the underlying ideology of keeping pastoralists settled rather than enabling them to return to active herding (Broch-Due and Sanders 1999), having increased people's dependency (Lind

2005) and having made them slaves of their stomachs (Reidy 2012). Experiments were made with new forms of relief-distribution, with the overall effect of turning emergency aid into a permanent survival strategy. From the 1990s, decentralised stores were built to improve food distribution, to be closer to people: where they live and where they move (Birch 1994). And also new forms of 'feeding camps', as labelled by Betti (2010), were opened, such as schools, dispensaries and churches distributing food to the so-called poor.

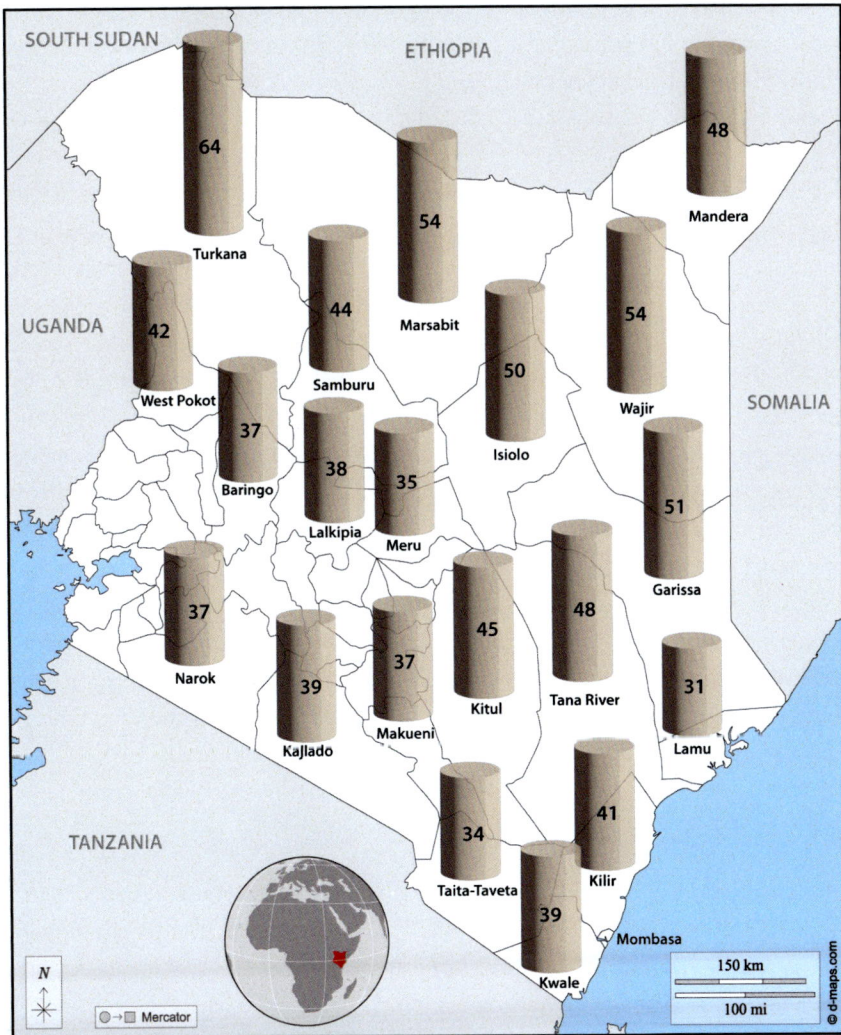

Figure 13. Resilience investments by district (year 2015–16). UNOCHA-EA (East Africa)..

Introduction

Since the early interventions, in line with dominant ecology theories of the time wherein pastoral strategies were inherently destructive for the environment, alternative livelihood schemes were also set up alongside relief-operations, by missionaries and development and humanitarian organisations. Under these schemes, nomadic pastoralists were re-settled along lake shores as fishermen, or along Turkwel or Kerio rivers as farmers, in the hope of promoting viable alternative livelihoods, other than herding. Through all these forms of intervention the main goal has remained unvaried since colonisation: to settle Turkana herders and transform pastoralism into something else. Especially following the catastrophic drought that hit the Horn of Africa (HoA) in 2010–11, a resilience agenda grew under renewed attention towards the drylands. Under the IGAD mandate, the Drought Disaster Resilience Sustainability Initiative (IDDRSI) signalled the beginning of the East Africa resilience agenda and used Turkana as first case study for their operations. Ever since, Turkana has received the largest number of resilience-labelled programmes and funds in Kenya, as reported by the resilience investment tracker-tool, an interactive platform aiming at mapping resilience interventions in the HoA and still operational at the time of my fieldwork. Turkana County appears the perfect laboratory for international organisations interested in *building resilience* to shocks and disasters, and in turn also a compelling case for this book that hopes to bring a more grounded, nuanced and rooted understanding of resilience in drylands. The empirical analysis presented here revealed the fundamental role of mobility in the lived experiences of Turkana herders. Mobility emerged as an integral part of everyday life, providing a new lens for the understanding of resilience which challenges dichotomous, linear and *bouncing* views of resilience. Instead, mobility, in its many manifestations, as a quality of space, as something people do, as an aspect of identity, allows for more fluid, dynamic and kaleidoscopic accounts of peoples' lives. I thus propose mobility as the site where resilience takes root and where a richer grasp of resilience, drylands and pastoralism can be found.

A nomadic approach to research

Mobility, as an overarching theme and analytical lens, emerged inductively at a later stage of my research. However, there are many aspects of my methodology which can be referred to as *mobile* from its beginning. I now refer to my own methodology as a *nomadic approach to research*: vigilant and sensitive to changes in the surrounding environment, flexible and unsettling, adaptive and open hearted. In the words of Hazan and Hertzog (2011: 11):

> She (the researcher) encounters incessant changes in the field which require her to be physically mobile, mentally alert, emotionally resilient and socially agile; she must be prepared to modify and revise her theoretical standpoints time and again; and she must cope with the frequent unpredictable mutations in the articles of faith as to the desirable management of knowledge.

Nomadism therefore becomes a crucial 'state of mind' for a sensible progression of research, 'resisting to settle into socially coded modes of thought and behaviour' (Braidotti 1994: 5) and showing, as pastoral nomads do, a 'continual adaptation to a changing world' (Marx 2006: 92). This form of nomadism is tied with my personal story. Trained in development economics, I began working as a Monitoring and Evaluation Consultant (M&E) for a UN agency in Somalia. I was involved in the implementation of a baseline survey to assess resilience interventions in the region and in the development of a new resilience index through a double-stage factor analysis (FA).[23] During that time, I developed interests in understanding more about both applied meanings of resilience and the computation techniques used. I had applied to a Ph.D. programme to pursue these objectives. Because of my twofold goal of both broadening the general understanding of resilience and developing an appropriate measure for it, I had ambitiously prepared to rely on a combination of both qualitative and quantitative approaches. I thus designed an *exploratory sequential mixed methods* research plan, organised around two rounds of fieldwork: the first round of field research for a qualitative exploration of resilience; and a second round of field research for the implementation of a quantitative survey aimed at the modelling of an improved quantification method. There is not an epiphany moment or one major factor which explains why my research changed so considerably in the course of my Ph.D. It happened more like a *drift*, through a slow and yet progressive realisation that quantitative measures would have never been able to tell the story in the way in which it was emerging.

The more I attempted to settle my own thoughts about what resilience could possibly mean, the more these possible meanings were expanding, enlarging and reaching composite aspects of human life. They were never static, never entirely

---

23. FA analyses assume that a causal relation exists between a set of observed variables and latent variables. In other words, the behaviour of a set of observed variables depends on some part of uniqueness proper to each variable and something else that is related to an unobservable variable (in this case resilience).

graspable. As a result, I had to keep on living, conversing, observing, documenting, participating in people's daily lives, and prolonging the qualitative phase of research into the second round of fieldwork, progressively turning my study towards ethnography. I have personally always been attracted to ethnographic immersive methodologies, openness to composite methods and compatibility with inductive research. However, it is only during fieldwork that I recognised I was 'doing ethnography' (Crang and Cook 1995) because it best responded to issues faced in defining resilience, and to my research questions: the exploration of the everyday, and the presentation of the perspectives of *insiders* on their lived environment, livelihoods and risks. Ethnography, defined as 'situated, long-term, empirical field research' (Malkki 2007: 164), explores systems of meanings from an experiential point of view (Campbell and Lassiter 2014: 120), and promotes an understanding of people's world-views and lifeways in the context of their everyday (Crang and Cook 1995). Several fundamental principles of ethnography guided my research throughout. The lines of enquiry I followed led me into the 'conditions and potentials of human life' (Ingold 2011: 3). The ways I engaged with people who welcomed and hosted me in their homes and villages led me to build trust and allowed experiential proximity to their lives (Procter 2019). The 'situated knowledge' (Malkki 2007: 163) I contributed to, whetted in the practices of long-term fieldwork and participant observation (Robben and Sluka 2007), permitted me to document the 'imponderabilia of actual life and to grasp the native point of view, his relation to life, and his vision of his world' (Malinowski 1922: 25).

The making of ethnography is undoubtedly *artisanal* (Clifford, Marcus and Fortun 1986: 6) and, indeed, I did not follow strict rules, but constantly re-invented fieldwork praxis, research methods and theoretical predispositions, following new paths which were opening in front of my eyes. I started crafting my own methodology, defined by a high degree of *experientialism*, based on my experiences and those of my hosts. Hence, I started burning charcoal; shovelling goat excrement; digging wells and carrying water; herding shoats[24] and camels[25]. I learnt weaving palm leaves for fences and hut roofs; milking goats; and cleaning cooking pots with sand and my own nails. I learnt cutting fish and removing entrails

---

24. Expression used to indicate mixed herds of sheep and goats.

25. The Middle East, the Sahara-Sahel belt and the Horn of Africa support a high population of dromedaries (*Camelus dromedarius*); they have one hump while, in Central Asia, proper camels (*Camelus bactrianus*) have two. In Africa, notwithstanding the difference, the use of the English word *camel* is prevalent, even in scientific literature.

with my thumbs; and repairing broken nets. I learnt cleansing maize and beans of the stones that come with them in relief bags. I learnt the taste of wild fruit and wild game. I learnt to be hungry. I gave food, I begged for food, I received relief food, and I ate it. And I walked, and while walking, I kept my attention on the eyes of herders. They were looking at mountains, grass, trees, footprints of wild animals, at clouds. They were observing how many cars were passing through dirt roads. The number of charcoal sacks piling along roads. They were noting if new buildings were under construction and were attentive to the sounds of mechanic water-drilling. To do this, I moved. The selected field sites lie along a geographic gradient moving from highlands of the Uganda Escarpment towards the lowlands of Lake Turkana, passing by the vast open plains of Turkana central areas. More precisely I moved between three sub-locations:[26]

- Urum (in Loima sub-county, Lokirimama division, on the border with Uganda), a mountain area where people practise what is still considered *traditional* pastoralism;

- Loregelup (in Turkana Central sub-county, Kerio division), central semi-desert low plains where people engage in camel and shoat rearing, agro-pastoralism, motorbike and pro-box services, petty trade and small business activities;

- Longech (in Turkana Central, on the shores of Lake Turkana, Kalokol division), lake site where fishing is the main livelihood.

Each sub-location contains an administrative *centre* and a number of small settlements and villages. Some consist of just a few isolated huts, kilometres apart. Some are concentrated around a farm, a water borehole, a school, an unused shop. Urum, Kambi Lore,[27] and Longech are the three administrative centres, respectively in the three sub-locations (Urum, Lorengelup, Longech). Imagine a small village with some level of administration (like the chief's hut), a dirt road cutting through, a school, a dispensary, drilled water pumps, a few shops and a food distribution point – where mainly elders and women with small children reside.

It was when I started writing that I realised this was a story of mobility. The methodological choice of journey showed mobility as ethnographically explaining the ways my hosts looked at their environment and living space and the ways they

---

26. Sub-locations are administrative units under the new constitution, cf. Ch. 2.

27. Sometimes abbreviated as Lore.

Introduction

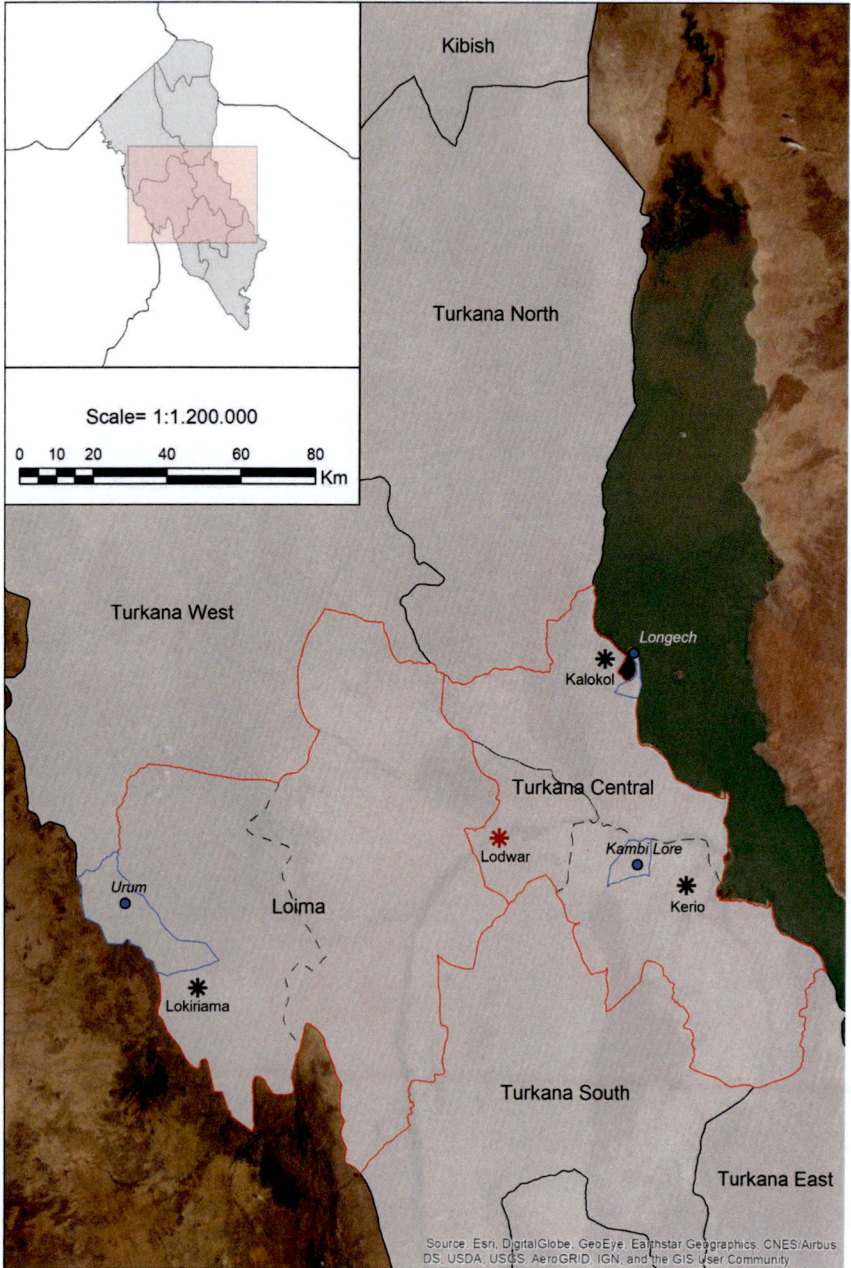

Figure 14. Map of field sites

were involved in its construction and destruction (Chapters 2 and 3). Mobility was acted out through daily micro and macro movements crafting a livelihood system that is inherently relational (Chapter 4). Finally, mobility was explaining the capacity to navigate across imagined social worlds as figuratively described between herders and town people and permeate flexible identities (Chapter 5). While mobility was emerging as an explicative variable, I began to ask myself how I could represent mobile experiences. Echoing D'Andrea and colleagues' question: what representational figures could I draw on for the description and analysis of movement without crystallising it (2011)? With my writing, I share the same goal announced by De León in his recent ethnography of Mexican migrants crossing the Sonoran desert into the USA: 'By drawing on specific details told me during fieldwork and filtering these descriptions for readability and flow, I aim to bring the reader phenomenologically closer to the everyday life in the desert' (2015: 43). Agreeing with Holtzman, I believe that this approach to writing renders my ac-counts more faithful to the realities of the field and more, rather than less, scientific (2009: 57). I thus decided to use *mobility* also as my approach to writing. The four empirical chapters unfold along a reconstructed journey which spanned the entire fifteen months of fieldwork. Journeying becomes a writing style, in order to avoid producing static accounts of mobility, having no intention of *capturing mobility* but rather letting it move. Journeying mirrors my experiences in the field and the 'junctures of wonderment, indeterminacy, and uncertainty of the field reality' (Hazan and Hertzog 2011: 2). Finally, journeying is an analytical tool to reiterate the significance of mobility, to express, represent and embody mobility in text. Journeying is an epistemic framework which ties writing to the interpretative process and leads the reader to the heart of my main argument: resilience is about moving.

Book roadmap

This book investigates the concept of resilience as lived and experienced by Turkana herders, and while it does so it sheds light on the values of drylands and pastoral livelihoods across the world. Chapter One opens with an overview of the concept of resilience, tracing its emergence in academic scholarship and mapping out its expansion into policy circles. It surveys the application of the concept of resilience by development actors in the context of drylands, drawing from the rise of the East Africa Resilience Agenda after the Horn of Africa crisis in 2010–11 and its translation into the Kenyan policy framework. The chapter shows that resilience is dominantly operationalised in the field of disaster planning, and that its translation into policy remains challenging and ambiguous. The chapter concludes by highlighting a set of conceptual and empirical puzzles in the resilience scholarship that the book aims to overcome by looking beyond the 'shadow of the crisis' (Bakewell and Bonfiglio 2013) and by searching for 'constructivist views' of resilience by using peoples' everyday lived experiences (Brown 2015). From Chapter Two, the journey across Turkana begins and will unfold until the end of the book. Chapter Two is a journey through the variable nature of drylands. Following Turkana herders moving across their territory, it shows how the drylands are known, seen locally and represented. Drawing from the *new rangeland paradigm* and theories of relational geography and mobile space, the chapter challenges common assumptions about the fragility, lack of productivity and remoteness of drylands and argues instead for another spatiality, for a space that is not static but alive, and moves through continual reconfigurations of spatial features. The liveliness of space emerges by enlarging the gaze over these vast landscapes, moving beyond micro-zonal approaches to space that limit interests towards the drylands to areas of so-called high potential. From a larger perspective, multiple spaces and multiple times appear while making and unmaking the territory. Resources grow, die and flower again in different places at different times; they are mobile. This chapter depicts a *nomadic space*, one that restlessly decomposes and recomposes itself. In the drylands, scarcity is a function of scale more than a state of absence, and it can be navigated by moving, through negotiations and by allowing real-time responses to changes in the environment. It is a space that holds great significance, that can only be learnt by criss-crossing it, becoming available for everyday inhabitants in symbolic terms as well, through beliefs, amulets and ritual life. Chapter Three looks at the *nomadic space* from another perspective. Using the vantage point of the huts that compose the villages popping up in rural Turkana, the chapter looks at the interplay of various forms of variability and the corresponding spatial practices that make and unmake, form and shape, places, through the creation of rural villages and how these are kept alive. I describe this space as pulsating in time with the variability in space (ecological, but also social and economic) and kept connected along socio-ecological chains. Villages are inhabited and abandoned, built and left to decay. The only stable element is variability. Chapter Four delves into the daily lives of Turkana herders, and their moving. It looks at what people do (practices and strategies), to restore a positive understanding of their mobility. The chapter employs mobility as the analytical lens to understand daily practices and it reconfigures livelihoods in relational terms. Mobility is the response to a mobile territory. Mobility is situational, tactical, strategical, ubiquitous and functional. By following Turkana herders in their everyday movements, the chapter offers a critical analysis of assumptions of uniformity and stability that permeate pastoral development, including in fixing people's livelihood strategies into rigid categories such as herders, farmers, fishermen or town dwellers, as well as mobile or sedentary. Chapter Five extends the analysis of Turkana herders' movements through various cultural environments. It uses the analytical lens of food to understand two different social worlds, that of Turkana herders and that of town dwellers. The image of food-insecure herders is replaced by one of ecological situatedness, endurance and a capacity to *stay-without*; whereas town dwellers are seen as vulnerable to the lack of food. After reviewing traits of these two opposed social worlds, from the standpoint of Turkana herders, around diet, fashion and other convivial habits, the chapter maps out how these constructed identities are nonetheless malleable by means of imitation, appropriation and adaptation. Chapter Five argues that solidarity (feeling part of a group) is a crucial aspect of resilience, as well as the capacity to respond to changes in the broader society.

With this book, I hope to bring to the eyes and hearts of readers a people who taught me so much about life and hope and laughter. Through the stories and voices of Turkana herders I wish to speak about wider 'herding cultures', as Ilse Köhler Rollefson refers to in her beautiful book *Hoofprints on the Land*, made up of skilled and intimate herd management, caring coexistence for the environment and all creatures upholding the web of life on earth, and relationships based on reciprocity rather than exploitation.

～ Chapter 1. ～

The resilience agenda

La resilienza è il più riuscito anestetico dei nostri tempi, l'antidoto più efficace contro ogni tentazione di resistenza.

Resilience is the most effective anaesthetic of our times, the most potent antidote against any temptation of resistance.

MARIANNA APRILE, LA STAMPA, 22 MAY 2025, P.25

Estee Lauder advertisement for 'resilience lift' crème product

doi: 10.63308/63891908548751.ch01

Background of a contested notion: resilience

Resilience is nowadays popular jargon. Programmes are broadcast about people fighting against hardship and traumas. It is part of the international banking language. The European Commission has issued a Recovery and Resilience Facility as centrepiece of Next Generation Europe. Resilience is referenced during television programmes about strategies of football teams, management of their supporters and the architecture of their stadiums. There are Facebook groups, musical bands, yoga retreats, self-help groups, *resilient cities, resilient crops, resilient dreams* and a countless number of research projects, initiatives, events, workshops designed around ideas of resilience. It has become so common that it is legitimate to wonder if it holds any meaning. With no doubt, the usefulness of the concept is debatable and the term itself contentious.

Derived from Latin *resilire*, to jump-back, it was first used by naval architects in the late nineteenth century to assist ships' resistance during navigation. It went a long way through engineering, ecology and psychology before crossing those disciplinary boundaries and entering development and humanitarian discourse. Here, definition after definition is proposed, contested, deconstructed and re-assembled by various agencies and organisations, resulting in great flexibility in the ways resilience is used. On the one hand, this flexibility is advantageous as it guarantees adaptability to specific contexts and the possibility to tailor interventions to situations on the ground. On the other hand, the amorphous term has allowed practitioners to attract funding without binding them to substantial scrutiny or transforming goals and approaches of interventions. As a result, debates about resilience have opened a turbulent stage of clashes: resilience represents an approach that challenges dominant policymaking and at the same time is meaningless jargon; resilience puts back people at the centre of discussion and at the same time maintains structures of power; resilience opens new opportunities for development and at the same time reproduces neoliberal agendas of self-responsibility; resilience encourages changes and at the same time promotes *status quo*; resilience makes use of metrics to be measurable, scaleable and comparable and, at the same time, metrics completely 'miss the point' (Levine 2014). There is, in other words, very little agreement about meanings and potentiality of resilience.

One of the very few shared acknowledgments I have found is that resilience is not a new concept, but is rooted in various fields of scientific research. As an academic term, it is said to have originated in the field of physics and mathematics, where it denoted the capacity of engineering systems such as bridges, buildings

Front and back. Family portrait at a wedding. Loima, February 2016.

and general infrastructure to absorb energy under pressure (Bruneau and Reinhorn 2006); or otherwise put: 'how fast displaced variables return towards their equilibrium following a perturbation' (Pimm 1984). Most applications of resilience, however, began in the 1970s in the fields of psychology and ecology. In psychology, resilience entails a positive outcome, such as employment, mental health, lawful behaviour or adaptation to disturbances such as adversity or trauma experienced during a lifetime. It was initially defined as a personal trait, then progressively tied to external conditions like the family or the social environment that facilitate the process of overcoming trauma. Research has more recently looked at how to create preconditions for resilience through preventative interventions and promoting competence and wellbeing. Despite ideas of bouncing to a state of *normality* remaining dominant, transitions to a better quality of life have started to be considered and resilience is also framed as a possibility for the flourishing of something not only new but also better than previous states.

In ecology science, it was first used by Holling Crawford Stanely, Emeritus Eminent Scholar and Professor in Ecological Sciences. Resilience was initially employed in studies of interacting predators and prey in relation to ecological stability theory (Holling 1961), and subsequently applied to several other field-based studies ranging from boreal forest dynamics (Ludwig, Jones and Holling 1978), grasslands (Walker, Langridge and McFarlane 1997), rangelands (Walker et al. 1981) and savannas (Ellis and Swift 1988), among others. Until the 1970s, ecology science was built on stability theory based on assumptions of one steady state and a single equilibrium (the balance of nature view). Such ecology theories were challenged in a seminal article by Holling in 1973, titled 'Resilience and stability of ecological systems', launching the beginning of ecological studies of resilience. Since, Holling has developed a theory of complex adaptation for which ecosystems are complex systems characterised by non-linear dynamics, thresholds (shifting or multiple boundaries), uncertainty and surprise. As reviewed by Carl Folke of the Stockholm Resilience Centre, and colleagues, many complex systems have multiple attractors (2010). This implies that a perturbation can bring the system over a threshold that marks the limit of the basin of attraction or stability domain of the original state, causing the system to be attracted to a contrasting state. This is no doubt qualitatively different from returning to the original state of equilibrium. Against stability (or speed of return to normal conditions), resilience started to be presented as the persistence of relationships within an ecosystem (Holling 1973,

1986). A return to a stable state is not only irrelevant but also impossible since there is no equilibrium state; rather, there are multiple basins of attraction across which systems fluctuate and flip-over. In ecology, thus, 'the emphasis is not on reaching or maintaining a certain end point or terminal condition, but on staying "in the game"' (Pickett, Cadenasso and Grove 2004: 373). Probably the most studied non-equilibrium grazing system is that of Turkana herders in the northern Kenyan arid lands, described by Ellis and colleagues. They found that rainfall levels affected all aspects of production, that rains were highly erratic, that droughts had occurred at least thirteen times in the fifty years prior to their studies at the end of the 1980s, and that the number of animals and stocking rates had very little do to with rates of loss in the flock and vegetation cover but were rather linked to the action of abiotic factors, like rain. Expanding their studies to other parts of arid Africa, they contended that, given these climatic patterns, non-equilibrium grazing systems prevail on many of the most arid rangelands of the continent. They concluded that these grazing systems are resilient, 'non-equilibrial but persistent, with system dynamics affected more by abiotic than biotic controls' (1988: 450).

The application of ideas of resilience to human systems is more recent. Adger, one of the most prominent scholars of social resilience, treated it as the ability of human communities to withstand shocks to their social structure arising from environmental stresses, or social, economic, political upheaval (2000). Broadly defined, resilience is used in various disciplines of the social sciences in the most disparate ways. In economics, for example, resilience is associated with consumption and production activities and resource allocations to withstand market shocks. In political science, it is used in relation to governance structures, laws, organisations to understand processes of internal change following institutional shocks. Most generally, resilience in the social sciences is used as a metaphor to indicate the capacities of businesses, institutions, communities or individuals to respond to adversity. In many disciplines, human actions were treated as external to the functioning of ecosystems, including herding, fishing, water harvesting, farming etcetera. Such division between social and ecological systems has been increasingly scrutinised, and it is today largely believed that many problems in natural resource use and management derive from failure to recognise that ecosystems and social systems are inextricably linked. In this way of looking at the world there is often an implicit focus on trying to resist change and to control it to maintain stability. But with the advancement of the Anthropocene, the modernist pursuit of command-and-control of the environment, of human superiority over the non-human, of centralisation and forecasting, is no longer tenable, as it harms more than it saves the planet. The notion of social-ecological-systems (SES) emerged to characterise cross-scale dynamics and interrelated social and ecological processes. Resilience scholarship then grew to inspire a shift in policies from those that aspire to control change in systems assumed to be stable, to managing the capacity of social ecological systems to cope with, adapt to and shape change. Berkes and colleagues formalised this shift in paradigm and coined the expression 'socio-ecological resilience', defined as the magnitude of disturbance that can be absorbed before a system changes to a radically different state, as well as the capacity to self-organise and the capacity for adaptation to emerging circumstances (2003). Resilience scholars started emphasising the necessity to learn to manage by change rather than simply to reacting to it, and the key role that individuals and groups or communities play in this context. Folke writes: 'It implies that uncertainty and surprise is part of the game, and you need to be prepared for it and learn to live with it' (2006: 450). This shift marked a further expansion of resilience studies toward a more explicit concern with adaptabilities and transformative abilities. Adaptability captures the capacity of a SES to learn, combine experience and knowledge, adjust its responses to changing external drivers and internal processes, and continue developing within the current stability domain or basin of attraction. By contrast, transformability has been defined as the 'capacity to create a fundamentally new system when ecological, economic, or social structures make the existing system untenable' (Walker et al. 2004: 5).

From the original backward-looking approach to resilience, used in a narrow sense to refer to the return rate to equilibrium upon a perturbation, trying to resist change and control it to maintain stability, there has progressively emerged a forward-looking approach, based on the capacities of intertwined social-ecological systems to persist, adapt and transform as part of the Anthropocene biosphere. Such a shift is gaining momentum in recent times. What has become known as the *relational turn* in the social sciences is also influencing resilience thinking. A focus on relations has the potential to overcome the ecological/social divide, putting emphasis on the patterns of relations that enable transformational change. From this perspective, resilience can no longer be treated as a fixed asset, nor as a characteristic or an attribute. It is not a *thing* that can be seized, held or managed. Resilience instead is the result of emergent relations themselves continuously made and remade in interaction with the past and the present. Darnhofer and colleagues define resilience as *becoming*, offering a dynamic view of resilience, one that focuses on change and 'navigates the adaptive cycle, rather than maintaining states and avoiding thresholds' (2016: 119).

This seems today all to be widely accepted. Yet it remains a challenge to fully account for such entanglements, to analytically represent resilience, and to put it into policy practice. In a recent article for the journal *Progress in Human Geography*, Arianna Tozzi contends that system-modelling approaches in coupled social-ecological systems end up reinforcing a functionalist view of the world as, yes, an interconnected whole, but unable to engage with the multiplicities of people's practices. The system approach reassembles objects (social or natural) and connects them at various scale of analysis. In this, she claims, it risks hiding the messiness, disjuncture and multiplicity that are key part of what resilience is ultimately about (2021: 1084). This is particularly evident in the field of development, where resilience has been defined as the 'new mantra' (Rigg and Oven 2015), a 'paradigm' (Kaika 2017), a 'buzzword' (Bouzarovski 2015), a characteristic individuals, communities and ecosystems must have to withstand shocks and minimise harms (Brown 2015).

Development translations

Focus Group run by DFID practitioners for a Resilience Assessment. Urum centre, Loima, January 2016.

Another agreed feature in resilience scholarship, besides its long history, is its extension beyond academia. Resilience is now popular in the policy lexicon as a central paradigm in policies and strategies responding to global threats, ranging from climate change to natural security, financial management, public health, economic development or terrorism. Prominent in the whole development agenda, resilience has been framed as the ultimate objective of development as well as the framework of intervention in the humanitarian sector. The way for resilience to turn so popular in policy terms was paved by many factors. Katherine Brown, an established resilience scholar, frames resilience as the *new sustainability*. She situates resilience roots in the policy arena in the publication of the Bruntland Report in 1987, and in the increased interests in global environmental issues in terms of conservation goals and global change. Acknowledging that current ways of using and managing global resources are no longer compelling, resilience frameworks in this domain reflect doubts about the capacity to meet future needs. As concerns development and humanitarian programmes, similar doubts surfaced when their effectiveness started being questioned in the early 1980s. The need to overcome the classical humanitarian-development divide emerged, favouring a *relief-development continuum*, referred to as the Linking Relief, Rehabilitation and Development approach (Mosel and Levine 2014). Later in the 1990s, a *contiguum* model emerged, aiming at increased coordination between development and humanitarian actors (Mohamed et al. 2025). In this domain, resilience frameworks work as a bridge between humanitarian actions and development programmes in response to persistent disasters through multi-sectoral approaches. Proliferation of resilience is also linked with the idea that now we live in a *time of crisis* and with a feeling of growing insecurity. This view is rooted in the idea of a *risk society* advanced by Ulrich Beck in *Risk Society, towards a New Modernity* (1992), referring to the complexity and interdependency of today's crises as well as reduced trust in human ability to control uncertainty. As a result, there is a shift in responsibilities away from national and local governments towards individuals and communities who are counselled to be resilient, vigilant and prepared – to some, a symptomatic shift of the transition from liberalism to neoliberalism. Several scholars in fact link the rise of resilience thinking in policy world with the hegemony of neoliberalism,[28] through a language of preparedness, adaptation and survivability. In line with neoliberal visions of state deregulation, reduced public interferences and celebration of individual freedoms to

---

28.   See for example Bracke 2016; Duffield 2012; Mcmichael 2009; Neocleous 2013; Rigg and Oven 2015; Walker and Cooper 2011.

make *right choices* to foster development and economic growth, resilience subjects are trained to accept and adapt to a world of endless risks (Bracke 2016).

The appropriation of resilience in the development and humanitarian domain was mobilised by a wide range of heterogenous actors, including several donors such as DFID, USAID, the EU, SIDA, OECD, some of which have even created specific funds for resilience programmes, as well as by leading institutions from the UN, WB, practitioners and international NGOs. Regardless of (or because of) its popularity, in the development sector there still is a general lack of understanding of what resilience means, how it should be promoted, applied and operationalised in the sector. It is generally used in reference to a *system* at different levels of aggregation: individuals, households, communities, organisations, states, etc. Programmes are generally developed around the identification of a set of characteristics which are deemed to *build* or *increase* resilience of the system. The goal is to present what a resilient system should look like by identifying what elements are critical for its resilience, and often, as shown by Matteo Caravani, lecturer in international development and cooperation at Roma Tre University, and his colleagues at Sussex University, the focus of interventions is on the prediction, management and control (Caravani et al. 2022). Centred around the notion of *crisis*, its prevailing operationalisation (how resilience is translated into practice) lies in the field of disaster planning. The rise of a new disaster culture first occurred through the Yokohama Strategy (1994) which marked a shift from reaction (Disaster Management) to prevention (Disaster Risk Management, DRM, or Disaster Risk Reduction, DRR), and secondly at the World Conference on Disaster Reduction through the Hyogo Framework for Action 2005–2015, *Building the Resilience of Nations and Communities to Disasters*, which highlighted the need to change the framework of intervention in disaster programming to something other than vulnerability, i.e. resilience; a goal which was re-launched in the post-2015 agenda at the World Conference on Disaster Risk Reduction (WCDRR) through the Sendai Framework for Disaster Risk Reduction 2015–2030. Generally, we can say that disaster risk responses aim to develop predictions for expected disasters, based on needs assessments, early-warning systems, anticipatory modelling, trend analysis and data-mining, and in turn plan for the outcomes, believing that more effective modelling and the resulting planning will reduce both disasters and the devastating consequences for those affected. 'Even if never accurate, the sense of being in control is important' (Caravani et al. 2022: 4).

Development translations

An appealing reason, especially for donors, for operationalising resilience as disaster risk reduction/management is that in this way it is ostensibly manageable (prediction, planning, management allows easy and linear budgeting) and measurable. Debates about disaster resilience are dominated by disputes on how to measure, monitor and evaluate resilience programmes, proposing different measurement models either based on characteristics or proxy indicators of resilience, specific implemented activities or functionalities (Levine 2014). It goes beyond the scope of my discussion to review the copious number of metrics proposed;[29] it is enough to note that the ability and methods to measure resilience are highly contested as it appears that no single tool, dataset or model is fully appropriate. In addition, tying resilience to disaster risk reduction/management is reassuringly similar to what was designed and implemented even before the mastery of the resilience agenda. In other words, it means organisations can continue business as usual, just tweaking language and re-labelling past interventions under the call for *building resilience*. This renders the whole resilience agenda more programmatically manageable because agencies will not have to think of entirely new content for interventions, or design completely new approaches. Rather, it will be enough to adjust and conform their programmes to the new resilience language. Yet, this leads one to question whether resilience, in development and humanitarian discourses, is a new idea at all.

Scholars have warned against an uncritical use of resilience. Since the Hyogo and Sendai frameworks, increasing emphasis has been placed on individual and community capacities to live with vulnerabilities. The risks of these approaches are the tendency to normalise and, especially for climate change processes, naturalise crises, casting them as of natural origin and sweeping under the carpet the legacy and ongoing pressures of capitalistic relations and political stressors (MacKinnon and Derickson 2013). Critics sustain that, through resilience programming, *therapeutic development* came to dominate, focusing on managing the effects of poverty and vulnerability by enabling and capacity building, rather than eradicating them (Chandler 2020; Grove 2018). This approach not only diverts attention and resources from real drivers of vulnerability (Bracke 2016) and downplays questions of power and politics (Scott-Smith 2018), as often sustained by critics of resilience, but, most critically, it is argued, it directly contributes to the problems of resource depletion (Chandler 2020). In these *soft* approaches, there is, in other

---

29. For reviews on resilience and measurement, see Schipper and Langston 2015; Winderl 2014.

words, a lack of understanding of the impacts of current approaches of resource management and extraction, while problems remained framed as external in search of internal solutions, through adaptive capacities, in order to maintain our existing modes of living.

'Now drought is in trouble': the resilience agenda in the Horn of Africa

The killing of the bull. Loima, December 2016.

While the difficulty of resilience in addressing issues of power, human agency or inequity has led to a questioning of the utility of the concept in development, there is little doubt that resilience has now become an 'all-embracing mobilising metaphor' (Pain and Levine 2012: 21), not least in relation to the drylands of the Horn of Africa (HoA).

The year 2010–11 is a benchmark in the humanitarian history of the HoA. Remembered as the HoA crisis, it can possibly be considered as the launchpad for the resilience agenda in East Africa. Many observers, governments and members of the international community refer to the 2010–11 crisis as *the Drought*, emerging from the failure of several rainy seasons. As we have seen, in this region drought is neither unexpected nor unusual, but in 2011 its effects were exacerbated by several other factors which led to a fast deterioration of events, including: high fuel prices, high and volatile food prices, poor governance, conflicts and lack of political commitment. As voiced by an assessment led by Maxwell and colleagues, across the Horn, an estimated thirteen million people were affected (2014). What shocked both internal and external observers at the peak of the HoA crisis, was the seeming inability of the international community to foresee the outcome of the drought (extensive famine) or act in time. Years of drought preparedness and disaster risk reduction plans bore little fruit and the resilience the international community had committed to supporting at the World Conference on Disaster Reduction, through HFA, five years earlier, was in short supply. As a result, the resilience agenda received renewed impetus from the evidence of past interventions' failure. The shift in policy saw the active participation of HoA countries themselves, who rushed to change their programming towards disasters to fully embrace resilience thinking and language, specifically addressed at Ending Drought Emergencies (EDE). Notably, on 9 September 2011 heads of states and governments in the HoA met at what is remembered as the Nairobi Summit with the goal to plan, harmonise and mobilise resources to ensure the next drought would not result in another humanitarian crisis. They defined the resilience agenda for the Horn, through the Drought Disaster Resilience Sustainability Initiative (IDDRSI), and the meeting ended with complacent confidence: 'Now drought is in trouble' (IGAD 2013).

IDDIRSI's aim has been for drought-oriented interventions to be more sensitive to long-term resilience building, protecting livelihoods through proactive early action instead of waiting for disasters to occur (Mohamed et al. 2025). Countries in the HoA have adopted national frameworks to end drought emergencies (EDE) and subsequently established national drought management institutions, such as Kenya's National Drought Management Authority (NDMA), that aim to provide early warning information and coordinate humanitarian and development interventions. Kenya's first early warning capacities were established in the 1980s. Samuel Derbyshire and colleagues retrace drought management history in Kenya in a recent article for the journal *Pastoralism: Research, Policy and Practice*, starting from the Turkana Drought Contingency Planning Unit (TDCPU), which was initially funded by the Norwegian government alongside wider Turkana Rehabilitation Project activities. In the late 1980s, the Drought Monitoring Project (DMP) emerged and expanded drought management in northern Kenya via partnerships with a wide range of other NGOs and new monitoring/assistance programmes in several other arid districts, including, for example, the World Bank funded Emergency Drought Recovery Project. The DMP was then complimented and ultimately superseded by the Drought Preparedness Intervention and Recovery Programme (DPIRP), which laid the groundwork for the Arid Lands Resource Management Project (ALRMP) to emerge in the late 1990s (Derbyshire et al. 2024: 5). However, general dissatisfaction with the centralisation of power and decision making in Kenya's national government culminated not only in the establishment of the National Drought Management Authority (NDMA) but also in seismic constitutional reform and the devolution of power to local governments following a referendum in 2010. Among all member states, Kenya has shifted towards the resilience agenda at the fastest pace, especially focusing on the arid and semi-arid lands (ASALs) located in the northern counties. The current policy framework in Kenya has indeed received a stronger push than in other IGAD states through the process of devolution initiated in 2010 with the new Constitution, which gave renewed powers to county governments, and through the private sector's interests over drylands, tied up with the discovery of large quantities of natural resources and minerals. As a result, areas historically marginalised with the label arid lands entered legal and policy frameworks, including the National Constitution as well as various acts pertaining to land, resources and national development funds.

Tom Campbell, a colleague from Maynooth University, and I reviewed the resilience agenda in Kenya for an article about the revaluation of pastoral practices and knowledge to combat climate change (2023). The Kenyan resilience agenda appears articulated in a complex policy framework made by several documents including:

- The *New Constitution 2010*, which includes articles 'to protect the interests and rights of minorities and marginalized groups, including pastoral persons and communities, whether they are (i) nomadic; or (ii) a settled community';

- The *Kenyan Vision 2030*, which represents the overarching Kenyan national plan;

- The *Development Strategy for Northern Kenya and ASALs*, also known as ASALs' policy 2012, which applies the Kenyan Vision 2030 specifically for the ASALs;

- The *Sessional Paper n.8* (2012) (National Policy for the Sustainable Development of Northern Kenya), which aims at closing the developmental gap between the north and the rest of the country.

- The *Community Land Act* (CLA) (2016), which aims at securing pastoral community land, and which Alden Wily calls the most progressive land legislation in Africa, and provides for communities, including pastoralists, to utilise and manage their land in accordance with customary norms (2018);

- Various county level *Livestock Strategies* (for example, the *Isiolo County Livestock Strategy and Action Plan, 2016*, which send a strong *pro-pastoralist* message);[30]

- Finally, the resilience agenda is also endorsed in the *Ending Drought Emergency Strategy* (EDE) 2012–2022, which tightly follows guidelines set through IDDRSI.

At the heart of this renewed policy framework there are two recurrent themes. The first concerns regional inequalities which primarily affect the arid north. These documents recognise the gap which separates northern Kenya, largely arid lands, from the rest of the country, mostly agriculture-suitable highlands and coastal regions. This gap is framed as a consequence of a political history of marginalisation and limited investments. Deliberately, the ASALs' policy and the Sessional Paper n.8 (2012), for example, challenge an historical and influential Sessional Paper, the sessional paper n.10 (1965) which perpetuated a biased distribution of resources and public investment towards the so-called *high potential areas* initiated under colonial rule:

> To make the economy as a whole grow as fast as possible, development money should be invested where it will yield the largest increase in net output. This approach will clearly favour the development of areas having abundant natural resources, good land and rainfall, transport and power facilities, and people receptive to and active in development (GoK 1965: 46).

The new policy framework identifies most problems of the arid north as political rather than ecological and aims at increasing national cohesion by closing the developmental gap created as a result of political and economic manoeuvres perpetuated from the colonial administration onwards.

The second common thread is the progressive discovery of the latent potential of ASALs. The Kenya Vision 2030 recognises a growing role for ASALs, even though these remain quite marginal in the general outline of the documents and confined to an aspired economic potential only achievable by boosting dryland agriculture, as implied by diagrams like the one below which states that of the

---

30. According to this strategy, pastoralism, 'if properly supported', remains 'the most appropriate land use and livelihood in the ASALs' (GoK-ICG, 2016: 15).

84 per cent ASAL land cover in Kenya only sixteen per cent can be considered as *potential*, reiterating a long lasting view of drylands as wastelands.

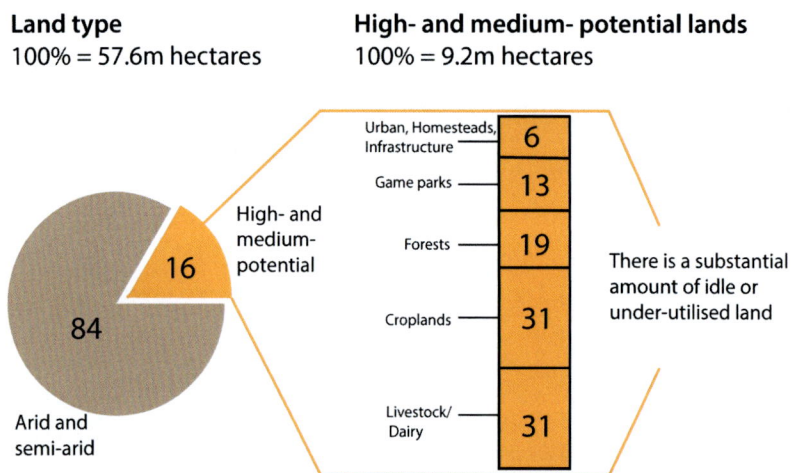

Land type
100% = 57.6m hectares

High- and medium- potential lands
100% = 9.2m hectares

Urban, Homesteads, Infrastructure — 6

Game parks — 13

High- and medium- potential

16

Forests — 19

84

Croplands — 31

Arid and semi-arid

Livestock/ Dairy — 31

There is a substantial amount of idle or under-utilised land

Figure 15. Dryland potential, Kenya Vision 2030: 47.

A more direct recognition of ASALs' potential comes from the ASALs' policy and the Sessional Paper n.8 (2012). Both texts target ASALs more specifically, as their economic role is increasingly understood. They highlight many opportunities arising from the arid regions, including: their strategic position within the Horn; domestic trade advantages and their complementarity with highland economies; natural wealth (oil, minerals, natural gas); and tourism potential. These documents also mention the opportunity to learn from arid lands populations how to manage climate change and variability; a rather different perspective from the unreceptive and passive agents described in the extract of the Sessional Paper n.10 (1965) reported above. The ASALs' policy is upfront in its endorsement of pastoralism, its critique of the historical neglect of ASAL and, notably, its emphasis on the problems of restrictions to mobility:

> Until recently, most governments viewed pastoral areas as net consumers of national wealth that offered poor prospects of return on investment. Pastoralism was therefore less valued than other forms of land use and less well-supported … Governments now recognise the strengths of pastoralism and have formed ministries or other authorities to enhance the contribution of pastoralism to food security, environmental stewardship, and economic growth (ASAL Policy 2012: 5).

The document continues: 'Pastoralists have successfully managed climate variability for centuries. Their skills and indigenous knowledge will become more valuable as the impact of global climate change becomes more pressing' (ibid.: 12). For the first time in a policy document, not only is the recurrent nature of drought recognised, but local capacities are also valued. The recent definition of pastoralism used in the Kenyan ASAL development policy is a good example of the way the understanding of pastoral mobility has also changed through time: 'As an economic activity, pastoralism is an animal production system which takes advantage of the characteristic instability of rangeland environments, where key resources such as nutrients and water for livestock become available in short-lived and largely unpredictable concentrations'. As also maintained by Samuel Derbyshire and colleagues, there is a general sense in which Kenya's institutionalisation of drought management and its commitment to ending drought emergencies is part of a broadly progressive process of political change, rather than leaving them purely to apolitical, technocratic management via a host of international (and largely project based) agencies and organisations (2014: 6).

Notwithstanding these progresses at policy level, problems remain when policies are translated into practice. A few years after these discourses gained momentum, there is still limited investment in pastoral economies. Some investments may even be pushing marginalisation and segregation of pastoral people in favour of a growing educated elite, sequestering resources for urban centres. Interventions proposed by the Kenya Vision 2030 as *flagship projects* are not particularly different from previous modes of interventions: early warnings, irrigation schemes, boreholes, school feeding programmes, market infrastructure, veterinary support, etc. Despite growing recognition of dryland populations' abilities and knowledge, they are still treated as vulnerable to their environment and in need of *development*. The EDE Strategy, IDDRSI milestone, a ten-year programme (2012–2022) aiming to end drought emergencies by 2022 and focusing on the 23 most drought-prone counties, is a good example for this observation, as it basically allows development/ humanitarian interventions to continue their legacies on the ground. Designed to add value to already existing activities, it was noted that 87 per cent of its funds are spent in standard sustainable livelihood projects and disaster risk-management activities, traditional policies linked to disaster reduction, now associated with drought resilience. For Mohamed and colleagues, EDE failed to practically end drought emergencies, partly due to inadequate coordination between governments, shifts in policy priorities and insufficient budgetary allocation (2025: 8).

The reiteration of past policies is seemingly transmitted also at county level, where EDE was anchored through the County Integrated Development Plans (CIDPs) emerging from devolution plans. Turkana County received the largest share of the EDE fund, with over $220m worth of projects invested in the region since 2011, and yet it did not lead to significantly different operations from the past. An assessment carried out by ODI has labelled CIDPs as largely aspirational documents with little evidence of effective programming and tied to budgets available at county level (Carabine, Jouanjean, and Tsui 2015). Embarking on the second phase of devolution, in Turkana, for example, despite the identification of the livestock sector as a policy priority, only approximately two per cent of the county budget is actually allocated to the pastoral economy, the same figure as in the previous County mandate. Instead, the largest shares of Turkana budget, in line with EDE's recommendations, are allocated to more classical interventions in dryland linked with water, irrigation, health and education sectors. Likewise, international aid linked to the EDE Strategy was invested in standard Disaster Risk-Management (DRM) and Sustainable Livelihoods interventions, as labelled in the *resilience investment tracker* (Figure 16). In these sectors, some of the largest programmes in Turkana are funded by the UK's Department of International Development (DFID), like the Arid Land Support Programme (ASP) and the Hunger and Safety Net Programme (HSNP). Also, a large number of NGO consortia have emerged to address the resilience agenda, such as La Nina Consortium (composed of Oxfam, ACTED, Concern Worldwide and VSF and receiving funding from the European Commission Humanitarian Aid and Civil Protection Office, ECHO); and Swift consortium, which operates through Oxfam and Practical Action, and promotes: drilling and rehabilitating boreholes; laying pipelines; constructing water kiosks; installing tanks and solar pumping systems; constructing and rehabilitating shallow wells; and equipping boreholes with low-maintenance Blue-Pumps.

From the 2018–2022 CIDP we can trace an ambiguous position towards pastoralism; on the one hand, it describes pastoralism as a specialised livelihood linked to a particular environment:

> For the past 400 years, mobile livestock herding offered the most appropriate production system to manage the harsh and variable environmental conditions found in the county (Turkana County 2018: 23).

But, on the other hand, pastoralism is seen as compromised by population growth, climate change and environmental degradation:

'Now drought is in trouble'

$224,299,961	63	57	16	8
BUDGET	PROJECTS	PARTNERS	DONORS	SECTORS

Sector

Donor by Budget

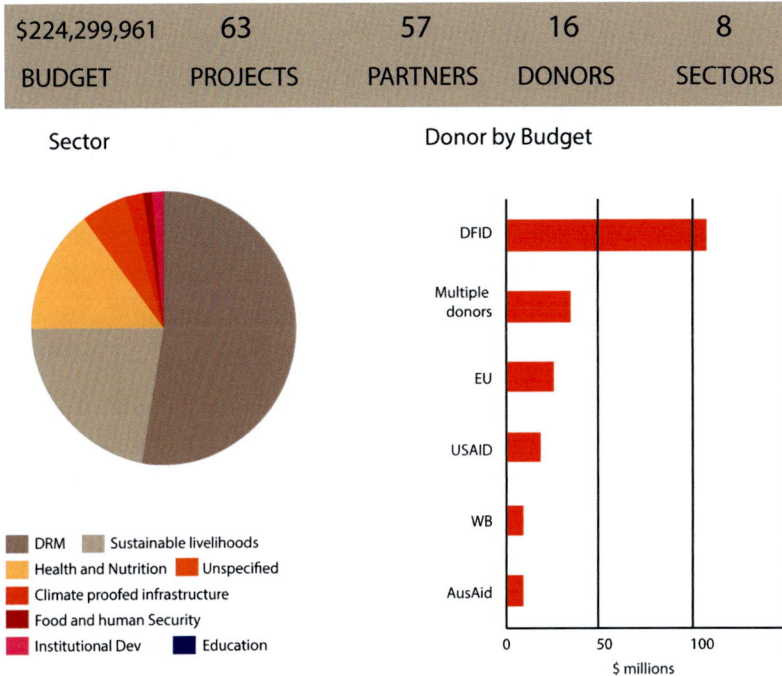

DRM   Sustainable livelihoods
Health and Nutrition   Unspecified
Climate proofed infrastructure
Food and human Security
Institutional Dev   Education

Figure 16. Resilience dashboard: investment tracker based on 3W Resilience Map, UNOCHA. (No longer available online).

… Over the past 40 years, the ability of Turkana people to secure their livelihood from nomadic pastoralism has come under pressure (ibid: 23).

And despite livestock being the major source of income, therefore supposedly a sector worthy of investment, solutions tend not to be found in strengthening the livestock sector but solving the lack of alternative options to pastoralism:

[there are] very few viable livelihoods alternatives to nomadic pastoralism, result-ing in high levels of poverty and food insecurity among the population (ibid: 23).

Scholarly changes in the views of pastoralism which stressed the importance of mobility, flexibility and adaptability for pastoral livelihoods have somewhat been lost in the translation into development practices which favour physical fixed constructions, provision of hard assets and promotion of alternative livelihoods. Overall, there has been a lot of emphasis on achieving agreements among nation states (regional transboundary agreements in both East and West Africa, for ex-ample) but little effort as regards their translation into national programmes by budgeting associated investments. There has been a general failure to incorporate these agreements into the wider national frameworks, resulting in inconsistencies among neighbouring states that can create disincentives to movement, if for example pastoralists no longer have access to resources or lose their rights if they temporarily vacate an area (Davies, Ogali, Slobodian, Roba, Ouedraogo, Velasco-Gil and Maru 2018). There have also been observed inconstancies within a single state policy framework when frontiers are closed despite regional agreements for terrorism or disease control (competing national objectives), or in the case of the recent Covid-19 pandemic restrictions (Simula et al. 2021). In general, these policies remain developed centrally and have a tendency to be imposed over a local population that therefore lacks ownership and control.

As it emerges, there is not much change in policy practices, confirming Brown's argument that resilience programmes tend to promote business as usual, notwithstanding the potentialities that could instead arise from new resilience thinking (Brown 2011). Such a conclusion does not really come as a surprise. Jedd and colleagues in 2021, in an article on the impacts of the Sendai framework in the Middle East and North Africa, have shown that, despite proactive risk management approaches promoted in the new disaster culture, drought management fundamentally remained anchored to crisis interventions (2021). For Derbyshire and colleagues, most problems remain with the negative characterisation of drylands pastoralism that has shaped interventions throughout much of the twentieth century and the general conceptual association of *development* with a shift away from pastoralist practices, despite scientific revaluation and progressive policy narratives (2024). The humanitarian architecture put in place after the 2010–11 HoA crisis treated the drought as a monolithic and dominant event, overshadowing people's everyday life, forgetting that drought is cyclical and part of life in drylands. Finding myself amid the 2017 drought as it was slowly approaching, I could see the progressive incorporation of droughts into the practices of my hosts. They continued their lives, building relationships, trading, hosting visitors (including myself) and more. It was evident that drought has long been a characteristic feature of their environments. They were prepared to manage such times of scarcity in a variety of ways, drawing on diverse social networks, skills and forms of information to strategically navigate a rapidly shifting terrain of constraints and possibilities. During the approaching drought, my hosts reinforced their sense of belonging and their identity of endurance and resistance in opposition to the weaknesses of those who instead flee and wail, like town people, demonstrating a strong culture of endurance. Conversations grew about footprints of the *enemy* (neighbouring pastoral tribes) found in the surrounding area, marking that moment in life in which people have to move closer, build higher fences around their huts, escort women to fetch water, guard animals. Relatedly, the increasing distance between homesteads and water sources at times of drought was the result of a local algorithm measuring water and grazing needs of livestock (and people) and increasing levels of insecurity around wells. Huts closer to water sources are more exposed to the danger of raids and attacks from the enemy. The usual kilometres-distance to water used as proxy for vulnerability and poverty was flipped, reflecting instead a deeper awareness of space built from within. Humanitarian policies fail to account for the strain and fear of digging deeper and deeper wells around which families ally, share duties and crucial information, and find conviviality. Outsiders' investments in boreholes and mechanic pumps break all this and translate in a form of emplacement, staying put, which encloses people, livestock and the lived space. I believe that it is important to follow the vantage point of Turkana herders in order to gain an understanding of resilience within, and hopefully provide the international community with the means to a more attentive programming, sensitive to insights, perceptions and voices of their targeted beneficiaries, mobile pastoralists, in this case.

Resilience in motion

Many critiques towards the use of resilience in the development sector concentrate around problems of definitions (Brassett, Croft and Vaughan-Williams 2013; Levine et al. 2012; Maxwell et al. 2014), fuzziness and its normative character (Brown 2015; Jerneck and Olsson 2008; Mitchell and Harris 2012). During my doctoral degree, Tomm Scott-Smith, Associate Professor of Refugee Studies and Forced Migration at my department, published an article in which he strongly affirmed that resilience should be resisted because 'too cosy, too diffuse, too prone to fuzzy thinking' (2018: 13). In 2013 the *New York Times* magazine declared resilience to be the buzzword of the year: attractive but meaningless, desirable but void of pathways and guidelines on how to get there. Others argue that the further resilience travels into the social sciences, away from engineering and ecology fields, the more 'its conceptual clarity and practical relevance is critically in danger', as original descriptive meanings of resilience are diluted in ambiguous ways (Brand and Jax 2007). Its applicability in social domains and dynamics is thus questioned as risking a fall into scientific imperialism and a silencing of the plurality of voices, especially from the least influential parts of society (Chandler and Coaffee 2015).

Herding shoats through Turkana plains. Turkana Central, November 2016.

Others warn against the conservative nature of resilience thinking and program-ming. We have seen how it can promote business as usual, re-packaging and re-labelling the same interventions, and maintaining the focus on the persistence of the system (structure, function and identity). In so doing, resilience language tends to be excessively technocratic and managerial. Discussion is wrapped around scientific definitions, metrics and technocratic responses which divert attention from the real problem at stake: reducing people's vulnerabilities (Levine 2014). Most interventions fail to underscore the root cause of vulnerability as historical marginalisation, a lack of political accountability and a general disconnection from local realities and planning and practice (Mohamed et al. 2025). This is mostly because strategies are often guided by views from above, divorced from actual livelihood dynamics (Semplici 2020). As reviewed by Mohamed and colleagues, Kenya defined a resilience strategy in 2011 through its Common Programme Framework for ending drought emergencies, with the overall goal of enhancing community resilience to drought by effective coordination of interventions between national, county and local communities. Yet the response to the 2022 drought has not been substantively different from previous interventions and significant disconnections continue existing between the availability of progressive policies for drought management and the practical implementations of these policies. For the authors: 'EDE clearly failed to end drought emergencies, as Kenya experienced severe drought (and concomitant emergencies) between 2020 and 2022. This drought was met with an exceptionally disjointed effort by both national and county governments and insufficient budget allocation for long-term livelihood support' (Mohamed et al. 2025: 11).

The development literature on resilience still considers disasters as episodes/events rather than a peak of a continuum, ignoring theoretical evolutions in the disaster literature whereby disasters can no longer be 'mentally exiled to an archipelago of exceptionalism' (Hewitt 1983).[31] For example, despite the idea of droughts in drylands as major disasters of exceptional nature having long been challenged, donors still continue to see droughts as exogenous and sudden events. Dominant frameworks emerging from resilience interventions still treat crises as

---

31. The literature on disasters has considerably evolved through time. Initially, disasters were considered to be *Acts of God* triggered by human sins. Since the Enlightenment, this view has changed (Manyena 2009). Increasingly, disasters were framed as *Acts of Nature*, or as a 'duplication of wars' (Quarantelli 1998), imputing catastrophes to an external agent against which human communities must react. This view has also considerably changed since researchers started recognising the social foundations of the evolution of disasters (Alexander 1997; Blaikie 1994; Hewitt 1983). Researchers now see disasters as caused by social conditions rather than by geophysical agents. As a result, disasters cannot occupy a specific phase within a classical cycle that moves from quiescence to warning and pre-alarm, to crisis manifestation, and finally rehabilitation and reconstruction. Rather, they are embedded within daily ordinary lives and are increasingly framed as normal orders rather than abnormal exceptions.

unforeseen singular events that disrupt normal life and require help from outside. The conventional framework of analysis in the development/humanitarian sector uses *the crisis* as the conceptual framework and analytical lens to explain people's behaviour and responses. Everything is discussed in the 'shadows of the crisis' (Bakewell and Bonfiglio 2013). As a result, resilience operates as a 'discourse of survival' (Jasanoff 2008) and reiterates ideas of coping as a main frame to understand livelihood practices. Matteo Caravani and colleagues sustain that the focus on shocks highlights 'events, moments of disruption and crisis', around which mobilisation of resources and actions must occur (Caravani et al. 2022: 4). The emphasis is not just on post-shock response, as forecasting and anticipation of events is a key part of the approach, central to building prior resilience. Events are predicted as risks, rather than seen in a wider context of unfolding uncertainties, and anticipatory actions therefore can be predefined and prepared for in a proactive response strategy. By excessively focusing on the *shadows of the crisis* one risks ignoring the social context and historical perspectives of the crisis itself. One also ignores the degree of embeddedness of crises in societies and the fact that people continue living their daily lives, despite it all. With this I am not implying that we should discard the element of crisis and accept/normalise it.

I do not wish to underestimate the suffering of many people in drylands when droughts strike. But to examine the nature of the crisis, I believe, we must also look beyond it. My last trip to one of my field sites took place in February 2017, it was the peak of the last drought hitting the HoA. All shallow wells in the area were dry, as well as most drilled boreholes. Water was only available from one windpump that had been drilled by UNICEF, if there was wind. I had gone to visit my host family, to greet them before I moved back to the UK. When I arrived at their homestead, located some kilometres away from the main road and settlement, only kids welcomed me. The three huts, for the three family wives, looked abandoned, goats' kraals silent. However, I quickly learnt that my host parents had simply gone to celebrate a friend's wedding. Kids stayed at home to look after the huts and the few remaining goats, as most of the herd had migrated long before with their older brothers and two co-wives. A couple of days after, my host parents arrived thrilled from the wedding and with plenty of meat. I spent my last days in Turkana, during the peak of one the most severe droughts in memory,[32]

---

32. Since the end of 2016 and throughout 2017 the HoA experienced a long-term drought. Media spoke of one of the severest droughts in living memory. See http://www.irinnews. org/analysis/2017/10/12/drought-pushes-kenya-s-pastoralists-brink Since, several other major droughts have occurred.

eating meat, playing games with kids during nights of the full moon and sharing countless anecdotes. Thus, to challenge the baggage of assumptions and stereotypes that shape dominant images of *drylands in crisis*, I urge moving beyond the crisis element, searching for every-day forms of resilience, such as the sharing of meat during a severe drought with my host family in Lorengelup, and 'attending to all possibilities for life', not just survival (Leach 2008: 309).

The centrality of the crisis in resilience interventions in drylands reflects equilibrium thinking rooted in engineering and classical ecology traditions. From equilibrium thinking, the main implication is that *bouncing* is ideal; an expression which is indeed very common in the application of resilience in the development sector. Emphasis moves from maintaining the status quo/returning to normal (reductionist approach), *bouncing-back*, to managing change and developing processes of becoming/transformation, thriving from crises (transformative approach), 'bouncing-forward' (Manyena 2009). If the *bouncing-back* analogy is clearly problematic for its little attention to what normality entails, and for hardly being either possible or desirable, the *bouncing-forward* metaphor is also questionable. In many circumstances it is equally unrealistic and, most importantly, it preserves ideas of discrete and stable states of change through crises (before and after) in which crises maintain central stage. Both, reductive and transformative approaches, imply an idea of progress as a linear path. Bakewell (2008a) showed that the practice of development has, not surprisingly, remained anchored to belief in *progress*, from one development status to the next (Bakewell 2008b). Once normality has recovered from the disturbing element of the crisis, a steady progress will unfold, generally illustrated by an upward line on a graph which shows increasing wellbeing and economic prosperity, while poverty ends. In contexts characterised by high variability, such as drylands, ideas of bouncing through stable states of progress are not only meaningless but also counterproductive. In these contexts, goals of linear development are perpetually hampered by what Emery Roe, policy analyst at the at the Centre for Catastrophic Risk Management of the University of California, called the 'mess paradox: The more mess there is, the more reliability decision-makers want; but the more reliable we try to be, the more mess is produced' (Roe 2013: 7). It is therefore suggested not to resist variability, but to move with it.

Mobility allows looking at fluxes and flows, processes and practices and imbedded relationality, rather than *bouncing states*, and, as an analytical lens, allows a better understanding of the behaviour of drylands and their inhabitants. I turn towards the use of mobility as the theoretical foundation for the understanding of resilience. The emerging picture objects to negative views of mobility and proposes mobility as part of the *solution*, as an integral part of people's lives and lived environments. I contend that, because mobility is so central to people's lives and places, analysis of resilience should be set in motion, and that attempts at constraining mobility can only increase vulnerability, undermining agency and reducing resilience. Rejecting a dominant 'sedentarist's metaphysics' (Malkki 1997) or 'sedentism biases' (Rodgers and Semplici 2023), implicit in development projects, which imposes order and fixity, I draw from the mobility paradigm which instead promotes a 'nomadic metaphysics' (Cresswell 2006), putting mobility first: not as a threat, nor as an obstacle or a sign of disorder or exceptional circumstance, but as a sociology of everyday life.

The relevance of mobility as an analytical lens explaining resilience in drylands emerged only from within, when I started seeing the world around me through the eyes of my host families. A corollary of this is the over-imposition of the views of outsiders over the perspectives of insiders on their own lives, consequently lacking the nuance of observations developed from within. Adding to more *objective views* of resilience as resulting from quantitative metrics, one should also pursue *constructivist views* of resilience by using people's own narratives and perceptions, as proposed by Katherine Brown in the book *Resilience, Development and Global Change* (2015). In other words, resilience should stop existing as a *category for outsiders*, as a view from above, but rather exist in the lived and imaginal experiences of people in their everyday, at their eye level; it should not aim at 'making a view of the world but taking a view in it' (Ingold 2000: 42). The next four chapters represent an attempt to highlight everyday forms of resilience. They come together, I hope, to provide a different narrative that rescues drylands and their inhabitants from the prejudices they are subject to, and to give resilience another possibility.

∼ Chapter 2. ∼

The nomadism of space.
An experiential journey through the variability of drylands

Possibilities are limited only by the power of the imagination.

TIM INGOLD (2000)

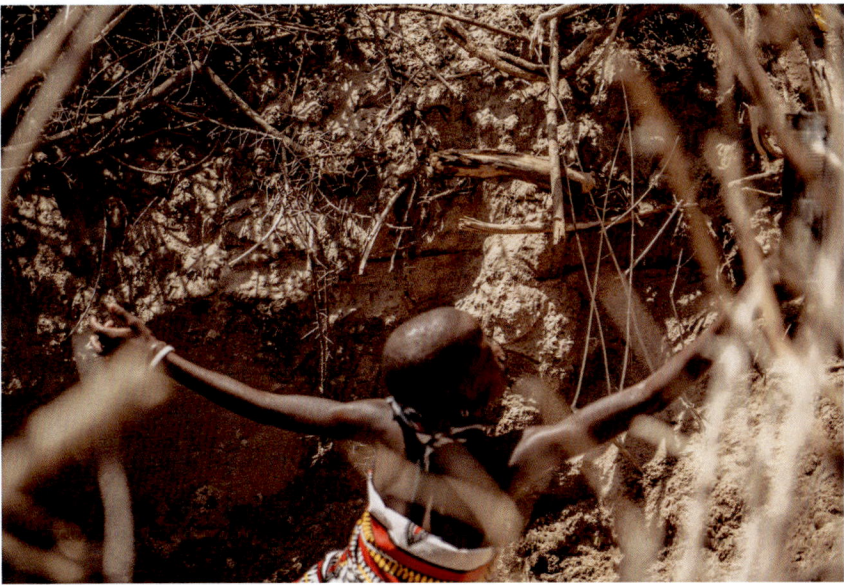

The well dance.

A girl fetching water at her family well. Lorengelup, Turkana Central, January 2016.

doi: 10.63308/63891908548751.ch02

The nomadism of space

Seeing like a herder

Not sunflowers, not roses, but rocks in patterned sand grow here. And bloom.

ROBERT HAYDEN, QUOTED IN TAIYE (2014)

Inspecting camel brands. Lorengelup, Turkana Central, November 2015.

'There used to be a time I could see the lake, and even beyond'. Akamaise once described her visits to her brother up the mountains in Lothagam in Turkana central, not too far from the eastern shores of Lake Turkana. When the sky was clear of clouds, she could see the other side of the lake. She could see Loiyangalani, and she remembered laughing at the reflections of metal shacks. This pleasant image was broken by concern in her face. 'I was scared', she continued. She described long waves shaking the surface of the lake, as if these could reach, take and drag her into the water. 'I do not wish to go close to the lake'. But she concluded by hoping the lake's waters could open to let her pass and reach the other side.[33]

33. The magical crossing of water, echoing the Jewish passage through the Red Sea, is a popular motif in Turkana mythology, which dates to long before Christianity arrived in their land. In Turkana the story is connected to the appearance of camels, thanks to a powerful diviner who saw in dreams animals as big as giraffes but with a huge hump. It was a time of drought and dying livestock. He went off with a large Turkana army towards the lake and opened up its water by beating the surface with his wooden stick. They crossed the lake, raided the camels on the other side of Lake Turkana, and ran back, closing off its water on the *enemies* who were running after them.

Akamaise is the youngest of the three wives of my host family in Lorengelup, a sub-location of Turkana Central. Currently settled within walking distance, approximately five kilometres, from the main centre, as locals call villages, she lives with two co-wives, their children, the husband they have in common, and a number of goats, sheep and camels; their cows stay with family friends along the lake shore where grass can be found. It is a relatively wealthy family. Although living mainly a pastoral life, they are also engaged in other activities, including charcoal burning, small trade at local markets, farming along the Turkwell river, and aid watching.

Akamaise is one of the best story tellers I have ever met. She enjoyed talking, chatting and showing me around while holding my hand. The night she talked about lake Turkana was not the first time she mixed her real-life experiences with mythological images. Unfortunately, that night we did not develop our discussion as far as tracing her knowledge of the Bible; nor did we talk about why she cannot see the lake anymore – either she no longer visits her brother, or something has changed in the landscape (taller trees, the lake has withdrawn further, buildings or construction are in the way), or she has never been able to see the lake from the Lothagam mountains. Either way, she was framing her notion of space. Her space is extendable (beyond what is reachable in her everyday living); her space has borders that can be dangerous to cross (or require negotiation if it implies entering someone else's land); her space is fluid and mobile, perpetually reproducing.

Space is a concept that encompasses geographical imaginations as much as policy and actions. Presumed to be relatively fixed and given, it has long been seen as a container divorced from a subject position (Livingstone 1992), a static nothingness which begins with some empty and innocent spatial spread, waiting for human activities (Casey 1996). Since the 1970s, thanks to Lefebvre's influential *Le production de l'espace*, the understanding of space has considerably changed (translated into English in 1991). Theories of relational geography emerged, pursuing an alternative imagination of space, that social scientist and geographer Doreen Massey called one of 'heterogeneity, relationality, and openness' (2005: 10). Space started being seen as a product of interrelations, constituted through interactions, a 'meeting place' made of multiple relations (Massey 1991, 2005). In opposition to a lifeless space, *relationalism* gave room to the understanding of dynamic processes of change (Murdoch 2006). Space could no longer be considered an empty container, but something only provisionally stabilised, under perpetual renewal. From these premises, mobile-space approaches have developed in geography and anthropology (Retaillé 2013; Walther, Howard and Retaillé 2015). Rejecting a 'metaphysics of sedentarism' (Malkki 1997) grounded in the tradition of maps (points, lines and areas) and based on a 'sedentary perception of the world' (Thrift 2006), mobile-space approaches started instead to focus on flows, exchanges and 'circulations' (Castells 1999), framing space as under incessant becoming, never complete but always under construction, highlighting the ongoing production of space, 'continually remade anew' (Adey 2006: 90).

These approaches are particularly relevant for the case of dryland environments, which work under laws of variability and disequilibrium. Uneasiness with classical ecological models in rangeland science began to grow in the 1980s. Until then, it was believed that, in the absence of grazing, each rangeland had a single state of equilibrium, called *climax*, achieved through a steady process of succeeding growth of vegetation, and corresponding to a well-defined *carrying capacity*[34] (Westoby et al. 1989). Exceeding the ecosystem carrying capacity was considered the primary source of degradation in arid and semi-arid lands, largely imputed to pastoralists and their herds because of overstocking and overgrazing (Brown 1971; Lamprey 1983; Le Houérou 1989). It was argued that pastoralists accumulate livestock more for their social value and prestige than for subsistence or economic reasons, something known as the *cattle complex*, first discussed by Herskovits (1926). In the absence of private property regimes or state regulations, the social desire to increase herd size leads to overgrazing. This case was presented by Hardin in his article 'The tragedy of the commons' (1968). Drawing from Malthusian population growth theories, Hardin argued that privately owned cattle grazing on communal land would inevitably lead to the overexploitation of resources and disruption of the environment, because no one is held responsible. Hardin's thesis had a significant influence on public attitudes towards pastoralist land-use systems and provided the rationale for sweeping privatisation and commercialisation of livestock production in the 1970s and 1980s. Writing the same year as the United Nations Convention to Combat Desertification (UNCCD), Swift argued that the *desertification narrative* had become widely accepted because it served the interests of groups of policy actors, including national governments in Africa, international aid bureaucracies and scientists (1996). In the 1970s, newly independent African governments were restructuring their bureaucracies and seeking to gain central control over natural resources. Droughts, and the assumptions about human-induced degradation linked to them, legitimised such claims and made centralised top-down planning seem a logical strategy (Swift 1996). For many policymakers in the post-independence period, pastoralists and livestock mobility were associated with a primitive past,

---

34. Size of different populations (plants, humans, and animals) that can be sustained through time in a particular area or ecological niche.

soon to be replaced by economic development and progress (Turner and Schlecht 2019). Their views were imbued with assumptions about the existence of a pristine space over which pastoralism acts as a source of disturbance, contributing to the encroachment of deserts.

In the 1980s and 1990s, the limitations of using conventional assumptions of equilibrium models started to emerge, prompted by Holling and colleagues (1973). Strong fluctuations in dryland ecologies were observed regardless of density related processes, indicating that an equilibrium point was hardly to be found and maintained (Behnke and Scoones 1992; Ellis and Swift 1988; Sandford 1983; Scoones 1995a; Westoby et al. 1989). Various alternative models have since been proposed[35] around the concept of non-equilibrium, emerging as a 'new rangeland paradigm' (Behnke et al. 1993; Niamir-Fuller 1999; Sandford 1983; Scoones 1995a). These new models allowed for a different understanding of drylands as 'resilient' (Ellis and Swift 1988): without an equilibrium but with persistent ecosystems. Variations in vegetative structure, ground cover and precipitation, corresponding to the concentration and dispersal of livestock, started being framed in terms of *variability* and were increasingly treated as structural features of drylands, where no stability to return to, or climax to achieve, could be found (Krätli 2015).

By bringing together the new rangeland paradigm with theories of relational geography and mobile space, it is possible to achieve an appreciation of space as alive, itself in movement, generating movement and generated by the movement of biotic organisms and abiotic factors. In this chapter, I argue that movement is constitutive of place. In this, I do not allude to a metaphor of the movements that occur over ground, but to a recognition that space itself is *nomadic*. For this, I mobilise Tim Ingold's vision of life as a 'phenomenon of lines' (2011: 12) produced by every human and non-human being moving in the world. He describes every organism (human and non-human) as a moving line, interweaving with other lines: earth and sky move, rivers and underground water; plants, seeds and wind; livestock and wild animals; land soils and surfaces. Everything moves and interweaves with each other. Space is never motionless, plants generate movement, trees flex, rocks drift, mountains glide, sand flows; 'the world breathes' (Ingold 2000: 21).

This perspective is missing in the development literature, which still largely, as we shall see, frames deserts as wastelands and inhospitable places, a static nothingness only disrupted by elements of fragility (droughts, disappearing water, land

---

35. Cf. Westoby et al. 1989 for state and transition models; Roe et al. 1998 for reliability models; Ellis and Swift 1988 for persistency models; NRC 1994 for rangeland health; Oba et al. 2000 for climate-plant-herbivore interaction model, among others.

exsiccation). Remote. Peripheral lands. From the perspective of urban dwellers, development indeed ends on the fringes of towns. Even the renewed attention given to the drylands today, brought about by discourses on *frontier economies* and *Africa Rising,* resulting in large-scale infrastructural investment and increased presence of extractive industries (Lind, Okenwa and Scoones 2020; Lind and Rogei 2025; Mosley and Watson 2016), reiterates an operational view of drylands as space strategically produced as a means to certain ends, otherwise valueless and desolate. Northern Kenyan drylands are punctuated by these forms of intervention (dryland extensive farming, geothermal power extraction, wind farms, oil drilling, mega-dams), which result in carving, enclosing, bordering lands, and reveal a struggle over the meaning of space and resources between *insiders*, everyday inhabitants, and *outsiders*. The latter attribute to drylands a role of deficit, as 'lacking in some ways' (Krätli 2013:1): fragile, unproductive and with scant resources, remote and peripheral to urban hubs and cities (see for example policy reports such as Cervigni and Morris 2016; Headey and Kennedy 2012; Headey, Taffesse and You 2014). This view is reinforced also by social media, which frequently reports drylands' populations as dependent on food aid and engaged in endemic conflicts over *scarce* resources, and refers to testimonies of pastoral dropouts to confirm ideas of drylands as *failed areas*, urgently requiring external action and innovation (see Shanahan 2016 for example).

How is the desert space instead seen by its everyday inhabitants? How do they learn, represent and perceive their lived environment? How do they experience variability? In this chapter, I turn my eyes towards the everyday practices of Turkana herders to show that far from being a *fragile nothingness*, desertscapes take on life. I depict a nomadic space that composes and recomposes itself in relation to the movements of human and non-human beings and abiotic factors. As a result, the nomadic space can no longer been seen as a *tabula rasa*, a static nothingness, but a rich and dynamic place. In other words, drylands are not uniform stretches of grassland but a sequence of dynamic patches, varying over space and time. From this perspective, scarcity becomes political: what resources are scarce and for whom? As argued by Ian Scoones in *Sustainable Livelihoods and Rural Development*, scarcities are always relational and constructed in particular social-political settings to the end of denying some people identified as *culprits* access to the resources on which they have long depended (2021: 64). In a nomadic space, scarcity depends on the vantage point and is a function of scale. My friend and colleague Ryan Unks, currently working at the Institute of Environmental Science and Technology of the Universitad Autònoma de Barcelona, in a recent article for *Landscape Ecology,* presents an innovative landscape ecology framework that considers scales that are relevant to rural livelihoods by understanding access, land use and landscape processes as intertwined (Unks 2023). Through such perspective, landscape ecology also becomes sensitive to power asymmetries, creating robust analytical linkages between social and ecological processes. Indeed, broadening the scale of observation, resources become available, in different places at different times, making accessibility (how to access resources? who can use them, when and for what purpose?) a crucial and highly political element of discussion, confrontation and negotiation.

By bringing together mobile space approaches, phenomenology of space, ecology science and, most importantly, the experience of everyday inhabitants, it is possible to rescue drylands from the fog of misinformation in which they are trapped. As argued by Massey (2005), this is an important exercise, because the way we think about space matters, it influences our understanding of the world, our attitudes, representations and politics.

A mobile territory through a live geography

The oaks marched north

...

If you open the temporal lines widely enough
everything moves,
nothing is static.

JAMES SCOTT (2020)

Back to the kraal. Lorengelup, Turkana Central, January 2016.

It is Christmas; we are in Urum, a small village at the border with Uganda, celebrating with a dik-dik soup and ugali *(maize meal). Together with my two research assistants, I am spending a few days here before starting to walk along the mountains separating Kenya from Uganda. We want to meet people living outside newly developed centres (what local people call villages) to learn about their connections with the closest centres, their narratives of problems faced, and responses adopted, and to move out of Urum, where village dynamics can be quite a strain for a young girl, as I was labelled.*

Seen in aerial photography, Turkana looks like a dull spot of desert, an arid savannah that welcomes nothing more than thorns and dust (Figure 17). Yet, looking at the region from within, moving through it, Turkana does not appear ecologically uniform. Turkana is a place where many ecosystems intersect, including plains and mountains, hills, piedmonts, sandy dunes, riverine sediments, lake shores, bushland, grasslands and forests (Anderson and Johnson 1988; Herlocker, Shaabani and Wilkes 1994). Such heterogeneity disappears with the adoption of a zonal model that organises space in homogeneous cells. Ecologists refer to *spatial controls* that are superimposed on land, with the side effects of partitioning landscapes and limiting access to land (Unks 2023). In these models, each spatial differentiation becomes spatial segmentation, and the earth's surface is divided into a mosaic of externally bounded segments. This reflects an old way of doing geography, referred to by Doel as pointillism (1999); the point dominates geographic practices by mapping surface into regular units of classification and identifying production systems within these units, losing connections and relations among them.

Development and economic interests in the drylands tend to be confined within some of these bounded segments, considered pockets of *high potential* from which resources can be extracted. Take, for example, the great emphasis given to investments in irrigation canals along the Turkwel or Kerio rivers in the recent Turkana County Integrated Development Plan 2018–2022, reconfirmed in the following 2023–2027 plan (Turkana County 2018, 2023). These types of intervention frequently entail the alienation and fragmentation of pastoral lands and reveal a continued misconception of pastoral land use. So do land confinement for oil extraction in south Turkana, or the vast fields devolved to the Lake Turkan Wind Power programme, or to the Northern Rangeland Trust conservancies (NRT). These are all interventions thought of in isolation, and carry the danger of altering lived

A mobile territory through a live geography

Figure 17. Turkana satellite map

geographies, creating a mosaic of enclosed territories and ignoring broader socio-ecological dynamics that take place in the territory at large. Certainly, herders are not limited by the imaginary boundaries imposed upon space by forms of 'enclave development', to refer to Ferguson's view of oil exploration in Africa, which divides land with 'bricks and razor wire' (2005: 387). Herders do not *hop* from enclave to enclave, but transverse the territory at large, flowing through diverse spaces and navigating change. They move beyond enclaves, taking advantage of multiple habitats across and within ecological niches. By following the herders' movements, it is possible to see the signs of connections between coexisting micro-zones in which resources grow, deteriorate and flourish again at different times. The Turkana

The nomadism of space

landscape, for example, is webbed with paths and footways: the tracks of birds, animals, people; the footprints of excessively loaded donkeys; the imprinted trails of motorbikes; the foils of hunted animals. By moving, Turkana herders respond to movements of their space, which restlessly decomposes and recomposes. They move between lowlands and highlands; between wet areas and drier areas during rainy seasons; they move following grazing itineraries, responding to the needs of livestock, water availability, away from ticks and flies; they move through a space that moves. In order to take all these movements into account and to compose a comprehensive picture of the territory, we need to look beyond – beyond our vantage point, beyond our categories and cartographies, beyond the micro zonal standard approaches to land and mapped borders – to take instead a broad view, to recognise the existence of a *large-scale ecology* and let a complex web of relation-ships, connecting heterogeneous ecologies, emerge.

Broadening the ecological scale also implies broadening the timescale. It contributes, in other words, to a renewed understanding of the temporality of the drylands: a *nomadic time*. Like space, time tends to be analysed as punctiform (Casey 1996), as if it could be fractioned in a linear and sequential range of dots displayed through clocks and calendars. In her doctoral thesis on the temporality of mobility in nomadic pastoral practice and culture, Natasha Maru also shows how the dominant view of time is as a 'point in time' (2022: 42). Following mobility turn scholars, like James Urry, she argues that 'modern time' is decontextualised, rationalised and abstracted, represented by the 'standardised, homogenous, and unchanging units of clocks and calendars' (ibid.). It is discrete and linear, whereby one moment follows the next, and the past precedes the present and the future. Such a view of time is opposite to the Lefebvrian *lived time* experienced through nature and socially constructed. Especially in variable environments, such as the northern Kenyan drylands, there are multiple and simultaneous timescales that are difficult to capture with clocks and calendars. For example, I tried to understand Turkana territory through seasonal calendars, mapping human activities across the year through a sequential organisation of time. This was never a success. Such a goal was continuously hampered by incredible variations in the months themselves, which I never fully managed to understand. Like 'The Nuer who do not use names of the months for marking the time of an event ... Time is a relation between activities ... Time does not have the same value throughout the year' (Evans-Pritchard 1940: 119–20), the Turkana also mark time by means of observations and corresponding actions. For the elaboration of seasonal calendars, I started focusing on the actual descriptions provided for each time sequence (extract reported in Table 2). Time appeared to be spatially defined with a focus on its spatial qualities more than its sequential order. Units of observations were colours, texture of soil, leaves, wind, clouds, the taste of water.

Sun and rain are the main markers of time. Turkana splits every solar year into two years, sun and rain, and gathers all rains that fall in one year into one single collective memory; it is the same for the months of *sun and wind*. Rain patterns are irregular and can make one Turkana sun-year cover several Gregorian years, until rain comes. The marker of months is the moon. I quickly started loving full moon nights in the desert. Not just for the white flood of light that transforms darkness into a game of shades and makes grains of sand shimmer, but for the significance, the excitement and expectations that a full moon brings to the community. It is a night of dances, migrations, raids, rituals and ceremonies. It is the night that signs a new month, when brothers exchange stock to look after, to obtain a full understanding of the *four legs*.[36] In this 'timescape' (Adam 1998), there is not a fixed November identical to every other November in every other year and across multiple socio-ecological niches. Rather, there is a moment in time when somewhere 'dry pods fall from trees, there is no rain, but a strong wind blows, and most trees remain without leaves'.[37] Time and space are no longer the negative of each other but have merged: what happens in the nomadic space (lands, grass, plants, trees, clouds, borehole drilling, road construction, school openings, creation of villages, food distribution) is translated into people's understanding of temporal cycles, and it prescribes actions. In Bakhtin's words (1981: 84):

> Spatial and time indicators are fused into one concrete whole. Time, thickens, takes on flesh, becomes artistically visible; likewise, space becomes charged and responsive to movements of time, plot, history.

When *dry pods fall from trees*, for example, time has come to prepare stocks for the advancing dry season and to reach a different location where space-time has a different representation. Such a relationship between space and time is what gives mobility to space through topological deformations caused by the many actors (humans and non-human organisms and abiotic factors) operating in the landscape. Space mobility is, in other words, the empirical observation, through the herders' eyes, of variability. By means of those empirical observations, Turkana

---

36. Complete herd: cows, goats, sheep and camels.
37. Focus groups discussion, Lorengelup, 11 Nov. 2015.

herders show an awareness of space that is within, and not above, the landscape. The landscape itself, through its continual deformations, makes people capable; it is a dimension of their agency. Turkana herders have thus managed to move beyond the characterisation of landscape as neutral and external to human activities. They do not simply observe space and time as a lay audience; rather, they participate in it and incorporate changes into their living. During my attempts to draw seasonal calendars, people were aware of what they are supposed to do when clouds move and reunite in the sky to prepare for rain, when pasture becomes green or soil turns into mud, when trees shed their leaves, when there is sun and wind, water withdraws and land is dry. The actual order of months did not really matter, because an order has rarely been seen, in the words of a focus group participant during my attempts to draw seasonal calendars:

> The characteristics of these months change all the time; we look at what happens around us and decide accordingly. We have learnt to see.

Followed by another participant:

> … Like now it should be the month of *Lorara*, but trees have already lost their leaves, and everything is dry, we know some wild fruit may have ripened somewhere and that we need to move our animals, water will end soon.

Decision making appears not to be an arbitrary choice but rather an account of changes. Through these recollections of space-time, it emerges that variability and change have always occurred in the landscape. And that variability itself is advantageous, rather than a sign of fragility. As reported by Odhiambo in a report entitled *The Unrelating Persistence of Certain Narratives: An Analysis of Changing Policy Narratives about the ASAL in Kenya*, the interaction between development actors and drylands often instead revolves around emergencies, feeding into a narrative of vulnerability characterised by disasters and food aid (2014: 10). For example, the Kenyan National Livestock Policy (2008) affirms that: 'The range environment is fragile and due to its inappropriate use, degradation of the range has been observed in some areas. This situation reduces the capacity of the land to support enough livestock in the rangelands' (2008: 21, reported in Campbell 2021). Similarly, the Kenyan Agricultural Sector Development Strategy (ASDS 2010-2020) describes the Arid and Semi-Arid Lands (ASAL) as '…fragile ecosystems with scarce and erratic rainfall patterns' (GoK 2010: 39). And, it continues by saying that

> the frequency and severity of drought has increased in recent years … coupled with overstocking and the degraded environment, this has had a devastating

effect on pasture regeneration and on the livelihoods of pastoral communities
... livestock migration has resulted in conflicts over use of pastures and water
sources, and in environmental degradation (ibid.: 40).

My hosts seemed to have a different view on the erratic character of their lived territory: 'God has a good plan in making these fruits available: when one is not ripe
you can find another one! There is always some wild fruit we can eat somewhere',
the chief's wife once told me in Lorengelup.

Variability increases opportunities. At a basic level of analysis, the different
combination and temporality of various plants allows some wild fruit to be available
always. Yet, variability can only be perceived as advantageous by abandoning ideas
of stability implicit in narrow scales of observation and favouring instead large-scale
ecology connections, accommodating the mobility of space. As reviewed in this
section, old approaches to space are still dominant in development practices by aid
agencies or governments that limit their interest towards the drylands to pockets
of high potential. These approaches hook onto dated ideas of ecological equilibria,
stasis of places and primacy of fixity versus mobility. Conversely, my hosts inhabit
a space that is alive, which they cross freely, benefiting from the variations that
occur over the territory. Benefits from socioecological variability can only occur
if people have access to land and resources through a *live geography*, one in which
space is not enclosed but maintained alive, constantly crossed, re-crossed, and
modelled. In a context of rising climate change concerns (Campbell 2021), mass
investments of the extractive industries (Lind et al. 2020), tightening of borders
and State authorities (Markakis, Schlee, and Young 2021), this access is turning
into an increasingly contested struggle.

The mobility of space renders conditions of accessibility of paramount importance. Certainly, to benefit from socio-ecological variability, land needs to be
crossed, resources found, relationships cultivated and maintained. Conditions of
access are thus not limited to physical dimensions, which may hamper (or facilitate) access to resources (can I get there with a herd of cattle or camels?), but also
climatic (will I find advantageous meteorological conditions?), ecological (will I
find food for livestock and human consumption and sufficient water?), territorial
(do I have the right of access to resources?) and social conditions (do I have social
relationships to grant me access or to host me along the way?). All these conditions
determine a constellation of possibilities and obstacles that are critical for a life in
variable environments. It emerges that access is a crucial and complex concept,
discussed in the next section.

The nomadism of space

Table 2. Seasonal calendar
Extract from Focus Groups Discussion held in Lorengelup sub-location (11 Nov. 2015).

Month	Meaning	Description
Lokwang	Derived from word *ekwang*, bright. It indicates the month of sun and wind.	Everything is dry. It is the worst time of the year. It is the month of suffering.
Lodunge	Derived from verb *Adudung'iar*, to close/fall. It is the month that marks the end/fall of the dry season and the beginning of the rainy season.	End of the dry season, there is some scattered brief rain in the surrounding areas.
Lomaruk	Derived from *Akimaruk*, formation of clouds. Early sign of rain. Clouds move in preparation for the rains.	Beginning of the rainy season, clouds come together (the clouds are moving fast).
Titima	Derived from *akititimare*, process of pasture germination/flowering. There is good grass for livestock.	Plants start flowering.
El-El	Derived from *akielarr*, to scatter/to blossom and mature.	Plants have matured. There are rains; flowers bloom and petals become big and can be seen even from far away, some plants also have matured.
Lochoto	Derived from *echoto*, mud. It is the month of heavy rains, the whole place becomes muddy.	Livestock are giving birth, they are healthy and fat. It rains a lot, vegetation is green and everywhere. This is the best month of the year. Most motor cars have problems crossing because there is too much mud.
Losuban	Derived from verb *akisub*, to make. This is the time for doing and for rituals.	Livestock has a lot to feed on. There are many ceremonies. People have plenty of food, grass turns yellow, there is no rain.
Lotiak	Derived from verb *akitiak*, to separate/divide. This is the month that divides the rainy season from the dry season.	The grass is yellow, animals ares till doing well. This is a transition month, end of the rainy season.
Lomuk	Derived from the verb *akimuk*, to cover. There is brief rain and the sky is covered by scattered clouds.	Most trees turn green, there are flowers and fruit. Trees are forming heavy shadows with their crowns. No rain.
Lopoo	Derived from *akipore*, to cook. This is the month of hardship.	Many trees start to flower, feeding animals with fruit and leaves. People gather wild fruit and cook berries for many hours, and drink blood from livestock.
Lorara	Derived from *aranaun*, make things fall off. This is the month when trees shed their leaves.	Fruits are ripe and start to fall from trees, no rain, strong wind blows, dry pods fall from trees, most trees remain without leaves.

Month	Meaning	Description
Lolongu	Derived from *along'u,* arid/dry. This is the month of livestock movement in search of pasture and water.	Very dry period. Trees start drying, there is scarcity of water, prices of food rise, animals are weak or die, even wild birds can be seen dying in the bushes. All trees become like skeletons, animals grow thin.

Accessibility, a relational approach to space

> *What makes the desert beautiful, said the little prince,*
> *is that somewhere it hides a well*
>
> ANTOINE DE SAINT-EXUPÉRY (1944).

Taking cattle to water. Urum, Loima, December 2016.

Drylands are seen and imagined as the realm of scarcity, places of romantic desolation where nothing grows and which possess little productive value (see for example: Neely, Bunning and Wilkes 2009; Oliveira, Duraiappah and Shepherd 2003). It hence may be a surprise to hear that drylands give the world its most important staple foods, including maize, beans, potatoes, sorghum and millet. They support woody vegetation, trees and tree products, greatly contributing to national economies (for example 74 per cent of total energy consumption in

Kenya). Drylands provide 44 per cent of the world's cultivated systems and fifty per cent of the world's livestock, and contain a variety of important habitats for vegetable species, fruit trees and micro-organisms (IUCN 2017). And they also host 2.5 billion people, with their complex societies and evolving cultures. Altogether, these features give another possibility to the drylands. They provide an alternative image of these environments, one that recognises their value, their contribution to local, national and international economies.

Development making in the drylands is instead often preoccupied with increasing their economic potential, by transforming land use into one considered more productive, for example through measures of agricultural conversion and irrigation schemes, or through large scale infrastructure and energy development. Hence, although in recent years we have observed a shift in policy discourses about drylands towards more positive frames (as reviewed in Chapter 1), a parallel emergent narrative is one that discursively constructs drylands as 'peripheral areas, empty and unproductive in ways that perpetuate old stereotypes and assumptions' (Mosley and Watson 2016: 455). Sites of unexploited resources, drylands appear now as a 'new frontier' (Odhiambo 2014), opened to multiple actors (States, transnational corporations, local and international NGOs, private companies and individuals, etc.) cooperating or competing with each other, no longer just to exert control over these regions, but also to transform them. Policies like the Kenya Vision 2030 or the Devolution Constitution of 2010, and projects like LAPSET, Lake Turkan Wind Power, GIBE III, NRT conservancies, as well as the prospective Lake Turkana resort city, can be seen in this light. Mosley and Watson maintain, for example, that Kenya Vision 2030 describes the country as on a 'transforming journey', giving great emphasis to technology, communication, infrastructure (2016). Roads, railways, pipelines, dams, irrigation systems, ports, airports are all indeed key components of the development of Kenyan drylands. Lind and Rogei reveal how beyond the alleged *public good* generated by expanding national energy production, the Lake Turkana Wind Power project in northern Kenya also brings conflicts of governance and authority concerning everyday lives and livelihoods (Lind and Rogei 2025). Beyond narratives of *green economy* and *social development*, these interventions often occur within pockets of high potential, those niches of high production found in strategic positions, near water or other key resources. The common assumption is that, beyond such zones of high potential, drylands would not have much to offer, being generally *unproductive*.

This assumption is strongly tied to the type of view inscribed over the territory. If the *Kenya Vision* were a vision from within, rather than a McKinsey and Co. type analysis, as commented on by Mosley and Watson (in that it resembles the vision for Rwanda, Burundi, Tanzania and so forth), maybe the potential of drylands for what they are and not what they can be transformed into would finally emerge: futuristic lands corresponding to, in Scott's terms, 'hyper modernist ideology' (1998); and local resource use be respected. The State's view is reinforced by the use of certain indicators that focus on 'discrete states', such as average rainfall or the length of the growing season (Krätli 2016), and effectively portray assumptions about emptiness. However, because of the uneven and variable distribution of resources in drylands, average values miss the point, failing to capture the full picture of what is available, when and where, and erroneously depicting an overall image of drylands as homogenous lands with *on average* scarce resources. On the contrary, 'it is the immediate context that matters to pastoralist households, not average values' (Krätli et al. 2022: 8). An alternative approach to socio-ecological systems research is one that adopts a process relational perspective, able to capture non equilibrium dynamics and relations among processes, moving beyond simple interdependence between states or system components, and taking change as core system characteristic rather than exceptional (Mancilla García et al. 2020).

In contexts of high variability, access to a varied selection of land types is crucial. Composing grazing itineraries across years, seasons, days and hours requires flexible access to multiple, overlapping sites, usually with different tenure regimes applying. As reviewed by Ian Scoones, drawing from multiple experiences across the globe, ranging from the Borana system in Ethiopia to grazing landscapes in Amdo Tibet in China, such rangeland governance cannot be simplified either into privatised systems, such as conventional fenced, individually owned ranches, or into common property use, free-for-all kind of use systems (2023). Rangeland governance according to a pastoral logic is an arrangement whereby relationships govern use, but boundaries are not fixed. In other words, rangeland governance appears more complicated, dynamic and flexible, enabling opportunistic access to multiple patches within a complex mosaic of land types. Tsering and Unks revolve to the notion of assemblage and bricolage to describe institutions that regulate land access in pastoral settings, where rules, roles and relationships between rangelands and their users are in a perpetual state of flux, 'deliberately destabilising current categories and definitions' (Aneesh 2017: 129 in Tsering and Unks 2024).

Amartya Sen greatly contributed to debates about accessibility when he described the famine in the Sahel at the end of the 1970s not as the result of food scarcity, but as a problem of *entitlements*. In *Poverty and Famine,* Sen overturned theories of famine and food security of the time by showing that starvation is the characteristic of some people not having enough food to eat and not the characteristic of there not being enough food to eat (1981). Poverty, market forces and policy frameworks were discussed as creating conditions of inequality of access resulting in mass starvation. So famine was no longer an inevitable outcome of drought or the result of livelihoods envisaged to be unsustainable, but rather the result of long-term marginalisation and state neglect (Derbyshire et al. 2024). Food studies and development approaches to food security have since been greatly influenced by Sen's theories. Nonetheless, these have not yet managed to change assumptions about resource scarcity in the drylands where the concept of accessibility is discussed narrowly, in relation to difficulties involved in reaching mobile populations, such as mobile pastoralists, in harsh environments. As Scoones puts it in the reformulation of the 2021 e-book edition of *Sustainable Livelihood and Rural Development*: 'Asking who owns what, who does what, who gets and what do they do with it allows for a nuanced understanding'. (2021: vi). These are questions of access and control.

What can we learn about drylands by embracing a broader accessibility lens? To respond to this question, we need first to understand what accessibility means for – in this case Turkana – herders. How is accessibility experienced by Turkana herders, and what can we learn in turn for service provision? I depict accessibility as the capacity and possibility to reach, appropriate and make use of resources (for livestock and people) and claim that it is a complex concept, experienced at multiple levels: the possibility of reaching pasture and forage with the herd (existence/location of pasture, level of security, low/no parasite infestation, conditions of the terrain and fertility, slope gradient, presence of water, low competition with other herds and predators); the herd's capacity to feed on it (feeding selectivity); as well as the time of access (accessibility of good quality pasture might be seasonal or depend on plants' life-cycles). Accessibility also refers to the presence of tenure restrictions and social connections. In the remainder of this section, I elaborate on the various dimensions of the experience of accessibility. The ultimate goal is to reformulate the classical equation of drylands with scarcity, claiming that scarcity is relational and a function of scale more than an absolute state, and the result of constrained access.

Accessibility, a relational approach to space

The multivariate experience of accessibility

Multi-level conditions of accessibility are constantly observed while on the move, shared and discussed by herders, as reported in the example below extracted from a conversation between one of my hosts in Urum, Lonyang, and a young boy, Lomung, who crossed our way during an evening walk to check all shoats[38] were back home.

> Lonyang: Where do you come from?
>
> Lomug: I come from Nayanaa Khatwan … I am in search of camels that went missing.
>
> Lonyang: Those camels were seen in Lotome stream two days ago where I was tending my goats.
>
> Lomug: Woi! Let's hope they have not gone past Locher Emoit, those wells pose great danger to animals. People dig too deep as wells continue to dry up.
>
> Lonyang: All villagers close to Locher Emoit are saying that those wells are dry … Now, tell me about your home, how are people there? Are your animals better than these ones here?
>
> Lomug: There is not much to say except that God has continued to fail us. Our animals are getting thinner and are dying every day.
>
> Lonyang: Did you cross river Kotome on your way here? I am told there is some rain there.
>
> Lomug: People there are not as bad as here. Their animals are eating green shrubs along the rivers and dry grass in Ngitiir. Their only problem is raids from the enemy.
>
> Lomug: Woi! and alcohol cursed the Turkana to react and defend themselves! … Is Nakua still in your village?
>
> Lonyang: Nakua, the wife of Lomerite?
>
> Lomug: Yes, I have a message for her from her people … OK, I really want to know where my camels are before dawn and then I will spend the night in your village …

Herders retain a complex baggage of information to make decisions about migration with the herd, where to settle a new homestead, or what itinerary to follow to reach certain resources. Lomug and Lonyang met along their paths, they were walking in opposite directions that in turn meant they were coming from different places. This was an opportunity not to be missed. As Volpato writes, 'This

---

38. Mixed flock of sheep and goats.

The nomadism of space

thirst for news is codified in nomads' long and ritualized greeting', which includes questions about the whereabouts of each party, family health, the state of pastures, the location and existence of rains, livestock diseases or the conditions of specific wells and routes. 'The underlying connectivity can be startling to the naïve eye, given the perception of dispersion and disconnection apparent with an etic gaze at the desert' (2025: 91). As emerges in their exchange, they do not focus on average values of resources, but on relationships and context. While Turkana herders are famous for their lying skills, and therefore would not necessarily trust all information they receive from others, through these lines of dialogue there emerge critical elements for the understanding the concept of accessibility in drylands. The lines contain important questions about rain, water and vegetation, health of livestock; the two men are marking territorial boundaries with respect to movement of each-other's animals as well as the advance of enemies and delineating social connections.

It is still dark when we start walking; a silver moon plays with the roof of the huts in Urum, creating long shadows on the ground. The first sunrays reflect on the village shacks we left behind as we divert from the main road to take a path that crosses sisal fields. Soon we run into a herd of cows and donkeys loaded with piles of empty jerrycans. I recognise those cows, or rather I recognise the women who are directing the herd. They are the co-wives of one of my host families from my previous round of fieldwork. I have heard they migrated towards Koomyo and I was excited to meet up with them soon. Yet, this is sooner than expected and worryingly so because they are going to water their animals at Kachaikol River, past Urum centre, back where we came from. I immediately become very concerned about the possibility that we would not find water along Koomyo River, and our 15-litre jerrycans will not last for long. We were warned about the persistence of drought, the lowering of the water table and the abandonment of several wells.

Luckily, this was a different story. The Lonyang family had camped slightly before the steep hills that lead to Koomyo River and its wells, known by the name Kotido. Despite Kotido wells being closer to their homestead, the hills are too difficult to climb with a herd of cows. Thus, every other day they take their cows to a well that is easier to access. Another reason is that the Lonyang family possesses wells along the Kachaikol River. They should fetch water from those wells, at least until they are dry. Furthermore, there are potential interests in passing through Urum centre to gather information about what may come from Lodwar, the capital town of Turkana, in case of aid distribution commencing soon; or to re-stock from local shops.

In this encounter, I am describing three different ways in which the Lonyang family is experiencing access to a needed resource: water. First, there is an issue of physical accessibility due to problems of access caused by a steep rocky hill. Bounded between the Great Rift Valley to the west, and the Samburu Hills in the southeast, most of the landscape in Turkana consists of low plains with elevation ranging between 300 to 800 metres (McCabe 2004). These plains are punctuated by mountain ranges, lower lava hills and flows. Volcanic rocks cover approximately one third of the county lowlands, the rest being made of sandy and clay plains, lakebeds and mountain foot slopes. Far from being uniform land, the German cooperation that mapped all landforms in Turkana identified at least 31 different types (Touber 1994).[39] The Turkana language has a wealth of terminology for small differences within land types that outsiders' eyes would perceive as homogeneous. With their language, the Turkana recognise the heterogeneity of their land and express it in terms of accessibility. Intensity, steepness, ravines, type of stones are all variables that affect accessibility. These descriptions are included in the topology of mountain' names, together with the colour, or warnings about past occurrences. Some examples are reported in Table 3 below.

Another way in which accessibility was experienced by the Lonyang family related to territorial rules that mediate access to resources. As stressed by Scoones, the role of institutions, organisations and policies in mediating access to livelihood resources and defining the opportunities and constraints of different livelihood strategies, is often overlooked, whereas it is 'access rather than simply resource abundance that explains some of the key resource management and governance dilemmas in the field' (2021: 51). In his chapter 'Access and Control: Institutions, Organizations, and Policy Processes', he argues that problems arise when designed institutions are imposed where institutions are assumed not to exist, as sustained by Hardin, for example, or to have been eroded, because too often 'user associations, management committees and so on have been developed without an effective understanding of existing patterns of use and access, nor of their institutional underpinnings' (2021: 48).

---

39. See Annexes 1–5 for compiled maps of landforms in Turkana County. Thanks to Müller-Dempf for helping find these maps.

Table 3. Examples of mountain names with descriptions

URUM: *Aurum* is a verb which means to hide and spy over something; it implies a place where people hide and spy over enemies.	**LOPETAKINEI**: *Peta* is to spread, *kinei* means shoats, *lopetakinei* is then a place where shoats spread while grazing and need little herding. The place is flat with pasture for shoats.
MORUANGADELIO: *Ekadeli* is a tree producing fruits called *ngakadelio*. *Emoru* is a mountain. Moruangakadelio implies a mountain with many trees producing *ngakadelio*.	**NALEMTOGOI**: *Etogo* means grass or small sticks tied together like those used to help climb huts for construction purposes. *Nalem* means flat. *Nalemtogoi* therefore implies a hill with *etogo* that is flat, or easy to climb because there is little obstruction like thick bushes or huge rocks.
MORULINGA: *Linga* means to mix colours. *Morulinga* therefore indicates a mountain that is half bare, half bushy.	**NAPEDO**: *Napeded* means hole; *Napedo* here implies hill or mountain that has a hole, as a passage way, a route through.
ERUS: *Erus* is another term for *echwa*; *echwa* is a place where water comes out of the ground; it implies that there are springs.	**MORU ANGKAATH**: Flat area with no bushes, herders can just relax and have an eye on their animals. *Moru* is a mountain and *ngaath* is a kind of a grass. *Moru angkaath* therefore implies a mountain that *ngaath* grows on.
KAAKAL: *Ekaal* means camels, it therefore implies a place where camels like to graze.	**KARAKARAYO**: Almost onomatopoeic, several small peaks making up a whole mountain range. Karakarayo is a sound made by stones when one steps on them. This place is called so because it has many stones that make this *kharakharayo* noise when stepped on.

Source: Developed by the author.

In Turkana, the management of land and resources is the result of a coexisting and overlapping set of claims and negotiations, disaggregated at multiple levels: type of resources (grass, trees, water), type of resource use (individual, household or animal consumption, commercial), season of use (shortage, abundance). These rules correspond to a different way of perceiving territoriality. As I see it, among Turkana pastoralists territory is the result of a reciprocal action of *marking* between space and people: space marks people and defines identities; and people mark the space they live in (territory as a cultural place).

On people and livestock these marks create identities. In Turkana there are two main social divisions, the *Ngimonia* in the west/south, descended from former pastoralists of the Koten-Magos group (Lamphear 1976); and the *Ngichuro* in the east/north, descended from the first Turkana immigrants who were agricultural Paranilotes (ibid.). This division is called *ekitela*, or ridge. *Ngitela* are geographical groups, called *territorial sections* (Müller-Dempf 1994: 179), membership of which is acquired by birth through patrilineal lineage from a common grandfather (Dyson-Hudson and Dyson-Hudson 1999:81). Territorial sections are distinguished by the way they perform *akiriket* (meat ceremony). This is the first identity-mark, incised on the *apol*[40] of a sacrificed animal.

Territorial sections are further divided into brands[41] (*emachar*), each with its own livestock branding. An elder in Kambi Lore once explained that 'the clan is like a numberplate on a vehicle. It serves identification purposes'; it controls laws, costumes, rituals and identities, as witnessed by Barret in his book *Turkana Iconography, Desert Nomads and their Symbols* (1998). The *emachar* is primarily an indicator of livestock ownership but also prescribes rules and taboos for specific groups of belonging. Brands are mixed over the entire territory and are exogamous. The brand-belonging is visible through a set of marks imposed on people and livestock. In the past, all Turkana people had three distinguishing marks on the forehead to signal their brand. The types of skin worn, the colour of clay applied or a hair style help distinguish different brands. Finally, men create animal identities through identifiable marks and cuts on their bodies, corresponding to the brand of the owner (Figure 18). In this way, families belonging to the same brand become livestock associates with similar branding marks (personalised at family level) on their animals. The relationship with livestock is dual: people mark identities on their animals, and animals give identity to people (every man, for example, takes the name of his favourite ox in the herd). The mixture of brands and territorial sections means a complex web of rules and customs. Newcomers must seek permission to access resources by establishing contact with brand-mates, or making friendships with local people (Müller-Dempf 1994: 182).

---

40. Section of kidney, muscles and fat cut from the hip of livestock. Each *ngitela* performs this cut differently.

41. Also called clans.

Figure 18. Livestock emachar

I also define a territory by the action of people carving out the environment, in turn determining rules and rights to access resources. I identified two levels of marks incised by people: material and invisible marks. Examples of material marks are family wells such as those Lonyang's wives were moving towards. Water holes are managed by those who have customary rights. The danger of fetching water, the strain of digging and maintaining and the paucity of water all determine the exclusivity of the well. Each family has several wells spread out in the territory, some active, others dry, others covered by sand from wind or a once flowing river. This creates a *geography of family wells*, the access to which must be negotiated, especially if used for livestock (Figure 19). The geography of family wells also allows for the control of stocking rates on pasture surrounding water sources – something that modern water points, such as boreholes, fail to do in ensuring permanent water access, generally mediated by the capacity to pay fees for water. This leads to a concentration of many animals from wealthier families, potentially causing conflicts and degradation. As suggested in a recent Handbook, *Pastoralism: Theory, Practice, and Policy*, it would be better to have many smaller water points in a network, ensuring livestock is well distributed and pasture is rationalised, rather than making water available from a fixed and permanent service (Waiswa et al. 2019). An assessment report on pastoral production practices in the neighbouring Sudan has shown how livestock mobility is a crucial production principle that turns environmental instability, in this case related to water availability, into an economic asset that makes pastoral systems economically successful and ecologically sustainable (Krätli, El Dirani and Young 2013).

Figure 19. Family geography of wells

Land, trees, bushes, even if unmarked, even if not clearly visible, may nonetheless belong to someone. This is part of what I term *invisible marks*, such as the extension of owned land around people's homesteads (always untraceable to me, but very clear to my hosts and neighbours). A young woman in Kambi Lore once explained,

> Newcomers introduce themselves to the elders and decide how much land to take: everything that grows in their land cannot be taken by others for productive activities. People can take fruit from trees to eat but not to sell, and people cannot cut trees to burn charcoal in someone else's property.

Selling, eating, gathering for livestock, cutting trees: these are all contingent rules in different communities, but commonly there is an extensive area surrounding the homestead that belongs to the owner of the homestead and defines the territory's invisible marks (Figure 20). My host father in Urum explained,

> *Ekwar* (land) beyond a man's home sets grazing boundaries, a place which by design of your area of residence, your animals are free to graze in, and others must ask permission; beyond that area the animals will be mixing with other people's animals.

At the same time, certain areas, like shores of rivers or grazing areas, are owned in common. In those areas people cannot build their homesteads or take private possession of resources in respect of common rights. The complexity of territorial rules increases because they are not static but constantly re-negotiated in the dynamic variability of dryland environments.

Figure 20. Invisible marks

Another way Lonyang's wives and cattle experienced accessibility is through social relationships that allow information sharing, gained from passing through a growing new centre, such as Urum. As Gabriele Volpato writes about the desertscape of pastoral Saharawi in his recent book *Desert Entanglements*, desert connectivity is also premised on a continuous gathering and circulation of news across camps, villages, wells and other gathering points (2025: 91). Social groups in Turkana facilitate crucial functions: protection from human and animal predators, information sharing, cooperation, socialisation, securing physical or psychological health. Social relations among agnates, affines, stock-associates, friends and neighbours enable people (and their livestock) to access resources spread over a vast territory by granting territorial rights or securing hospitality. The basic social group in Turkana is the *awi*, the household, a 'legally independent, stock-owning and more or less self-sufficient' group' (Gulliver 1968: 353). In actual life *awi* do not exist in isolation, but are related to other families, including neighbours, friends and distant relatives. Ecological conditions in Turkana as well as the processes of diversification cause a widespread dispersal of extended families, 'a number of households linked together by a web of genealogically defined social bonds to form a more amorphous group' (Gulliver 1968: 353), as well as of stock-associates and bond-friends. This social web enhances accessibility to rangelands, water points, grass plains or other resources (including, for example, food aid, or cash in towns), easier to access if these areas belong to neighbouring or familial groups. Social relations also serve as a vehicle to pass information, a valuable commodity across a *large scale ecology*. It is possible therefore to delineate a socioecological system of relations, which guarantees reciprocal access to different places through channels of sharing, trading, reciprocity, marriage, splitting families and the search for allies. These networks form pathways that determine access to resources. However, as conditions change and families move, networks are continuously re-created, and the social rules of access are often negotiated through elders, to ensure safe passage and the utilisation of rangelands across district or national boundaries.

The movement of Lonyang's wives and cattle to fetch water in Kachaikol reveals the many ways accessibility can be experienced, which I refer to as physical, territorial and social experiences of accessibility. Physical accessibility implies the capacity to reach resources, depending on landforms, terrain and soil conditions, and distances to be walked with the herd. Territorial accessibility refers to the rights to use resources, depending on tenure systems and customary rules. Social accessibility influences both the possibility to reach a place, for example by being hosted along the way or being informed about the presence of good resources, and the rights to use resources if permission is needed. The experience of accessibility also depends on other factors, such as climatic and ecological factors, including water and forage resources.

Comforted by the assurance that wells in Koomyo are not dry, we proceed. We cross several dry streams; the path starts climbing up and the sun is scorching. We are directed to the Kotido wells to refill our jerrycans. Next to the wells, a big tamarind tree sits grandly in the middle of the dry wadi. The tree's shade is used for important meetings and all the main elders of the area have gathered there. A cleansing ceremony is taking place to redeem a case of adultery in the community. A bull is sacrificed while chanting takes place. The ceremony ends with the drinking of the blood refreshed with sugar and water. In the evening, we walk to the homestead with Logiala, our newly met host. There is still excitement in the air from the ceremony and plenty of meat to be eaten. When we wake up the following morning, the camels have already gone. Some of these animals must be lactating, despite the peak of the dry season, because it is the sound of the calabash of ng'akibuk *(sour milk) being shaken that wakes us up. We are offered some tea with milk. Logiala sits with us on his* ekicholong *(stool) when two young men walk into the homestead. They come from Loima and are looking for rain.*

The two young men were scouts sent to 'look for where grass can be found, a water point, a secure place where huts can be built'. Herders who need to know whether they can reach a certain grazing field by a certain route (physical experience of access), also consider whether the grass they are going to find has adequate nutritive values or if they will find water at the destination and along the way, partly dependent on the interplay between precipitation and the condition of both soil and terrain. Thus, in addition to discussion about landforms, rain becomes another major topic of conversation.

Indeed, we spoke about rain in every setting. Rain was in the goat's entrails inspected to foretell the future. Rain was danced for on full moon nights and whispered along human chains emerging from deep wells. Rain was dreamt, remembered from the past, prayed for in the future. Rain was in morning teas, in meetings between chiefs and in children's games. Rain was in green sprouts, dry pods and in the skeletons of trees. Rain was in every word, and beyond words. Rain was in the grass, the plants, the rivers, the animals. Rain was God, life and death. I took note of most discussions about rain and realised that rain was rarely the direct object of discussion (Figure 21). Talking about rain is talking about its relationship with people, animals, grass and the future.

Figure 21. Meanings of rain. Developed by the author (Nvivo.11)

Primarily rain is about animals and 'good grasses' that grow. 'When it rains, it rains life, all the different grasses grow, and the animals survive'.[42] Grass is one of the most limiting factors for herders, more than water. Livestock can last several days without water (particularly camels), but to survive dry seasons they must eat. Following rain means finding better grass to maximise food intake for the animals. Humans then use animals as a means of production to convert otherwise useless resources, such as grass, into edible food. Thus, rain is also about people. 'When rain disappears, the only thing to do is to migrate … Our stomachs will speak and say where we will go to survive'.[43] I was often told, 'Nothing will change, until it rains'.[44] Rain is often said to *bring* something. The future is the domain of God, *mandeleo* (development) or rain. The future concerns change, and change is often brought about by rain, recognised as one of the most influential vectors of spatial mobility.

---

42.   Male elder, FN, Lorengelup, 19 Jan. 2016.

43.   Middle-aged woman, III, Lorengelup, 17 Jan. 2016.

44.   Old woman, FN, Urum, 24 Dec. 2016.

The nomadism of space

Rain is associated with lack of rain (seasons and drought). Rain comes seasonally, but not as well marked as expected. Dry seasons contain *ng'irupei* (short showers); wet seasons are interrupted by the sun and *ekuwom* (wind). Dry-season and rainy-season co-evolve, temporally and spatially (See also older ethnographies: Galvin et al. 2001; Oba 1992; Soper 1985). Rain in Turkana is so erratic that no one can predict when, where or how much it will rain with any degree of accuracy, represented in old ethnographies, such as:

> In the Ateker region a normal rain pattern is said to start at the beginning of April … this is more exceptional than normal as the amount and incidence of rain varies considerably. (Dyson-Hudson 1958: 6)

Nonetheless, climatic variability is often used as a *discourse of crisis* in terms of climate change, based on the increased frequency and length of droughts in the region (HRW 2015; Schilling et al. 2014). The underlying risk of these debates is to reiterate old assumptions of stable ecologies and to ignore historical cycles of fluctuating rain patterns in drylands where weather variability and unstable environments should be understood as the norm. Indeed, droughts represent one of the most widespread hazards in the region (NDMA 2015); as Glantz puts it, they are 'a part of climate and not apart from it' (1987). As a result, the vulnerability to climate change may be due to more socio-economic imposed restrictions of access than due to changes in climate (Semplici and Campbell 2023).

When Turkana herders speak about the seasonality of rains, they not only refer to lack of rains, but also imply that at times it rains too much. When they speak of *akamu* (dry season) and *akiporo* (rainy season), they do so in relation to herd conditions and the accessibility of pasture, not of the average quantity of rain. Drought is defined by the timing and location of rains, and whether these occur in circumstances that allow grass to grow. Certainly, they cannot change the amount of rainfall; they can instead change the experience of climatic accessibility of pasture by means of mobility (Krätli 2016). What herders are concerned about is the distribution of rain, remembering that 'a good rain season is when there is enough water and it is well spread' (Krätli 2015).

In drylands, average rain predictions are rarely reliable and also largely meaningless: the amount and distribution of rain varies tremendously and, when this unpredictability is combined with different soil types and a complex topography, there is even greater variability, creating scattered and volatile niches of moisture to support plant growth as rainfalls move over the territory. In other words, the interplay of landforms and conditions of the terrain with climatic variables contributes to the construction of heterogeneous and dynamic ecological niches, including water and forage availability, which determine another way to experience accessibility.

A key resource that herders must access is water, and this can be strenuous. In Turkana, water supplies for animal and human consumption are mainly taken from watercourses. After rain, depending on the conditions of the terrain, ponds form, rock pools are filled and local springs gush. After a period of sun and hot wind, these sources are exhausted (Gulliver 1968: 348). Water is thereafter found by digging deeper wells fetched from underground water storage networks. Several studies have shown that Turkana is well equipped with water supplies (Cuthbert et al. 2017; Gernote 1994); nonetheless any major humanitarian intervention in Turkana, starting from early missionary works to contemporary development programmes, has dealt with the lack of water and entailed the construction of water points. These approaches treat water as a necessary starting point for development and one that has to be made available via a fixed and permanent service. Such an approach fails to acknowledge the variability of hydrological landscapes, or, in other words, that water must also end. The end of water is fundamental as it allows human and livestock relocation, which in turn contributes to saving the environment from degradation and overuse, and guarantees the reproducibility of resources (Salza 1997). Several scholars argue that part of existing degradation processes, which include the lowering of the water table and land impoverishment (HRW 2015), is because of the construction of permanent water sources (and permanent service infrastructure) (De Jode 2010; Khazanov 1984). Permanent wells also disrupt adaptive local strategies to water management. Powerful families settle around the borehole and start controlling flows and the use of water by others. This creates social stratification and population pressure (human and livestock) that will erode land, deplete its nutrients and divert water from other nearby sources (such as seasonal rivers or downstream wells). Accessing water is a more complex task than simply switching on a water tap. It implies accepting to let it flow, having the skills to find it again, at the right time and in the right place, taking both present and future needs into consideration. Digging wells and watering livestock is, as Volpato describes, one of those human activities that make the desert habitable, also to a host of species beyond humans (2025).

Variations even of a few millimetres in soils, landforms, rainfall and hydrological landscapes have crucial impacts on forage distribution, creating a variable and patchy vegetation structure (Ellis and Galvin 1994: 383). Forage is indeed another key resource for herders. It is commonly believed that the migration of pastoralists is driven by pasture shortages. Conversely, when they move in search of feed for their livestock, they generally do so in search of high quality forage and not because of a low quantity of forage (De Jode 2010). For example, I was confused when, migrating with the two eldest brothers in my host family in Lorengelup (Turkana Central), we arrived at a place called Lokitela to graze their family shoats. Lokitela looked dry and not very different from the rest of the surrounding landscape.

Akiru:[45] … A dry place, why do you take goats to a dry place?

Lopwenya:[46] It is in that place where grass can be found.

Akiru: Therefore … is it not dry?

Lopwenya: There are shrubs, when it rains those shrubs become green.

Akiru: Is Lokitela now green?

Lopwenya: Lokitela is now green and goats graze.

Lokitela, a flat dusty area close to Kerio in Turkana Central, was *green* and I could not even see it. To outsiders, grasses, shrubs, trees, may all look the same, but in fact the quality of pasture varies on a daily, seasonal and annual basis, and it is not evenly spread across the landscape. Vegetation in Turkana ranges from barren land to annual grassland, and evergreen forests. Browse plants are found almost everywhere in Turkana, varying only in quantity and quality. Even the worst of the central shrub desert regions affords some browsing in the wet season and extensive areas of the plains provide forage throughout the dry-season (Gulliver 1968: 349).[47] At times ephemeral vegetation is triggered, producing flowers and seeds in different places at different times.

---

45. My Turkana name.

46. Lopwenya was the oldest son of my host father in Lorengelup. We spent a week walking with him and his shoats through Lokitela grazing area while they were making their way towards the mountains at the horizon.

47. See Annex 2.5 for a map of vegetation distribution in Turkana.

We decide to follow rain together with the two brothers sent to scout potential family destinations to Lokorokipi wells. It is a long march, at the end of which Lokorokipi wells appear like an industry. The watering act itself is a choreography and a ritualised staging of life in the desert, made up of repeated and synchronous tasks. There are two wide and deep wells, dug next to each other. Columns of people emerge from the wells. Some dig sand to make the well deeper, and chase vanishing water. Some fetch water to pour into troughs for the animals. Some shovel all around the well to make it safer for the animals to access. Livestock line up. We have the name of an elder of the area, but Emoru theatrically tells us to wait: he is busy coordinating all the well operations. In the evening when the animals start being taken away, Emoru calls us. A group of elders have gathered. They want to know who we are and what we want to do. They listen and reply gravely, 'We are facing one of the hardest periods of our time.[48] *Water is refusing to come. Grass died. We fight to give our animals something to eat, and we are killed by the enemy'.*

These variations occur spatially and temporally and determine highly dynamic grazing ecosystems to maximise food intake for livestock. In *Valuing Variability,* Saverio Krätli explains such spatial and temporal dynamics very well (2015). Spatially, distinct pulses of plant production are followed by long periods of plant dormancy. This happens among different ecological zones as seasons alternate (spatial co-evolution of dry and rainy seasons), and within the same ecological zone thanks to certain combinations of plants. Different ecological habitats evolve when the same species of plants are richer or poorer in nutrients because of, for instance, the different incidence of pests and diseases, differences in soil properties or plant lifespan. Temporally, the ecological variability of nutrients is determined by alternating seasons, by the lifecycle of plants[49] and by the time of day when the plant is consumed.[50]

---

48. Turkana County was starting to face a severe dry season, officially declared a drought in February 2017.

49. Nutritive levels vary according to the plants' lifespan. For this reason, if it rained in the same way everywhere, livestock would eat progressively less nutritive food. The fact that rain is distributed irregularly in a wide territory, allows differential plants' cycles and pastoralists could potentially find the most nutritive plants for their livestock.

50. In the evening plants have lower nutritive values than in the morning due to photosynthesis processes.

The nomadism of space

To conclude, it emerges that accessibility is an important factor in the drylands, and that it is experienced in multiple ways. These many ways of accessibility experienced in pastoral drylands can be very informative for development planners. Resource management emerges as a more complex affair. It is not limited by availability and quantity, as per more standard indicators of resource management. It is also about distribution and access, which respectively in turn depend on the variability of dryland ecologies and on the rights, technologies and abilities to reach and use resources, socio-cultural institutions and politics. Not only should development planners maintain an open and wide reach over a territory at large (beyond micro locations of interventions), favouring broader dynamics and relationships, but they should also plan to accommodate local needs and interests in accessing resources. In this section I have reviewed at least five ways in which accessibility is locally experienced: physical, territorial, social, climatic and ecological, and certainly there are many more. Access depends on the conditions of the terrain, on the distances that can be walked with animals to fodder, on the availability of water for people and animals and on the availability of pasture. It depends on the location of kinsmen and other relatives. All this feeds into the multi-functionality of space as seen by Turkana herders. Statically, resources may even be scarce but opening up to variability, letting resources move across a large-scale territory, creates new possibilities for the drylands. By employing this lens over Turkana territory, resources would no longer appear as scarce but unevenly distributed across a vast territory, and mobile as they grow, die and flower again in different places at different times, in co-evolution with the movement of human and non-human inhabitants. It then emerges that scarcity is relational and a function of scale, more than an absolute state of being of the drylands, and it is managed through live geographies, as opposed to confinement of land use into enclaves of high potential.

Indeed, a fixation on states or levels obscures how people and resources move between places and across scales, constructing ever more complex livelihood pathways (Scoones 2021). The mobility of both resources (a nomadic space) and people (a mobile livelihood) is key. While moving, following the movement of space, herders also create the outward form of their lived space (physical, and ecological accessibilities), its identity (cultural territory), and its internal structure (social accessibilities). Therefore, the herder's mobility is not a natural trait, nor an act of disturbance, or a coping mechanism, but a process of world-making. It is not mere physical motion, but a relational strategy to access land and resources, connecting geographies and sociologies, but not in a deterministic way, as it is involved in the co-production of the same resources and the same space it is moving along with. Such a way of moving across while managing rangelands' resources through complex institutions is critical for the future of rangelands themselves, for pastoral communities across the world, and also for the rest of the world through the benefits that pastoral livelihoods provide, including key commodities (meat, dairy, leather, manure), biodiversity conservation, reducing erosion, preventing wildfires, dispersing seeds, allocating nutrients, defragmenting landscapes, preserving cultures (Herrera, Davies and Manzano 2014; see also Chapter 1).

A space in which resources are in constant motion, a space which is itself mobile, like the one my eyes were opened to while living with my hosts, is a space that can only be learnt by moving, 'wayfaring', using Ingold's terminology (2000). It is in fact by moving that my hosts taught me their landscape and it is by moving that they develop an *alternative science*, based on processes of meaning generation that mould a *sense of place*, as I show in the next section.

We spend a few days with Emoru. Our new host informs us that soon they will celebrate the wedding of one of his sons. We are asked if we wish to attend the ceremony and see the killing of the white bull. We are awaiting the new moon, and enthusiasm is rising. Dances and songs are performed, ostrich feathers are cleaned, dresses and decorations tried on. Liquor is brewed in the huts as excitement is increasing both for the expected feast and for moving. Finally, the new moon rises and the trek to the wedding site in Lobei begins.

Perceptions of remoteness

> *Belief in witchcraft is quite consistent with human responsibility*
> *and rational appreciation of nature.*
>
> EDWARD EVANS-PRITCHARD, (1977)

Geography from the top of the hut. Lorengelup, Turkana Central, November 2015.

Emoru calls me from the front line: he wants to teach me his landscape. While we walk, Emoru points at some camels on the horizon and asks me to say 'e-ka-l' (camels) and the name of their emachar *(clan mark) as readable from the scar on their bodies; he points at some mountains and wants me to say 'e-mo-ru' (mountain or rock) explaining that he is thinking of moving there soon because the grass looks new and a good green in colour; he prevents me from drinking from a new borehole:* 'na-kha-ba-ran' *(salty-water) and points at a shallow-well along the dry-stream where water is fresher and tastier.*

During the journey to reach the ceremonial site for the wedding of my host's son, I watched the vigilant herders' eyes acting in their lived space. The purpose of movement was ceremonial, but the act of moving served several functions. Because resources are mobile and conditions of accessibility are mutable and under perpetual renegotiation, the best way to know the territory is indeed by moving. While walking, the eyes of our travel companions were manifestly alive, inspecting, scouting, surveying and mapping in their minds new grass, the state of rivers, the shade of trees, the footprints of wild animals, whose livestock was seen and where. My GPS was totally useless. My hosts knew where we were and where we were going. They were not simply marching *in the middle of nowhere*, as outsiders who venture to the drylands would often term it. Some of the extractive interventions described in the previous section, and others including interventions of so-called *green grabbing*, whether linked with biodiversity, conservation, ecosystem services or ecotourism, build on discourses of marginal lands and, as shown by Fairhead and colleagues, 'are assisted by satellite imagery that occludes people, livelihoods, and socio-ecological relationships from view' (2012: 251). In other words, they depict remote lands, difficult to access and void of particular meaning other than desolated, faraway and harsh. On the contrary, thanks to my Turkana hosts, my eyes were opened to drylands as full of significance, places of knowledge construction, transmission and modification.

A number of scholars have shown that movement is a way of knowing (Habeck 2006; Humphrey 2003; Ingold 2011). Ingold, for example, argues that it is not possible to detach movement from the formation of knowledge, because it is not possible to lift the mind from the surface of the world and leave the body wandering around: knowledge is embodied in the place-to-place movement (2007: 102). The best way to know the everyday landscape is by being there, by trekking, when the environment is perceived along a path of observations. Far from being a point-to-point collection of information, the herders' knowledge develops 'alongly' (Ingold 2011: 154). As Salza says: mobile people do not enact *in situ* but on the way (2014). This was clear during the walk with the groom and his family: the journey was equal to the destination, for what it could instruct us about the nomadic space. While travelling, as a novice herder, I was shown specific features of the environment and underwent a process of knowledge creation, through a mixture of watching, listening, smelling and experiencing (Ingold 2000).

Turkana herders have a very practical view of the environment. They know most benefits and dangers that come from it; distinguish fruits and herbs; know nutritional qualities, patterns and distributions of plants; how to read traces to find resources. The environment itself is a school of life. Elders (like older animals in the herd), having proved that they have mastered their environment, are the main transmitters of such knowledge. This explains why forms of power take the shape of a gerontocracy based on a generational knowledge. The elder's knowledge translates into authority as well as into a higher degree of freedom to choose where to go and what to do, on the basis of cumulative experience.

Knowledge about space is in fact not static. Rather, it is subject to change through moving, discoveries and shared experiences; as such, it is better understood as a process rather than an archive. Herders' viewpoints are not timeless or changeless; on the contrary they are constantly changing and reviewing the images by which the world was seen (Humphrey 2003: 140). For example, they offer detailed information about frequency and length of droughts, number of days separating seasons, reduction of clouds and whitening of the sky; about reduced grass quality, and bush encroachment in crop fields or along rivers preventing access to water sources; about lower water table and increasingly dangerous deep wells; and about the disappearance of wild animals 'except the hostile ones', referring to hyenas and jackals attacking small stocks.

New knowledge is perpetually re-organising around observations of an ever-changing landscape. For example, many told me that 'prolonged droughts happen because of urbanisation. In the past there were no vehicles and modern things, there was rain and grass'. Others believe that 'God has gone missing, angry at people because we started adopting a modern lifestyle and God does not want to let water down'. Others blame local diviners: 'The *emuron* (seer) pretends to know more than God and requests a lot of sugar and *etaba* (tobacco) to do God's job. The emuron of the past were good, they were not greedy. Nowadays they only worry about money and alcohol ...' Others instead pointed out that 'noise and modern things are responsible for the lack of grass, now, no grass is growing even if it rains' (which may very well be linked to reduced mobility because of many factors, leading to the perception of reduced rain or grass). Others complained: 'This deep hole here [referring to a drilled borehole], this is stealing our water!' In other words, local knowledge adapts to observed changes. Attending to the formation of new local knowledge is therefore a way to learn about changes in the lived landscape. Changes in the environment, climate and society are not only noted and observed by herders (making them highly valuable informants about ongoing processes in their landscape), but also accounted for and incorporated in their understanding and perception of space. Through their observations and narratives, we can learn to see the factors co-implicated in the production and reproduction of the drylands: roads cutting through bushland, the expansion of settlements, drilling of boreholes, policies of restrictions and enclosure, changes in social behaviour (modern clothes and alcohol), among many others.

A struggle over land or water is not just about access to the material resource but also a range of other less tangible factors. Land is intimately linked with history, memory and cultural meanings. As Scoones argues, 'These socially embedded negotiations are part and parcel of livelihoods, but because they are so deeply ingrained, they are often not grasped. Practices thus create institutions, just as institutions create practices' (20021: 54). Turkana herders encode their knowledge in the environment, in the form of beliefs, amulets and ritual life. For example, direction and placement (inner, outer, back, front, west, east) have local meanings which go beyond pure cartography. Traditionally in Turkana, West is badness and wilderness, while East is the place of goodness where God lives (Betti 2010). This can be rooted in the historical Turkana conquest of their current eastward territory (Figure 22).

West symbolised the old, the place from where the Turkana were pushed away and where the sun dies down. East symbolises the good, corresponding to the new conquered territory where they established their own power (see the Introduction for a short history of the Turkana). These beliefs are reproduced in practices performed by some to this day. A Turkana homestead is oriented according to the sun: the kraal opens eastward, the men's sleeping area faces the kraal and wives' huts follow all around clockwise. One must face east in *agata* (prayer), in the direction from which life emanates; or sleep with one's head towards the east to avoid *longapen* (the disease of craziness), that comes on if west is faced. Similarly, *akiriket* (meat ceremony), if followed by chanting and praying, may end with throwing the *aburo* (walking stick) towards the west while saying 'may all bad things set in the west with the sun, and never come back'. The ending of *amok,* the ritual performed after defeating diseases (to push all bad spirits away to where they came from) or to cleanse deviations from the path of tradition, involves walking counter-clockwise, towards the east, raising the hands and saying: 'What makes you hot? You should cool down, may new things come with the sunrise, may you start afresh…'

These practices reveal the degree of embeddedness in place of Turkana herders. East is not only where peace is found, and God lives, but also where there is shade and freshness, refuge from everyday struggles. Scorching sun, dry wind and heat are associated with evil forces, which rest in the west where the sun sets, a psychological construct to make sense of the lived environment. Indeed, the more the sun moves towards the west, from its rise in the east, the hotter and thirstier the

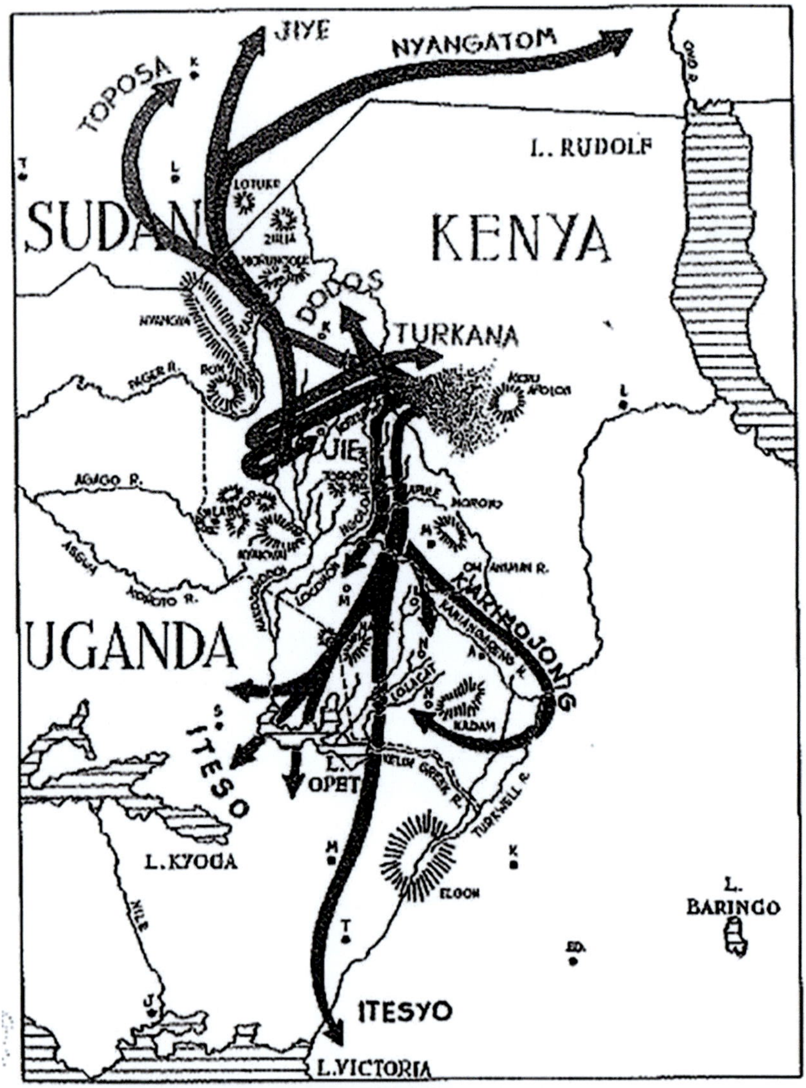

Figure 22. Nilotic population dispersion.
Source: Novelli 1988. Courtesy of Missionari Comboniani, Verona.

day becomes. Beliefs and rituals about space serve to emplace the individual, both physically and spiritually, within a landscape of larger significance. They are used to train new generations of herders, protect them and instil strength. This is how I was taught what to fear and what to enjoy. I could only possibly learn about the danger of thorns that *steal skirts (and hats)* by walking through them with the risk of being cut by their poisonous tips; about hidden demons among mountain rocks tripping travellers, by climbing through them and feeling my legs hurt; about the evils in the wind, by being lost in the middle of sandstorms. Living with Turkana herders was as if the variability of the landscape took on its own agency.

In response to the agency of space, Turkana herders have developed different scales of practices of divination, to regain control over their land. These include, for example, forecasting and rainmaking, both through the help of diviners (*ngimurok*). The former, which I witnessed myself, can happen through the inspection of a goat's entrails. Turkana represent their territory over goat's intestines curled in upon themselves (Figure 23). Intestines are laid on the ground by diviners and spread to take the shape of the surrounding landscape. Elements of the intestines such as arteries, cysts and clots represent landforms, creeks, mountains, plains and Lake Turkana. From irregularities in the entrails, seers find visual representations of

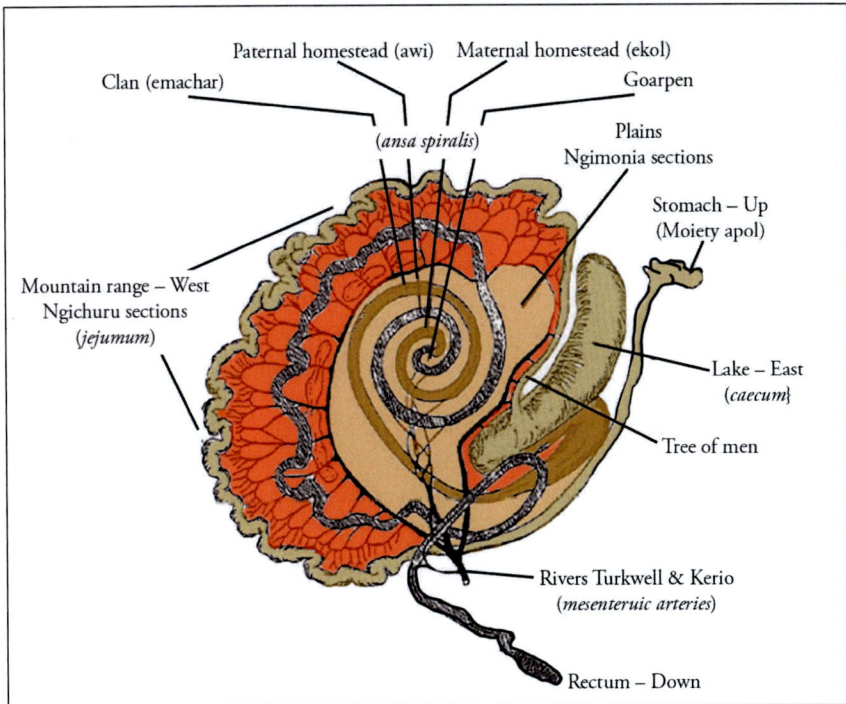

Figure 23. Entrails map
Source: Broch-Due and Schroeder 2000. 63.

future events, such as impending drought or the danger of a raid by neighbouring communities, or other transformations in the landscape. This shows not only the high investment of Turkana herders in the representation of their territory, but also a fluid perception of the same (Broch-Due 2000). By using soft animal material, the entrails map is necessarily flexible; topographic features become signposts and not fixed elements in the representation of space as seen from within and not from above.

Another way to forecast future events is through messages sent by God *Akuj*, a monotheistic deity, to the *emuron* in his dreams. These dreams are visions, visions of the future. They can be joyful dreams with rain, milk and fat, or they can predict bad events to come: diseases, droughts, raids. A local *emuron* in Lorengelup explained,

> We do see it in visions. We predict bad disasters. God tells several *ngimurok*, from different corners. Especially human and animal diseases, droughts; we can also see the good seasons to come, when people have plenty to eat.

If the scale of the bad event is large, involving entire communities, several *ngimurok* receive the same visions and collective action is required. The intervention performed in the case of a bad drought, for example, requires the reunion of powerful elders and *ngimurok* together with members of parliament (MPs) and other government representatives, who collectively pray to *Akuj*.

> We heard all traditional leaders were gathering next to Kalobeyei, next to Moruanayece, where the Turkana believe they come from.[51] We went there. MPs and government people were also there. And then it rained, I still cannot believe it.

The quote above is from a non-Turkana UN official, who recently moved to Lodwar. I could not tell how much of his excitement was raised by the sense of the *traditionality* he witnessed, or by the fear and delight when real drops of rain fell after the ritual was performed. Whether the ritual made it rain or not, for a non-Turkana this is a spectacular performance. For Turkana herders, this is a way to perceive their environment and make sense of it. As such, space, as the Sahrawian *badiya*, described by Volpato, is not only the result of multispecies agency but also of multispecies feelings that spring into action (2025). Similarly, often when there is a strong dusty wind, some people will stretch out their right arm and shake their hand against the wind, saying *taman kayaye* (return to your land, or go away, evil!) to the devil/spirit carrying the wind. Turkana herders

---

51. About the myth of origin see Barrett (1998) and Chapter 5.

the wind's potential dangers through a shared performance, teaching the novice herder what to be careful about, offering protection and strength on the crossing of unpredictable spaces. Protection is also offered by amulets and talismans. It is not rare to see herders, including small children, wearing a small piece of wood (*ekamuka* or *ebata*) around their necks, wrists or waist (women), as a protection against bad things (snakes, scorpions, spiders or the *evil eye*).[52] Others wear *epira*, a rubber ankle/wrist bracelet, around their arms or legs, which is believed to produce a certain smell that chases snakes away. There is also a plant root locally known as *ekeriau* (*Cyperus articulatus*); once bitten, chewed or ground into fine dust, it can be spat on the ground in the direction warriors will move towards a raid. The root will offer protection by making them invisible (or prevent the enemy from noticing them), while they can see the enemy.

All these examples show how space holds great significance, in symbolic terms as well, and is used to encode knowledge, transmit it to new generations and provide strength over an agent's space. Questions of how people interact with the resources of their environment to obtain a livelihood are normally treated separately from how life is imaginatively constructed in mythologies, ceremonies and rituals (Ingold 2000). This separation holds onto a distinction between the natural and the cultural; that is, onto the belief that there is a real environment (independent of our senses) and a perceived environment. In contrast, as this chapter has shown, ways to act in the environment are also ways to perceive it. In other words, the landscape also becomes the realm of the imagination. The ecological realm is thus not only connected to but inseparable from the economic, the spiritual and the personal (Rotarangi and Russell 2009). Without, I hope, falling into Evans-Pritchard's famous caveat described by Holzman (2009) – 'We know, of course, that witches do not exist' (Evans-Pritchard 1977) – I claim that the level of engagement with the lived space shown by my hosts and interlocutors through beliefs and ritual life is a sign of a 'grass-root resistance' (Anderson and Saxer 2016), one which defines collective identities[53] and marks a distinction from the expanding forces of modernisation. Perhaps this is a different form of resistance from that alleged by Saxer and Andersson's paper, and yet Turkana herders also find in the remote a refuge for ritual life amidst the rising forces of modernisation that emanate from urban centres.

---

52.   See Chapter 5.

53.   See Chapter 5.

The nomadism of space

Turkana representations of their environment yield a different perception of places that are often framed as remote because they are peripheral or seen as desolate, harsh and hard to reach, like the animate *badiya* in Volpato's book on Sahrawi camel husbandry in Western Shara. The *badiya*, the desert, Gabriele writes, is 'conceived as a fertile and animated landscape: it is a relational mode of dwelling under an ever-shifting configuration of rains, sand, plants, soil, water, camels, goats, sheep, and nomads; it conjures liveliness there where the word "desert" implies lifelessness' (2025: 1). The *badiya* is the result of a constellation of multispecies tasks in which everyone and everything plays its part. This constellation of tasks, Volpato writes, 'is in itself a process of place-making' (2025: 86). By walking with Emoru's family I learnt the level of engagement of herders in their landscape, their efforts to learn it, and give meaning to it. Cognition can be said to be both motion-sensitive and site-specific (Macfarlane 2012), and draws from an alternative science (knowledge), based on a sense of place. As Scoones puts it,

> with such a perspective, we can see how institutions are not fixed or designed, nor are they the result of simple, rational responses to economic incentives. Rather, they are dynamically reconstituted, reproduced and reshaped by the continued actions of multiple, located actors (2021: 54).

Resilience and the nomadism of space

Representations of space, 'conscious reflections on or about place', are born from the relationship between individuals, groups and the environment through everyday practices and the experience of inhabiting it (Hammond 2004: 9). By seeing like the herder, clouds are transformed into mobile shade; thorns turn into needles and nails; stones become gifts to the mountains; rain is the word of God; plants are medicine for hunger and weapons against disease; water drops sprinkle purification; trees and roots offer protection; paths are borders of friendship and enmity. Seeing like the herder means seeing more than a collection of resources spread over a geographical area. It means celebrating differences given by the heterogeneity and variability of resources; it means recognising space as mobile and moving along.

To most westerners and Kenyans, the Great Rift Valley, which includes Turkana, is unwelcoming. To most Turkana, this region is the place called home where they live and herd animals. By unpacking the territory occupied by Turkana herders in terms of large-scale ecological connections, live geographies and relational accessibilities, another possibility for the drylands emerges. In this, Müller-Dempf is correct: nature in Turkana offers both relative abundance and scarcity and hunger (2014a). Rather than seeing this variability as a constraining factor, I urge us to see its potentials.

In this chapter I have shown how drylands are not static stretches of nothingness, with scant resources and remote; rather, they are alive, movable and inscribed with local meanings. The nomadism and richness of drylands, however, only emerge if we begin to *see* from within. Conversely, abstraction, at bird's eye level and away from the ground – and homogenisation of places into zonal cartographic representation – fail to include such an understanding. In it there is no sunlight, and no moonlight, no wind, no thorns, no enemies, no neighbours, no relatives or friends; it is devoid of people and static in spatial features (Ingold 2000). 'Seeing like the state',[54] in drylands, means looking *at* the *remote* and not experiencing it. Scott argues that these views reflect a way of seeing that sought to impose order on the chaos of life and replace 'views from somewhere' with 'views from nowhere' (1998).

Acknowledging *views from nowhere* as views from within, new insights and interpretations of space rise which make resilience a matter of perspective, a quest for sight. A renewed perspective on drylands would help move beyond a representation of their inherent variability as solely a manifestation of crises. Rather, it would become a representation of space nomadism. From this renewed perspective over drylands, we could conduct 'better science' (Ingold 2000), not only based on *high scientism* but also on a *sense of place*.

Development planners can make use of such re-evaluations of the drylands by thinking about development at large, exploiting existing large-scale connections and relationships that weave together space mobility (variability), peoples' movements and decision making. This could improve the experience of accessibility of resources rather than constrain it into well-defined and bounded zones that will never reach sustainability when thought about restrictively in equilibrium terms. Planners can also rely on the herders' lived knowledge of a territory, which, far from being remote and desolate, is rich with significance and under continual transformation.

The changed form, shape, demography, liveliness of Urum village upon our return, made me realise that perhaps the variability that Turkana herders have learnt to manage and appreciate goes beyond the socio-ecology realm. It is rather a key trait of their everyday lives. From their perspective, and not from the desks

---

54. Scott 1998.

of planners in capital cities, everything is uncertain and variable: people cross paths randomly; vehicles appear fortuitously on remote dirt roads; development programmes are funded, delayed, expanded and abandoned. Aid, like rain, following the same laws of uncertainty, generates the mobility of space as produced and re-produced by the movement of its inhabitants. This is the content of the next chapter, where I discuss social, economic and political dimensions of variability through the lens of village creation, destruction and re-creation.

To see like the herder entails re-thinking about our *own* ways of comprehending human actions, perception and cognitions, and about our very understanding of the environment and our relations and responsibilities towards it (Ingold 2000); in Mbembe and Nuttal's terms, it entails starting a project of 'defamiliarization' (2004). To see like the herder entails a new way of thinking. Leave our conceptions, leave our homes and place ourselves 'down below' (de Certeau 1985) at eye-level. From this renewed position, I could experience the variability of space and see its nomadism. Space itself moves, and mobility becomes a quality of space.

After the wedding in Lobei we return to Urum, exhausted from the long trek and little food, and dusty from the lack of washing. Going to the drilled pump next to the dispensary to refresh ourselves, we find out that the new blue-pump technology tested in Urum had stopped functioning some days earlier. We go to the Kachaikol seasonal river instead and dig water out of the ground. There is still tumult in the village because of food distribution that happened just after we left the village at the beginning of our journey. One of the women takes us to the hut built as storage for the food distribution. The wind had blown the sisal-structure down. Sacks have been lying on the ground since a few days after Christmas when a government car brought them. No one is responsible for the distribution and people are kept waiting. Those who came from far away, hoping to get a share, are now leaving to go back home, no longer hoping that food will soon be distributed. Every sack has a tiny hole broken through the plastic strings, grains of maize spilled on the floor creating intertwined lines away from the storage area. People are walking to the horizon with small bags on their heads.

～ Chapter 3. ～

The nomadism of settlements. Aid like rain

We know, now, that we are in the presence of myths.

GRAEBER AND WENGROW 2021

Urum, a village along the Ugandan escarpment, at the far west of Turkana County. January 2017.

doi: 10.63308/63891908548751.ch03

Nomadism of the hut

Human mobility is a complex phenomenon but one that traditionally has been over-generalised and often analysed in terms of simple dichotomies.

JONATHAN BAKER (2001)

Rope jumping. Lorengelup, Turkana Central, January 2016.

Weeks pass and Urum seems dormant. The greatest excitement was created by our attempt at accessing our luggage from the hut of our previous host in Urum. When we when we walked out into the area surrounding Urum village we left some of our belongings in the hut belonging to our host in the village. On our return we had found that they had left, chained the hut's door and locked it up. The only thing we could do was to break the lock, but the many people who had gathered around us had different opinions, expressed eagerly and loudly. James, an elder of Urum who accepted to host us in this difficult situation, reassured us that everything would be fine. Eventually, thanks to my satellite phone, I reached the owner of the hut and agreed to buy a new lock in exchange for theirs, as well as leaving some money in exchange for their having kept our luggage in the hut while we were away. This event remained in the village's gossip for a few days, but otherwise the village was rather calm, emptier and quieter. We were also tired from the long march and starting to look for a chance to return to Lodwar.

Urum comes into view when emerging from a deep and sinuous wadi. The dirt road from Lokiriama runs for fifty kilometres before reaching the village, 150 kilometres away from Lodwar town, the capital of Turkana County. A ridged surface, waves of stones, the undulation of riverbeds all feed in to the fluctuating bouncing of overloaded pick-ups. From a distance, it is possible to see the blue roof of the primary school and the corrugated sheet roofs of the shops in the village. There is no electricity or phone network in the village. There is hardly any evidence of what is called *development*. Urum lies in a valley close to the border with Uganda, surrounded by mountains. Urum is a labyrinth; narrow alleyways intertwine around closely built sisal huts. Fewer than 100 inhabitants live here. A renovated dispensary, where no doctor wishes to work, is a little separate from the village, in a flat area once used as a landing strip by small aircraft, a memory from colonial times. Nearby, a recently introduced blue handpump for water is hard and dry most of the time. In front, there is a food distribution store made of grass and recycled relief-bags.

Urum is one of the many small villages that are springing up in rural Turkana along improved roads and telecommunication infrastructure. These types of villages are called *loline* by the Turkana, *along the line*, with clear English influence in the naming of something that perhaps, because of its temporal nature, did not need a name before colonisation. *Lolines* are small villages, often organised around a road with some levels of administration (for example a chief homestead) and some basic services (an infant or primary school, a dispensary, some water pumps, a few shops). *Lolines* are generally used for food distributions, village meetings (*baraza*), Focus Group Discussions (FGDs) by government or development agencies, and are where mainly elders and women with small children nowadays reside. The rise of *lolines* in rural Turkana can be taken as signalling the changing status from nomadic to semi-nomadic pastoralism, on a path towards sedentarisation and urbanisation. Such a view is rooted within dominant recollections of human history, whereby humans used to live in small, nomadic, egalitarian bands of hunter-gatherers, then, several thousand years ago, they domesticated plants and animals, discovered agriculture and grew sedentary, eventually erecting cities, which gave rise to civilisation. David Graeber and David Wengrow in the recent book *The Dawn of Everything* (2021), contest this linear story, claiming that societies of early humans were in fact wildly heterogeneous and complex. They demonstrated that a given society might alternate between farming and foraging, settling down for one season and on the move the next. This is the story I wish to tell in this chapter: *lolines* have living bodies.

During my sojourn in Urum, the village changed configuration several times: the number of people living there, the liveliness of the place, its contours, form and sounds. When I returned from the march along the Ugandan escarpment in the surroundings of Urum, I found it rather animated by the presence of the many people who had arrived for the food distribution. Shops were open, people came and went from the village selling goats or bringing sticky bottles of aloe vera oil collected from the plants that grow in the area. They had joined their relatives or friends and continued their lives in Urum until some decided to leave, having lost patience or hope to wait for the distribution to take place. When leaving, they did not forget to take some share of the maize brought by the government and left in big relief bags in the storage hut. Others remained, still others continued their errands somewhere else. Sitting in the yard of the homestead of my new host, I saw the village flourish and wane. From the perspective of the village itself, if we were to look at the world from the perspective of the huts it is composed of, Urum was never motionless. Rather, it was constantly formed and deformed in response to changes and elements of variability in the socio-political and economic domain: in response to aid, market prices, infrastructural development, for example. My hosts, other villagers, people I met along the way, constantly incorporated into their understanding of space elements of variability, also beyond the socio-ecological realm as discussed in the previous chapter. They were attentive and open to changes in society and economy. In other words, variability is systemic. I began to see aid, like rain. Following the same laws of variability, aid generates the mobility of space as produced and re-produced by the movement of its inhabitants and their practices of space-making. And contrary to dominant thinking, villages became, to my eyes, places of mobility, while the nomadism-sedentism dichotomy was progressively losing significance.

The scholarly literature about sedentarisation is abundant and very sparse. Since its beginning, the study of pastoralism has dealt with relations with the settled world by seeing the categories settled and nomadic as representatives of two opposite realities (Irons and Dyson-Hudson 1972; Khazanov 1984; Monod 1975). Classifications of pastoralism still today draw on the dichotomy nomadism *vs* sedentism, by which nomadism is the movement of an entire household during the annual round of production activities, and sedentism is the settlement of those productive activities over a single location. Sedentarisation is the change from nomadism to sedentism or, as defined by Salzman, a 'process of socio-cultural change' (1980: 10). Describing this process of change as a global phenomenon, the tone of much of the literature suggests, with a good dose of fatalism, its inevitability, irreversibility and perhaps desirability. Throughout modern history there have been countless attempts to settle pastoral nomads. Persecution of nomadic people through the world has persisted since antiquity (Shaw 1983) as they were seen and described as 'an abortive line of history' (Khazanov 1984) or a 'thorn in the sides of states' (Scott 1998: 1). Colonial and post-colonial states, religious, developmental and humanitarian organisations have all managed pastoral populations while pursuing different goals (taxation, administration, conversion, service delivery) but engaging in the same methods: keep them in place and establish control. Emeritus Professor Dawn Chatty describes these efforts as emerging from late Victorian ideas of civilisation and later theories of *modernisation*, in which sedentary lifestyles are superior to those requiring movement (2007). Maryam Niamir-Fuller, in the prologue of a recent special issue for the journal *Nomadic Peoples* that I co-edited with my friend and colleague Cory Rodgers, 'Sedentist Biases in Law, Policy and Practice', well describes how, during the industrial age, the concept of efficiency further strengthened sedentism. She claims that it started to be more efficient to centralise than to decentralise, to settle than to be mobile, to consolidate rather than disperse (2023: 316). The benefits, she remarks, appeared higher than the costs because the costs were transferred to the pastoralists, who have lost access to customary pastures, have been subjected to burdensome bureaucratic regulations and fees, or feel forced to settle to take advantage of aid and development programmes or land rights but thereby undermine longstanding forms of land governance and livelihood (ibid: 316). In the same special issue, we collected articles that show contemporary forms of implicit but pervasive attempts to settle mobile peoples – either through the centralisation of social and economic services (health, education, markets), or through legal and procedural state tools that undermine the flexibility, reciprocity and porousness of land use, or by creating fixed boundaries between communities, mobility patterns keep being disrupted even today. As such, Cory and I argue that discrimination is occurring to date, in some contexts less overtly than in the past, through interventions that are incompatible with mobile livelihoods and lifeways and continue seeing sedentism as a 'normative way of imagining and pursuing progress and betterment' (2023: 155). Many have warned against the negative impacts of sedentarisation that could outnumber its benefits: damage to culture and traditions, density-related problems (diseases and degradation), impoverishment and destitution, and political questions along the lines of *why should they settle?* With respect to development goals of economic growth and prosperity brought by sedentarisation, it is not uncommon to read that pastoralism has 'survived despite development schemes, not because of them' (Dukhan 2014: 75).

It hence appears that agreement over the impacts of sedentarisation has yet to be reached (McDonell 2016). What is certain is that sedentarisation is not a recent phenomenon or a unidirectional process and has occurred in many regions of the world at different points in history. From the Biblical Abraham in the Middle East to the Saami people of Northern Norway, nomadic people have always transited towards settled life, in and out (Barfield 1993; Khazanov 1984; Salzman 1980; Vrålstad 2010) and seeking alternative livelihoods (Anderson and Johnson 1988; Homewood 2008; Scoones 1995a). Hence, interactions and shifts between settled and nomadic lives become a feature of pastoralism rather than a sign of change from an ideal, or idealised, form of pastoralism as self-sufficient and largely isolated, an image that seemingly remained crystallised since early ethnographies (Dyson-Hudson 1966; Evans-Pritchard 1940; Gulliver 1951; Jacobs 1965; Stenning 1959).

In the literature as much as in popular conceptions and representations, aside from some interpretations by mobility turn theorists of fixed infrastructure that serve modern high mobilities, there is little acknowledgment that sedentism and sedentarisation do not preclude mobility, and that people in settlements, as well as settlements themselves, can even be very mobile. Certainly, as I was getting familiar with my field sites and started working without the help of a local assistant hired directly from the visited communities to show me around, it became more difficult to find people to interview in villages than in the shrublands of camel and goat shepherds, or in the mountains of cattle pastoralists. In villages, people's homesteads were unattended most of the time, livestock kraals were open and social gathering places like shops or the shaded of certain big trees were not very busy. Then, I started hearing. I heard whistling coming from river bushes and maybe the sound of the bells of oxen; kids laughing and running after each other while going to the shops to buy sugar; I heard whispering around wells and water points; I heard digging sand, dropping sweat, and pouring water which echoes in empty jerrycans; motorbikes rumbling; I heard fire lighting and wood burning; tree branches breaking, axed and tied together, and then I heard them falling from someone's head, and someone else starting to laugh loudly.

Nomadism of the hut

Every sound resonated as an action. Every sound was a verb, a tireless movement. Following these sounds, I realised that both, villagers and villages, move. As such, the initial dichotomy of nomadism *vs* sedentism is itself misleading, as claimed by Humphrey and Sneath in *The End of Nomadism?* (1999: 182), failing to reveal the dynamic and fluid character of pastoral societies. It ignores that nomadic pastoralism still exists in the twenty-first century (Fratkin and Roth 2005) and has not permanently settled; rather, it might even be gaining new momentum (Meuret and Provenza 2014). It forgets that settlements themselves, if viewed from their foundational action, from the perspective of a hut, are expression of a process, a dynamic act of settling (La Cecla 2011). Thus, a better way of looking at sedentarisation is, as proposed by Sneath and Humphrey, 'the material form of individual strategies, a complex process of dwelling and settling' (1999: 179), as this view includes all the sounds I heard, and allows movement and change, constructions and destructions, to be accounted for.

I must recognise that the nomadic-sedentary opposition has long been questioned. Nonetheless, it persists in the epistemological infrastructure of research in pastoral areas, as a category of reference that in turn influences policymaking through measures that privilege emplacement over mobility: permanent borehole drilling, grand and static infrastructure, residence-base service delivery, private land ownership and so forth. With reference to Jeffrey Kaufmann's concept of a 'sediment of nomadism', for which pastoralism is still, implicitly or not, essentialised to *pure* degrees of mobility and *pure* food economies centred around livestock (2009), in this chapter I claim that sedentism is equally essentialised. I therefore question the relevance of ideal types of *pure sedentism*, from the perspective of a hut. I base my reflections on the daily, simple and complex, practices of people in drylands, who – with their actions – build, shape and re-shape the localities where they live and the societies they represent. Inspired by the phenomenological bent of place-making as an act of 'being in the world' (Heidegger 1971), and by using the framework of the body to explain city transformations (de Certeau 1988), I look at the spatial practices that make and unmake, form and shape, villages popping up along improved roads and telecommunications infrastructure in rural Turkana, the *lolines*. The subject remains, throughout the chapter, the village itself as expression of space-making.

The creation of villages

> *When we reject the single story, when we realize that there is never a single story about any place, we regain a kind of paradise.*
>
> CHIMAMANDA NGOZI ADICHIE, 2009.

Huts under construction. Lorengelup, Turkana Central, December 2015.

Leaving Urum is not an easy mission. There is no public transport in Urum, and days pass without any car running down the dirt road that crosses the village. People from the village start making promises: 'a car is coming to restock my shop shelves' says one, passing his fingers over the dust of his counter; 'my motorbike stopped functioning, I called my brother in Kakuma to come with a car to help me fix it. You will be able to ask for a lift!', a neighbour alerts us. But days pass, promises vanish in silence, and the village is quieter and quieter. Suddenly, one day, a rumbling sound from a car's engine reaches us. We run. Three pickups are stuck in a bend of the dry river just before the road enters Urum.

In Turkana, small towns started to be built in the early twentieth century with the arrival of the British. Before colonisation there were hardly any urban settlements, except some small fishing villages along the shores of Lake Turkana and trading centres in South Turkana. Nomadic pastoralism was the dominant and most suitable livelihood strategy given the climatic and geographic conditions of the Turkana basin. Housing structures were built with branches or other materials found in the environment and were meant to last only until the next move. The composite profile of the landscape allows for complex patterns of mobility inward and outward, from and towards the outer mountain ridges, through the vast central plains and lake shores. Livestock husbandry was commonly integrated with various forms of gathering and hunting, as well as fishing in the waters of Lake Turkana, rain fed agriculture and exchanges with farmer communities along riverbeds. The first permanent settlements were born out of the encounter with the colonial administration, whose action was not only limited to countering the expansion of Abyssinian forces, bureaucratisation of society and introduction of trade and taxation, but also aimed at extending control, militarily if necessary, over grazing fields and water sites. Since around the same time, the mid-1920s, relief assistance has also been brought to Turkana, marking now over hundred years of humanitarian and development interventions. As recounted by Reidy (2012), this process started with colonial paupers' camps in the 1930s (where free cereals were distributed), moved to mission-run famine camps (which became a near permanent feature by the 1950s), expanded into large scale emergency relief operations in the 1980s (when about half of the population was receiving food aid), and gradually evolved into the multi-agency distribution efforts of today. Around these meeting points between nomadic pastoralists and outsiders (administrative sites, police stations, water points and distribution centres), settlements started growing, and over time they became towns. Much of sedentarisation history in Turkana has focused on the development of large towns, like Lodwar, Kakuma or Lokichogio. Such prevalent attention to large towns betrays a sedentary view over processes of growth and ignores the current proliferation of small towns and minor centres rapidly spreading, springing-up and senescing, in the rural countryside, the development of which is situational and contingent on the interplay of many factors that permitted variability and experimentation. In the history of these minor centres we can trace the indigenous critique identified by Greaber and Wengrow, whereby colonised people launched a consistent moral and intellectual assault on European society. (Graeber and Wengrow 2021). It shows ingenuity and skills to live off uncertainty and exploit changing and unpredictable resources, including aid and other socio-economic and political resources. The volatile, uncertain and fluid nature of *lolines* is a trait of variability, which is as much ecological as socio-economic and political. This emerges clearly from the many histories behind their creation, which, unlike evolutionary views of growth and civilisation, bring to the fore their contested, mutable and multiple meanings.

The literature of nomad sedentarisation refers, for the most part, to conventional push-pull and gravity models derived from old migration theories (Harris and Todaro 1970; Lee 1966). These theories generally focus on disparities in conditions between place of origin and place of destination, suggesting that migrants are pushed by low incomes in their countries and pulled by better prospects in more affluent areas. Similarly, in sedentarisation models there are pushing-out and pulling-in factors. Push factors may include loss of common land, livestock raiding, shocks, droughts, resource competition, population pressure and conflicts. Pull factors are normally cited as availability of services (water, schools, dispensaries), food relief and economic opportunities (petty trade, wage labour). Models that rely on these forces of attraction and repulsion prove insufficient to understand a phenomenon as complex as sedentarisation. Baker (2001), for example, warns against the risk of dichotomisation proposed by push-and-pull theories that seem to imply the absence of free will, aspirations and dynamic decisions. In addition, the literature is polarised around the ambiguous role of settlements as both refuge and entrapment, seen as a step either towards modernisation or towards the creation of places of poverty and destitution (Broch-Due and Sanders 1999). During my sojourn in Urum, in the time that was freed up while waiting for a vehicle to return home, I could enquire about the processes that led to the creation of the village and it progressively became clear that social processes bridging a nomadic to a settled way of life are diverse, and multiple (at times contradictory) spatial imaginaries were created. The chief, for example, presented a rather *chief-centric* view of the creation of Urum. He described finding a desolate area waiting for 'good development', which he transformed into a vibrant place, much more 'developed' than before, and holding great potential for further growth.

> At that time, there was nothing here. I was working as veterinary officer in the area, when I decided to start recruiting people to come to live here, so that I could ask for registration of voters and establish the village in 2009. The only distribution point at the time was in Lokiriama [approx. 50 km from Urum], and with the enemy still around it was very dangerous to walk in that direction. I wrote a letter to WFP and World Vision to implement a food distribution point. Food distribution began in 2011 and more people settled since, now we can find water here and a few shops have opened.[55]

---

55. KI, Urum, 2 Feb. 2016.

The creation of villages

Urum is a relatively new village, established in 2009 and developed along the road to Kakuma. Before my arrival in Urum, the national government had built a dispensary, a primary school and an early childhood centre but, overall, there is still little evidence of *development* in the area. The chief explained that before 2009 there was no permanent settlement; people used only to temporarily camp and plant sorghum when it rained, or to form defence clusters (*arumrum*) when the enemy was raiding. To establish Urum as sub-location,[56] it needed to have its own administrative centre where a chief could operate. This reconstruction resembled the search for a 'settled identity', as described by Saverio Krätli and Jeremy Swift, as a way of securing administrative visibility (2014). The chief of Urum started holding *baraza* (village meetings) instructing people to build permanent homesteads. Once Urum was recognised as a sub-location, and following the death of three women who were walking from Lokirima back to Urum for a food distribution, the chief convinced WFP to build a road to connect Urum with Lokiriama and to start a food distribution programme directly in Urum. The opening of shop – the chief's shop was the first one – and drilling boreholes further contributed to the growth of Urum.

The story narrated by some villagers differed, adding layers of contested meanings to the creation of Urum. They downsized the role of the chief; if anything, the process was reversed: '… and then the government brought the chiefs'. Only after the village was created, and because of its creation, was the chief appointed and sent by the government – according to some, compromising elders' authority. In many interviews people argued that the village started as a collective *arumrum* or *adakar*: the settlement of multiple families within a common fence. Explanations I was given for these settlements varied. Families living in the same *adakar* are connected by kinship, affinity, friendship or spatial proximity. For some, it forms a grazing community; families living in the same *adakar* share the same water sources and responsibility for maintaining them, and take animals to nearby forage. For others, families come together mainly for security reasons, especially in border areas. Many others referred to *adakar* as a grouping that emerged for dancing purposes – somewhere youths would travel to, especially during full moon nights, to sing and dance away the tiredness of the day. Others instead remembered the time spent in *adakar* as the 'time of sharing milk between many families'. In the *adakar* in Urum, conflicts and the search for security brought people together under

---

56. Sub-locations are small administrative units under the New Constitution.

a small hill called Urum, which literally means *coming together* within a common fence against the enemies. *Arumrum*. Hence the name: Urum.

> The enemy was all over the place; there were a lot of conflicts. A lot of people died in these mountains [pointing]. There are many graves around here, and bullets in the trees. People moved together mainly because of the enemy. We had to stay together to protect each other.[57]

Only afterwards was the government informed that people were living there and sent a chief who started building structures (school, dispensary, hand-pumps). Food distribution was then brought to Urum, and a higher number of people have since settled, *in line with relief*. A common view of these processes of village creation is to be walking the way of urbanisation, civilisation and progress. Chiefs, NGOs, development agencies tend to see in the growth of villages the opportunity to open the minds of people to the possibilities of business as an alternative to pastoralism. As explained to me by the chief in Urum:

I intend to raise the number of associations in Urum to show those people who are still moving around with livestock that there is an alternative. They have other ways to make a living. Here there is a very fertile soil, for example, that they can utilise for farming. They also have forests which they could use for bee-keeping and harvest honey. Or they can collect stones and sell them. There are so many other alternatives they can explore in this area, like mining gold.[58]

From these accounts, villages appear as a stage of permanent change and are taken as evidence of a local wish for change, to raise living standards and find a more comfortable lifeway. Villages are the locales where development agencies can invest to foster growth. Here is the frontier where development actors do venture, meet local communities and bring services. It is unusual that the same development actors move beyond villages as it is also rare to hear them speak in support of a mobile lifestyle and livelihood that remain, to them, trapped in the imaginary of the uncivilised, the pre-modern, and hardship.

Sedentarisation is not a homogeneous experience. People's decision can rarely be reduced to one single factor – rather many factors interplay, inform, influence and modify each other. Most importantly, it is not a static process that can be described as a single action. This lens ignores that settlements evolve, change through human activity and can acquire many levels of contested meanings. There is, in other words, a difference, as in de Certeau's 'panorama city', between the

---

57. Elderly man, FN, Urum, 23 Dec. 2016.

58. KI, Urum, 6 Feb. 2016.

imagined, *planned town* (by development or government planners) and the *lived town* of herders. *Lolines* are, in reality, complex, always changing, locales, where stories overlap. De Certeau writes that the images that *tell* a place are those down below, with those whose steps *write* the city (1988:93). Placing myself *down below,* I tried to listen and observed the trajectories which formed and deformed the localities where I was living. And suddenly, after repeated visits of different lengths over many months, I could feel the pulsations that characterise these places. These villages became to my eye highly dynamic, surprising and resourceful; never the same, physically (in terms of housing structures, buildings, pathways, extensions, etc.), demographically (density and demographic composition), emotionally (liveliness, quietness, noisiness), and always under constant reconstruction.

The materiality of variability

> *Sono arrivati dall'altipiano* / They have arrived from the uplands
> *uomini e donne con lo sguardo assorto* / men and women with rapt eyes
> *dei seminatori di grano* / people of the wheat
> *ed hanno lasciato quello che non c'era* / and have left that which was not there.

GIANMARIA TESTA (2006)

The making of charcoal. Lorengelup, Turkana Central, January 2016.

As maintained by Emery Roe, the socio-ecological landscape is heterogeneous not just because it contains a variety of different land uses, habitats, ecosystems and vegetations. 'It is also heterogeneous because households, communities and other sub-landscape levels of analysis are varied in their practices, relations to and impacts on the environment and natural resource base within the landscape' (1998: 33). The changes I could observe in the villages where I lived during fieldwork were responding to laws of unpredictability as much as rain does. Some were in response to grand international schemes of changing relations which fund, withdraw or extend relief aid, and allow maize to be sent to Urum as happened over Christmas, but not to be distributed until a month after its arrival, for example. Surely, away from the desks of planners, this is a difficult process to grasp, understand and foresee. Take the example of Kambi Lore, a village in the central Turkana plains. Because of its relative proximity and better connection to Lodwar I was able to visit the village several times at different moments of the year. I could hence better observe its constant deformations. The first time I arrived at Kambi Lore at the end of October 2015 I noted in my diary:

> Kambi Lore lies in the dust, next to a mirage. Air trembles over the hot cracked soil. Blue hills shape the horizon line. All you can see around is flat, golden sand. Tall trees and dense bushland thickly follow dry creeks, like sinuous snakes. A white signpost informs travellers they are entering Kambi Lore, 45 kilometres away from Lodwar. The dirt road cuts the village in two: on one side there is a primary school, a dispensary, latrines, broken water-tubs and a few huts; on the other side, the village expands, where approximately sixty families live. Dome huts made of woven dried palm leaves are built next to each other; pathways marked with human and goat footprints signal busy days. There are a few shops made of mud and iron sheets. Rays of light reflect from solar panels leant on the walls of the shops. You can charge your phone and find tepid light at night. There is one black water tank standing with a single pipe directly feeding into the chief's homestead. Another tank is rolling on the ground, empty. Grains of sand fall from a water kiosk, which has not seen water for a long time.

In December 2015 I returned to the village for the second time:

> The village is growing fast. Since my first visit, the water kiosk, which looked dusty and crumbling, is now working, having been connected to a nearby borehole. There is also one small *hoteli* (restaurant) where now we can buy chapati and eat something at lunch time; another one is under construction, and people are bringing palm leaves and wooden poles to the owner for a small payment or food to bring home. There is also a new big structure made with mud, with no roof yet but corrugated sheets are lying on the ground which I

assume will be the future ceiling. People inform me that someone is building a video-saloon to show movies for 50 shilling a show. There is an unexpected and contagious ferment. People seem very busy; it is difficult to find them in their homesteads for interviews. People believe that in a few years they will all have water in their homesteads and houses will turn from being built with palm leaves into mud and iron sheet. Kids play loudly every night, and I can hear music coming from one of the shops where youths have gathered. During the day people are busy: some bring their small herds to the river, others prepare sacks of charcoal to replace those sold along the road, motorbikes go and come bringing eggs, which we could not find two months ago, and beers from the bigger centres …

When I returned once again in February 2016, it appeared very different, like a ghost of itself:

… I recognise Kambi Lore, but this time it is different. Not even sand flies. With my research assistant, we stay in the sub-chief's homestead. She is not here. It seems she has not been here for a long time. I remember her *boma* (homestead) being always full of people sitting in the shade of the *mwarobaini* tree (neem tree). Now it is only us. Part of the fence has fallen down, there are spider webs in the hut, and silence instead of music, at night. The small business activities started last year have closed or failed. Only one *hoteli* now opens, when money from cash-transfer programmes is distributed. Shops have closed or have empty shelves. The water tank feeding into the kiosk has broken and is spilling water everywhere. One extra water tank was brought by a politician who passed by and saw they had no water; the tank is now lying down on the ground, empty. It seems to me there are many more fences around the houses; the number of charcoal sacks along the road waiting to be sold is impressive; but fewer people are around.

This situation was once again different by the time I went back, for the fourth time, in November 2016, a year after my first visit. During this whole time, Kambi Lore was anything but still. Such changes represent the crude and material dimension of uncertainty. The failure of contemporary scholarship and policymaking to describe the novelty of these processes, and to imagine places as fixed or sedentary is due to the lack of understanding of what Membe and Nuttal called the 'creativity of practice': the compositional acts that give life to places (2004). The dynamism which emerges from the extracts provided above is what makes settlements highly mobile. This movement is rendered visible by its embodiment, first, in the villagers who move along chains of relations and by moving create and connect places; and second, in the villages themselves, which throb to the rhythm of uncertainty.

The vehicle stuck in the river creates sudden ferment in the village. A few people run to help, while a group of 'town people' get off. Mostly youths, and an older couple. They have come to Urum for their asapan (initiation ceremony). The older couple is the current county minister of health with his wife. One of the young guys is their son. The youths are spending a few days with their 'bond family[59] *in Urum, before the ceremony can begin. Afterwards, they will return to Lodwar. We think we have found a way back, and also a rare opportunity for me, outsider, white and female, to assist in an initiation ceremony.*

Connections: variability along social chains

Ugo Fabietti describes the Arabian Peninsula as a 'land of mobile men' (1989). Alberto Salza speaks of 'mobile people', referring, among others, to the people from the Lake Turkana basin (2014). For these authors, mobile people themselves become one more cardinal point in the maps of their movements. 'Mobile people are the centre of their world, and the horizon moves with them; themselves turned into a map of their territory' (Salza 2014: 3). The social maps of the people I encountered or lived with are no doubt very complex, intertwined and expandable. Their mobility acts as a means of connectedness and relationality across large territories. For example, Loporucho, an elder in Kambi Lore, envisioned his future while talking to me:

My youngest children will go to school in town where some relatives can take care of them. One day we will all meet in my home; people will come from far away, those with animals will come and bring some for us to eat together, those from town will also come and bring sodas, and my newborns will return from their jobs in the foreign land. I will be very proud of my family that day.

The intertwined paths of Loporucho's family members give shape to places woven into a vast net of relations, a web of connections. 'As the spider spins its threads', rendering space possible, habitable and walkable, 'every subject spins his relations to certain characters of the things around him and weaves them into a firm web which carries his existence' (Uexküll 1957: 14). Like spiders, human beings weave webs. Webs of relations along which it is possible to move. Thus, relations connect places as they spread and enlarge over different areas, creating

---

59. Closely related families tied together by obligation bonds, important for alliances, mutual aid, support, defence protection.

more and more tangible locales along the web. For the villages I visited, social webs have important implications: first, as I realised after several visits, most people in the villages are related to each other. They are currently in the village because they know someone or were brought by someone they know, or because they have heard from someone they know about a successful business. Close relatives, extended families, family friends, adopted relatives, borrowed children, friends, friends of friends, tight, loose or distant connections could be established for each villager I met within the village and its surroundings and beyond the village; beyond regional borders up to the mountains and lake shores, North Turkana, West Turkana, South Turkana, Kitale, Moite/Loiyangalani/Marsabit on the other side of the lake, *down-country*, the rest of Kenya.

The ceremony takes place for a whole day. It is a day of meat, prayers and chanting. It is not difficult to distinguish the town youths from their rural fellows as they are the only ones keeping their pants on. Eleven naked youths line up in the middle of a small forest next to the dry creek. All elders from the area have gathered. I recognise some of my hosts from the march along the Ugandan escarpment. Women are not allowed at the ceremony. Only a few sit quietly further ahead, in the hope of receiving some meat to bring home. Around the fireplace, the elders have sat in a semicircle. Sacrificed goats are burning on the fire. Eleven goats for eleven initiates. First their fur is burnt. Then, the goats are taken out of the fire and cut open to let blood percolate into the chest, it may be drunk warm, but also collected into a big wooden bowl and let cool down under the shade of a tree. The goats are cut into pieces that one by one are sent back into the fire to finish roasting. That is the meat ceremony, akiriket. *The initiates sit outside the circle and are offered pieces of goat meat. The first bite is spat to the ground, for the ancestors. Once the entrails are eaten, the initiates are let into the circle, while* ngujit *(chyme)* [60] *is spread on their bodies, each by the* mzee *(head of household) of their bond family. The ceremony ends, after a long day of chanting and rituals, with the final prayer by the* emuron *(seer):*

Emuron: *Tell hunger to depart from these children. Has it moved?*
   Choral response: *It has moved*
Emuron: *Let all bad things depart from that home, have they departed?*
   Response: *They have gone*

---

60.   Semi-fluid mass of partly digested food taken from the stomach of the goats.

Emuron: And the place where the herds are grazing, let all come back in coolness
     Response: Cool
Emuron: Let calmness prevail and plenty of food
     Response: Yes
Emuron: Let us pray for calmness in the land that our cattle have spent the night,
let it be cool. Hasn't it calmed?
     Response: It has calmed
Emuron: Let the cows be met with rain
     Response: Let it be
Emuron: Curse all bad things away from those cattle. Eehei!
     Response: Eeehei!
Emuron: Defy the eye [61] *Leave and go, go back to your land. Follow the sun as*
it sets to darkness.

The second implication of social webs is that sedentarisation does not result in a sharp break between pastoral, fishing, farming and urban communities. Former pastoralists living in towns, for example, often own livestock in rural areas herded by friends, relatives or hired workers, or have split family members accordingly; town dwellers travel to rural areas for coming-of-age rituals and various ceremonies which involve their bond-families; herders have relatives in towns whom they can visit when they need money to pay debt-food[62] in local shops, or to whom they can send their children during school periods; town relatives inform their rural family members when cash is distributed through cash-transfer programmes or host them on market days or when they have gone to town to sell various products. Social networks spread across many different livelihoods. During times of abundance, the different livelihoods complement each other (livestock being exchanged for grain for example). During times of scarcity, family members survive by turning to whatever in their repertoire of activities is still tenable.

Social ties are maintained by marriage, initiation rituals and exchanges of various kinds, which serve to keep communities integrated and expanding; the networks they create allow for continuous movement between various places, making mobility part of the essential nature of places. Following this perspective, the emerging image of the villages I visited reveals stories of connections, for, as Ingold writes, it 'would be quite wrong to suppose villagers are confined within a

---

61.   The evil eye, witchcraft.

62.   A common practice of borrowing food from shops and delayed cash or in-kind payment.

particular place or that their experiences are circumscribed by a restricted horizon in a single place' (2007: 100–101). Their mobility is the first foundational act, a primary condition for the reproduction of the social formation of the villages. In this, I reiterate Ingold's question: 'how could there even be places if people did not come and go?' (2007). This means not only that villages are created through movement, but also that movement gives life to the villages, which are, in turn, always under construction. There is not a single image, a single snapshot, I can provide of the visited villages because the villagers I met, spent time with on several occasions or never encountered again had the capacity to continually produce something new, singular and unthought of. This leads me to my second point: village pulsations.

Pulsations: the variability of huts

If we understand sedentarisation as the material form of dwelling and settling (Humphrey and Sneath 1999), then, when villagers move, villages do too. Along webs of relations, networks enlarge and integrate into existing relationships in a specific place. People build, call on friends and relatives; villages pulsate. Villagers, in de Certeau's term (1988), 'spatialise': they create discreteness. Spatialisation occurs at the rhythm of different uncertainties. Has food aid been distributed? How are market prices? Is there a conflict? Are resources available and accessible? From another perspective, we could see spatialisation as being part of a 'programmed destruction strategy': at times of crisis/opportunities people gather, while during quiet periods human settlements spread and vanish (Retaillé 2013). This was seemingly evident after the Turkana Rehabilitation Project in the 1980s, for example, which started as a famine relief operation in response to a severe drought, but soon disclosed its true objectives in the form of a five-year land rehabilitation plan, encouraging mobile herders to settle permanently into sedentary riverside agricultural schemes (Derbyshire 2022). This, as officers envisaged, was a more sustainable way of getting along. However, as soon as the climatic conditions improved and nutritional security was re-acquired, most people departed the famine camps and returned to a semi-nomadic lifestyle, one which allowed livestock husbandry and self-agency. The famine camps were a *pulse*, a dynamic interaction with emerging resources at times of uncertainty. *Pulsations* work like the *actualisation of various possibilities*, or the *materiality of variability* in its very flesh. The villages where I have lived have undergone tremendous transformations throughout my fieldwork. Forms of things, their materials, shape and varied usages, arose, transformed and died along with people moving in and out, and villages throbbed. This dynamism is, put simply, what is needed in a place that has never offered predictability and where variability reigns.

'People in this village are like seasons' is what an elder from Longech, along lake Turkana's shores, once told me. People gather when they have heard there are plenty of resources available around certain villages including grass, fish and rain – a village expands – and leave when there is scarcity of those resources – a village contracts; people gather when there is conflict, in search of a safe place – a village expands – and leave when peace has been restored – a village contracts; people gather when word has spread about food distribution or construction of water facilities or enrolments in cash-programmes – a village expands – and leave when these are completed or have moved somewhere else – a village contracts; people gather when they hear they can earn money selling charcoal, liquor and brew, livestock, basketry along roads – a village expands – and leave when roads are no longer used by vehicles or have been diverted – a village contracts.

These pulses are not unidirectional (only moving in), but multi-directional (including: in, out and several other ways of layering these motions). Pulses are heterogeneous and not single-factored. Pulses are dynamic. These pulsations are the materialities of variability, the different configuration of *lolines* in response to socio-ecological-economic and political variable factors. Different sounds, objects, buildings and facilities were created and destroyed throughout all my visits in the three villages. Silence, or deep and vibrating music from drums during night church ceremonies increased as drought was striking, and people were moving closer to the villages, hoping relief food would be distributed soon, meanwhile praying God would help. The sound of vibrant children's laughs and screams while playing at night came when stomachs were full. Loud pop music played from cell phones of youths who gathered when shops were running and had shelves full of beers and sodas. The sound of beans poured into a pot. Mechanical drilling. Huts up. Fences down. Plastic bags flying. New churches; new constructions; a new dispensary room; abandoned homesteads and kraals. New water pumps, broken ones; piles of charcoal sacks.

By materiality I mean 'the tangible stuff' (Ingold 2011: 20), of production, destruction, degradation, erosion, corrosion, wear – which came into being by sawing palm leaves, threading strings from relief food sacks, burning wood, digging sand, building huts, carving iron sheets, knapping stones; bringing things to life and death, responding to changes in society. From the perspective of Turkana herders and pastoralists, not only rain and pasture are variable, but everything is: people met on the way; vehicles passing through the dirt roads; the number of charcoal sacks that will be bought; development programmes which are funded, delayed, piloted, failed, expanded; water drilling, borehole construction and borehole exsiccation; food distribution. With humanitarian assistance that disappears with the first rains or falls from the sky,[63] the similitude with rain is easy to grasp. Like the seasons, aid is factored into the understanding of space, and it is discussed, shared, searched for.

Scouting for aid entails the movement of parts of households towards distribution points and the subsequent creation of places for as long as food is distributed and seen as a source of opportunity. Phenomena of *densification* (the expansion of villages, together with an increase in the number of people and huts, general noise and liveliness), are mixed with phenomena of *fluidisation*: when food stops arriving and villages contract, houses are abandoned, fewer people remain around, leaving silence and dust. Similarly, when there are election campaigns, candidates drive through rural areas and hold meetings and assemblies. And then they leave, having distributed cash, brought water tanks, promised irrigation schemes and school development. Rumours spread. The village throbs and densification starts. And, after a period of time, water tanks roll over the ground empty. With no international oversight of funding, or coordination of interventions, facilities (like boreholes, cattle dip stations, trade centres, schools, fishing industry along the lake shores) fall into disrepair and become the symbol of the unpredictability of aid to which Turkana herders have learnt to respond by making and unmaking their lived space.

The sun is setting, and we start walking back to our host's hut, thrilled and tired at the same time. Our path is crossed by a group of women, whom we do not know; they do not seem habitual residents of Urum. They are walking fast, with determination, to the centre of the village with empty jerrycans. We follow them and try to understand what is happening. A big truck that we did not see or hear arriving is parked outside the chief's homestead. Two men are confronting the many women gathered around. They all seem aggressive. Voices are loud. Jerrycans are lifted and shown to the men. One of the women explains that the men have been sent to start a new maternity centre next to the dispensary. 'We are demanding they use and pay for our water for the construction materials, 50 shillings per jerrycan', less than 50 Euro cents.

---

63. The Royal Air Force used to drop food from the sky in the 1960s (Reidy 2012).

Aid, like rain, is a metaphor for forms of social, economic and political variabilities in the landscape: it shapes people's accounts of space and contributes to their decision-making and creation of the world. Variability is thus material, and its materialisation is apparent in village pulsations. Contours of villages are movable, as if villages themselves are breathing. A villages is not just a stop but also a crossing point, a junction which grows, shrinks and shifts; a 'discrete permanency' (Harvey 1996), a temporary arrangement of cohabitation that may break when the season changes and people migrate, where space contracts when time dilates in vain. After leaving, people are replaced by ants which take over the places created during the peaks of the pulsating movements; when people gather again, they will start afresh, and the centre takes on a new body-shape; it moves. As Akai, an old woman living in the surrounding area of Kambi Lore once told me:

> When it rains somewhere, people will go there. Ants will eat away all our things and houses; when we return, we will have to start afresh … this that you can see now (pointing around) will no longer look like this and will be eaten away.[64]

Figure 24. The dying hut.

The abandoned hut in *Ngiturkan* is called *awi a ng'orot*, which simply means *home of long ago*. By wayfaring through Turkana, it is possible to see many *awi a ng'orot*. The same happens when someone dies. My host family in Kambi Lore grieved the death of the *mzee's* mother. She lived her last months enclosed in her own hut, with a glass of water and one of milk, if available, brought to her every day, too old to even stand; the family feared she would injure herself by crawling on the ground if she was let out. The mourning of the old woman was haunting our nights. Upon my return, after several months, she had died and her hut turned into a gigantic grave where she was laid to rest, a collapsed dome which once used to be her home. A dying hut (Figure 24). The abandoned hut, however, is not a

---

64.   HI, Kambi Lore, 26 Nov. 2016.

dead hut, as its appearance may initially suggest. Upon closer inspection, the same material with which the hut was built, drops off and takes root, creating a new growth of living material. Houses become alive after they are abandoned. Huts, villages, paths, shops, churches, schools – they are all living organisms (Blier 1987 cited in Ingold 2000: 187). The influence of human presence prevails, they look like buildings, but slowly less so as non-humans advance. Building is therefore a process which goes on continually, with no final form (Ingold 2011). And settlements are never really settled.

Resourceful dumps and quicksilver economies

All good things follow the roads.

YOUNG MALE HERDER, AKUDET, 15 NOV. 2016

Selling charcoal. Kambi Lore, Turkana Central, January 2016.

The following morning, one of the men from the dispensary comes to inform us that the lorry should be back tomorrow to bring more materials, and we could return to Lodwar with them. We are also told cars will be sent to pick some of the initiates. After an extra week in Urum, we finally think we will soon return home.

The nomadism of settlements

In *lolines*, it is difficult to see livestock. Elders and women with young children settle in the newly formed villages while livestock is mainly kept far away. In *lolines* there are only a few shoats, weak or lactating ones, because 'it is not possible to live a life with no animals' and because they may 'not be strong enough to move long distances over rough terrains'. Most livestock are taken away by male youths, 'the strong and energetic ones' and their wives (if they have no children yet) who move in search of better pasture using temporary satellite camps (*abor*). The households (*awi*), the principal production unit among Turkana pastoralists, split, like a drop of mercury.

The creation of *lolines* has brought up an extended model of space use which includes pasturelands, mountains, rivers, lowlands, and also roads, markets, towns. To make use of all these spaces, the household necessarily splits. In other words, space extension entails social fragmentation and household re-organisation, including household splitting and new types of mobility. New villages, new opportunities and new food gave families the ability to separate, thus making simultaneous or prolonged use of the multiple coexisting spaces, while earlier the whole family had to stay together. As explained by my host mother in Kambi Lore:

> Today one burns charcoal and takes it to the road. When drought comes, the animals migrate, and we remain behind like now. Before, when it was livestock alone to keep us alive and the world was still good, we used to migrate fully [the whole household].[65]

Since the household splits, struggles are equally faced among members of distant mobile household units. Splitting implies a separation from wealth which today has the shape of a bull but also a radio, a metal foil, or maizemeal every night. Life becomes equally hard, for those who migrate and for those who stay behind.

> Here in the village there is *akoro* (hunger). Animals are kept far away, and we do not get enough animal products to sustain a decent life. Only those who still migrate get good food and can enjoy life.[66]

> People who migrate nowadays face a lot of struggles; there is not food for them, no fat, they eat only *engol* (palm fruit).[67]

In the face of these struggles, families provide reciprocal support. People who stay behind, those who remain in *lolines*, send someone to visit those who migrate,

---

65. FN, Kambi Lore, 18 Jan. 2016.
66. Elderly men, FN, Urum, 2 Feb. 2016.
67. Young woman, KI, Kaikol, 17 Nov. 2016.

and vice versa, to inform each other about herd condition, state of animals and destination of migration. Those who stay behind bring a bag of beans and maize to those who migrate when they buy or receive it from the government; alternatively, those who migrate pass through *lolines* to buy food, when they finish their stock, with money lent by their relatives in towns, or go to collect their cash transfers from the government. Those who migrate also bring an animal when they hear that people in villages are struggling for food.

These relationships, within the households and with the surrounding environment, define what I imagined being a *Quick-Silver Pastoral Model*, made of fluid human and animal groups, characterised by continuous fusion and fission phenomena in response to changes in society and the environment. Households are organised in mobile units defined by movement, autonomy and flexibility in order to provide quick responses to rapid external changes which occur in space, environmental, social, economic, and political variations. Rather than the end of pastoralism, this shows its constant evolution, the re-organisation of a livelihood in order to access both cash-based opportunities and the livestock-focused resources of the pasturelands.

This occurs differently from case to case – here some examples (Figure 25):

- Compass model: one nucleus of the family is placed at the heart of the village and other parts split, moving along a circumnavigation radius at a reduced distance from the village.

- Decentralised model: one nucleus of the family moves from the village but remains within a short distance from it while other parts of the family move around the decentralised centre at a reduced distance from it.

- Long range model: regardless of the distance from the nucleus of the family to the village, the other family units split into cells depending on the number of species owned and size of herd and travel long distances away from their centre.

Turkana herders continue moving so much that these are obviously just some notes about the households' organisation during the time of my presence or what was described in household interviews; it is in reality neither stable, continuous or definite. The ways households organise and re-organise their moving are ever changing in accordance to needs, contingencies and household capabilities. Though there are various ways in which households split, *lolines* remain commonly used as places to buy goods, collect food-aid, seek health services, pay visits during the day to meet friends, or gather news and be updated about things happening

The nomadism of settlements

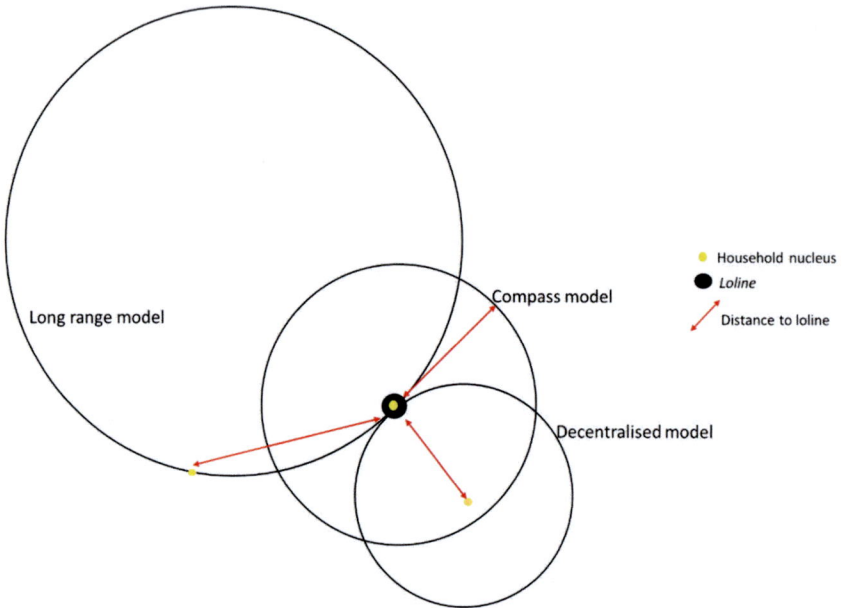

Figure 25. Quicksilver pastoral model. Developed by the author.

around, information being an additional resource to utilise in a multi-resource economy (Chatty 1996; Hobbs 1989). They are mainly used as *resourceful dumps*, to store people considered unable to perform pastoral activities (old people and young children). I came to understand these places as *old age homes*, for old people to rest and intercept, capture and share forms of social, economic and political variability; and *children's training grounds*, for helping grandparents with house chores and other errands, attending government school and learning how to herd from the few animals left behind before they take full responsibility for the herd and start their migrations in one of the various family nucleuses.

In *lolines* people learn 'the ways of the government', as Akamaise, my host in Kambi Lore, once told me. This echoes other exchanges with people in settlements:

> Most people did not know how to make mats and baskets or how to burn charcoal when there were not roads and *lolines*. We started learning these new things since more cars pass through here …[68]

> Before the government arrived, people were migrating away from the drought; now we run into it.[69]

---

68.   FGD, Kambi Lore, 13 Nov. 2015.

69.   Elderly Woman, KI, Lorengelup, 18 Nov. 2015.

By 'learning the ways of the government' and engaging in farming, wage-labour, entrepreneurial activities, market opportunities (charcoal, liquor, basketry, livestock) or aid-watching, people are bridging the cash-based economy of towns with the livestock-based economy of pasturelands to quickly respond to various forms of variabilities, creating a complementary, *hybrid economy*. Müller-Dempf has introduced the idea of a hybrid economy in Turkana, 'where the pastoral and non-pastoral sectors become more and more linked, and people in both sectors are increasingly cooperating' (2014b: 14). As a result, urban markets become part of the pastoral landscape, and food purchased from livestock sales becomes part of the livelihood strategy. Women have also pursued new avenues to earn an income, including the collection and sale of wild resources, firewood and charcoal; weaving palm leaves to make mats/brooms/basketry; or opening shops to sell various products including maize and beans, tobacco, drinks, beads and modern utensils (plastic plates and cutlery, mobile phones, torches). As noted by Fratkin and Roth, sedentarisation does not imply one type of lifestyle or economic activity, but includes a range of economic choices (Fratkin and Roth 2005: 10). People mobility is what allows the simultaneity of urban and rural spaces, by being here and there, through physical movements and widespread connections.

The growth of a complementary economy does not, however, lead to a uniform process of general 'enskillment', to use Ingold's terminology (2000); rather, this occurs unevenly according to idiosyncratic possibilities and other contingent factors with the risk of creating new forms of inequalities and stratification, and sense of exclusion. Akamaise fears that,

> … The person who has not gone to school, the survivors of the new changes of life [those who maintain a pastoral way of living], nothing can suit them. Nowadays people survive with casual labour, and those who are not learned [those who did not go to school] grow thin

Indeed, as *lolines* grow, spread and proliferate, next to new economies, expectations rise too, which can drive further space-making, but can also transform into frustrations and fears, when these remain unmet.

The following morning no car arrives. The workers at the dispensary insist it will be there any minute. Our luggage is ready and standing next to the road. Nothing for hours. Also, from the initiates, there is seemingly no movement of preparation for leaving. Tiredness and frustration blend.

Clearing bushes: a note on expectations

Armed with shovels and sickles, I was once approached by a group of people in the surrounding of Urum, along the Ugandan escarpment, who were going to open up their own road, 'so that food aid can come here as well, and they can bring schools and *mandeleo* (development)'. The proliferation of *lolines* creates new expectations and ideas about development, shaped upon urban lifestyles. There is, in other words, a form of pre-emptive sedentarisation that occurs when pastoralists anticipate government-mandated policies (Nyamir-Fuller 2023). Chiefs and development agencies/NGOs working in rural Turkana have played their part in the spreading of these imaginaries. Many have shared a vision of growth which takes Lodwar, the Turkana capital, as the model of urban evolution.

> With the school and development there will be changes. Urum will grow like Lodwar.[70]

> There will be more people and the road will be tarmac and development in general, like houses with corrugated-iron. Many more people will go to school and those who are in school now will have finished and will bring development back here.[71]

People envision a future where the number of inhabitants will increase, *even more*; the number of constructions and permanent structures (corrugated-sheets and mud houses, 'one day even concrete ones!', restaurants and lodges, schools, medical facilities) will also increase; more shops, more jobs, more business; there will be big market areas and trading centres; roads will be tarmacked; there will be lights; and water in all houses. These expectations drive further creation of place, clearing bushes with one's own hands and shovelling roads which are seen as paving the way for development in many parts of rural Turkana.

Expectations also shape aspirations of younger generations. One day, with my host family in Lorengelup, I was trying to understand how they choose to send Itiiri, one of their daughters, to school and not another one:

> Akamaise: It was the same Itiiri who has always said to her dad 'put me to school; dad if you put me to school, I will buy the motor car'.

---

70. Middle-aged man, HI, Koomyo, 28 Dec. 2016.
71. Young woman, HI, Nangorichoto, 27 Nov. 2016.

Itiiri: I will drive it to this place that is your home and stop at that acacia tree (pointing). I will bring sugar, rice, beans, and tea leaves and give this all to you, who are my father.

Problems rise when expectations of returns from school investments remain unmet, as another family explained to me, and it was not a rare sentiment:

The *mzee* (household head) sent his kids to school with the expectation to be helped once they get a job. I want my kids to know that we used our livestock for their education and that there is no more livestock left; we are old now and do not have strength to look for food; we want our camels to be returned.[72]

There is a thin threshold which transforms expectations into disappointments, sense of abandonment and resentment.

We have been forgotten. We ourselves have to struggle. Rains do not come any more. We cannot farm and we are forced to sell our animals to buy the food of the enemy.[73]

In many of these centres there are understaffed schools, inadequately stocked dispensaries, several inoperable water pumps. Much of this infrastructure can provide a material basis for expectations of transformation and integration – but often falls in despair like derelicts of development and can create contestation and anger. In Urum, for example, prior to our journey along the surrounding hills and mountains, we assisted to a *baraza* (village meeting) called by the chief. It served to write people's names down (*to pen*) for enrolment in a newly sponsored programme for social entrepreneurial activities. Soon after the *baraza* began, Ewal, a renowned elder of the area, stood up and with vehemence said (addressed to the local chief):

They [outsiders, people from town] call us 'reserve' [sic], 'drunkards', but they are not giving us any direction. I once went to Nairobi and found that there were tractors cultivating farms for the people living there: why then are not they cultivating our farms here as well? Why they do not request a tractor for us to irrigate our farms? Where is the person who demarcated Nakuru [south Kenya], and made it the source of maize that you now scramble for [during distribution of relief food]? Where is the person who planned a village, and it became a true habitat [grew into a town]?

---

72. Elderly women, HI, Loreamatet, 26 Nov. 2016.

73. Middle-aged woman, HI, Ngichwae, 10 Dec. 2015. Among Turkana herders, emoit (the enemy) indicate both neighbouring pastoral communities (with long history of reciprocal raiding), and foreigners (mainly wazungu, but not only). Sometimes it is used also in relation to Turkana people (or Kenyan town elite) who have abandoned the herd and settled in town, behaving like non-Turkana. It thus broadly indicates outsiders.

When we see a tractor here [when tractors are brought to this place], it comes to create valleys that destroy land.[74] You are busy enlarging your farms [private plots; meaning that the chief is preoccupied only for his own wealth], what has happened with you? Come sunrise and Akuapua remains Akuapua [one of the small settlements around Urum], nothing has changed; comes nightfall and Urum remains Urum. We are not expanding in advancement [we are not seeing any lasting development].

It is being said that there will come a pen [we are told people are coming to write our names down][75] from Kakuma, and that pen will develop this place. I have come here in front of chiefs because I want you to see where I belong. I voted for councillors [Members of County Assembly] who are blind, who are without eyes; and chiefs, who are blind, who are without eyes; and members for parliament who are blind, who are without eyes. They all are blind.

I say they are blind because which of these old women here have you assisted? I recently went to Lodwar and I found old women benefiting from old age support; which of these old women are beneficiaries here? You! The maize that is meant to be fairly distributed, it is what you instead want us to beg for,[76] and you are even saying to do us a favour!!!

But let me tell you that we are not blind. I thought that a nominated chief was supposed to call all these men and women under a tree and ask them to share their problems with him. And then you would go and forward our needs ahead to the relevant authorities. But instead, what are you doing? Nowadays you make deliberations at your doorsteps. How will you understand our needs, the

---

74. Referring to the flat area in between the village and the dispensary which during colonial time was used for a small aircraft landing strip, and now it is an unused area, where crops do not grow, and the drilled borehole is dry most of the time.

75. Expression used to indicate enrolment into a development or government scheme.

76. Maize is the most common form of food distributed in Turkana. I assisted several food distributions during my fieldwork and could observe how unevenly these occur from place to place. Sometimes there are people in charge of the distribution, other times this is delegated to local elders, other times chiefs are in charge. The process of distribution itself is normally very confusing with the ration arbitrarily varying and people fighting among each other to have more or running away to empty the sack to go back and pretend to have not been given anything. Also, most of the time, food distributions happen unexpectedly with rumours spreading in the area a little in advance and people marching towards the expected food distribution point with uncertainty. When food distribution is not universal (i.e. covering all households in a given area), selective targeting is planned but often not understood by local households who complain about being left out. A final typical comment is that food which finally arrives to the distribution points has been reduced through its own journey from Lodwar, being *eaten* by authorities and elites along the way.

problems we have at home? Is it not the responsibility of the chiefs to bring the people together and deliberate with them?

These are the problems of Akuapua, these for Namoru-areng'an [a small settlement in the surrounding of Urum] and these for Urum. Just leave us that way, ignore us! You may write with pen on a piece of paper, but we write curses with our hearts.

Someone once upon a time said [local proverb]: 'take care of the thorns, be careful of the thorns, this side you have thorns, and that side you have thorns, there are thorns all around you, thorns are in front of you, and thorns are behind you'. I thought, if here and there we are all surrounded with thorns, why should we tire our mouths speaking, *ng'imoru* and *ng'irithai* [generational clan division] – why should we tire our mouths, what are we saying? What are you saying? These are the same words of all the time (we are repeating these issues time and again), go and we shall perish with you.

Who will redeem us? Who is going to advocate for us, who will stand amidst us and defend us? …

I have quoted this speech at length because it does justice, better than thousands of my own words, to the sense of frustration felt among some elders in the peripheries of Urum. Ewal opens his speech by sharing a sense of persisting denigration about their lifeways, a persistent misrepresentation promoted by media, policy actors and academics who still relegate rural livelihoods into the domain of the pre-modern, hardship, the irrational. Ewal instead is very eloquent, and precise. He addresses issues about the past, the present and the future: lack of support, aid and development; bureaucratisation of society; corruption; loss of tradition. In his speech he discusses issues of old-age cash transfers, and problems with the school system which leaves children alone after early care with no primary and secondary school available to let their knowledge grow. In his speech Ewal speaks about the damage to the land of certain interventions, about privatisation and marketisation penetrating into interior Turkana lands, and fostering unequal development, which does not reach everyone and creates social divisions. He insists that development ends at the doorsteps of chiefs, he claims that government, officers, chiefs, do not know how the people are living but nonetheless make decisions for them. He addresses problems of aid targeting. He points at the volatility and insecurity of the support they receive. He compares *pens*, symbols of development, with *thorns*. Yet pens often do not reach everyone, as chiefs, members of parliament, governors, all are blind and greedy, taking most benefits for themselves, and the future where the village will be transformed into a *true habitat* never gets closer.

However, the future is far from static. In response to the sense of uncertainty shared by Ewal, villages throb, people observe, learn and replicate what is happening around them. Similarly to the autonomous creation of a road near Urum with which I opened this section, villages are popping up along the Turkwel River, one of the two permanent rivers in Turkana. People are learning from funded irrigation schemes nearby how to dig their own canals and are buying seeds from their neighbours to start their own agricultural fields.

> There are farms along the river now, but we have to fight with *Prosopis*.[77] We dug canals ourselves to plant tomatoes, spinach, sorghum, maize. We started digging when the government taught people in Nadoto and we copied from them. In Nadoto they went to dig with machines, here we just copied them and did it ourselves with our own tools.[78]

In response to a combination of complex variabilities, expectations and frustrations, people pick up their tools and clear bushes to cut roads through their landscape to allow development to come, and villages spring, like flowers, along new trajectories, but, like flowers, they wither and die too. As Scoones writes, this is not only significant for resources directly important for livestock production, such as grass and water, but also for the markets that allow pastoralists to realise cash income (2023). Navigating across these uncertain, unruly materialities is a central feature of pastoralists' strategies. Questions of access therefore also arise in relation to material uncertainties, for resources are not fixed features but are socially and politically constructed. Thus, it is structural and historical relationships, along with the wider political economy, that influence who gets what and so how vulnerabilities emerge, and uncertainties are experienced.

Resilience and space making

Because of the proliferation of small villages in rural areas of Turkana, there is a growing sentiment that the Turkana are changing from nomadic to semi-nomadic or semi-sedentary lifeways. For some this is a sign of a local desire for modernisation and integration into the civilised world. For others, it signifies development and

---

77. *Prosopis juliflora*, introduced in Turkana in the late 1980s, is an acacia-like tall bush, imported to East Africa from America (mesquite) by development agencies for re-forestation purposes. Now it has become an invasive plant, dangerous even to livestock because of its unpalatability and infectious thorns; its encroachment blocks mobility, and Kenyan authorities are launching eradication programmes or alternative uses (charcoal).

78. Middle-aged woman, FN, Loreamatet, 20 Nov. 2016.

improvement of living conditions. It is remarkable that processes of sedentarisation are deployed as metaphors for change, evolution, progress and betterment. In contrast, nomadism remains confined to an imagined past. It represents immobilism of culture and production; resistance to change. These accounts treat traditional pastoralism as a static or unchangeable livelihood system only involving roaming around with livestock. Conversely, the creation of *lolines* is the expression of people's capacity to incorporate elements of change in society (i.e., various forms of social, economic, and political variabilities, such as the sudden food distribution or construction of the maternity centre in Urum), through the making and unmaking of their lived space, their social networks and their broader livelihood. As Chatty has shown for the Bedouins in Oman who started using trucks to transport livestock through vast desert lands, 'their adaptation ought not to be regarded as evidence of system decline' (Chatty 2013: 139). Similarly, the creation of *lolines* shows a system which is continuously changing in response to variations in environmental, socio-economic and political conditions, always adapting to new factors, always 'potentially modernising' (Chatty 2013: 139). The capacity to incorporate elements of change is part of the story of resilience I learnt with Turkana herders, an entanglement with the nomadism of space.

Lolines, as expression of space making, represent the fluidity of both space, through the making and unmaking of their inhabitants, and livelihoods, through a process of enskillment geared towards the creation of complementary economies centred around cash and aid. *Lolines* are places of movement, construction, destruction and reconstruction. Relationally, dryland centres move together with the movement of villagers. The creation of settlements does not result in a sharp break from different lifestyles than those of village dwellers, but rather the village itself lives through nets of relations and connections, as a spider web which renders space habitable and walkable: people walk in and out of *lolines* by means of connections. Physically, dryland centres are never the same in contours, extension and liveliness. Villages pulsate through the movement of people who transform spaces into lived places according to their imaginaries; as Olwig writes, 'it is time we recognise that human beings, as creatures of history, consciously or unconsciously, create places' (2002: 52–53). Turkana herders have managed to transform settlements into living bodies, constantly in movement and breathing. In a review of *The Dawn of Everything*, Michael Robbins writes that capitalism has dissolved the older forms of collective relations that permitted variability and experimentation in communities (2022). To concur with Scoones, as shown in this chapter, 'uncertainties are not simply the result of 'natural' processes, but are produced via material relations, through human and animal bodies and emerge as a result of social and political dynamics over time and across scales' (2023: 1). By seeing like the herder, social, ecological, economic and political variabilities, seen as threats by outsiders, become instead different forms of mobility of space which take various shapes in coevolution with the moving, building and unmaking of its inhabitants. The mobility of space translates into a different understanding of place, in which uncertainty is a way of life, as when the 'muddyscapes of hazards' of the river islands described by Mukherjee and colleagues become 'muddyscapes of opportunities', and ultimately a possibility for resilience in the options opened, 'along "situated adaptive practices"' (Mukherjee, Lahiri-Dutt and Ghosh 2023: 9). From this vantage point, we can perceive drylands beyond vulnerability and instead as viablescapes. Interventions targeted to fix the nomadism of space, to enclave multiple spaces by imposing borders or permanently stabilising features (permanent boreholes, permanent irrigation, permanent food distribution and the like), have shaped and aggravated volatilities by impacting on lives and livelihoods, while frustration and malcontentment rise, and people's capacity to be mobile decreases along with their resilience.

Out of nowhere, a pickup materialises in the yard of the chief's homestead. My assistant and I run to the vehicle. There is already a loud crowd gathered around the pick-up. The town initiates, the health minister and his wife and a few residents of Urum. It looks like a fight. Everyone wants to get in the car, an unusual opportunity to leave, reach a bigger centre, possibly get some business done. We manage to sneak in. On the open back of the pickup, 25 people squeeze and battle with thirteen goats, which the initiates are bringing back home. I am literally standing on the back of two goats, one foot on each. Some people are hanging from the sides of the pick-up. Every turn of the dry creek, every bushy hill that we need to cut through, is a struggle. The pickup swings from side to side. Most people have to jump down from the pickup when it gets stuck, push it and run fast ahead in order to recatch it when it takes off, not to be left behind. Halfway to Lokiriama, the closest bigger centre, still some 25 kilometres away, the minister and his wife get off, too scared to continue further.

∾ Chapter 4. ∾

Practices of mobility

Our nature consists in motion; complete rest is death.

BLAISE PASCAL (1678)

Holding the net while setting it in the lake. Longech, Turkana Central, April 2016.

doi: 10.63308/63891908548751.ch04

Navigating variabilities: mobility to mobility

It starts with a step and then another step and then another that add up like taps on a drum to a rhythm, the rhythm of walking.

REBECCA SOLNIT (2001)

Crossing Lake Turkana. March 2016.

We approach Lodwar when the day becomes night. Dust flies over the road in a dazzling cloud. We get off in front of my favourite Somali restaurant in town, and silently share an enormous pilau with sukuma *(kale), potatoes, cabbage, onions and tomatoes; and a cold bubbling soda. We are too tired to even speak.*

The journey so far brought to light an understanding of space as complex, dynamic, always changing under the incessant fabrication of humans, animals, insects, plants, water, terrains, rains. This is a typical scenario of the rangelands of the world. Whether the high mountains in Central Asia and Latin America; the dry savannahs in Africa, the Middle East and South Asia; mountains, hills and plains in Europe; or the arctic tundra, these socio-ecological systems work under laws of variability and non-equilibrium that turn them into highly dynamic contexts.

The sequence of dynamic patches, where nutrients for livestock become available in unpredictable and ephemeral concentrations, where markets are mantled and dismantled, where social networks, friends, kin, *enemies* expand and contract, where development aid is distributed and withdrawn, all varying over space and time, requires specialised and skilled management, which is fundamental to make the difference between scarcity and abundance, within the same ecosystem (Krätli, El Dirani et al. 2013). There is great debate over such management, which Ian Scoones recently streamlined in two opposed approaches: control and care (2023). Mainstream development in pastoral areas has, from time immemorial, aimed at creating stability and asserting order; the underlying narrative, through colonial, postcolonial, neoliberal language, is recursively one of crisis, vulnerability and coping; variability has been treated throughout as an obstacle. Owing to a tendency to control, track and tax populations, states privilege settled farming over mobile pastoralism. From this perspective, interventions revolve around fencing to create ranch-like paddocks, feedlots, reticulated water points, fixed markets or single location service provision, with the side effect of restricting movements and in turn undermining pastoralists' capacities to respond to uncertainties. Confronting these approaches, there are those centred around care, in which openness, attention to change, flexibility and responsiveness are central ways of life, making productive use of variability rather than fighting against it. Such caring approaches are a much-needed evolution towards *farming with nature*, to work with nature, function with the natural environment and, as supported by a recent FAO report *Pastoralists: Making Variability Work, a Promising Avenue for Innovation* (2021:13), to emancipate from fossil-fuel economies.

This chapter dives into the daily practices that constitute the caring approach to uncertainty and form a pastoral livelihood. Daily is not to be confused with simple. On the contrary, pastoral livelihoods are to be thought of as highly sophisticated approaches to production, with history and situated in place and politics. It is not a stylistic choice when Saverio Krätli speaks of 'specialists', or when Emery Roe refers to pastoralist populations across the world as 'professionals'. That is, it takes a lifetime to develop knowledge, capacities and resources, including cultural and social resources, to perform pastoralism sustainably and efficiently, even handling situations of the greatest difficulty. Pastoralist systems evolved to incorporate adaptive mechanisms for managing variability and uncertainty, across socio-ecological, economic and political dimensions. These mechanisms are various, including herd diversity, selective breeding, flexible resource management systems and tenure arrangements, extended social networks, specialised institutions and cultural assets, and are always under continued experimentation and innovation.

The most salient feature of a pastoral livelihood is mobility. Mobility is central to pastoral strategies; as Krätli and Shareika put it, pastoral mobility is essential to 'live off variability' (2010). That is, mobility is the core successful strategy in highly variable environments, in ways that no sedentary system could aspire to perform. It involves the movement of animals across a range of different environments at different times to reach water, pasture and minerals for livestock, or to respond to other socio, political and economic opportunities and needs. The costs of immobility are high in non-equilibrium systems, requiring for example high fossil fuel and/or water inputs. Forecasting and measures of control are almost impossible, are counter-effective and are accompanied by high negative externalities (Herrera et al. 2014; Krätli 2015; Law 2007). Instead, mobile pastoral systems, with high levels of specialisation and minimum inputs of external resources, are proven to be more productive: livestock feed better, produce more meat and milk, are healthier and have more calves than sedentary animals (Abel 1993; Behnke 1985; Breman and de Wit 1983; Catley, Lind and Scoones 2013; De Jode 2010; Western 1982).[79]

My journey continues to the lake site, to a place called Longech. Bags are packed and ready, when my research assistant unexpectedly shows up on the doorstep in my home-base in Lodwar. He was selected for a job as enumerator for an NGO and they leave tomorrow. I need to quickly find a new assistant. A couple of phone calls. A short interview. Ekwee is my new partner for the lake. After a few days we squeeze into an overloaded pro-box driving to a growing town called Kalokol. Lake Turkana once used to reach Kalokol, but now plains, punctuated by Prosopis, separates the port town, seat of the once growing fishing industry,[80]

---

79.   Also note that 26 studies in 9 countries in East, West, and Southern Africa found returns per hectare several times higher in mobile pastoralism than in ranching (Ocaido, Muwazi and Opuda-Asibo 2009; Scoones 1995a).

80.   Norad and the Italian Aid Fund (FAI) helped the newly independent national government develop a fish industry in Lake Turkana. They established fishing cooperatives and branches along the western shores, a fish-road which connected Kitale to Kalokol, ice-making and cooling storage, training and provision of modern fishing gear to Turkana people. A range of factors varying from political clashes with the Kenyan government to poor managerial capacities led to the collapse of the fishing structures in Kalokol and expulsion of NORAD from the country. Most facilities opened by Norad remain abandoned to this day.

from its waters.[81] *Another pro-box, with dry fish in its internal pockets, takes us to Natirae,*[82] *the mainland shore which overlooks Ferguson's Gulf. Longech sits on the other side of the Gulf.*

Mobility among pastoralists has long been an important topic of discussion in literature and policymaking, one that has undergone profound changes through time, never really fading from interest and with current renewed attention in international forums and scholarship. From early accounts in classic works, which described pastoralists as wanderers whose mobility was seen as backward, unproductive and harmful, there progressively emerged a view of pastoralists as adept decision makers and environmental managers, giving particular emphasis to the role played by the environment in determining pastoral decisions concerning mobility, largely framed under the overarching umbrella of survival or coping strategy. From the 1960s and 1970s, there was a growing recognition that ecology could provide only partial answers, so that the role of economics and exchange (Marx 1967), political oppression (Elam 1979) and facilitation of social relations (Gulliver 1975) began to emerge as co-constitutive elements of pastoral mobility, none of which could be thought of in isolation but rather as a constellation of highly diverse, contextual and contingent factors. An enormous variation at individual, community, regional and international level started to be observed, leading prominent scholars as early as the 1980s to claim that classification of pastoral movements into transhumant, nomadic, semi-nomadic or semi-sedentary risks resulting in a 'sterile enterprise' (Dyson-Hudson and Dyson-Hudson 1980).

With the affirmation and consolidation of the 'new rangeland paradigm',[83] pastoral mobility came increasingly to be seen as rational, opportunistic and adaptive (Chatty 1972; Roe et al. 1998; Westoby et al. 1989), leaving the survival language behind and seeing variability as a productive advantage. The focus has shifted from seeing mobility as a way of life (a trait of identity), to seeing it as a complex

---

81. More recently the water level of Lake Turkana was observed rising (Salza 2023, UNDP 2021). The concomitance of drought, floods and water-level rising around Lake Turkana is baffling. As Salza writes, the Lake Turkana socio-ecosystem is liable to alteration by man-made structures; The Turkwel Gorge dam intercepts highland waters, the Gibe dams affect the Omo river basin, in Arsabit County a wind-farm forms a barrage extracting kinetic energy from the air, and therefore reducing the wind force possibly altering alter the net water balance (Salza 2023: 96–97).

82. The name *natirae* indicates a place where many *etirae* trees grow (*Prosopis*).

83. See Chapter 2.

practice at the core of the system of production. Such a view was consolidated in the framing of 'strategic mobility', defined as the ability to arrive in the right place at the right time to take advantage of unpredictably variable grazing opportunities (Krätli et al. 2022: 10), and one among a range of real-time strategies developed as *process variance* in the face of *input variance*, where availability of inputs is variable. By comparison with the functioning of control rooms that juggle multiple changing factors to ensure that critical services are sustained, Emery Roe contends that pastoral systems also employ means of process variance, including strategic mobility, to achieve stable outputs (2020; 1998). Moving these debates forwards, Niamir-Fuller proposed a 'mobility paradigm' in the book *Managing Mobility in African Rangelands*, repositioning mobility as the 'foundation of future sustainability' as opposed to a 'remnant of the past' (1999: 1). In this, she aligned with a burgeoning group of scholars, showing mobile pastoralism as a land management system providing food, livelihood security and a whole range of what have now become popularly termed ecosystem services. Pastoral systems, in fact, when left to operate according to their own logic, bring important contributions to the conservation of biodiversity and carbon sequestration, they connect ecosystems by transporting seeds, grazing improves the water-holding capacity of grassland, reduce the risk of forest fires and restores and maintain soil fertility through manure. Pastoral rangelands are therefore far from being natural in the sense of pristine wilderness because they have been shaped by millennia of management with respect to ecosystem functionality. As a result, livestock mobility can be useful in the management and restoration of landscapes, which demonstrates its relevance as a tool for the United Nations Decade on Ecosystem Restoration (2021–2030). From this perspective, pastoral mobility purses productive objectives as well as a culture of care, which regard animals and the environment as co-creatures rather than objects and whose relationship is based not on exploitation but on reciprocity. As Ilse Köhler Rollefson writes in the wonderfully poignant book *Hoofprints on the Land*, pastoralists engage with livestock in ways that are simultaneously good for animals, people and the planet and, in fact, they are essential to upholding the web of life on Earth and ensuring its future functioning (2023: 12). These emerging views flow into a recent reframing of pastoral mobility by Ian Scoones, as care, involving a sensitive disposition to uncertainty central to daily life, deeply embedded in livelihood practices considered as a universe of socio-economic, cultural, emotive and political complexity (2021, 2023).

Navigating variabilities: mobility to mobility

Practices of mobility, as discussed in this chapter, are a response to a mobile space, following logics of situationality. Mobility refers in this chapter to something people do, resonating with Habeck's focus on movements, as 'mobility acted out' (2006). It is through a close inspection of people's daily movements that we can gain a nuanced insight into how herders see the world that surrounds them and how they interact with these surroundings while doing their work. From this vantage point, mobility (of practice) matches mobility (of space) through the art of navigation, mobilising knowledge and a wide range of socio-ecological relationships among humans and more-than-humans, where trust, social bonds, forms of collective solidarity, reciprocity, sharing and mutualism are all important. Using the framework of navigation proposed by Vigh (2006, 2009), I intend to discuss a social practice entailing movement through, within and along an environment which is itself in motion, as *an effort to gain directionality*. Navigating variabilities entails moving across intertwined domains of variability and finding directionality in the mess of possibilities emerging from the nomadism of space.

This is still an important claim to make. Even if together with scientific revaluation of pastoral mobility, a positive reframing is also gaining purchase in some international organisations and policy circles (see for example: AU 2010; FAO 2021, 2022; UNESCO 2019; IFAD 2018; IUCN 2012; UNDP 2011 the Transhumance Protocol promoted by IGAD in 2020, regional declarations such as the N'Dajema and Nouakchott declarations in 2013, the rise of the pastoral codes in West Africa: Mauritania 2000, Mali 2001, Burkina Faso 2003, Niger 2010, among others),[84] institutional inertia or contradictory legal and policy frameworks as well as competing economic interests, continue leaving pastoralists behind. Several policies continue to marginalise pastoralists even today, either directly or inadvertently restricting their movement even when intending otherwise, as the authors of the special issue *Sedentist Bias in Law, Policy and Practice* argue (Rodgers and Semplici 2023). As argued by Micheal Odhiambo and Pablo Manzano in a recent FAO report, *Making Way*, in the absence of legislation that protects and regulates mobility, pastoralists enter into conflict with other resource users at the risk of increasing livelihood insecurity (which comes at a cost for nation states) and increasing grazing pressure in other areas, reducing the environmental benefits of pastoralism (2022). Thus, mobility has yet to be fully endorsed, protected and promoted, and this has long term effects for the future of pastoral cultures too,

---

84. A list of declarations, legislations, and policy reports is provided at the end of the book, Annex 6.

modifying perceptions and attitudes towards mobility. The role of culture is not to be overlooked. Saverio Krätli, in the FAO report *Making Variability Work,* shows that cultural assets such as customary institutions for resource management, local knowledge, social capital and a culture of endurance are important for effective livestock mobility and in turn for production and the provision of ecosystem services. Most of the variability pastoralists embed in their system is aimed at supporting mobility. In the rest of the chapter, I reflect on the ways mobility is thought, dialogued and practised by Turkana herders, including negative views of mobility and the perception of stasis. I aim to offer insights into how, by following herders' movements, we can recentre the importance of cultural and social assets and recompile an understanding of livelihood as relational, moving beyond superimposed categories and classifications. It is the very act of moving that weaves together composite socio-ecological worlds.

Dialoguing and imagining mobility

Would you tell me, please, which way I ought to go from here? That depends a good deal on where you want to get to I don't much care where Then it doesn't matter which way you go… if you only walk long enough.

LEWIS CAROLL (1865)

Celebrations in preparation for moving. Urum, Loima, February 2016.

Dialoguing and imagining mobility

Ethnographic literature about Turkana often reports that Turkana herders are among the most mobile of pastoralists; moving frequently, over long distances, and always to different sites (Leslie and McCabe 2013). Undoubtedly it remains so even today. Turkana herders move so much and in such contingent ways as to make difficult any attempts at categorising their mobility. This is what is reported by researchers of the Feinstein International Centre, Tufts University, currently re-examining early warning systems and humanitarian responses in pastoral areas across the Sudano-Sahel and Greater Horn of Africa. Even so, I have found myself doubting this statement several times. I once wrote to my supervisor at the time: 'Now they don't move anymore!'; or I replied to a message from my friend Elena Dak, an Italian writer who had recently published a book titled *Io cammino con i nomadi* (I walk with nomads) (Dak 2016), that: 'These nomads do not move as much'. Having prepared to fieldwork with one of the *most mobile groups* in the world, I could not map the images of mobility I had projected in my mind to the empirical reality I found. Neither could I explain the litany of complaints about moving so often shared by my hosts and their neighbours. Salzman in the 1980s wrote that pastoralists move because they have to, not because they love it, but they indeed also love it (1980: 174–78). Where was such love for long marches, loading donkeys, across vast stretches of golden landscapes? Where was such love when I was told of the many dangers and fears associated with moving? In the evenings or during interviews, people often narrated, with empathetic suffering, stories of migrations with livestock, or long walks to collect aid money or join food distributions, or exhausting marches with heavy luggage to market towns to sell basketry/charcoal/firewood/livestock. They recounted days with no food and water. Days of scorching sun. Encounters with scorpions, snakes and hyenas. Days of shame, needing to beg for food. Getting lost. Entering hostile communities. Equally counterintuitive was the shared desire for a settled house, 'made of mud and iron sheet'; with 'permanent water pumps feeding directly into everyone's hut'; or market days in their villages, 'so that we do not have to walk long distances', and irrigation schemes, 'to have our own farms and stop all this moving around'.

They also expressed a sense of immobility that I found especially in *lolines*:

'From morning to evening we just sit here looking at the lake shrinking'.[85]

'We do not move anymore [herding livestock], we just sit and wait'.[86]

---

85.   Male elder, KI, Natabaa, 12 Feb. 2017.
86.   Elderly men, KI, Lokorokipi, 2 Jan. 2017.

I mistake flamingos for goats. Along the shores of the lake, there is a lot of movement. Cars half-way into the lake waters; open boots, boxes and packages moving in and out along chains of arms. Bicycles with piles of yellow jerrycans tied on their backs. Boats. Plastic boats, wooden boats, engine boats, rafts. Nets. Women throwing fish entrails into the water. Queues of motorbikes waiting for rides. Skinny cows wetting their hoofs in the lake. Kids running after seagulls. People queueing to enter passengers' boats to cross the gulf and reach Longech.

Sitting and waiting became a recurrent narrative. Charcoal sits and waits too: 'Sacks already filled are sitting and waiting along the roads'. As Natasha Maru writes in her doctoral thesis *Explore the Pace of Pastoral Mobility*, waiting is an inevitable occurrence in pastoral lives, whether waiting for rains, for crop fields to be grazable, for markets to take place or aid to be distributed – as happened with the food distribution in Urum over the Christmas holidays. But such waiting is different from being in limbo. A lot more than being immobile is happening, while *sitting and waiting*. As discussed in the previous chapter, some of the emerging sense of immobility is rather associated with a sense of separation from the people who do migrate with the family livestock, and the obligation to eat tasteless food,[87] while levels of expectation and frustration raised by the meeting with outsiders increase. The relationship between mobility and immobility nests in such separation. Scholars from the mobility turn have long objected the binary representation of mobility and immobility (see for example Adey 2006). They are co-constitutive and emerge together, as highlighted through the expression *(im)mobilities*. In other words, some mobilities immobilise others. And vice versa. The stationing of the elderly and women with young children in villages, or of women around the *awi*, or in mobile camps, enables the daily movements of flocks and the amplification of the family livelihood to include other economic and social resources flowing into the villages. The perception of immobility can also be temporally confined to a present state of not moving, but not really considering future states that instead would reveal dynamic (im)mobilities. For example, my last trip to greet my host family in Lorengelup before returning to Oxford occurred in the midst of the 2017 drought. At that time, I found only one of the three wives living in the compound. The others had long gone to other preferred locations for times of drought. No-one had previously told me that this might happen. This should not be a surprise,

---

87. See Chapter 5.

given that, as highlighted by Krätli and Swift in an assessment of survey methods to count pastoral population in Kenya, that decades of policies and interventions promoting sedentarisation are likely to have made pastoralists reluctant to classify themselves as mobile (2014). In addition, even from the perspective of those who remain fixed, we in fact rarely stayed still, sitting and waiting. Despite my host families often telling me not to move anymore, we walked every day to graze small shoats they were keeping near home, or to go to marketplaces and towns, to meet kin and neighbours, to check on cultivated fields, to provide for friends and relatives when in need of help. Mobility thus emerged through nested quotidian pathways. These are the lines that 'develop freely, and in their own time "go out for a walk"' (Klee 1961: 105 in Ingold 2007).

If we think of mobility as walking (the gesture of a walk), its ubiquity can be appreciated by looking at everyday practices; it is acted out unnoticeably but constantly. Mobility re-enters the narratives of my informants and friends, discursively, even when just scratching the surface. 'We cannot sit and wait if we want to eat', explained a woman in Nangorichoto. She then listed the many tasks she performs each day to ensure a meal to her family, all implying walking, moving. 'Let us rest now; but nothing is like resting in this place', is what my host father in Lorengelup, Lopangach, once told me when we finished watering his shoats. He then explained the number of activities we still had to do before resting: gathering *engol* (palm) leaves for their kitchen hut under construction; clearing maize of the stones it comes with in relief bags to cook for dinner; finding the 'brown camel' which had gone missing; refilling the small goats' water bowl; and collecting *ngitit* (acacia pods) for goats at home to feed on at night. All these activities involved a different movement and took us in multiple directions, tirelessly, for the rest of the day. Mobility is hidden in people's everyday practices, beyond its discursive representation. Mobility nonetheless emerges in people's everyday walks, micromacro movements enacted for a variety of reasons and in a variety of directions. As explained by a woman I met in Lorengelup:

> Mobility has changed. Nowadays we move to bring charcoal along the road, or to sell in the nearest centres to buy food. We pay visits to friends when we miss them and, if they can, they will give us something. We move looking for water which is more and more difficult to find as rivers dry up. We move for marriages of relatives and friends we are invited to. We go to Lodwar to sell mats. We move in search of lost animals.[88]

---

88.   HH, 17 Nov. 2016.

Practices of mobility

The most common way my hosts explained their movements is *ewote* or *awesit*. Both verbs imply movements that involve people and their livestock. Search for good quality pasture, salt and water. Avoid enemies and diseases. Reunite with friends. Choose migration routes according to the availability of grazing resources, especially water, along the way and the spread of social networks. Alternatively, often people would talk about movement in terms of *aperor*. This means sleeping away, visiting, being away from home just for a short time, a few days. It is an individual movement, with no livestock, generally performed to visit friends, to check on animals in kraals, to be updated on the destination of migrations, or on happenings in nearby towns and villages. Then there is *eloto*, the journey to ask a woman's hand for marriage. It implies bringing sugar, tea, tobacco, goats and sheep to the bride's family, and it also includes movements performed to seek contributions for the dowry. It is walked by the groom, his friends and relatives, as the first official step towards *akuuta* (wedding), after months of courting and studying the bride's family: their *emachar*, family lineage, wealth and reputation. *Akireb* means to scout. It is the movement performed to better understand a place or a situation. It can be used to indicate the search for rain, pasture and water when changing location of the homestead, or the search for the location of the enemy's kraals, their weapons and internal organisation, to prepare for or defend from raiding.

Even if mobility can be discursively represented as a struggle or as something people do not aspire to do, their daily actions tell otherwise. Not only are Turkana herders are engaged with various and intricate forms of mobility in their everyday, but great excitement also arises in preparation for migration with livestock (*ewote*) or *eloto* (marriage proposal), as witnessed by the happiness of the faces in the opening picture of this section. It was shot in the days days before our departure to reach the wedding site of the elder son of my hosting family in Urum. The homestead was filled with alcohol, dances, storytelling every night in a countdown to finally moving. Additionally, mobility is metaphorically reflected in an imagined lifeworld. Such imagining is crucial to understand people's lifeways because it not only influences people's way of thinking, but also their way of acting upon the surrounding world, creatively engaging with it. Sanders, in a chapter on magical migration in Tanzania, suggests using cultural lenses to understand how people provide meanings to their own world, and their moving through it. Likewise, I infer Turkana's understanding of their lived world as well as of their mobility by drawing on the links between the body and healing practices.

Dialoguing and imagining mobility

The anthropologist Vigdis Broch-Due, who worked extensively in Turkana in the 1970s and 1980s, showed the importance of the body in Turkana culture (1991, 2000). A site where practices are grounded (Bourdieu 1977), the body is shaped by healing practices which also contribute to cultural understandings of mobility. The Turkana health system is imbued with a set of meanings indicating potential threats and healing practices, both linked with ideas of mobility. Potential sources of harm derive from a cultural repertoire embedded in a particular geography. For example, disease may come from mountains or water points, both seen as dangerous sites. Other harms may instead be carried by *ekuwom* (wind) and its *ng'ipian* (evil spirits) and belong to the supernatural realm. Finally, other diseases belong to the social environment and correspond to social disharmony in the form of the *evil eye* or bewitching associated with broken customs or moral codes.[89] Despite modern medicine being now widespread in Turkana, not all diseases can be treated by such means. Many diseases both for humans and livestock, especially *edeke a akuj* (disease of God), *edeke a ngikapilak* (diseases of witches) and *edeke a Turkana* (diseases of the Turkana) require specific interventions often with the help of a local healer (*emuron* or *akapalan*). These diseases are often described through some general symptoms, such as bloating, high temperature or reduction of appetite, but the most striking descriptions focus on the subject's immobility; *akimookin*, to stay still, to stagnate, to be immobile.

You can recognise *emany* when the animal doesn't eat and stays still.[90]

…and then, *lomoo* came. Animals were dying standing.[91]

Akitoweken is something like malaria for the animals, the animal stops eating and has fever and just stays still, standing and no longer moving, until it dies.[92]

Not to be able to move implies death. Not to be able to move is a dangerous symptom that can affect both humans and livestock. Movement guarantees survival. It is through movement that, in fact, such diseases are often treated. Practices and rituals such as *akimad* (burning process), *amok* (opening of goat's stomach while it is alive), certain incisions around the kidneys (*ngingalur*), lungs (*ngiukoi*), spleen (*etid*), swollen legs (*sir*), every 'opening', adopting Salza's terminology, is done to

---

89. On the evil eye, see Chapter 5.
90. Young man, KI, Kaichakol, 24 Dec. 2016.
91. Young man, KI, Akudet, 14 Nov. 2016.
92. Elderly woman, FN, Urum, 2 Feb. 2017.

control sinister dangerous forces which have entered the body of the sick animal or person (2000: 4). By cutting, the way is opened for the bad spirit to exit, leave the body and return to where it came from; again, the idea of movement. What can really cure those diseases, freeing the affected subject from its status of immobility, is allowing the movement of forces and energies. Immobility is the diagnosis, and mobility is the cure.

Figure 26. Lung and throat scarification/ cheloids

I lean to the side of the boat to play with water. As we are reaching Longech the colours of water transform. Past mud and dirt, carried by seasonal rivers flowing after the rains and colouring the water with a dark brown/red tonality, the lake becomes blue as a dark night and then green like jade. Approaching Longech, a new microcosm opens to my eyes. A piece of desert surrounded by water. Restless and burning. Hot and humid. Smell of fish. People with red eyes and golden hair. Docked on the peninsula, sand burns under our feet. We run, with our luggage, to the chief's homestead, which is also his office, and a big shop, run by his wife Akai.

Moving

If you're going through hell, keep going.

ATTRIBUTED TO WINSTON CHURCHILL

Walking east. Urum, Loima. February 2016.

It is early morning. A gentle wind carries an illusion of freshness. Salty tea and mandazi, before we meet Simon. Simon is a young man who has studied to become a health worker, but, failing to find employment, returned home in Longech. We asked Simon to take us around to start knowing the peninsula during our first days. Our walk ends along the shores which look at the 'big lake' (as people referred to lake Turkana, compared to Ferguson Gulf, often called 'small lake'), in a place called 'Equity', the bank of fish,[93] because of the plentiful fish that can be found within easy reach. There are a few improvised bivouacs and temporary shelters. Families who live along the shore, with simple palm-leaf structures where fish is put to dry, tangles of nets and rafts. Ekwee is not keen to talk with them: they are drunkards, 'nomads'; they follow fish.

---

93.   Equity Bank is one of the most widespread in Kenya.

Practices of mobility

If the space is nomadic, people move to meet emergent opportunities: peaks of feed nutrients, new springs, favourable market prices, ripening fruit and crops, food or cash aid, old or new kin and fish. Families living in Equity move as water flows, sending a scout to assess fish availability when rumours have spread, and then they follow fish and wind; and travel very light with all their luggage on a small raft which is 'our donkey', as they explained. They will stay in Equity until there is fish. Then scouts will leave again to find a new destination. Pastoralists can do this because they are equipped with a mobile capital (livestock) and a flexible territory. Foremost, mobility is the vector to link multiple habitats, enabling the relationship between people, animals and the environment. And it is an imperative: 'all those with animals must move', respondents agreed in some semi structured interviews my assistant Peter Ewoton conducted over the 2024 summer. Presented with the current possibility to buy feed for animals ('if you had money, you could still rear those animals by buying grass and avoid moving'), people remained firm about the necessity to move: 'these animals have their own lifestyles that cannot be restrained with this idea of feeding them with certain types of food and having them settled in one place. These animals need to move for their health'.

Besides mobility, pastoralists achieve resilience by embedding variability in most of their processes of operation. Turkana herders raise a variety of livestock species: sheep, goats, zebu, dromedaries and donkeys. Herd diversity is one of the recognised strategies of *process variance* that allows making use of 'environmental heterogeneity rather than attempting to manipulate the environment to maximise stability and uniformity' (Behnke et al. 1993: 14–15). This is achieved through livestock breeding and livestock separation/concentration. Livestock populations in pastoral systems are bred to make use of permanently changing landscapes. The focus, as Scoones writes, is not on uniform individual production but on the ability as a whole to make use of the environment successfully, combining genetics with behaviour change (Scoones 2023). Thus, breeds are also permanently in the making, including not simply genetic diversity but multiple, complex and rapidly adaptable combinations of animal behaviour and performance (Krätli et al. 2022: 10). In addition, Turkana herders, like most herders in other parts of the world, separate herds and guide them to feed off multiple habitats, matching them with dietary requirements for different animals. Broadly, cattle (grazers) need grass and certain types of associated herbage; camels (browsers) prefer leaves and stems of bushes and trees; sheep (grazers) love low grass that grows at the roots of plants; and goats (browsers) eat the leaves on top of shrubs. Differences in grazing patterns of different animals creates both ecological separation, when different herds are taken to different areas, and ecological concentration, when different herds are taken to the same areas (depending on the coexistence of multiple habitats within an ecological zone and degree of competition or facilitation between species). Therefore, goats and sheep are generally kept together (and in English can be referred to as *shoats*) because they are not competitive in a shared habitat. Cows and camels could be kept together, but cows cannot be found in Turkana central plains where grass is rare, and they are often separated and grazed in the mountains.[94] Camels, being more drought-resistant, are taken to the central low plains to protect mountains from over-grazing and benefit from shrubs found between distant water points in Turkana's central areas.

While migrating, herders respond to the needs of the individual animals composing the flock. Sometimes they leave behind lactating animals (*namanang*), old animals and the sickly ones that can give people challenges during movement.

> There are small animals or lactating ones that do not move fast. These are left back in the village or moved early ahead of rest of the flock. They also create disturbance whenever they want to suckle their mothers and so it is necessary to have them ahead of the herd. They can also be killed by the intense sun and so they are driven in the early mornings or late evenings. Those that move as fast as people, such as calves, are driven with all other animals. If the place is bushy and difficult terrain, then they are all driven at once slowly as they graze. Donkeys are set aside for carrying very old or sick people, children and even other animals such as young goats.[95]

Livestock separation and concentration is also occurring today between villages and grazing areas, denoting livelihood adaptation to social changes.

> Some animals are kept behind while others migrate. Back in villages we keep those animals that can manage nearby bushes. Those that can eat *ngitit, ngakala-lio* [plant species]. Those that would not strain us looking for grass. They are mostly catered for by young children, women and the old who find it difficult to move around with the animals because of age and health issues. They keep a few shoats with them in the villages for emergencies such as medical care, or to provide for some food. There are also those who have settled in villages with a few animals so to access services that are provided by the government such as cash transfer and easy access to healthcare and food.[96]

---

94. Small cattle herds are also found along the shores of Lake Turkana.
95. SSI with a group of herders, Sept. 2024.
96. SSI with a group of herders, Sept. 2024.

Another reason for livestock separation or concentration is conflict.

> In places with enemies, we move together with all the animal species together
> to safeguard them against theft by the enemy. Others sometimes fear having
> all the animals moving together because they can be taken by the enemy. The
> young animals are mostly the ones that are kept moving around in search of
> pasture and we leave some behind such that, when these are stolen, at least the
> old ones will be at home.[97]

Pastoralists are like 'desert chefs', as eloquently described by Meuret and
Provenza in *The Art & Science of Shepherding* (2014). They recreate grazing itineraries at a variety of scales, so that livestock feed better than without a herder, while
taking advantage of environmental variability. Attention to animal nutrition is
critical. This resides in their situated knowledge and ability to identify sites with
prime fodder plants, in terms of palatability and proteins, and accessible water.
Animals themselves are of course also skilled in eating what is more nutritious for
them. They feed selectively following the herders' instructions but also their own
experience of the territory, external factors leading to distraction, stress or fatigue,
and their own preferences, likes and dislikes. Yet, the role of herders remains crucial
to help livestock balance the available forage across various ecological niches, to
stimulate herds' appetite by being attentive to livestock behaviour, having developed fine skills of interpreting animals' feedback to feeding. Also, herders support
their animals in places and times of reduced pasturage by providing them selected
food such as *ngitit* (acacia-pods) which grow in dry seasons. A good herder was
defined to me as someone who is hardworking, quick witted (*achoan*, the capacity
for inventive thought and quick understanding, keen intelligence) and observant
(*akiit*). A good herder wakes up in the morning and goes to the animal's shelter
and looks at the animals to see if they are all present. Because of the skill of *akiit*,
he or she can easily tell which one is missing. Thanks to such observation skills, a
good herder can tell that an animal is sick by looking at its skin. When the hair of
an animal seems to stand up on the skin, he or she knows the animal is sick. Also,
herders observe how the animal feeds. If they notice a change in feeding habit,
they will know that the animal is sick. In the morning, before the animals leave
for grazing, there are people who observe how they walk, they also observe the
animal waste to assess their health. This is not an innate skill: 'every herder must
be keen enough to note these changes'. It involves commitment, motivation and
experience. 'We know these things because we are with the animals most time'.

---

97.   SSI with a group of herders, Sept. 2024.

'A person who is *echoana* can know every colour of a goat among a herd of 400 animals'. Herders' knowledge of the herd is down to each single animal that makes up the flock, at a very personalised level (including their footprints, as demonstrated when we followed a specific lost camel in the midst of hundreds of other camel footprints). In exchange, the animals' trust in the herders is key. The resulting human-livestock relationship is very complex, based on care and reciprocal learning.

> My animals need me. If all animals were left on their own, they would not know where grass or water is and that is when they would die. They need me all the time also because wild animals can kill and eat them. I also need them; that is why I work hard to see them survive. When I get sick or when I am hungry or whenever I need to marry, I will need them too. That is why I need to provide animals with grass and water.[98]

Such intimate reciprocity could inform a future farming in which the relationship with livestock is one of caring coexistence. People reunited for the semi structured interviews that Peter conducted over the summer 2024, with their distinct Turkana irony, joked that: 'there is no way people would be if animals did not exist. People would turn green because of eating too many plants!' It is not only herders who learn from and guide livestock, but also livestock that become knowledgeable through experience. New entries in a herd are aligned with older and more experienced ones to learn to eat only 'the right things' and the ways back home from grazing. I was initially very surprised to see various stock walking back home in the evening, alone. Even more so when I was asked to take the hundred-camel herd from my host family in Lorengelup to the river Turkwel. I had no idea where the river Turkwel was, but the camels did, and took me there, more than the other way around. This recalls the Sahrawian camels described by Volpato, which know 'the direction and distance of each *bir, hasi, guelta,* and *hegla* from which they drank in their life, and even of the wells where their mothers drank while pregnant!' (2025: 97). The social hierarchy within the herd and the skilled, caring and intimate animal rearing approach pursued by pastoralists across the world help to lead livestock along grazing itineraries without pressure and stress, which in turn improves production through successful grazing. And as Volpato argues, the ability to find the route to pastures, rivers, wells becomes a 'multispecies skill whereby each knows a piece of the puzzle, whereby each mental map is continuously recomposed as a multispecies map to navigate the desert' (2025: 97).

---

98.   SSI with a group of herders, Sept. 2024.

Practices of mobility

Movements along grazing itineraries occur day-to-day, across relatively short distances to reach close-by water points and patches of available forage, and are also timed with changing seasons, mobilising a great understanding of the patterning of resources at a variety of scales as well as a sophisticated sense of timing. Seasonal movements see animals marching longer distances towards high quality/low volume forage in seasons of abundance and turning less selectively to high-volume forage to meet nutritional requirements in seasons of scarcity. This is a movement that I have found elicited in the metaphor of the heart and lungs by Alberto Salza (2014): lungs expand and compress in the same way pastoralists aggregate around wells and pasture during dry seasons and disperse when rain comes, and the rangelands breathe. Attention to nutrition is not only confined to the places of destination, but the route also has equal importance, with regard to animals' needs, as well as to minimise problems with other communities and/or to gain access or receive hospitality and support along the way from friends, cognates, affines, livestock associates or clan members.

> Even the route we follow is considered. The routes change every time depending on the destination. There are places that are known to have enemies, we avoid them. There are those that are known to provide water for animals along the journey and these are the preferred routes. You can even use a route you have never used because you are going to a destination you have never gone to; you just ask for people to guide you along the way. These days with phones we do not have difficulties knowing where to go because we make calls and inquire about status of this and that and we decide. There are routes that we know that have been used by our forefathers. We still use the same routes because we are familiar with them. If there is grass and water that is the best route, as people and animals need water.[99]

While reconfigured to incorporate elements of change such as the creation of towns and villages and the interaction with foreigners, including the same county government perceived as *other*, such movements continue happening with great intensity.

> The number of times we move is uncountable because we move a lot. We can stay in a place for one day, there are places we can stay for days and also months. We move a lot. Especially when the people herding the animals are young males, they can move a lot: they want their animals to touch every grass in Turkana.[100]

Some perceive this intensity to have increased:

---

99.   SSI with a group of herders, Sept. 2024.

100.   SSI with a group of herders, Sept. 2024.

Moving

We can nowadays move many times and longer distances because of the reduced instances of rain and intense sun that kills grass quicker. Shade for animals is also reducing because *etirae* (prosopis) does not provide much unless the huge *ewoi* (acacia) is found along the rivers.[101]

There is today little space as some places are now towns and with people rearing animals in town every pasture around town has been exhausted and we have to move more frequently and longer distances.[102]

When it is time to move, people gather and share roles to start the journey. It can be decided that the *big animals* such as cows and camels go first so that they can get to water points fast. Then goats and other animals are brought slowly as they graze because they are more resistant to thirst. Those that go ahead can build shelter for animals before the arrival of other people and the rest of the animals. In places with enemies, Turkana herders tend to move together so that they can safeguard livestock against raids, forming what is known as *arigan*. *Arigan* reunites people from an extended family encampment (*eree*). From the *eree*, people can form, one, two, three or more *arigan*, depending on number of people available, livestock needs, external conditions in terms of grazing resources and security. Each related family sends at least one member per *arigan*, but if, for some reason, they cannot contribute labour force, they will assure assistance and cooperation back in the encampment. *Arigan* is formed especially at times of rising tension with neighbouring tribes and when insecurity strikes.

For the journey, woman usually carry food and water using donkeys. Small children who could not walk long distances are put in the *asajait*, a sort of donkey saddle for transporting belongings, as well as children, young animals and people if they get sick along the way. They must travel light. The material culture of a nomad loading her donkey (or raft) is controlled by three main limiting factors: weight, volume, versatility (Figure 27). All pastoralists' efforts, therefore, tend to reduce weight and volume and to enhance the versatility of objects (Salza 2018). A nomad is the epitome of behavioural flexibility and reduction of objects to a minimum.

---

101. SSI with a group of herders, Sept. 2024.
102. SSI with a group of herders, Sept. 2024.

Figure 27. Shepherd's possessions

They head to a place they know has grass. Along the way, they can gather information from people they encounter, who they know and trust, or sometimes they send scouts to assess the status of a place. Or these days, as attested in the quote above, they can make great use of mobile phones as means to obtain information. When it gets dark the migrating group builds up temporary camps. It is the eldest who normally decides where to camp. Some people nowadays carry tents that they can easily source at the refugee camp, but the majority still use animal skins, branches and thorns found in the surroundings. In these cases, people split and surround their livestock to provide security. The young goats and cows are tied to the donkeys overnight so that they do not run away. And they can also use *ngakulorto* (pegs) to tie stubborn animals down so that they do not move around. On other occasions, they find 'households of the past' (*awi ngorot*) that still have kraals and huts that can be used instead of building new structures. At *awi ngorot* or in mobile camps they can stay for as long as the place is good for the animals. However, nobody stays in *awi ngorot* for long because they don't know why the owners left in the first place. Indeed, there could be bad spirits left by the previous inhabitants. When they are in *awi ngorot* people remain vigilant. They have to look around for possible enemies and wild animals that could eat livestock or injure people. If it is a dry place, they move on quite rapidly with the journey.

When a place offers good conditions, they build what in the Turkana scholarship is referred to as 'satellite camp' (*abor*). Cory Rodgers in his doctoral thesis *Rural, Remote, Raiya* writes:

> Young *raiya* men describe with pride the hardship they derive living on the remote satellite camp (*abor*), where they watch over their cattle and survive on blood meals procured by puncturing (*akigum*) the neck arteries of living animals. Life on the satellite camps is difficult, but raiya men are adjusted (*enaikinete*) to the hunger and thirst. (2018: 122).

While at mobile camps, in addition to livestock-related movements for grazing and water, as well as hunting and gathering, there are also movements to and from villages, no matter how distant these are: 'a few people are sent to buy whatever is needed, in this way people in villages are also updated on where the animals have reached and we can give them some meat or milk as the old nowadays remain at home'. Some satellite camps nowadays are equipped with solar panels to charge mobile phones and to provide some tepid light at night. When they hear that the place they come from has good pasture they go back. When returning, the route is once again chosen depending on the water and grass it can provide for the animals and people on the way. And the time to arrive home is also a function of how situations on the ground evolve.

Nothing appears pre-fixed but rather expresses distinct situationality rooted in the experience and knowledge of the leading herders. As Salza says: 'Mobile people do not enact in situ but on the way' (2014), turning themselves into a live map of the social territory they inhabit. Turkana pastoral society, like most pastoral societies in the world, is formed and moulded by communities of kin, following a rather broad and flexible understanding of kinship – based on a more fluid arrangement of relationships than blood or lineage (Ohta 2007) – or herd ownership (Gulliver 1955), that cross ecological boundaries. These networks form pathways. It is through these spread networks that mobility across the territory is made possible, food shared, a secure place to rest found, information obtained, access and rights to livelihood resources granted. As a corollary, it is by moving across the territory that social networks are kept alive and new friendships initiated. Diversity of assets is surely another strategy of *process variance*, and livestock are not the only assets. Large networks of kin and friends spanning rural and urban contexts in often distant locations contribute to bonding and bridging ties within and outside communities and support pastoralists in their mobility both on their routine routes and in exceptional migrations (Krätli et al. 2022).

We return to Equity to visit one of the families living there. In the evening, when the sun is no longer scorching, we help them mend their net, which is often broken by the engines of bigger motorboats, while seagulls sing for the fish which will come. Erot is a friendly young man who recently married and has no children yet. He moved with his wife to Equity not long ago. In their bivouac there is also uncle Kapus who has joined them because his home in interior Turkana has burnt down due to an accidental fire in the village and he is now looking to start his life again. There is also a younger kid, from some distant family member, to help with family chores: collecting firewood for cooking, fetching water and helping with processing fish to sell. Erot's father also joins us from Kalokol, where he went to collect his HSNP[103] share as an elderly vulnerable person. He now laughs, holding in his hands only a small portion of the total amount he just withdrew. The rest has gone to pay for debt food[104] borrowed from local shops and also to friends met along the way back home. Erot smiles at him, with the look of someone who knows how these things work, and continues mending his net.

Social networks are woven together by means of the generosity and hospitality that are an intimate part of the social fabric of nomadic Turkana culture, within the cultural framework of reciprocity, as in most pastoral societies of the world. Gabriele Volpato, for example, writes about the nomadic Sahrawi that 'the same existence of nomadic life in the desert is premised on social connectivity, it is no wonder that the use of hospitality principles, generosity, and sharing abounds among nomads and refugees in seasonal nomadism' (2025: 89–90). Generosity implies sharing. From richer to poorer households, from aid-targeted households to non-aid-targeted households, from households whose small crop-field was successful to those whose crop was eaten by birds, from households whose kids hunted a dik-dik at night to those who sleep a second night 'just like this' (with no food), sharing is a daily practice and customary norm among the Turkana. The act of sharing thought of in its most practical dimension involves the act of moving. Moving to give and donate. It is an altruistic movement, enacted to gift someone else, the benefits of which will outweigh its costs, as a gift today will probably yield a greater gift in return in the future; or even more simply performed out of affection among

---

103. Cash transfer programme; see Chapter 1.

104. Typical practice among my hosts: borrow food from local shops and re-pay them in cash (or in kind, with charcoal or livestock) when possible.

friends, family members and neighbours. Relations built through reciprocal gifts are perpetual, as long as the *debt* is never extinguished. The same existence of a *debt* between two parties keeps the relationship open; as a result, gifts are never equally matched with future exchanges: it is important to return a little bit more or a little bit less than what was once received, so that the relationship remains active. Inability to share signifies the failure to participate in the community life, while sharing (and a reputation for generosity) is symbol of wealth and power in the social hierarchy of the communities I visited.

Many times, I have seen my sugar or tobacco gifts for my host families being split in several small bags to be given to and shared with neighbours. Other times, I have seen relief food being collected at food distribution points, walked back home, and then shared with livestock. I have seen young boys coming at night into the homestead and quietly waiting for their mothers to give them some food to bring back to where they are attending to the livestock to be shared with their fellows – at times they brought a bottle of camel milk which they left behind for the people in the homestead, when by morning they had already vanished. I have seen mothers caringly packing some food and money in a wrapped cloth and starting to walk towards the horizon where they knew their children were resting with the animals; or they met around wells, grazing or crop fields, where young daughters were spending nights to watch against birds. Children are also shared. They are shared between mothers and grandmothers to help with family chores. They are shared with distant relatives to diversify one's family economy. They are shared to lighten the family budget. The moving of children among families complicates the idea of household. Families' ties are very loose and mobile, households change constellation of members frequently as members move in and out (agglutination), separating and re-uniting into spread units non-boundedly defined, on the base of contingent factors, individual or family needs/desires. By the end of my fieldwork, I had no certainty about the composition of my host families because connections among members continuously changed and people in the homestead kept on moving throughout.

Nights along lake shores are long, especially when the moon rises late. When the sun sets, many fishermen reach the shores to lay their net in the lake. Erot explains that people prefer fishing without the moon, in the hope of catching more fish. Moonlight would show fish their way out of the net and let them free. One night, after two rounds of setting and hauling the net, I walk, exhausted, back to our host family's bivouac to fetch the mkeka *(mat) we use for sleeping. And I notice them. Two men, I think. It is very dark, and I cannot see very well. They have been sitting close to our host's shelters the whole day, quiet and still. They are visitors from interior Turkana, waiting to be attended, which I have learnt can be a very long wait.*

Hospitality entails visiting and visiting entails asking for something, *akilip*. It is rare for people to visit someone and not ask for something: livestock, food or even cash. When rains come, and the season of plenty has started, when people are happy and engage in ceremonies, when there is food and time to rest, some members of the families engage in long distance movements to visit their acquaintances and ask for a contribution to their sons' dowry; to ask for money to refund debt-food borrowed during the season of scarcity; to collect previously incurred debts in the forms of livestock or other favours. Visiting is also important in the season of scarcity, as I was able to observe in my second round of fieldwork during the onset of the 2017 drought. During this period, almost all the families who hosted me had visitors at some point in my sojourn. Quietly sitting at the back of the homestead, waiting to be received. And hopefully to be given what is asked. At the same time, however, my hosts confided their increased difficulties in meeting the requests of their visitors because of the strains they were all facing. Because of the drought, stocks were depleting, livestock was migrating far and money was scarce.

Visiting as a form of socio-relational movement that permeates the Turkana social fabric also comes along with social-pressure, expectations and implications for future exchange flows. People visit also benefactors and politicians sitting in Lodwar. They ask for help with school enrolments, with participation in development/humanitarian programmes, or for local problems such as broken water pumps or failed food distributions. People visit their relatives, especially those who are now employed in town, in the hope of being given part of their salary. I once met Lopangach, my host father in Lorengelup, with his wife, Akamaise, and one of their daughters walking along the streets in Lodwar. They had gone to visit some relatives to ask for a share of their salaries. Unfortunately, they arrived in the middle of the month when income was not yet distributed and only received 2,000 shillings, not enough to pay back their debt with Ndyo, a local shopkeeper in Lore centre. They were disappointed because of their own *illiteracy* in not knowing 'these modern things'. But they were also disappointed with their relatives for the lack of help. Not being able to help visitors is perceived badly. As a result, generosity and hospitality in assisting kin are not mere symbols of solidarity, but also a form of covert social pressure that ensures those who have share and, in so doing, acquire power and respect. Strong social bonds are part of those cultural assets and customary institutions that are so relevant, both culturally, as shown by Casciarri and Ahmed in a special issue of the journal *Nomadic Peoples, Pastoralists under Pressure in Present-Day Sudan* (2009); and economically/productively, as discussed by Krätli and colleagues in a report about Sudanese pastoralists' wealth (2013).

Among cultural assets and social norms there also are institutions that regulate access to resources such as water and grazing. Certain places in proximity to villages like *lolines* or family encampments like *eree* can have delimited grazing areas kept in reserve for the dry season. These demarcations are invisible to the eyes of outsiders, including other groups of herders or practitioners, members of the government or foreigners. If someone defies and grazes his or her animals in such restricted places, then they will be fined, for example through a goat that is eaten by the elders of the area. The same level of protection of local ownership is arguably more difficult to enforce when such areas are targeted for irrigation schemes, or fall under new regimes imposed by oil companies, or are of interest for other development interventions by public or private actors.

Water is also heavily regulated by customary norms.

> Wells are sometimes protected by the owners. You need to ask for permission to use them. If people join hands to dig a well, then they can share with their in-laws or even people of their *emachar* (clan members) and friends. There are travellers who may be in need and they can be allowed to water their animals only after the owners have watered theirs. In some cases, they are asked to give a goat for them to access the well. If a traveller on his journey stops and waters his animals without permission and is caught then sometimes people fight, and the travellers can pay a fine with a goat, sometimes he may be forgiven after stating his case. If a traveller comes and helps the owners to water animals as he waits for his turn then he does not even need permission to use the well because he has earned his right to use it that one time. There are people who are rude

and use your well even before you water your animals and do not even bother explaining, these ones are beaten and even taken to the elders.[105]

In places with shallow water that is more easily accessible, everyone can have his/her own well with personal rules of access, but it is always better to ask permission before using water from wells in Turkana, especially if you plan to use it to water livestock! In other cases, the water table is very low, difficult and dangerous to reach. In this case, people join hands to dig and as a result co-own the well. This is especially true when the construction of the well needs what is considered serious labour, when there are stones and a human-ladder of six people is needed to reach water. This is when people join forces. Such an apparently strenuous job can turn in a festivity. Someone can decide to sacrifice a goat so that people sing and enjoy the work: 'all you need is to kill an animal, cook some *unga* (flour), or provide local brew. People will make it more of a celebration than actual work'. The same level of participation, ownership and attention to sustainable use is arguably difficult to find in relation to drilled water pumps that usually work via outside committees with little local recognition and use cash as their regulating mechanism.

Considering patterned livelihood resources, including feed and water for livestock and spread social resources with their underlying cultural norms, moving requires substantial planning. It implies a choice about time, direction, distance and destination. It is the result of a process of assessments, information sharing (and hiding) and exploration and scouting. It is also the product of structural differences (herd composition and labour availability, for example) and personal perceptions, attitudes to risk and general preferences. As a result, moving is a choice characterised by great variability. In Lorengelup, for example, I travelled with two old brothers and their family shoats in Lokitela when all other families had already gone to the 'blue mountains at the horizon', showing a different strategy towards migration. As part of the same family, I had also grazed their camels together with a larger herd of camels merged from several families. And I had listened to stories of their cattle along the lake shores, herded by family friends who also engage in fishing. There is not a single best choice, but a variety of possibilities. Movement is not the simple means by which drylands' heterogeneity is put to use, but also, as termed by Krätli and Schareika in an article on the intelligent animal production of dryland pastoralists, an 'experimental framework' for a complex relationship between humans, livestock and land (2010). This perspective fundamentally

---

105. SSI with a group of herders, Sept. 2024.

challenges views of pastoral mobility as a coping strategy; rather it is essential to seizing fields of opportunity.

Mobile livelihoods

Imagine that mobility is border crossing, as though borders came first, and mobility, second. The truth is more the other way around.

DAVID LUDDEN, 2003

The livelihood net

We are now starting to regain a view of the movement of Turkana herders as a ubiquitous part of their livelihood. But more than that, their moving crafts a *livelihood system*, and renders it complex, articulated, dynamic, mouldable and changeable. Since their introduction in the early 1990s, livelihood approaches have become mainstream in both academic and applied fields, especially in rural areas of the global south.[106] Resilience programmes have fully endorsed a livelihood language, as it is nowadays widely accepted that, during crises (domain of resilience programming), livelihood-based strategies are important for both recovery and development. The resilience scholarship contributes to enriching the understanding of livelihoods beyond reductionist goals of economic or food-production nature, to embrace larger social, cultural or political issues that are equally important in the lives of people in crises. Vice versa, the use of livelihood approaches in crisis contexts is beneficial for many reasons. Above all, I believe, the greatest contribution lies in the incentive to open our eyes to the complexity of the world and try to understand needs and aspirations from local perspectives, recognising the variety of resources, capabilities and entitlements. In Ian Scoones' words: the appeal of livelihood approaches is simple, 'Look at the real world, and try understand things from local perspectives' (2009: 1). Livelihoods approaches fostered interdisciplinary collaborations, beyond sectoral boundaries. They allowed a different development practice, countering monovalent approaches that had dominated. They permitted a deeper and more critical reflection for looking at complex development questions, aggregating individual analyses into livelihood strategies and pathways of change. Despite these strengths, many of the claims of the livelihood revolution in development practice remained more ambition than reality. Even if it wants to

---

106. Livelihoods thinking has a long history that precedes the influential paper by Robert Chamber and Gordon Conway in 1992, *Sustainable Rural Livelihoods: Practical Concepts for the 21st Century*. However, the 1991 IDS working paper is often referred to as the starting point for what came to be known later in the 1990s as the *sustainable livelihoods approach* (SLA). The transformation of sustainable livelihoods from an approach (SLA) to a framework (SLF) occurred though the 1998 publication by Ian Scoones: *Sustainable Rural Livelihood. A Framework for Analysis*. The move from diagrammatic checklist to the SLA and SLF diagrams happened also in 1998, with the establishment of the Department for International Development (DFID) in the UK and the creation of an advisory committee, led by Diana Carney of the Overseas Development Institute in London, together with researcher and NGO representatives. From that time onward, with money and politics behind it, the concept could travel, gaining incremental momentum and, as admitted by Ian Scoones, a large dose of misapplication and misunderstanding along the way. Critiques piled up during all this time, perhaps the most recurrent is not being sufficiently political. But the framework remains alive, and expansions, reformulations, adjustments keep being proposed to date. For example, Ian Scoones set up an extended livelihood framework in his 2015 *Sustainable Livelihood and Rural Development* book (made open access in 2021). Natarajan and colleagues proposed a reformulation of the framework, foregrounding a structural, spatially disaggregated, dynamic and ecologically coherent approach to framing rural livelihoods (2022). Hanrahan explores the potential contribution of a feminist ethics of care to livelihoods approaches (2015).

be a tribute to diversity, for example, too often it slides into the establishment of homogenous human groupings, defined by their belonging to a livelihood group, from which people are, at best, granted the possibility to *diversify* income streams; and reiterates a teleological approach to lifeways, aimed at pursuing material and simplistic objectives.

The *borders* of the opening quote of this section become a metaphor for the perimeters drawn in livelihood-zone maps; imaginary lines defined by the adoption of rigid labels and categories to capture people's identities and lifeways. The metaphor of borders allows us to use mobility analytically. Pastoral moving enables everyday practices that transcend categorisations imposed by outsiders. It allows people to move beyond categories. And it crafts livelihoods. It forms a livelihood system that incorporates a broad range of non-livestock production activities through a variety of socio-economic relations enabled by the very act of moving. So, we can say that moving allows a view of livelihoods as relational.

Mobilities theorists like John Urry, Mimi Sheller, Tim Cresswell and Alice Elliot have long critiqued the sociological imaginary of the world as an array of separate societies and bounded entities. Pastoral scholars have also long argued that pastoral livelihoods are better seen as a continuum along which individuals and groups move through time, back and forth from herding to cultivating to gathering, and increasingly also into national economic structures through trade and employment, with an almost indefinite range of variations. There is also great evidence that it is not the individual but the household, the co-wives, the many children, the brothers, the cousins, the cognates, the affines, that make up a complex relational livelihood system. Taking these arguments forward, to understand daily economic life at the heart of a livelihood system, I suggest following everyday moving and letting the meshwork of livelihoods, activities, identities relationally emerge in the form of a livelihood-net that encompasses a large-scale economy. In employing the metaphor of a net, I consider that nets are created by threads coming from multiple directions and wrapped together around connection points (knots), taking the shape of a network; they contain all geometrical elements (points like *lolines*[107] and other sites of connection: wells, ceremonial trees, marketplaces and so forth; lines that can represent people's lifeways and their moving across the territory; and surfaces, namely the territory); and form a container of variable geometry. Nets are also resistant, permeable and deformable into the shape of the prey; and transportable. Their ultimate scope is to catch (something, an opportunity, a possibility).

---

107. See Chapter 3.

Practices of mobility

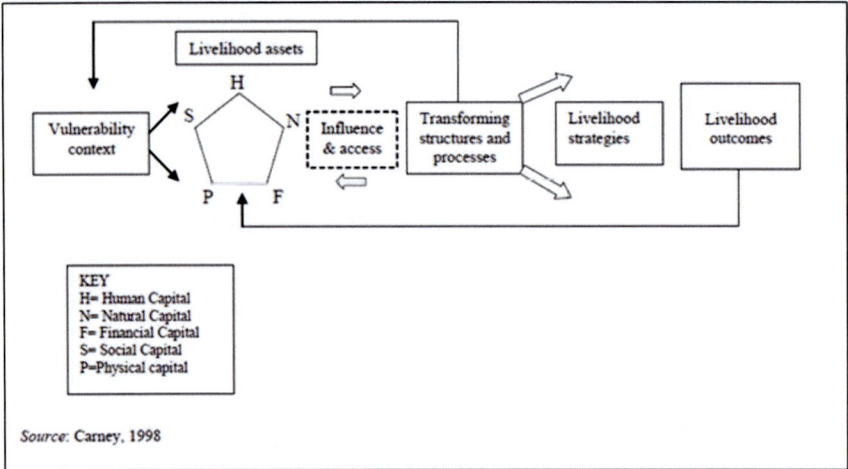

Source: Carney, 1998

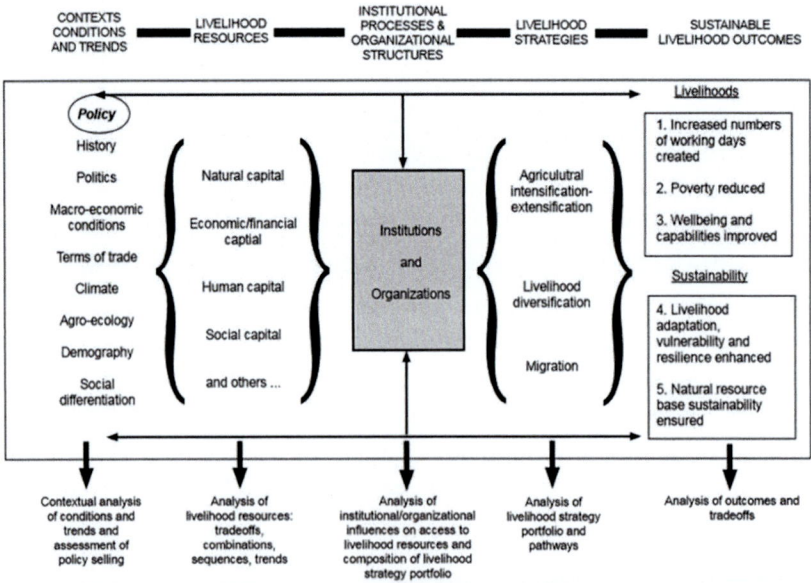

Source: Scoones 1998.

Figure 28. Sustainable Livelihood Approach and Sustainable Livelihood Framework

---

The two men come from Lokorokor, a small village down the peninsula. It is early morning, and they are returning home after having had a small share of HSNP cash from our host, and also a bag of maize. I am curious to see how life is over there, where palms and bushes grow in large number, and ask if we can walk with them. We leave behind the village business of Longech and venture down, walking along the shores. The water is a flat mirror of a pallid sky. Groups of women and young children are shrouded by fish. Cutting, removing entrails, washing in the lake, and carrying away. Floating entrails and plastic bags play with water. Seagulls and black ibis guard all fishing operations. A woman walks resolutely in the opposite direction. A bucket over her head. Her face is entirely covered by small drops of sweat. She comes from Wadite, one of the last villages along the peninsula before it turns into mainland. The sweat on her face reflects sunlight. The bucket is filled with ngichok *(palm fruit seeds), which she wants to sell to the 'rich Turkana in Longech'.*

The woman from Wadite left home and began a movement intended (also) for selling goods she possesses. The 'rich Turkana', in this case, are Luo women who have migrated from Lake Victoria and run the monopoly of smoked fish in Longech. Palm fruit seeds serve to start a fire which, once covered with a metal grill and old *mkeka* (mat), releases dense smoke to cook the fish. The woman from Wadite had planned to ask hospitality from her friends in Longech and find, in this way, some food and company.

At the heart of Turkana herders' economic life resides the art of trading, in the barter or monetary economy, as in all pastoral societies of the world. By trading or exchanging, Turkana herders fare through and forge relationships across their territory at large.

In the past, 'the people without animals' used to collect *engol* (palm fruit) and crush it into flour. They used to exchange it for blood with 'the people with animals'. At that time, when 'the people with animals' knew it was raining, they were asking 'the people with *shambas*' (gardens) for some of their harvest in exchange for animals, blood or milk.

This is how Akalale, one of our hosts during the journey around Urum, remembers her past in the mountainous border with Uganda: a common practice of exchanging

Figure 29. Drying fish

livestock for agricultural products, to supplement diet and stock up for the season of scarcity. With the monetisation of local economies, these exchanges started to take place between *people with animals* and *people with shops*. Pastoralism scholarship has progressively recognised these forms of economic exchange, moving away from structuralist ideas of nomadic pastoralists as autonomous self-sufficient peoples with little or no interaction with other livelihood groups, to emphasise their increasing integration into the market economy. All families I stayed with in Lore, Urum and Longech were involved, in a way or another, in market activities that connect and relate different spaces and livelihoods, starting to form the livelihood-net. Markets in Turkana can take various shapes. For example, they take the shape of local shops now found everywhere in rural Turkana: from bigger towns to smaller centres, to dispersed homesteads deep in rural areas. People, at times, turn their huts into temporary local shops, by investing aid-money, by selling big livestock or by receiving remittances from their town relatives.

Mobile livelihoods

Figure 30. The shop

In these shops there is everything: sugar, tea, tobacco and *magadi*,[108] maize, rice, beans, flour, milk powder, biscuits, salt, *shuka*,[109] *bananas*[110] and beers, razors, soaps, cooking oil, jerrycans, matches, *royco*,[111] chewing gums beads for necklaces, and paste colours which women use during ceremonies. There can be all of this, or just some extra oil the owner of the shop could afford to buy and now sells back to their neighbours. In these shops, people go to buy what they need; or to sell small stocks, which shopkeepers will then sell at bigger markets; or people go to barter charcoal, firewood or aloe-vera oil for what they want from the shop.

Markets also take the shape of a road. Driving through Turkana, as in most parts of rural Africa, even throughout apparently desolated bushlands, it is easy to notice charcoal sacks leaning on each other or piles of rocks and firewood, unattended and waiting to be sold. The road has become a market; and when roads are unused or less trafficked, goods mount up. In addition, in each administrative location I visited there are bigger centres which hold market days. People leave their home and walk to these markets, carrying goods to sell (*mkeka*, baskets, livestock,

108. Pieces of dried salt to chew together with tobacco.
109. Herders' clothes.
110. Imported sachets of alcohol from Uganda.
111. Stock cube for flavouring food.

herbal medicines, clothes, crops and livestock) with the hope of making some money to pay for a lift back home on local motorbikes or buy necessities for their families. People also engage in longer walks to towns, like Moroto or Kakukma for the families in Urum, or Lodwar for the people in Lore and Longech. Here, they wish to sell their bigger livestock (cattle/camels) or roam around to make some money (or find some food) to take back home. Here, people also go to replenish their shops, when stocks have run out.

A final form of markets is mobile markets in the shape of itinerant traders. 'These days the buyers are all over the place'. It is common to see traders coming from down-country selling tobacco or tea leaves, even in the remotest of places. One can also see people walking along dry creeks selling alcohol sachets smuggled from Uganda to herders watering their livestock. Others walk with buckets of lumpy liquids, or colourful powders or wooden sticks for medical purposes. Along lake shores, middle-men drive to collect stakes of fish to sell to the Congolese in Kalokol. Or people go to collect *fagy* fish, rotten, wasted, leftovers from bigger fish, to trade with Luo people who grind it and use it as feed for chickens. Along lake shores, anonymous foreigners from Japan come to trade dry stomachs of Nile perch used as biodegradable thread for surgical purposes. Chinese traders also come to interior Turkana regions to buy donkeys' hides and skins. And there are also those who go around looking for livestock to buy. Indeed, the increased number of *hoteli* and restaurants in the growing towns results in increased demand for meat and in turn in an increased number of slaughter houses. This has also contributed to the creation of new professions responding to such emergent demand for livestock products: 'Today to sell animals we do not walk long distances to towns like before because amongst us there are those that are known to be doing this business on and off. Whenever there is an animal to be bought, they can buy from you and drive them to the market themselves'.[112] In other words, commodification of livestock is occurring.

We do sell our animals all the time. Whenever we have a sick person or even when these animals are sick, and we need to buy medicine we sell one or two to cater for these needs. We sell animals that we know will give us good money, but we are careful not to sell the ones that are good.[113]

Selling occurs mostly in the dry season, when it is painful to see 'animals turning thin' and people's needs also may rise, but this is also the time when prices

---

112. SSI with a group of herders, Sept. 2024.
113. SSI with a group of herders, Sept. 2024.

drop. For example, a male goat, of grade 1, which is three or four years old and relatively fat can be sold at 10,000 or 9,000 Kenyan shillings (approximately seventy or sixty euros) but, during the dry season, the price can reach as low 7,000 shillings (approximately fifty euros). A male goat of grade 2, which is two years old and smaller in size, can be sold between 6,500 to 7,000 shillings (approximately 45–50 euros), and the price can reduce to 4,000 shillings in the dry season when most livestock reach the market (approximately thirty euros). A male goat of 1.5 years is normally sold around 4,500 shillings, but during the dry season can reach 2,800 shillings (approximately twenty euros). Of course, prices are also determined by the size and health of the animal that is to be sold: 'that is why you must make sure that they are always eating good grass and drink water so that they remain not only big but also the skin should show that it is healthy, and that one can get good meat from it'.

Here there re-emerges a predisposition for care and hard work that the market economy is seemingly yet to eradicate, though it is spreading its long invisible hands over the remotest possible places. For example, in Urum I spent my last weeks in the main village, while waiting to find a way to go back to Lodwar.[114] During this time, I lived with an elder called Lorot. Lorot arrived in Urum after years of working in the gold mining business. He grew up as a herder boy around a place called Gold. During his childhood, he admired gold miners whom he saw, as he said, 'growing big', starting to change their clothes, progressively adopting modern dress. Then they started owning motorbikes. Finally, they started running parallel businesses, selling various items, and making money; until they were able to run their own shops. Out of admiration, Lorot left his herd and followed their path. When he arrived in Urum, a few years before my fieldwork, he was opening his second shop. The first one is in Kakuma, with his second wife. Yet, in Kakuma there is a lot of competition, with many new businesses opening recently. Hence, he decided to expand his activities to a place where there was less business rivalry. His third wife runs the business in Urum with their three children. Lorot's first wife stays with livestock, not far from Urum. He visits her frequently, with his motorbike, checking his animals and bringing supplies. He also brings livestock bought from neighbours and other villagers, to augment his herd. When his livestock is fat enough, he rents a truck and transports it to Kakuma and sells it to local *hoteli* (restaurants). Finally, he is saving money to buy another building in Kakuma to rent out, in order to have a pension when he is older because 'life should continue

---

114. See Chapter 3.

being good also at that age'. Lorot's story is thus a form of spontaneous livestock commodification where the herd is devolved to the family economy and commodified for material ends other than the pastoral economy. Even so, the value of animals is far from being overshadowed by merely economic meaning:

> Even if it is very dry, we try our best and let the drought take its share as we wait for the rain. After all, the drought is not a new phenomenon as we have had it before, and we have always come out of it even with a handful of goats and were still able to grow a herd out of the few that survive. It is you people [points at me] who know money that can think of having animals in any form other than animals themselves. Nobody herds money in the bank like we herd our animals here.

This was said with laughter and pride. Laughter and pride in having animals instead of money in the bank. Animals are valued much more because they keep one busy, unlike money, which, as a metaphor for the people who value money more than livestock, just sleeps there, in the bank account. Selling an animal is the result of complex decision making around necessity, opportunity, affection and customary norms. Turkana families ensure they keep records of every animal lineage in the flock, especially those derived from dowries or gifted by friends. These animals are considered special, and people tend to keep them in memory of important relationships.

> If you look at those goats [points me at his goats grazing in the compound where Peter is running the interview]. I brought the red goat from home. That goat gave birth to two goats, the yellow one and the brown one. Now, that red goat is pregnant, and both her daughters are pregnant, that means that very soon I will be having six goats from one red goat. That is why I love that red goat.[115]

Herders have the tendency not to eat or sell animals that have borne twins so that they can continue growing their herd, with a sense of love. Those that have problems like getting sick are more often sold or eaten compared to those that produce offspring. When one gets into a situation that requires selling animals then it is those that are not good at production that are sold. However, and perhaps inevitably, the market is continuing its side job of altering values and creating needs.

> In the long-gone days, we used to sell very few animals because there was plenty of food! There was milk and there was plenty of grass for animals. These days, people are eating these town foods and that needs money. We no longer eat animals and animal products alone like before. We cannot go a day without

---

115. SSI with a group of herders, Sept. 2024.

food these days. In the morning children are already crying. People prefer to sell a goat instead of slaughtering because there are other needs that need money.[116]

Figure 31. The killing of a camel at a wedding ceremony. Urum, Loima, February 2016

We stop in a village called Lokwar, a fishery for the night, sleeping along the shores. We wake up when the sun rises, surrounded by many women who have reached the shores for their morning activities. They take some fish from one of the piles along the shore and put them in small, mended nets. Their scales sting. They walk into the dirty and muddy water and dunk the small net, wash it quickly and bring it back to the shore. I am introduced to Antony who came to buy the fish cleaned by the women. We help him carry it home. A red bucket full of fish over my head. Antony tells us that the job I am doing would normally be paid 50 shillings per bucket. This is the version of the migrant me who steals work from locals; I happen to think. We take the bucket to his homestead. As we enter, a strong smell of dry fish assails us. A catch of hundreds of small fish is drying over an improvised mat of grass and palm leaves. On one side, a pile of fresh fish, where we throw those from the red bucket.

116. SSI with a group of herders, Sept. 2024.

Practices of mobility

Turkana herders' everyday economic life is imbued with practices that form a moral economy nested in networks of friends and neighbours (see also Mohamed 2023). During my fieldwork along the lake shores, I was long frustrated by a common statement: 'Here, if you do not work, people will not help you!' Searching for collective forms of resilience, this was not an ideal answer. But there was a different story hidden. Along the shores of the lake, small jobs have been created for the needs of richer people (like boat owners or shop keepers) in support of poorer people, in line with the economy size. Hence, many small jobs, called *commissioned work*, have developed, including transporting fish to people's homesteads, cutting and cleaning fish, bringing firewood or carrying water jerrycans from wells, or making fences for people's homesteads, in exchange for a small payment or some food. These are activities that involve a movement enacted for an economic end, but also hold meanings of local support and contribute to building community cohesiveness through complex patterns of assistance. This is the story, for example, of a woman we met in Wadite along the peninsula. Following a lived trauma, she does not remember where she comes from and why she came here. Neighbours saw her arriving to the shores alone, in a very bad condition, many years ago. 'She had nothing with her and her clothes were torn', some of the villagers told me. She spent a long time roaming and wandering along the shores. Slowly, people started calling on her for small jobs. Collect water. Transport fish. Weave a mat. Bring *ngichok*. A little money was given, together with many new relationships and friends. Such an economic fabric is similarly found in the desert plains around Lore and in mountain areas in Urum, where commissioned work is often referred to as 'pieces of work': build a hut, fetch water or firewood, gather wild fruit. The woman in Wadite can be considered an *ekedalan*: someone who does not have anything. The term is used to refer to people without family like orphans and so considered without resources. *Ekedalan* make a living working for other herding families and are paid with animals or in-kind. Some end up becoming part of the family, like a son or a daughter, marrying in the family or building close friendship. While I could observe this practice as constitutive of the communities I visited, my hosts also shared a sense that nowadays there are no more *ekedalan* because there is employment in town that pays them in cash with which they can buy animals if they want: '*ekedalan* are no more because of the ease of finding employment in town'.

Continuing walking along the shores, the next village we enter is Jaap City. We are attracted by a noisy group of young herders, crowded on the side of a small hoteli. Epuu is particularly eloquent. He is in Jaap to work. His home, the place he considers home, is in the rural areas with animals. Here he comes to work when he needs to supplement the herding economy, when he hears there is good fish in the lake. He learnt how to fish from local fisherfolks and then became very good at it. He now comes every year for a few months. Initially, he used to stay with friends who could host him. Now, one of his wives lives permanently in Jaap City. They have three children. One of them lives in Kalokol with some relatives while attending primary school. One stays with the mother, helping her with house errands. They will decide whether to send the last-born to school or to their home with the livestock. Epuu says it will depend on the kid's own skills, on the needs of the animals and on God's will.

Through everyday movements, Turkana herders' economic life appears imbued with relations that transcend a narrow focus on livestock rearing. Turkana herders farm, fish, hunt, go gathering, burn charcoal, weave mats, take waged employment. Epuu came to the lake in search of resources he heard were available along the shores. He came to the lake thanks to his initial connections who could host him, and he became a successful fisherman thanks to the new friends he made along the shores. Finally, Epuu came to the lake to respond to an economic need to support his families; at times his livestock was not enough. The settlement of Turkana people along the shores of the lake, in some cases, does not transform them into fishermen but rather into part-time fishermen who continue investing in the livestock sector as they can. In some other cases, conversely, 'those who left never came back because they are used to town life now'. Permanent or temporary economic shifts are very common in Turkana. Such movement occurs within Turkana or beyond Turkana to *down country* or outside Kenya. One of the young men driving passenger boats from Natirae to Longech once told me he was new to the lake, having been sent by his family to look for means to support them. He is now waiting for some friends to call him from Doha where they have managed to find good occupations. He wants to follow them and see what the world can offer him 'beyond fish and salt'. These forms of movement, therefore, not only reveal the economic flexibility of livelihood groups, but also larger aspirations shared by peers. This is possible also thanks to new technologies such as motorised vehicles, mobile phones and GPS, which have opened-up new mobilities and techniques of practising pastoralism and combining pastoralism with other types of work, as Ariel Ahearn describes the changing work relationship in rural Mongolia, a country renowned for its pastoral tradition (2016) and Dawn Chatty recounts of Bedouin in a modern world, who made trucks into their new camels for transportation (2013).

All these micro and macro movements allow Turkana herders to navigate emergent opportunities and constraints. The mobility of their livelihood enables the creation of livelihood-nets made of multiple relations across and within over imposed categories, and in turn signifies the ingenuity, flexibility, hard-work, saving attitudes and courage to follow broader aspirations that I was confronted with during my journey through Turkana. If this is not resilience, then what is?

Resilience and moving

Categorisation is a basic mechanism within social sciences and policy circles. My supervisor at the time, Oliver Bakewell, wrote a paper in which he warns us of the risks of conflating what he termed 'academic categories', developed by scientists while doing their research as important mechanisms of ordering reality, especially when this is dominated by complex dynamics and blurred boundaries, with 'policy categories' (2008b). The latter, in fact, tend to be superimposed and remain fairly invariant over time and space. Policy categories end up producing bureaucratic labels which *stick* to people. In other words, they tend to give dichotomic interpretations of people's lives: pastoralism, agro-pastoralism, farming, fishing, and also categories like mobile and sedentary. These clear-cut categories never really existed. Even more so today, with technologies and aspirations for modelling lifeways that swing over time between categories conceived as fixed. Categories end in this way masking reality rather than revealing it. Worse than that, in a context where successful production expects flexibility and dynamic adaptation, the abstract rigidity embedded in this classification makes it inadequate and potentially misleading for informing policymaking and the economic development of rangelands and pastoralism.

Migrating away, the act of walking, is seen in such thinking as a local response or coping strategy for problems that need to be solved to preserve the natural state of being, conceived in terms of stability. This logic is arguably reversed in drylands where, for example, positive environmental change (land flourishing, increased precipitation, peaking nutritive values) generates mobility. Pastoral mobility acts as a complex vector of socio-spatial and socio-economic connectivity which serves to navigate variability. As a result, livelihoods are better conceived as a web of relationships, which disrupts livelihood borders by seeing different livelihoods not as absolute states but as co-constituting each other and woven together into a broader livelihood-net and multi-resource economy. Relational theorists reject the notion that there are discrete and pre-given units that can be used for analysis. The world is not constituted of static things, but of dynamic, unfolding relations. Livelihoods as the quotidian unfolding of peoples' lives therefore must be relational to. And their relationality is enabled by our (yes, all our) moving in the world. During fieldwork I encountered fishermen with cows and pastoralists with shops; everybody had a small farm and did farming any time they could as long as there was some rain; I met pastoralists with nets and boats; local seers and diviners in new catholic churches; teachers who also herded and raided; politicians who participated in initiation ceremonies; herders smuggling Ugandan beers into Kenya; fishermen crafting goat skin skirts woven with palm seeds and fish bones. There is no herder, no household, no family history, no needs, goals and aspirations which are the same. The heterogeneity of space is reflected in the heterogeneity of decisions, lifeways and movements performed by herders in their lived environments. I decided to represent such messiness of lives by drawing from my journey along the shores of Lake Turkana. This is a deliberate decision because it is only from the lake shores that I could see the large scale of geographical and socio-economic connections shaping livelihoods in Turkana. As such, this may be seen as at odds with the most typical image of herders in desert plains or mountainous areas with large stock. Again, this is a deliberate choice, as it allows me to contest the 'sediment' of ideas of 'pure pastoralism' (Kaufmann 2009), and force readers to imagine pastoralists with fishing nets. Following Ingold, in his book *Being Alive*, the livelihood-net is not a 'network of interconnected points' but a 'meshwork' of interwoven lines, in which life is along (Ingold 2011: 151). Each node in the net is a tangle of lines, and each thread is multidirectional and multidimensional, following complex forms of mobilities employed in several simultaneous domains. The net is deformable, taking the shape of the *prey*; and is movable, transportable. By means of various forms of movement, pastoralism becomes better defined as a complex, heterogenous, fluid and interacting system which crosses multiple spaces. The intertwined lines of people's movements determine the degree of economic integration, social circulation and socio-ecological connectivity as well as the degree of incorporation of complex forms of variability. Their mobility can be, in other words, an important manifestation of their resilience, seizing opportunities and relationships.

I do not aim to convey a picture of necessarily harmonious societies. In line with Massey, I do not aim to generalise mobility as a universal benefit (2005). I met people who struggle leaving a certain place because they cannot leave their old parents alone. I met people sorrowful because someone had left and never been in touch again. I met parents who invested all their camels for their son's education and disappointingly are still waiting to be refunded. And I met youths in town ashamed not to be able to support their parents back in the villages and thus avoiding going back home to face them. I also met youths in town who felt embarrassed at the lifestyle of their parents and hence also avoid going back to their villages. I had local assistants who left me in the middle of a mission because they could no longer accept certain living conditions. I met people who struggle with learning 'these modern things': weaving, charcoal burning, driving motor-bikes, managing shops. I met people who cannot move far away because of their disabilities. I met people who have been cursed by their jealous brothers and lost all their livestock; they stopped migrating with the animals and remained with nothing else to do. I met people who failed in their business because of increased competition and now beg for a living. I met people who struggle with receiving relatives and visitors and acting as good hosts in support of kin mobility. Mobility is a socially differentiated phenomenon, differently experienced and mediated by a wide range of factors. Massey writes: 'Some are more in charge of it than others, some initiate flows and movement, some are more on the receiving end of it than others, some are effectively imprisoned by it' (1993: 61). Mobility can create ruptures in society, jealousies, rivalry and greed. It is nested into power relations and personal capabilities and entitlements. There is competition over resources, over few opportunities in the labour market, over entrepreneurship activities. In Urum, for example, the marketisation of aloe-vera by Somali traders pushed most shop keepers also to engage in the business. Somali traders were eventually overcome by local merchants and retailers whose success pushed the Somali to leave and pursue their business elsewhere. Along the lake shores, middlemen run fast with their pick-ups to buy most fish from local fishermen and have larger power in negotiations with Congolese dealers. Newcomers to Longech may find hard times contending with Luo women if they wish to start a business with smoked fish. In Lore there are fights for water rights around shared water pumps among several villages, for those who get shares from payments to access water. Thus, with this chapter I do not argue for an uncritical privileging of pastoral mobility. Rather, I argue that mobility, if unconstrained, can be an important part of resilience in everyday life.

Mobility enables pastoralists to arrive on the forage at the time when nutrients peak. Mobility also allows them to manipulate exposure to drought and other stressors, climate-related and not – for example, social and political insecurity – as well as taking advantage of distant market opportunities. The importance of pastoral mobility for both productivity and resilience, including in the face of climate change, is widely recognised, albeit with little follow up in practice (Krätli et al. 2022). Moving across the territory at large enables successful livestock production while caring for the environment and the animals, and it creates and maintains substantial economic and social ties. This complicates the idea of livelihoods as bounded categories, as well as the idea of identity as something neatly identifiable, anchored to tradition. Turkana herders' navigation skills go beyond the *situational* (the contextual everyday), to also encompass a navigation of the *social imaginary* and the self, as opposed to the *other*, as an expression of coexisting multiple cultural environments. As is perhaps already emerging from this chapter, the next one will show the construction of a sense of solidarity among Turkana herders in opposition to *town people*, a divide which is felt very strongly but is nonetheless very fluid and bridged by means of imitation, appropriation and adaptation. Resilience rests in both: in a strong local identity used as social construct of belonging, and in its responsiveness to changes and distinctive fluidity and malleability – or, in other words, in the mobility of identities.

We are now reaching Namukuse, the very last village of this stretch of desert surrounded by water. Hot air trembles over soft dunes. Lake water slithers, low. Apart from gulls singing their chant of hunger, silence. Unexpectedly, between one palm tree and another, big houses painted with bright colours appear. Shops. Churches. Private houses and villas. There is an invisible wealth, hidden among palm trees. Rafts on the small lake slalom among growing etirae (Prosopis) *in shrinking waters. On the 'big lake', bigger boats in search of bigger fish. We swim at sunset watching Central Island and, for a few minutes, forget crocodiles.*

∼ Chapter 5. ∼

On food and no-food. The mobility of identities

Food is a song and dances. Food is a pot, and charcoal and matches.
Food is the route walked to reach a friend no matter how far, when you have no food.
Food is a prey to the clouds. Food is a berry collected when goats are drinking at the river.
Food is a woman, a calabash, and milk. Food is money, a shop, and big white bags
'USAID'.
Food is the strings of those big white bags when empty and re-used to thread necklaces.
Food is local brew. Food is a road, and cars.
Food is your children who now have another mother.
Food is also those other children of yours, who now look like street children.
Food is the lack of food, food is no-food.
I have learnt to stay-without.

FIELD DIARY, 2016

Milking. Lokitela, Turkana Central.

doi: 10.63308/6389190854875l.ch05

Flipped narratives of vulnerability

To live, we eat death …
And eventually we'll stop eating bucolic,
between picnics and disasters.

ALBERTO SALZA, 2025

Edonga. Urum, Loima, February 2016.

Loporucho welcomes us with an apology. 'Nowadays, the sun does not let us to treat visitors properly'. He means he cannot slaughter one of his goats for us. Not that he would really do so, as he is unsure of the purpose of our visit. However, the sun has little to do with his inability to offer us a goat. He is old and has now parted from his livestock. He moved to within walking distance of a growing *loline* and hopes to gain something from the road and shops. We learn he has multiple large livestock, 'some of which must be already in Uganda by now', amid the dry season. Nonetheless, such a non-offer was enough to act, to perform, as wealthy families ought when receiving visitors. He wears a single line necklace with big red beads matching the colour of his hat. A pink e*chuka* (blanket) around his hips, folded on his legs as he sits on his *ekicholong* (head stool). Around his wrist he shows an *abarait*, a circular knife protected by a piece of stretched goat skin, used to cut meat during *akiriket* (meat ceremonies). *His aburo* (herder's staff) and *esebo* (hunting club), of which I have noted an increased display in times of impending drought, both lie on the ground next to him. Finally, a ram-horn where he stocks his tobacco, hangs from his left shoulder. As we talk, he is definitive in asserting that he does not know the 'things of town' such as schools and 'those modern ways to earn shillings. For us *raiya* is all about animals and making *ng'akibuk* (sour milk) in *etio* (gourd)'.

While identity is an overlooked dimension in resilience scholarship and in development practice, Lopurocho was making a statement on where he belongs through the reproduction of a social imaginary of what *being Turkana* entails. He was embodying his Turkana being through the reproduction of a collective performance of the self while also enacting a process of othering, with reference to growing urbanities and town dwellers. As much as the immediate, the contingent and situational context that drives mobility in the everyday, discussed in the previous chapter, the social imaginary, in Vigh's terms, also requires navigation to gain directionality (2006). Vigh's book, *Navigating Terrains of War*, offers us an anthropological understanding of the relationship between agency and structure, specifically focusing on the ongoing negotiation with, and within shifting *social terrains*. Among Turkana herders, navigating the social imaginary implies, beforehand, the construction of local identities as imagined, produced and reproduced in relationships within and outwith groups of belonging and solidarity, or, in other words, the construction of a skilled way of being, considered to be attuned, accustomed and rooted to cultural places. Secondly, it implies the ability to cross and bridge over varied imagined cultural places (in this chapter across rural and urban areas) and their respective characterisation.

We trace our steps back to Lodwar: a boat to Natirae, a pro-box to Kalokol, and a second pro-box to Lodwar. Always when approaching Lodwar I experience mixed feelings, but this time they meld into a broader sense of nostalgia for soon leaving Turkana and going back home. I smile at the thought that in my research design I had planned to go to Nairobi once every couple of months to rest and socialise. I never went. If Lodwar already felt so distant from my host families in the rural areas, I was worried that I would be more traumatised than comforted in Nairobi.

Flipped narratives of vulnerability

Based on the conceptual underpinnings of cultural resilience, various recent ethnographies have sought to pursue analyses of social dimensions of resilience by looking at the ways in which cultural traits survive despite a rapidly changing world (see for example Fortier 2009; Galaty 2013). As discussed by Derbyshire in his ethnography on Turkana material culture, these studies maintain a restrictive approach to resilience by lingering with a tired dichotomy, tradition–modernity, that does not account for the changes that occur within culture (2020). With this chapter I aim to show that resilience rests in both: in the local identity used as a social construct of belonging and solidarity (thus similarly to other ethnographies), but also in its responsiveness to change and distinctive malleability, or, in other words, in the mobility of identities. The chapter shows how, far from being statically anchored in tradition, identities are flexible, disrupting dichotomies built up along what Lesorogol used to call 'symbolic boundaries' (2008), and are accommodating change.

The need for a group identity as well for an underlying flexibility of this identity is particularly important in contexts of rapid socio-economic, political and cultural changes, such as those occurring in Turkana. From merely being known as one of the world's richest archaeological sites and cradle of human beings, the arid and most north-west County of Kenya is now subject to great international attention. In this context, power is shifting away from the ruling authority of elders and local seers, who used to manage and control the region, to progressively (irreversibly?) go into the hands of urban elites. This is a long process, which started during British colonisation, as recounted for example by Casper Odegi Awuondo in his book *Life in the Balance: Ecological Sociology of Turkana Nomads* (1990), or Vigdis Broch-Due and Todd Sanders in *Rich Man, Poor Man, Administrator, Beast: The Politics of Impoverishment in Turkana, Kenya, 1890–1990* (1999). Social change has not stopped since these early studies, and in fact one could say that it has accelerated. A recent e book by Jessica Hatcher, *Exploiting Turkana: Robbing the Cradle of Mankind*, reports a growing feeling among Nairobi citizens that Turkana 'will be one of the best counties in terms of investment and development' (2014: 37). This sense of economic growth is associated with devolution plans emerging from the 2010 new Constitution, with the nascent oil industry in the south of Turkana (Okenwa 2020) and with expanding refugee operations in Kakuma and Kalobeyei camps, referred to as models for the international community (Betts et al. 2019). By the end of my fieldwork, there were numerous low-cost flights connecting Nairobi and Lodwar, the Turkana capital town, several times a day, landing in the newly built small airport. Lodwar town was growing fast, with increased sections of tarmac roads and streetlights, and an increasing number of hotels, restaurants and tourism companies. Streets were full of *boda-boda* drivers (motorbike riders) coming from other parts of Kenya, 'because in Lodwar there are more opportunities', as one driver once explained when, out of sheer curiosity, I asked why he came from Kitale to Lodwar. When I left, I had the feeling of leaving a town in ferment.

In response to changes of such magnitude, as well as to find a position in *relation to* them, referring to Bourdieu's theory of *distinction* (1984), there emerges a need for a *feeling of belonging* and solidarity based on a shared identity. Such identity is built *relationally*, within a group, but also outwith a group, in relation to what is perceived as *other* by means of *symbolic boundaries*. Such a sense of identity is, however, never static as it undergoes perpetual re-articulations. In other words, precisely because of the incessant expansion of towns, development and modernity, a strong sense of localised identity is necessary to maintain meaning and purpose, so as not to lose your compass, and to find support from peers. But it is also important to develop skills to confront, to respond to, to adapt to such changes. In this way, it is not only livelihoods that diversify, as documented in many studies about resilience and pastoralism (see for example Little et al. 2001; McCabe et al. 2014; McCabe, Leslie and DeLuca 2010), but identity, material culture and ritual life also undergo processes of continual adjustment. Resilience, then, rests also on such skills of re-adjustment, which I will refer to as *capacity for change*.

Derbyshire warns us that changes taking place in Turkana, while promising to many, are also accompanied by an 'impenetrable fog of misinformation and distrust' (2020: xiii). Those who promote development interventions are rarely familiar with Turkana people, their livelihoods and societal dynamics or the socio-ecological context. From the perspective of town dwellers and other promoters of change in Turkana, what explains the life of Turkana herders remains tied to a sense of tradition which inhibits growth and development, while also, as argued by Natasha Maru, creating 'an oppressive affective atmosphere' (2022: 176). However, tradition has little to do with Turkana herders' lifeways. What more strongly emerges is the reproduction of a collective social imaginary through everyday performances of being *raiya*, as they refer to it: a person who lives in the reserve, a herder, an original Turkana. *Raiya* is a polythetic category, one which holds several meanings, including a livelihood (pastoralism), a place (the bush), a behaviour (those who uphold custom).[117] By understanding how people construct their collective identities, in this case the *raiya* category, and how these flexibly respond to changes in the surroundings, one can understand resilience. A fundamental dimension of the *raiya* identity is played by food, or better *no-food* (lack of / absence of food), and the relationship with hunger. Contention about meanings of food is a salient node between Turkana herders and their urban counterparts and development planners. Food security, as well as water development as seen in Chapter 2, is an overarching goal of most development masterplans. Guiding development interventions worldwide, the Sustainable Development Goals include: 'By 2030, end hunger and ensure access by all people, in particular the poor and people in vulnerable situations, including infants, to safe, nutritious and sufficient food all year round'. Before global development goals, food security has long been an objective of development and humanitarian interventions dating back at least to the early 1970s (Maxwell and Smith 1992). Initially framed as a simple problem of supply (Gross et al. 2000; Valdés 1981; WFC 1974), food security was increasingly recognised as a question of access thanks to the critical work by Amartya Sen. As we have already seen in Chapter 2, Sen described the famine in the Sahel at the end of the 1970s not as the result of food scarcity, but as a problem of *entitlements*. In *Poverty and Famine,* Sen overturned theories of famine and food security of the time by showing that starvation is the characteristic of some people not having enough food to eat and not the characteristic of there not being enough food to eat (1981). Food then started being discussed also in terms of cultural preferences and food uses (WFS 1996). More recently food security and nutrition issues have also entered the heart of resilience discourses (see for example: FAO 2013; Hoddinott 2014; Von Grebmer, Klaus et al. 2013). Food security is often used as a proxy for resilience, generally measured through indicators of nutritional values (caloric intake), dietary diversity and consumption scores (Barrett 2010; Coates 2013; De Haen, Klasen and Qaim 2011). Nutrition and food security of vulnerable populations, especially in crisis situations, have been a priority for humanitarian interventions and, as reported by Czuba and colleagues in an assessment of food assistance to pastoralists in Africa, these usually involve the provision of food in-kind (2017), increasingly also including cash-based interventions believed to enhance people's

---

117. For a nice reflection on the meanings of *raiya* I suggest reading Rodgers 2020, 'Identity as a lens on livelihoods: Insights from Turkana, Kenya', published in the journal *Nomadic Peoples.*

resilience either by directly preventing starvation or saving depletion of assets through the selling of capital to buy food.

The strongest manifestation of food insecurity is hunger. I cite the FAO report *Anti-Hunger Program: Reducing Hunger through Agricultural and Rural Development and Wider Access to Food*:

> Hunger is the most extreme manifestation of poverty and human deprivation … Hunger breeds desperation and the hungry are easy prey of those who seek power and influence through crime, force or terror (FAO 2002).

Food insecurity through its emotive counterpart (hunger) has become a symbol of vulnerability, an equation particularly stringent in the context of drylands where food shortages are considered a constant threat because of cyclical droughts. And yet, I heard rather different narratives from Turkana herders through the performance of their identity.

A large part of being *raiya* entails the capacity to *stay-without* food, as a wider signifier for toughness, endurance and ecological-situatedness. Food insecurity among Turkana herders is not a synonym of vulnerability, but a marker of belonging and sign of strength. Hunger is turned into a matter of pride. Through their hunger Turkana herders perform a distinctive collective identity which is different from the 'lazy and weak town people', as they were often described to me, spoilt and vulnerable, always whining, incapable of walking long distances, and only thinking about food; this collective identity of being *raiya* resonates against images of poor and vulnerable herders commonly portrayed in policy documents.

Drawn into a flipped narrative of vulnerability, I use food as a way in, an analytical lens to understand people's representation of their own vulnerability. However, I quickly learnt that food signifies much more than food per se. That the significance of food is not limited to its dietary intake is well established in the anthropology of food. Holtzman in his book *Uncertain Tastes: Memory, Ambivalence, and the Politics of Eating in Samburu, Northern Kenya* explains vividly that food is social, emotive, psychological, political, economic, religious, gendered, symbolic and sensuous (2009). Many anthropologists have shown that food is a key element in the construction of personal and collective identities (Diodato 2001; Guptill, Copelton and Lucal 2017; Monsutti 2010); it marks membership in some groups and signals outsiders. I contribute to this scholarship by focusing on meanings of no-food (hunger, lack) and what role they play in the construction of identities, which, as argued also by Kristin Phillips in *An Ethnography of Hunger: Politics,*

Subsistence, and the Unpredictable Grace of the Sun, remains, amid a huge literature on food, largely underexplored (2018).

In this chapter I present the distinctive sense of solidarity built around hunger and the capacity to stay-without, and then expand on other features which determine belonging in terms of dietary, fashion and other convivial habits. Rodgers, in his doctoral study of social differentiation associated with the expansion of urban centres and impacts of development in Turkana, discusses *raiya* also in terms of 'skilled performances' (2018). Following this approach, I focus on the relational aspects of these performances as forming a collective personhood which I argue represents a hidden dimension of resilience. In other words, Turkana herders have turned their vulnerability into a group survival-strategy, based on a sense of community. However, identity is not absolute, uncontested and static, as manifested through incongruities between presentations of the self and daily practices. With this, I do not argue that presentations of the self are an invention or that they do not hold significance. Rather, I want to show that identities are malleable and can move across cultural environments. A *mobility of identity* is employed to cross varied environments and navigate socio-cultural landscapes. By unpacking contradictions and ambivalence between memories, narratives and practices I show responsiveness to changes, and the coexistence of fluid identities among Turkana herders, *raiya*.

On my way back home from the pro-box station, Lodwar streets appear lively, noisy, crowded. Young herders with their walking sticks and Masai blankets around their hips, come from the peripheries of town for a cold beer. School boys and girls run back home with their uniforms and backpacks. Young professionals walk firmly, in suits, to their appointments. Some women weave palm leaves into mats to sell. Motorbikes speed up in all directions. Some beg. An aircraft flies over town.

On food and no-food

Solidarities of hunger

> *Have you experienced fierce hunger,*
> *cold which penetrates bones,*
> *heat which leaves breathless?*
> *…*
> *Humbly, yes.*

> Roberto Bolano
> (interviewed by Mónica Maristain 15 July 2003,
> released a few days after his death).

Offering a drink. Lorengelup, Turkana Central, November 2015.

> *Aponopono: you could have told her that there is something known as thirst*
> *you could have told her that there is something known as sun*
> *you could have told her that we have learnt to stay-without.*[118]

We were preparing my visit to the sons of one of my host families during fieldwork, who were migrating with family shoats. We met at their family wells on a day we knew they would be taking their animals to drink. Aponopono, the elder brother,

---

118. Lorengelup well, 19 Jan. 2016.

was worried: if I joined them, I would lack the comforts he (rightly) assumed I am used to, like cool water and shade from the sun. At the same time, he was praising his own ability to survive despite undesirable hardship. In Turkana, herders have grown accustomed to a lifeway which takes them to walk long distances in danger of scorpion bites as well as fighting with sharp thorns while herding livestock, fetching water and firewood or gathering wild fruit. While carrying out tasks, they have adapted to a modest diet largely composed of fresh or fermented milk, sorghum or millet when available, small berries and fruits, occasionally meat, and blood at cattle camps during dry seasons. They have adjusted to hunger and thirst. They describe with pride the harshness they have grown accustomed to. Those who are not adjusted do not belong (yet). For my hosts I have (at best) remained a young girl who is still training, learning to adjust. For most, I have continued to be a town girl (still of young age because of my thin body and lack of husband and kids). This certainly caused a few problems while trying to get as close as possible to my hosts. Like the time I was left sleeping when all family members of my host family went to *edonga* (village dances) one full moon night. My host mother understood my sadness the following morning when I realised what I had missed. There was empathy in her eyes, when she took my hands and explained she was not sure 'my feet had adjusted to the tough terrain, when at night is easy to step on thorns and be injured'. To belong implies firstly acquiring a certain skilled way of being, only achievable by *going-through*, adjusting, and overcoming problems: *anaikis nghichan*.

Going-through

Mama Aruk, a strong woman and wife of the chief in Lorengelup sub-location called me back a few steps after I had departed from the village to begin my first experience with the *real Turkana* or *raiya*. Mama Aruk called me back and gave me a spare charcoal stove she was no longer using. 'They, *raiya*, do not use this for cooking. They survive on bushes and cook only with firewood, otherwise it is only milk and blood out there', she explained, while portraying a collective imaginary of being *raiya*. As I thanked her and promised to bring the stove back on my return, I felt uncomfortable. With her kind gesture, what she really meant, perhaps rightly, was that I would have struggled in the bush because I was not strong enough and had not adjusted yet.

There is an image of being tough and stoic which was constantly presented to me throughout the entire fieldwork, also reproduced in the reconstruction of event calendars.

It was *ekaru emuudu* (the year when everything got finished). It was a very dangerous period, a year when most animals were attacked by diseases in a scorching drought. Before, people were rich and healthy, grass and trees used to reproduce in large numbers. Conditions got worse. Rains disappeared. Grass withered. Wild fruits went absent. Disease became fierce and dangerous, and killed people and animals.

I was asking John Lopua, an elder from one of the small settlements born in the surroundings of Lore centre, to share with me one of his worst memories.

People started eating dogs because they lacked food to eat [laughed someone else].

Dogs were not the only things we ate. We also ate dried animal hides (*ejomu*). We used to soak them in water to make them soft and later they were cooked in a pot.

Others roasted it.

By then, Lopua's story had become a collective recollection of tragic details to which a group of people who had gathered under the big *ewoi* (acacia)'s shade contributed. Multiple voices echoed:

People sent their children to work on the farms in Kitale.

And then rain came. But the grass that followed was not good grass as the surviving animals were getting sick with diarrhoea.

… Many houses were destroyed. Animals died both in the field and in kraals. Most trees fell, floods carried away many properties. That rain was not a blessing. It was accompanied by thunderstorms. Both, cold and thunders killed our animals.

From this account, one of the many I collected, there emerges an underlying story, one which goes beyond the struggle and the suffering. There was something unnoticed; something initially difficult to grasp that was also present in the concern felt by Mama Aruk when she saw me leaving Lore centre for the first time. In some ways, and despite the tragedies narrated, Lopua's story was not a story of vulnerability, at least not in the ways it was recalled to me. From the choice of words, from the tones of voice, the collective laughter and the gestural behaviour of the people gathered under the acacia tree, there emerged a certain pride in *having gone through*, having survived and persevered to arrive at the season of plenty.

John Lopua Lourien and his friends agreed: 'we are used to this place'.

To be used to this place questions whether we (outsiders) would manage to survive what they have repeatedly faced in their personal history. It triggers a change of perspective to reveal strength and toughness as opposed to vulnerability and poverty. As I tried to understand what this implied, responses aligned around a skilled way of being (tough), to go through; and indeed *to be used to this place* was generally followed by another expression: *anaikis nghichan*. This was translated to me in various ways: having endured, adjusted or got used to challenges. The underlying meaning was clear: to be accustomed to place; lamenting difficulties among fellows would instead be taken as a sign of weakness or would expose one to the risk of being accused of witchcraft.[119] Place becomes an inherent part of one's own being. In rural Turkana this takes the form of a *survivor identity* around which Turkana herders have built a collective persona: *raiya*. *Raiya*, as a social construct, gives strength, value and meaning to one's own life in the everyday of her environment.

In societies where food shortages are chronic threats, the way one eats and does not eat is fundamental for the construction of the personhood, as also argued by Holtzman in his ethnography of food among Samburu pastoral communities in northern Kenya (2009). Turkana herders of both genders frequently and explicitly (and often laughing at me) pointed at their ability to abstain from food, sleeping hungry, and yet never failing in their daily responsibilities. They often told me that town people were weak and vulnerable because they cannot go without food, presenting a flipped discourse of vulnerability, when instead we hear about herders drawn into famine camps because of their hunger. For *raiya*, it is more the other way around: town people cannot survive without food, unlike *raiya* who can move with their cattle camps and find comfort wherever they go even in the absence of food. It follows that the western paradigm that 'no one should be hungry at any time' is a meaningless paradigm in Turkana. Rather, Turkana herders have built a distinctive social imaginary around the ability to *stay-without*.

Stay-without

One of the predominant outcomes of getting used to a place like Turkana is to learn to *stay-without* since hunger is a salient part of the experience of being *raiya*.

---

119. This behaviour is different towards outsiders or in relation to *things* of foreigners (i.e. aid food). In these cases, weeping, begging, lamenting, asking for more, is all very common and locally understood as correct behaviour, part of an optimal foraging strategy (not a sign of weakness) and subject to different rules and norms than among fellow insiders. That is, begging is external not internal.

On food and no-food

The primary absence to sustain is that of food; that, however, also signifies many other lacks (rain, water, grass, mobility). Making sure we would eat something in the evening became a daily concern during fieldwork, especially while the 2017 drought progressed, and daylight hours would pass entirely without meals. It became an even more prominent concern when I realised that I was the only person really worried about food. No one from my host families showed any interest during the day about their food intakes. Only a few curious ones accepted my offer of dates and peanuts carried to sustain long hours without food. Most replied that it was better I saved that food for me, as they were *used to staying-without*. Others ended up spitting out the strange food I was offering, with disgust and laughter. At the same time there was humour and interest in my reaction when trying greasy mixes of wild fruits and animal fat (*akimiet*) or caloric residues from a local brew fermented from sorghum and maize (*adakae*) or roasted wild game. Food and no-food became a point of interaction.

In his famous essay *Toward a Psychosociology of Contemporary Food Consumption*, Roland Barthes introduces the idea that food is not only about eating – 'it is also a system of communication, a body of images, a protocol of usages, situations and behaviour' (1961). The analysis offered by Barthes on the psychological dimension of food behaviour also applies to the no-food behaviour that I have found among Turkana herders. The capacity to stay-without is firstly an internal *system of communication* and socialisation. It results from the relationship with the lived environment, one where food is a gamble, and from a livelihood that takes individuals on long marches while living in remote satellite camps where blood and milk are the only diet during dry seasons. It is the result of the *weight-volume-versatility* dimension of the material culture of herders loading their donkeys, discussed in Chapter 4, which results in a system of communication to ask for food, often confused for begging. Begging for food or water while migrating with livestock is normal and generally accompanied by pointing to one's stomach and saying: *akoro*. *Akoro*, the most typical representation of Turkana interactions with white communities working in Turkana, is a recurrent quest in the streets of Lodwar town. But *akoro, I am hungry*, is not only addressed to *wazungu* (white foreigners) in the hope of receiving some food; rather, it is multidirectional and an expression of a lack which is primarily a livelihood output and originates under nomadic conditions. *Akoro* is different from begging (among fellow insiders). It is an expression of ecological situatedness and a relational system of socialisation to ask for food, when lacking it.

Showing to ability to stay-without also reproduces a *body of images* drawn from the collective imaginary of being *raiya*, a solidarity built around hunger. Among Turkana herders, abstaining from food is not a matter of shame or a way to hide personal greed, as presented in other ethnographies of hunger (see for example Kahn 1986; Riesman 1977). Rather, it is a distinct personhood accustomed to hunger. Lacking the capacity to understand that there is no food, small children cry helplessly, while I could observe an evolving attitude towards absence of food with aging. Salza in *Bambini perduti* (2010)claims that in pastoral societies children typically have not yet fully acquired the status of personhood. In Turkana, in fact, as one grows, attitudes towards food change. The cry for food is first substituted for resignation towards absence. 'These children do not speak; they are still learning to be thirsty', explained a woman who intercepted my thoughts towards a group of silent children surrounding us during an interview close to Lore centre. Those children may have been shy because of my presence, and yet, with these words, the woman explained that older children undergo a sort of enculturation to stay without and sleep hungry as they become adult. I could observe this attitude in many children who, as they became more confident with my presence, started showing their skills at herding, hunting, recognising wild fruit, carrying heavy jerrycans on their heads with pride transcending the discomforts of a day spent without food. Adulthood was finally presented to me as the ability to sustain hunger without lamenting and without praising the ability to survive it. For Turkana herders, the *no-food person* is a cultural mirage to tend: it embodies the epics of *staying-without*. The whole story is simply a way to *digest* no-food, to make no-food the armour of a hero who, one day or another, is going to be dragged in the dust behind a chariot (Homer 1924). To cry for food, to be silent and resigned, to show pride in abstention are different stages in the construction of the *raiya* personhood reproduced in the collective imaginary.

Finally, the capacity to stay-without responds to a *protocol of behaviour* in the context of scarcity. It not only proves strength against weakness, but is also an invitation to share and prevents one from falling under the accusation of being a witch. Hungry people are in fact not only pitied because weak, but also feared because their jealousy can transform into a curse. Stories of jealousy and bewitching permeate daily life of Turkana. When food is too scarce to be shared, it is eaten hiding inside huts to avoid *the bad eye* of jealous people. Most of the herd is kept far away from villages, to hide the size of the stock from neighbours. Future plans of migrations are revealed only partially. Jealous people are dangerous, because they can curse both people and animals and cause bad events in terms of health or wealth. Food lodges in the throat. Livestock dies. People get sick. Cursing can start when, for example, people see others eating. They can wish to eat the same. Such a strong feeling is enough to harm those who are eating by making food choke them. Alternatively, it can be whispered when neighbours see that others are wealthier. It is a soft rustle, which can take everything away from wealthy families. Or it can involve actions intended to harm. Stealing small objects, gnawed bones, a chunk of hair, a pinch of tobacco. Burying these items close to targeted families, one can curse them, their livestock or their properties. To prevent all that, one never eats in front of others without offering. The heads of the households who hosted me during fieldwork were often guiding the ceremonies I attended and were always those who ended up eating the least, publicly showing their generosity in feeding others the most exquisite parts of the meal, before themselves. Failing to adhere to prescriptions on food sharing is arguably the most common source of misfortune and cursing. Turkana herders deny greed and repulse jealousy, both moral qualities which should be understood against a socio-ecological context where dry seasons can at times bring extreme scarcity.

In the praise of being able to stay-without, my hosts never missed the opportunity to highlight the appropriateness of a typology of food suitable for *raiya*, which feeds into a collective social imaginary of being *raiya* by eating the *right* food.

'Milk we drink every day, meat we eat every day'

'Milk we drink every day, meat we eat every day' is how one of my host mothers described their diet with a sentiment that an epicurean approach to food would entirely dismiss. And yet this is the food considered most appropriate, satisfying and delicious (*ebob*), the most suited for pastoral living. There indeed is a food which was presented to me as the 'food for the Turkana'. A diet that satisfies hunger, allows undisturbed nights of rest and days of walking under the hot sun. This diet is represented by the pastoralist triad (milk, meat, blood), but not only, as it also includes a large variety of berries, sorghum, millet, wild game and other supplements.

Despite the limited vocabulary of taste, my hosts were enthusiastic in narrating how much they love the time of the year when milk flows from all animals and can be mixed in the *akurum* (calabash). Milk is drunk fresh (*ngakile*), sour (*ngakibuk*) or dried (*edodo*). Sour milk is prepared through fermentation. Milk is placed in a gourd (*etio*) suspended on a rope, and some cow urine-grains (*ngachoto*) are added to boost flavour.[120] This is then shaken firmly until the butter fat (*akidedet*) separates. The mixture is poured into a wooden bowl from which the solid matter is separated using a wooden spoon (*akaloboch*). *Akidedet* is used to make porridge with blood or to add flavour to other cooked foods, or dried and conserved for the dry season. The watery part is generally drunk fresh or mixed with seasonal small dryland fruits. Butter can also be heated to further remove water and produce ghee (*akimiet*). *Akimiet* is used for cooking, but also to smear on the body and beads as a cosmetic, or to soften leather and skin products, or to treat wood used to carve utensils and attire. Oil will last longer than butter through the dry season and is used to add flavour to dried wild fruits and cereals. The solid residue that remains at the bottom of the pan after cooking is called *akibot* or *emur* and contains proteins and minerals. They also make milk powder (*edodo*) by sun-drying milk curds on rocks or hides; this is kept in skin bags for the season of scarcity when it will be mixed with water or blood. During the rainy season, milk is alternated with fresh sorghum stems harvested from farms, which is as sweet as sugar cane. Otherwise, sorghum is dried and kept in big sacks made of hides (*ng'ichwei*) for the dry season. Leaves and edible shrubs that grow during the rainy season are also added to the seasonal prevalently milk diet.

Livestock is rarely slaughtered unless sick or killed by predators, or when required by rituals and ceremonies, or to welcome visitors. However, meat (*akiring*) is the most preferred food. Skin, fat, humps are generally the favoured parts because they are tasty and filling. The pot and boiled meat belong to the realm of women, while roasted meat over live fire is for men. Meat is also stored for times of need. It can be cut int long thin strips which are hung and dried under the sun (in some cases adding salt to hasten the process). It can be cut into tiny ball-shaped pieces which are deep fried and then sun dried (*enyath*). Or it is minced and then sun dried, stored under oil or mixed with oil and seeds such as maize or sorghum. In Turkana, nothing from an animal goes to waste. This includes meat from sick livestock (from diseases which are not communicable to humans) and animals found killed by wild predators. For example, while marching in Urum we encountered the carcass of a striped hyena found in the bushes. Or in the kitchen hut of my host family in Lorengelup we found an unfortunate hedgehog fearfully curled in a ball and hiding behind a small rock. It was left hanging on the hut's

---

120. The urine is tapped, then left in the sun until it obtains a colour called *emug*, 'the colour of strong tea without milk'. *Ngachoto* is put in milk for scent, but some respondents also say it is sweet *ebob*.

branches for a few hours, and then boiled until its meat became white in colour and so soft as to be eaten with a spoon, by children for breakfast. When migrating with Aponopono and their family shoats in Turkana central, the herding boys hunted several squirrels which we roasted at night. And the price of hunted dik-dik in Urum was as low as 100 *shillings* (approximately one dollar) during the dry season. I found only a few food taboos, and these are not well specified. Indeed, as also reported by Holtzman: 'Turkana are well known to eat almost anything: birds, fish, reptiles and all manner of games, donkeys, donkey blood' (2009: 95), following the principle of *better than nothing*. In addition, most attires and home objects are obtained from livestock parts including skin, bones and horns, or wood from available trees.

Blood supplements this diet. Especially during the dry season at cattle camps, livestock are bled while alive, a practice called *akigum*. This is done through a small incision close to the nose for shoats and on the neck for cows and camels. In this way it is directly sucked, and it 'tops up human blood, like a soda', as the son of one of my host families tried to explain. Otherwise, it is collected in a wooden bowl (*atubwa*) and allowed to clot for some time under the shade of a big tree, to then have water or milk and sugar added and be drunk fresh. When an animal is slaughtered for *akiriket* (a meat ceremony performed by men) blood is not wasted. It is let to flow from the open abdomen of the animal after having burnt the hair on fire. Men bend and follow each other to drink it warm, directly from the animal's chest.

All this food is sweetened by adding crushed wild fruit which accompany all seasons. I have found that wild fruit is one of the most crucial components of a pastoral diet, and it is not just coping food as hunting and gathering wild fruit is an important part of daily living. In two early publications, *The South Turkana Expedition: Scientific Papers X. Sorghum Gardens in South Turkana: Cultivation among a Nomadic Pastoral People* and *Ethnobotany of the Turkana: Use of Plants by a Pastoral People and Their Livestock in Kenya*, Morgan records 47 different plants for food and 62 for medicinal purposes (1974, 1981). Throughout my fieldwork, people have never lacked details about the wealth and variety and tastiness of edible wild fruit. It also finds a central role in ceremonies like *akuuta* (wedding), when it is eaten mixed with *atap* (porridge) during the final prayer (*agataa*), and also in the myth of origin of the Turkana tribe when it parted from their Nilotic allies:

Figure 32. Drinking blood

There was a place, a mountain, called Moru a Nayace, which divided the land. Turkana people arrived there originally from Jie in Uganda. They had parted while travelling eastwards to an *abor* (satellite cattle camp) when they lost a bull and started searching. At the same time there was also a *mama* (married woman) from the Jie who got lost while gathering wild fruits. She arrived at Moru a Nayace where she found a lot of fruit: *edung, engomo, edome, epat, ngakalalio*. Loving such food, she decided to settle. One day, the mama, returning to her new camp after a day of gathering wild fruit, found bull footprints. She burned a tree and laid the wild fruits to dry next to the fire as she was preparing for the season of scarcity. The bull smelled the fire and came close to the mama and slept there. The young warriors who were still searching for their lost bull, found the old woman and the bull, living nicely together. There was water and good grass and a lot of wild fruit. Hence, they decided to split from the Jie and stay with the mama and the bull in the area now called Turkana.[121]

The striking relevance of wild fruit in my hosts' daily life implies that it is the reduction of wild fruit gathering that signifies increasing hardship and not its increase. As the drought progressed during my fieldwork in 2017, people increas-

121. Elderly man, FN, Urum, 24 Dec. 2016; (see also Lamphear 1988).

ingly lamented the difficulty of finding wild fruit or the discomfort of walking longer distances to find some, compromising the quality (in terms of taste and sweetness) of their diet.

As in many other pastoral cultures, there are gender and generational roles attributed to food behaviour. This is certainly true among Turkana herders who spent a long time explaining how parts of slaughtered animals are distributed among family members of different age and gender. However, no-food behaviours (staying-without) are transversal. Both genders must adhere to the no-food behaviour and show adulthood through their ability to stay-without. It is equally masculine and feminine to persevere amidst scarcity and train the youngest to perform alike. Food studies fall into the danger of adopting western epicurean lenses of analyses. It is difficult for us to think of no-food, and yet no-food (lack) plays a crucial role in the construction of a sense of solidarity within a pastoral system in which seasonal hunger is frequent, and in which hunger is not only a problem of supply, or of accessibility or preferences but a quest for belonging and identity.

The form of solidarity built around hunger, food and no-food behaviour is accompanied by what I have termed *everyday performances of being raiya*, which includes dietary but also fashion and other convivial habits discussed in the next section.

Gendered performances of being *raiya*

There is no feline who doesn't say: I'm beautiful.

A Samburu proverb

ACHILLE DA ROS (1994)

Beauty.

Gendered performances of being raiya

The concept of a performing identity is drawn from Victor Turner's idea of *Homo performans*. *Homo performans* reveals herself in the 'basic stuff of social life' (Turner 1987: 13). To be *raiya*, as well as the capacity to stay-without, there are other elements of quotidian life which define belonging and personhood. I conceptualise personhood as relational, drawing from Brewer and Gardner in their joint essay 'Who is this "we"? Levels of collective identity and self representations' (1996). They promote an idea of the social self as a more inclusive self-representation in which relations and similarities to others become central. A relational identity becomes a performing identity when everyday practices of dietary, convivial and fashion habits define mainstream cultural traits of belonging. In what follows, I describe those everyday practices performed by a *raiya* woman (for which there is more wealth of detail available, because of my positionality as a young girl) and a *raiya* man, addressing their performing attitudes, possessions, code of aesthetics and norms of behaviour. The portraits reported below were drawn during a mixed focus group (in age and gender) held under the shade of a big *ewoi* (acacia tree) along Lorengelup stream.

In the first drawing, we sketched a 'strong and successful woman'. In this drawing there are many elements that point to the distinctive identity of a Turkana woman. What strongly emerged from conversations during the focus group, which seems particularly important to emphasise, was the full participation of women in herding activities. The mixed group of participants in the focus group praised her ability to *multiply* the number of livestock. She knows how to take good care of her animals, she recognises each individual and will provide for the weakest. She wakes up when the moon is still high, lets out the baby goats and milks their mothers. The sound of *ngakibuk* shaking in the gourd wakes the rest of the family. She has a lot of livestock covering all the *four legs*: cows (*aite*), camels (*ekaal*), shoats (*ng'akine*) and donkeys (*ethikiria*); and she walks with e*bela* or *akeat* (depending on her brand/clan), a walking stick used also for herding. She always has a lot of milk in the house conserved from the season of plenty and is very generous with visitors.

She is hard-working and does not like sleeping in the house when men are herding livestock. She fetches water, while gathering wild fruit and checking on the herd. She fetches firewood from *ekadeli, ethekon, edome* trees to build huts and utensils. Her *ekol* (sleeping hut) is neatly woven and the entire homestead is clean and spacious. And mostly, she is tireless, independent and speaks the truth. Participants in the focus group were assertive about her qualities of being hardworking, trustworthy and generous. Then, they started to engage in long discussions about stylistic features of women's dresses, adornments and other articles deployed performatively by Turkana female personas as signifiers of their wealth. Undoubtedly, Turkana women pay extra attention to the refinements of their home utensils, decoration of their body and dress. For example, when I asked Akai, a friendly young woman living in Kambi Lore, to take me around the village showing me places she considered important, she took me to her house . The homestead, as a symbol of women's resourcefulness and their art skills, is the realm around which Turkana women construct their collective personas as queens of the *boma*.

Akai praised her crafting ability showing, one by one, a large number of articles concealed in the crannies of her huts. And she was not the only one. Many women showed emotive affection for these objects and responded to my queries about their most preferred object by running into the hut and displaying their favourite ones.[122] For each article, Akai acted and performed for me the ways in which they are correctly utilised. These objects were shown to me as traditional and therefore something I, an outsider, needed thorough explanations of. The institutionalisation of particular appliances as *traditional* expresses a distinctive sense of belonging which automatically excludes all those who do not belong and reinforces self-identification as part of a group. Akai proudly concluded the home tour:

> Because some of you *emoits* (enemies and foreigners),[123] when you come here you think these things are dirty and do not like using them. Hence, we will serve you with plates and mugs. But the rest of us, who are used to these things, we serve from these.

These articles therefore acquire a double meaning of symbolic participation in distinctive socio-economic and political structures, and practical engagement in the everyday necessities of living.

---

122. See list in Table 4.
123. On the enemy, see note 54.

Gendered performances of being raiya

Figure 33. Wealthy Turkana woman

Participative drawing from a focus group along Lorengelup stream, Turkana central. I prepared the shape of the person and participants added details in line with the conversation we were having on the representation of a wealthy Turkana woman.

On food and no-food

Figure 34. Home utensils and articles

Women also ally around a distinctive sense of aesthetics. Their beauty was also much discussed as signifier of their wealth during the focus group in Lorengelup:

> She is beautifully dressed, with plentiful beads. When men choose a wife, they look at how she dresses, how she behaves and speaks to peers, and how she manages her duties.[124]

The wardrobe of a Turkana woman includes several garments like skirts and dresses worn differently according to age and marital status: *abwo* and *adwel* (front and back skirt for married woman), *eleu* (long skirt sewed together from multiple hides differently patterned, worn by girls), *egolos* (long front dress).[125] Time is spent making those dresses unique and beautiful, by adding colourful beads or sewing together hides from different coloured livestock. Once, I assisted in the slaughtering of a goat under direction of the one of the wives because of the colour of its skin, imagining the glamorous dress she would afterwards obtain.

---

124. FGD, Lorengelup, 13 Nov. 2015.

125. See more in Table 5.

Gendered performances of being raiya

Table 4. Home utensils and articles

Item	Translation	Example of usage
Agulu	Clay pot	Pot made from clay, used for boiling cereals like maize, wild fruits, etc.
Akaloboch	Spoon	Serving spoon, it is carved from wood into various sizes and shapes.
Akurum (and akurum naibole)	Gourd	Elongated round shaped container used to store fresh milk, and to start fermentation before being transferred into *etwo*. It is also used for carrying milk while moving around to sell in the villages. The long lid (called *ibole*) is used to serve milk.
Akutwam	—	Round shaped container made from animal hides into a dried ball. It is used for storing liquid fats from animals, for example ghee *(akuring)*.
Atubwa	Bowl	A home plate/bowl, or livestock drinking trough. It can be carved in many shapes. Small ones serve as plates and the largest can serve as a water trough for the animals to drink water. It is carved from woody trees
Ebur	Container	Used for storing/preserving fatty pieces of meat, to be eaten in the future
Egech	Stirring stick	Made from fixing one end of a wooden stick to goat or sheep spine vertebra. Used for stirring soup inside a large pot so that the oil does not float, or to stir porridge or blood meals during cooking until fully cooked.
Ejomu	Sleeping mat	Made from skin and hides. It occurs in many sizes but hides of big animals (cow, camel, donkeys) are preferred due to their large size and long lasting.
Elado	Whisk	Made from several cow tails, it is well organised to form a big thick tail fixed on a short stick; the handle is made from skin. It is used during traditional dances, being wagged or swayed from side to side, or in all directions, during the dancing to move the dancers in unison, to give order or harmony to the dancers, to control the pattern of dancers. Mostly used in all celebrations, weddings, village dances, welcoming prominent leaders, etc.
Elepit	Milking can/jar	It can be carved in different shapes, but most often it looks like a tall wooden glass. It used when milking livestock, where initially milk is gathered, before being transferred to *akurum*.
Etwo	Calabash	Round shaped and used to shake milk every dawn, after it has undergone fermentation, to allow milk, its fats, and coagulated particles to break, and mix properly. Clean pieces of rocks are sometimes added to allow the break-down of the fatty layer or coagulated layers.

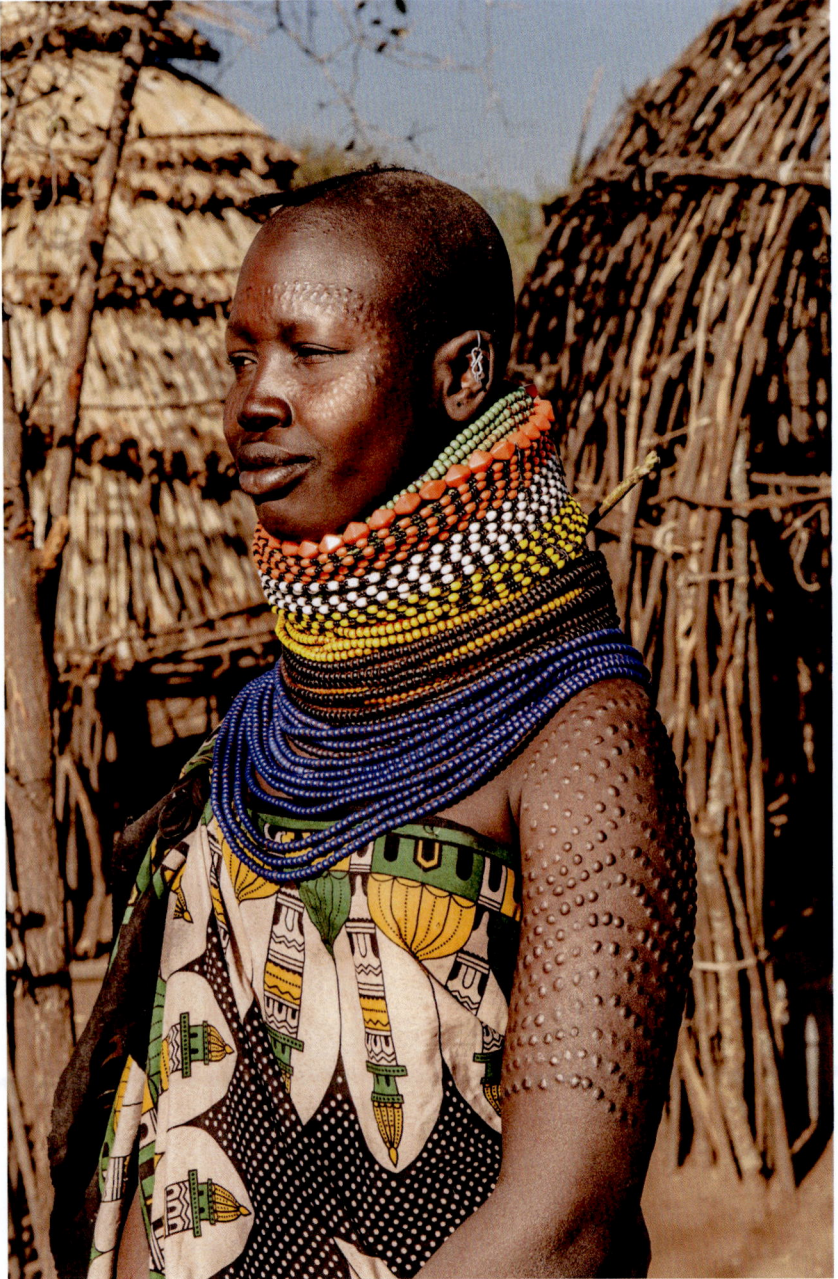

Figure 35. Turkana young woman

She has beautiful beads (*ng'akoromwa*) from which she chooses her favourite colours and wears *alagai* (necklace for festivities) during ceremonies. If married, she carries a copper or aluminium ring (*alagama*) above her beads to mark her status. She smears her body and hair with clay, *aruak* (fat from cow stomach mixed with coloured clay) or burnt cow hair mixed with butter cream (*akidedet*) or fat (*akimiet*). She also removes two front teeth and scarifies her body (*ng'ageran*) around shoulders or eyes to enhance her beauty. Clothes, together with artisan jewellery, earrings and other ornaments, become a symbol of cultural belonging around which gendered solidarity is performed.

Table 5. Attire and adornments

Item	Translation	Example of usage
Abwo	Back skirt	Half skirt made of animal hide in a specific pattern, with hanging extensions on the sides. It is worn to cover the back, stretching from the waist to the feet.
Adwel	Front short skirt	It is worn at the front by women, stretching from the waist to just above the knee.
Akoloch	Calf teeth	Calf teeth used as ornaments worn by ladies around their heads.
Aruak	Animal fat	Solid fats; most fats come from animals' stomach or other parts where fat deposits occur (under the skin, around the kidney, heart, intestines, etc). Turkana women and men mix *Aruak* with the red clay(called ochre) and apply on the hair.
Aruba	Belt	It is worn around the waist by ladies, it is like a big belt, and it is commonly used during dances. It is made from skin and patterns of small beads.
Egolos	Long front dress	It is made of animal skin and covers the entire front part of a woman, from just below the beads and stops just below the knees. It Is normally decorated with beads or multiple patches of skin.
Ekude	Headband	It hangs on the head with small decorated beads up to the face.
Ng'akoromwa	Beads	Beads arranged in a thread and worn around the neck.
Alagama	Wedding ring	Large wedding ring made from copper or aluminium wire; it is worn around the neck on top of the beads as a symbol of a married woman. It can be silver or golden depending on the age group.

On food and no-food

We started talking with the participants of the focus group along Lorengelup stream, about *wealthy* men too (see Figure 36). A strong man works hard. His toughness, trustworthiness, knowledge of animals and surrounding environment are praised among his best qualities and reasons for his success. His home is lively, with many wives, children and visitors. All are happy and given plentiful good food: sour milk, ghee, dried meat mixed with berries. Like women, he also spends time on his looks. Many young herders migrating with livestock carry a mirror and a comb (Figure 27). His most representative attire is a colourful *echuka* (blanket), tied around the waist or around the shoulders during cooler hours. Its multiple uses, for clothing, sleeping or as a wrap to carry *ngitit* (acacia-pods) for shoats, is a manifesto for the practical implications of being *raiya*. The *echuka* is generally matched in colour with the hat and beads he displays in plenty. He walks with a bare chest, or wears collared shirts. During ceremonies he wears a hat with ostrich feathers, carefully protected from dust in a hand-made wooden container (*atoroth*) during the rest of the year. He never parts from his *aburo* (herder staff) and *ekicholong* (head stool), the appearance of which is also an expression of his skills at crafting as they should be smooth, straight and strong. Hence, he spends time on their maintenance and takes good care of these articles. Next to rubber and plastic armbands, he wears an *abarait*, a circular knife used to cut meat. He has many wives and children. He has a favourite animal, generally an ox or a ram, about which he performs songs to praise its beauty and strength.

Days pass between transcribing my field diary and packing, getting ready for my departure. I search for gifts to bring back to my friends and family. I walk through market streets where laying on the ground on large fabrics one can find hard plastic kitchen pottery, wood ekicholong (head stool) and metal circular knifes for akiriket (meat ceremony). Lines of metal shacks display plastic beads for the necklaces of rural girls, and modern jewellery for town girls. I go to eat ugali, beans and sukuma (kale) at my favourite hoteli (restaurants). I try to absorb smells, flavours, sounds as much as I can. Some evenings one of my flat-mates takes me out for a drink or to chew some khat (in Kenya called miraa). Lodwar offers a quite lively night life between bars and night clubs, which stands in stark opposition to the nights of chatting while lying on skin mats under a pitch-dark sky in rural areas.

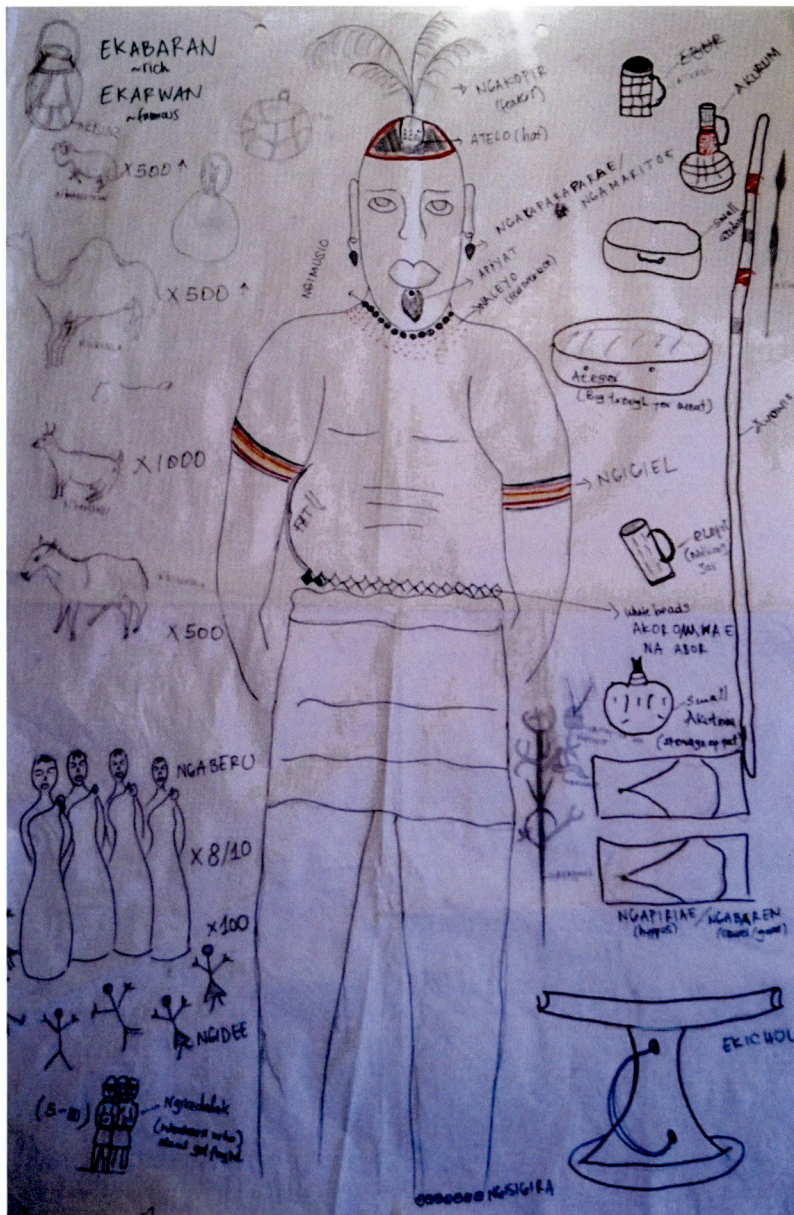

Figure 36. Wealthy Turkana man

Drawing from focus group, Lorengelup stream.

On food and no-food

The relationship between men and their favourite animals signifies a large part of their pastoral identity. Many hours around shallow wells in Urum were passed in praising the qualities of favourite animals, pointing at their horns or big humps or beautiful skin colour. For example, Nawuoi, a young boy in one of my host families in Urum, was responsible for the family cows, at the time of our visit. Next moon[126] he will be moved by his father to look after shoats. He explained that being with the cattle is more a strenuous and demanding task than herding shoats. However, this is the time of year he loves the most. Cattle confer pride and respect, and he is allowed by his father to choose one as his own to grow and take care of. As he is pointing to his favourite one approaching the well, he stands up and starts singing, while others around the well echo.

Ooh, iiii yeaaaah (solo)

Ooh, iiii yeaaaah (choir)

Erithia

Eeya ngalima lomeria

Elim e ebua

Lomeri ngorokoo

Elim ngithepionoo

Emalaa loa Epetet ee

Kimala ekitoa angakinei aa Kaile

This song is about his bull which has spots like those of a leopard. It is big like a mountain compared to the cows of his friend Kaile, which next to his bull look like goats.[127] His bull is like a lion, a leopard, a hyena; all feared animals to which his bull compares in ferocity. If the bull is under a tree, it will be the first thing to be seen from faraway by his friend Epetet who was sent to see the bull.

Lobokoera ejie ka ngimanikoo

Igooro ngithulua ang'opikinete

Lobokoera utuirianikin nyutaako

Lobokoera utuirianikin nyutaako

---

126. On the lunar calendar, see Chapter 2.

127. Turkana have moieties, leopards and stones/mountains, that also can explain the meaning of this song.

The song praises the fertility of the bull since its youth. The bull has few eyelashes around the eye and normally faces down searching for its eyelashes. It has big bones in its body and a huge hump.

Athur ngimoe katokanga

Ngesi aramunie ekarisia lolimaa

Even if this bull were raided by the enemy, Nawoui would be able to follow its footprints to the horizon and beyond, attack the enemies and return the stolen bull back home. Together with the bull's qualities he is also praising his own qualities as a warrior. As also pointed out during the focus group in Lorengelup, a successful man's wealth can derive from raids. And indeed, a successful man is also a skilled warrior. Turkana manly solidarity builds around stories of raids, gun battles and epic chases after stolen animals. His bravery brings him fame and prestige. Much of the pastoral identity performed by Turkana herders is constructed around raiding, which therefore is more than a means to acquire cattle for weddings, secure new resources or expand territory. It also plays a role in the performance of being *raiya*. Such warrior identity, and the reputation of fierce fighter, is rendered visible on the warrior body by a set of marks cut over his skin to cleanse away the blood of the enemy which entered the fighter's body at the moment of death.

Gendered performances of being *raiya* (both masculine and feminine) are infused with everyday practices of attention to livestock (as manifested in the affection felt by women and men for their animals), aesthetics (as shown by the attention to beauty and attire employed by both Turkana men and women) and epic (as shown by the warrior profile aspired to by young men and general capacity of both genders to sustain hardship). Additionally, through the portrayal of wealthy Turkana herders, a distinctive moral personhood also emerges, one which entails diligence, hard work, thorough knowledge of the environment, trustworthiness and generosity. Vigdis and Todd in the famous book *The Poor Are Not Us* also describes how, among Turkana herders, wealth is woven into a moral economy (1999), and a variety of key ethical values are central for the construction of *raiya* as moral personhood. Both profiles of successful woman and man show a moral code implicit in being successful *raiya*: hard work, pride and dignity, integrity, hospitality, generosity and responsibility. It is around aesthetics, epic and ethics that the 'basic stuff of social life', going back to Turner, of being *raiya* is organised and a collective identity performed.

Such an ideal type acts as a threshold of reference. Turkana language does not have a specific word for poor, as reported by Müller-Dempf: *ekechodon* (temporary lack of animals), *elongait* (no relatives), *ekebotoonit* (no animals) (2014a). Poverty is explained to outsiders (so that we can understand) by subtraction of what it means to be successful, and it entails rotten morals which break costumes, bring disrespect and transgression. As reported by participants in the focus group in Lorengelup:

> A poor woman wears clothes which are worn out and her single child is mal-nourished. She is poor because she is lazy and does not do much during the day. Her children do not have a father. She wears acacia thorns as earrings, as she cannot afford beads and bracelets. She is dirty, she forgets about hygiene and flies follow her. Her house is messy and her stock very small. At most she has three goats, no donkeys or camels or cows. She begs, steals and drinks. She does not have love for herself and cannot be helped. If one tries, she will take advantage to steal from the supporting household.

Described in these terms, a poor woman appears hopeless and helpless, stuck in conditions of poverty without room for manoeuvre to uplift her living standards. Conversely a poor man is seemingly always accorded the possibility to redeem his status, and thus is described with slightly more sympathy by the FGD participants:

> He has only one wife and few children. A small stock and dogs can be found in his house. He is very irresponsible, cannot be trusted and does not take his duties seriously – not even looking after his stock that gets lost or raided frequently – and this being the major reason for his poverty. Nonetheless, he is very friendly and talkative. He knows how to impress people who will offer him support. As long as he is not lazy, he can make his way out of poverty because of his good skills at crafting articles which he can sell or finding wild fruit that he can stock to sustain his family through the dry season, and his good attitudes towards learning new things.

Figure 37. Poor Turkana woman and man

Drawings from the focus group along Lorengelup stream.

Traits of aesthetics, epic and ethics, as well as stoicism and toughness through hardship, are unwritten scripts of being *raiya*. These scripts were presented quite definitively to the extent of becoming stereotypical characterisation of themselves, especially when in opposition to urban counterparts. As they convey notions of membership and belonging, collective identities encompass endless comparisons between in-group and out-group characteristics (Brewer and Gardner 1996) and these dynamics inevitably foster processes of othering. Membership of a group implies self-stereotyping by the individual member, and the emphasis on the *we* category, as elucidated by Brewer and Gardner, through specific collective character-istics implies the 'need to belong' to a certain group as opposed to another (1996).

In the next section I explore how *raiya* see town dwellers and also how they cross the divide of their reciprocal constructed identities in the social imaginary, that of being *raiya* and town dweller; this is not a comparative analysis of *raiya* vs town, but a representation of the *social imaginary* as portrayed by Turkana herders.

On food and no-food

Identities in opposition

Anything that belongs to the locals is better left for the locals; what belongs to the
foreign home is better left to the foreigners.

MALE ELDER, 2016

The guys of Lore centre. Lorengelup, Turkana Central. October 2015.

Everybody is laughing loudly. They are laughing at Ejomu when he exaggeratedly jokes, 'you would die of starvation if you travelled with her!' Everything started when people were amused to see me and my assistant, Ejomu, drinking a whole mug of tea with salty water and fresh goat milk in a single sip. It was midday and this cup of sugared tea contained our first calories of the day. People who were hiding from the midday sun with us inside someone's hut could not believe a town girl (and *mzungu* too) could drink goat milk. Beyond towns and road settlements, only the strongest can possibly make it, while 'town people eat children's food'. *Raiya* believe town people cannot cope with hunger and thirst and would let themselves die craving for food if they lived as *raiya* do. Sentences like 'they went to sit and earn; they are lazy and do not walk; they only worry about food'; proudly framed the conversation around our sugared tea, broken by sonorous laughs. The social imaginary of being *raiya* also prescribes what being a town dweller entails, to the extent of reproducing a flipped narrative of vulnerability. Such a dichotomy between *raiya* and town dwellers is reproduced in narratives and memories of *raiya's* collective past. However, dichotomisation of being is not as strongly performed in the everyday: practices of appropriation, adaptation and imitation show great responsiveness to change and the fluid character of constructed cultural identities.

Town dwellers

Raiya markedly distinguish themselves from their urban counterparts. Differences in behaviour, taste, diet, fashion and convivial habits become expressions of different social worlds which *raiya* use to position themselves with respect to the broader society. Town life is firstly imagined as a life of absence. Absence of livestock, sense of community and one's own purpose.

> If it is that difference you needed [I was asking Akamaise about the difference between pastoral and settled life], what I forgot to tell you is that I am not missing anything. This is the traditional way of living. I have all the traditional things including *akurum, etio, akutwom*, I have animals. Someone who lives in town is the one who knows the absence and wants to have a chair, a permanent house, buy land [a plot].

Even though family separation and mobility have always been part of mobile pastoralist livelihoods, as described by scholars such as Ahearn-Ligham (2016) and Chatty (1996, 2013), absence, 'that which is not there' and 'that which is missing' (Bille, Hastrup and Sørensen 2010; Meier, Frers, and Sigvardsdotter 2013), is learnt and known in settled spaces like towns and road settlements, as Akamaise, one of my host mothers, clearly points out in the extract from our conversation reported above: to fill up such absence people buy, own and build. From the perspective of *raiya*, the first absence experienced in towns is that of animals. Animals give food and money and thus provide a double access: to rural spaces where they belong; to towns when converted into means (fungible value of livestock). Livestock also gives much more. It gives respect, honour and the right of belonging to a community, which town counterparts lack: 'We can celebrate weddings with animals and have the right to participate in *akiriket*'. Animals, in addition, provide good and meaningful food: 'You can enjoy the good taste of fresh milk'. Food eaten in rural areas is tastier, healthier and makes people stronger. As also narrated about other pastoral societies in the world, like the Bedouin of *Mobile Pastoralists: Development Planning and Social Change in Oman*, described by Dawn Chatty (1996), livestock has a dual value: material and symbolic. The symbolic value plays a significant role for the wellbeing of pastoral societies, signifying their independence and sense of purpose. Livestock is also essential to welcome visitors and build one's own reputation for generosity.

In towns open spaces are also lacking as people build their homes crowded together. Life is expensive because 'you pay almost for everything': you pay for rent, you pay for food, you pay for medicines, 'you even pay for toilets!' People in town are idle, lazy, bored. Livestock keeping is recognised as a hard task, but also a beautiful and fulfilling one which 'keeps awful thinking away' and helps find solutions to problems on your own with no need to 'wait for salaries'.

Perhaps the biggest absence in town is one's own purpose. 'People in town only worry about food and money. In town you cannot get animals. You work to have money to buy food. This is all you care about'. This inevitably leads to loss of dignity and self-respect. It leads to a tame life where 'there is nothing [important] to do'. Settled life is described as a life where you 'sit and wait', with no real goal or important tasks to accomplish. 'Real life is when you build your house, shake your milk and eat the product of your animals'; which is not possible in towns. Missing a reference identity – feeling part of a group, and traditions – harsh staying-without is also experienced by town youths.

The paradox of absence[128] in town is signified by *things* owned to replace what is lacking: animals, milk, fat, free space, purpose and feeling of control over one's life. When all this disappears, 'when the world disappears, then we will squeeze next to the government, but space will be too little', Akamaise continues. Town life is imagined with fear. To 'have a chair, a permanent house, buy land [a plot]', is not an easy task, as Akamaise concludes her reflection on settled life:

> … the person who has not gone to school, the survivors of the new changes of life, nothing can suit them in the new life in town. Those who are not learned [those who did not go to school] grow thin in town.

In towns tradition has got lost, forgotten in a cooking pot of alcohol: clothing changes, language change, habits change. Alcohol distracts men (and women) from their jobs and often this causes fights and there are often conflicts in towns. *Raiya* also believe that 'people in urban places dress poorly'. Many explained how trousers, shorts and modern clothes are refused by *raiya* because they are not considered appropriate. 'Moral decadence in towns is high, for example town people drink excess alcohol and don't follow the norms of tradition'. They do not have

---

128. In the geography and anthropology literature of absence, absence is considered to have paradoxical qualities referring to the *presence* of absence in people's lives.

a sense of respect towards elders, and do not adhere to traditional customs. They do not know how to treat visitors and are generally lazy and irresponsible, lacking the moral personhood and toughness typical of *raiya*, who instead can walk long distances, stay without food and water and still carry out their daily tasks.

Town people have no knowledge about or care for the environment. Town is dirty, polluted, noisy, crowded, 'and if we kept animals there, they would be eating paper and old clothes, instead of grass'. Many approach town people, their habits and their customs, as causing the degradation they can observe over their land. Towns have diverted grass.

> Prolonged drought I think may happen because of urbanisation. In the past there were no vehicles and modern things, rain was in plenty and there was grass – now there is no grass.[129]

> … pollution from towns prevents rain from falling and grass from growing.[130]

Finally, in towns, urban centres and along roads, relief aid brought by the government or by foreigners ostensibly reduces, little by little, until nothing reaches the targeted beneficiaries in rural areas. People who do not live in *lolines* walk long distances during distribution days and often go back empty-handed: transportation people, distribution people, chiefs, shopkeepers, villagers, are some of the people blamed for taking too much from aid distributions; in some cases, selling it back to locals or using it for their own livestock.

The dichotomisation between *raiya* and town dwellers emerges even more strongly in a context of fast changing socio-economy and politics, in a world practically full of urbanities, one which sees pastoral livelihoods turning into a marginalised majority against expanding town elites, as described in the doctoral thesis by Cory Rodgers *Rural, Remote, Raiya: Social Differentiation on the Pastoralist Periphery in Turkana, Kenya* (2018). The existence of a collective identity is thus used to position oneself within a broader society which is fast changing, especially since devolution. In this context, a process of othering in relation to growing urbanities is also reproduced in the polarisation of memories skewed towards a plentiful past compared to a shameful present of decay and scarcity, in which food becomes a 'locus of historically constructed identity' (Holtzman 2009). In such memories, despite strong elements of *cultural nostalgia*, taste serves as an assessment of the social world which manifests through food, and as a marker of identity.

---

129. Young man, FN, Ngiipae, 14 Nov. 2016.
130. Young man, FN, Kaikol, 17 Nov. 2016.

On food and no-food

Memories of taste

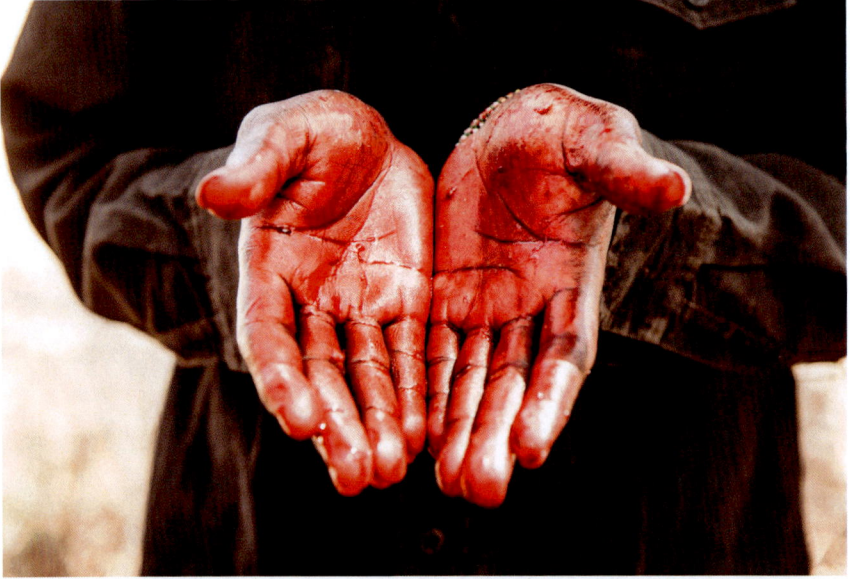

Hands after the slaughter of a bull, Urum. December 2016.

Hands while cleaning maize from stones, Lorengelup. January 2016.

In an article by Emily Keightley, memory is defined as the 'process of making sense of experience, of constructing and navigating complex temporal narratives and structures and ascribing meaning not only to the past but to the present and future also' (2010: 56). Some scholars have shown food as a valued artefact for inner sensory memory (Counihan and Van Esterik 2013; Monsutti 2010; Sutton 2001). And indeed, with a good dose of nostalgia, through continuous swings between an imagined or real past and present, Turkana herders have reconstructed their past around the distinction between a happy past of plenty and a shameful present of poor food and dependency brought by town dwellers, and outsiders more generally.

Years of plenty

'I was born in *ekaru amuje kimet*, the year to eat fat', remembers Alaar, one of the elders in the village, while walking through Lore plains.

> It was a time of plenty, animals were big and healthy and produced a lot of fat. That's why we called it the year to eat fat. All this land you see here around us, this was all grazing land. Those years we were eating a lot of meat and there also were many *alogita* (age group dances) during which we were given livestock to slaughter and celebrate. I met my first wife in one of those dances. She was beautiful, with red ochre on her body and beautiful beads. During the dry seasons *ewoi* (Acacia) would still be full of ngitit, out of which our animals survived and never suffered. And we were drinking their blood without fear of making them weak. When it rained, we planted millet and sorghum along Turkwel River which we would stock for the dry season and eat together with animal fat and blood. All the food was so delicious and filling. And there was so much that people did not fight. Many crossed these lands when it rained, and we stayed together in peace because we were all Turkana and there was enough for everybody. I remember eating meat soup every day, and milk. People enjoyed the life of milk. We did not know about relief food. We were depending on our own. We did not know about money. Our animals were enough. Women wore only animal skin dresses and men were fierce. That time was a time of happiness. Children were happy and listened to the elders. Our food was so satisfying that we could stay the whole day looking at our animals without being disturbed by hunger.

Years of plenty, as it emerges, are not only valued for their nutritional intake (plenty of meat, meat soup, fat, blood, milk and wild fruit), but also, and mostly, for the emotive and social effects these years had on people. Years of plenty were years of happiness when people could dance without worrying; when people were full of energy; they were strong and proud as they did not need to be helped, but 'depended on their own'. Social friction was minimal. Many met their partners in years of happiness during village dances by the light of full moons, or during migrations with livestock through new places. Plenty of food induces good behaviour, fosters moral personhood and leaves people time to rest from stresses. Pastoral food creates inherently better behaviour. It is generally more satisfying and is conducive to a morality of being that is compromised by the expansion of the *enemy's* foods. A good past of plenty is marked in contrast with an impoverished present when food is lacking, and behaviour has degenerated. Their living has transformed into mere surviving when they have been made slave to their stomach due to food aid.

Years of shame

'And now we live in these years of shame', Alaar continues after my exhortation to tell me how those years of plenty compared to today.

> Almost everything is now lost. There is no grass, no livestock, no *ngitit* (acacia pods), no rain. Now we are eating the government [what the government brings]. We are eating ground maize and salt, and our body grows thin. We have stomach-aches, and adding salt is burning our body. When we drank blood, our body became strong, we ate milk and got fat; when we ate meat there was nothing else to add to your meal. The oil we are using now leaves glue at the bottom of the bottle. The same happens in our stomachs! *Mandeleo* (development) brought us shame. Children have back pains like old people and remain with appetite in the heart [hungry].

A whole set of somatic meanings clustered around notions of health is attributed to *new* foods, which spread through relief operations and *mandeleo*.

> Current food is full of diseases, like *edeke moruariiwan* (stomach pain).[131]

> All body parts are in pain. When we eat animal products our body becomes light and one can even decide to run. But nowadays after we have eaten these new foods, we have known their bad effects and we refuse to eat them.[132]

These were some of the words spoken about *new* foods of which maize is the most significant – perhaps because the most disliked, or because the cheapest to purchase, or the cheapest to distribute for relief organisations and hence the easiest to find in someone's home. Maize is not liked because it is associated with diseases, which were absent in old foods, and because it is tasteless, not like eating meat

---

131. Middle-aged woman, FN, Nangorichoto, 15 Nov. 2016.
132. Middle-aged woman, FN, Lorengelup, 16 Jan. 2016.

when 'there was nothing else to add to your meal'. It is also extremely difficult to cook, it takes long hours and yet remains 'hard as stones' (and it also comes with stones in the relief bags – carefully removing these one by one is a newly introduced everyday practice).

> Akamaise: Someone puts *githeri* (beans and maize) on both sides of the mouth, tries to chew but spits maize out.

> Nawoi: That's why the goat is following her like a dog!

> Lopwenya: It has become the goats that are feeding on that white maize, just like a bird.[133]

Maize leads to compromising one's own identity, even that of goats, now acting like dogs or birds. Indeed, *new* foods entail several changes of alimentary structure and family social organisation. Cooking for longer hours implies reduced time for fetching water, wild fruit, firewood. Eating hot food implies reducing distances from the homestead to serve it. And certain cooking utensils have come into use also at cattle camps where men are nowadays 'entering a woman pot'. With these words Lopangach, my host father in Lorengelup, meant that, nowadays, herding boys have learnt to cook like women; while in the years of plenty there was no need for these cooking practices because blood and milk were enough and men could remain men, and not act like women. *New* food has thus not only brought nutritionally less valued intakes but also a whole set of moral degenerations that bring shame, as echoed in an endless litany of laments regarding current years of shame: women are promiscuous because of alcohol consumption, *ngimurok* (seers) reside in towns and become greedy, children lack respect for elders, men are no longer fierce. All these behaviours were absent in the years of plenty.

These statements sounded definitive. A *raiya*, a real Turkana, repels *new* foods brought by the *enemy* [outsiders] and deprecate the social world they have brought through their foods as a world of general decay. And yet, these two imagined worlds are way more intertwined than stated in these accounts. One can imagine the confusion I felt every time I was asked to tell the government they needed more food aid; that all 'good things follow the road, and here we are left fighting with thorns'; or that my hosts wished to have permanent houses, a business and money to buy food; or my disorientation during the fights I saw around food-aid distributions to grab more maize, the same maize that was so much disliked. During these episodes, I assisted in the origination of what Hobsbawm and Ranger

---

133. FN, Lorengelup, 16 Jan. 2016.

called 'counter-narratives' embedded in the implementation of new practices and traditions (1992), which linger over a representation of the self as pure and detached from 'things of town and modernity', but are in reality embedded in daily practices which draw from both social worlds, those of *raiya* and town dwellers, indicating a broader process of social, economic, and political transformation and the coexistence of fluid identities.

Sometimes I have the impression of being the stereotype of myself, and beyond myself. Some mornings I even go jogging along Turkwell river with our adopted dog. Something that I have rarely, if ever, done before. I am performing an identity that in reality is confused. I am white, I am a woman, I enjoy the paucity of rural life but I am also physically and mentally tired and I hold on to my flight back home. I prefer eating local, but I love flavours from many parts of the world. I study and try to do most things that I can with my hands. I travel and wish to grow a garden. In the mixed lives that open to my eyes while walking through Lodwar streets, I lose and find myself several times

---

Ambivalence and fluid identities

Anthropologists have adduced evidence for the discontinuity between self-descriptions and social behaviour being the norm rather than the exception (Santopietro 2015), an incompatibility which Turner calls 'social drama' (1987). Mainstream narratives, such as individual sense of solidarity with a certain social identity, do not necessarily correspond with the same individual's everyday practices (difference between ideal and actual behaviour). Greater variation and heterogeneity emerge within everyday performances of being *raiya* beyond its dichotomisation against urbanities as reproduced in the social imaginary. By 'stylistic playing', as reported in Rodgers' study of Turkana herders (2018: 149), or by reproducing slow social change, as argued by Holtzman (2009) about Samburu identity's adaptations to modernity, *raiya* are also incorporating foods and traits representative of their urban counterparts. However, I like to emphasise that such contradictions found in people's narratives do not imply those accounts shall be discarded. Rather, this shows how reformulations of the self and collective identity undergo multiple, at times contradictory, processes. Contradictions, between principles and practices, are not mutually exclusive. Rather, they show the coexistence of multiple identities

and an underlying fluidity of social worlds, which are not organised by dichotomies but navigate across imagined social boundaries. This is a salient dimension
of personal resilience.

The pastoralist diet (expression of physical potential and beauty, independence and integrity, as described above) is now at odds with an 'identity built
around maize' (Holtzman 2009: 1). Ground maize-flour (*epocho*) and beans have
become a very common staple food and are found in most homesteads. Grains
are not entirely new to the Turkana diet, having always played an important role
in exchanges with agriculturalists, but the variety of white maize made available
through the provision of relief food and the spread of small rural shops, has only
emerged in the last sixty years and has entered daily and ritual food practices. For
example, *akuuta* (wedding ceremony), one of the most loved ceremonies, concludes
with a big pot of *epocho* (mixed with wild fruit), signifying the incorporation of new
foods within *traditional* practices. Tea and sugar have been so much incorporated
into daily practices as to have now acquired the status of *traditional* food despite
being born in faraway plantations and equally as imported as other new foods. It
is not rare, either, to find salt, vegetable oil and *Royco* (stock cube) and, in some
families, even rice and spaghetti. All the herders I met or stayed with depend on
purchased food, regardless of how much they dismiss it. While I was migrating
with two young brothers and their shoats in Turkana central plains, we were hiding
our bags of maize and beans in holes dug in the ground to prevent squirrels stealing them from us. And we also diverted our route to restock our provisions from
a small rural shop known to be outside someone's hut. But mainly we diverted
to charge their mobile phones through solar panels leant over the shop's walls, a
service which cost them 20 *shilling* (approximately 20 cents). We watched music
videos and listened to phone ringtones at night while lying on a carpet of shrubs
and sand, next to an improvised *anok* (kraal).

Contradictions between declared hostility to what comes from towns and
daily practices of imitation and incorporation of town habits and articles is not
confined to food practices but affects all aspects of social life as western items are
replacing *traditional* ones. In the following picture (already shown in Chapter 4
about the lightness and versatility of herders' possessions), I now want to highlight
another point. Among the few objects the two shepherd brothers were travelling
with were a pot and a discarded bit of metal with a wire as holding ring used to
cook maize (as well as a plastic bag which contained maize and beans).

Figure 38. The herders' possessions

The young herders explained that they had bought the pot at a local market, and expressed pride at having found the discarded metal next to an abandoned building site. They had incorporated into their daily practices articles from a repertoire belonging to their urban counterparts, and with distinctive resourcefulness were weaving together two counterposed lifestyles in their social imaginary. The same approach to recycling was often explained to me in regard to abandoned plastic pipes once meant for borehole or irrigations schemes never brought to final implementation. The rubber is re-used in multiple ways including to make blade covers, small tobacco containers, armbands and other decorations.

Turkana herders have also incorporated items into their wardrobe and accessories in addition to the attires and clothes described earlier in this chapter. Skirts, trousers and shorts are not rare to see even in remote bushlands, as the catalogues of products sold in rural shops display. Many women asked if I could give them my bra and admitted not to using 'real clay from the base of the mountain, but a coloured paint bought in shops'.

Figure 39. The fuchsia garland for akuuta

Another striking example of outfits which do not suit a *raiya's* closet was the adornment shown by Lokir during the wedding of his son. He wore his favourite collared dark green shirt and exhibited long and well cared white feathers over his head. Hed had a black *elado*, from the tail of an ox in his hands to shake during *edonga*. Around his neck he wore a fuchsia garland possibly found abandoned on the ground at the end of some formal event. It made me smile, but I soon realised how resourceful such a gesture appeared to other attendees at the wedding. The disdain for urban life was overcome with the appropriation of attires and articles that felt glamourous, like the improvised scarf worn by Lokir, and practical, like the discarded metal used by the shepherd brothers. The capacity to select specific traits from the culture of *rayia's* urban counterparts 'removing the meaning conveyed and replacing with their own' shows that the constructed *social imaginary* remains fundamentally open, polythetic and with 'fuzzy borders', as Roma scholar Piasere puts it (2009: 91). All this shows features of constant reformulations of the self and the malleability of *traditions* and social positionalities, as well as the possible harmony between combinations of narratives and practices, starting from food practices. Monsutti, speaking about young Afghans, argues that food becomes an arena in which identities are negotiated in their complexity and shows the coexistence of multiple narratives (2010). The emphasis on a *raiya* diet and the omission of other types of food not perceived as strictly *raiya* reinforces the idea of a cultural identity, a sense of solidarity around one's own imagined and performative living: a nomadic lifestyle where food available originates only from cattle, camels and flocks. Claiming that one disdains foods from outsiders is a clear identity message, a performative resistance to expanding urbanities. Hence, on the one hand, maize represents all which is lost: a nutritionally superior diet; a culturally greater people, tougher and exhibiting more moral behaviour. Through this perspective, *mandeleo* (development) is seen advancing together with poverty and tasteless food – foods that signify cultural decay eroding aspects of moral personhood as represented in the memories of *years of shame*. However, on the other hand, these changes are also seen as signs of progress. Thanks to these new foods, people nowadays no longer die from hunger. This food is easier to obtain, without the endless struggles of follow-ing livestock. 'We can rest from all these movements' (migration with livestock). I explain these counter-narratives and ambivalences on the basis of the inherently mutable character of *tradition*, a word that Hobsbawm and Ranger claim was in-vented by anthropologists (1992), and on the skills to navigate the complex *social imaginary*, weaving dichotomies together.

First, being in the midst of broader social, economic and political changes one finds oneself grappling between one's ideal behaviour and a changing land-scape which imposes new practices. With this perspective, I confirm Turner's and colleagues' idea that self-categorisation is inherently variable (1994) and highly dependent on contextual shifts (Brewer and Gardner 1996). The *raiya* identity is adaptive to changing conditions as their way of interpreting *modernity*. Pfaffen-berger, cited in Chatty (1996), says: 'every human society is a world in the process of becoming in which people are engaged in the active technological elaboration, appropriation, and modification of artefacts as the means of coming to know themselves and of coordinating labour to sustain their lives'. What appears as *spontaneous change* in any society is often the result of limited but continuous and ongoing experimentation (1996: 126).

Second, social identities are fluid and malleable. Being *raiya* is more flexibly performed in the everyday in which multiple identities coexist and can be acti-vated at different times. The ability to navigate the social imaginary corresponds to Brewer and Gardner's theory of relational identity, by which the *we* category, *raiya* in this case, coexists with one or several self-categories that can all be used at different times, creating flexible self-representations. The *raiya* category can thus be better described through a 'fuzzy epistemology' (Piasere 2009), a categorisation that is not based on the principle of contradiction or on bounded socio-cultural groups, but on a kaleidoscopic set of cultural traits that, on a case by case basis, come together differently, creatively borrowing features from urban counterparts when these are perceived to be in their own interest.

Through the ambivalences and contradictions presented in this section, Turkana herders have shown a great responsiveness to changes in the surrounding social landscape, including the growth of non-pastoral populations, as well as the fluid nature of their being. Admittedly, this is easier said than done. As argued by Ferguson, people can surely shift among different styles as long as they acquire the ability to do so competently (1999). He thus recognises the difficulty of altering identities, and indeed many complained of the difficulties of town lifestyles and the new things they would have to learn. To recall Akamaise's feelings about towns:

> … the person who has not gone to school, the survivors of the new changes of life, nothing can suit them.

However, regardless of how difficult this is, I believe such flexibility of identity proves useful in negotiating relationships among dichotomies in a changing and variable social landscape. The ability to negotiate their own identity gives Turkana herders larger access in a highly variable lifeworld. As argued by Rodgers (2018), the resilience of pastoralism does not involve the persistence of its forms, but the ways it re-articulates itself in the face of contemporary variabilities. As many others have argued, longstanding pastoralist practices and relationships should be examined not as fixed elements underlying a flexible set of responses, 'but rather as things that are themselves perpetually under construction, always open to redefinition in the face of a changing world' (Derbyshire et al. 2021: 18 see also; Galaty 2013; Lesorogol 2008). Turkana herders' lifestyle and livelihood are not tragically disappearing by being incorporated in the corrosive hands of modernity; rather Turkana are creatively reworking their values, sensitivities and self-representations to make a meaningful living. As argued by Chatty, we can no longer support theories of conservatism towards change (2013). Conversely, Turkana herders show a flexible identity which engages with forms of *modernity* while maintaining a sense of solidarity around certain distinctive traits of food, no-food, fashion and convivial habits. That is, in the negotiation of identity, Turkana herders show intrinsic mutability but also a degree of resistance and determination never to be free from *themselves*, as in the song by Bob Dylan: 'Are birds free from the chains of the skyways?'[134]

---

134. 'Ballad in Plain D'. 1964. Track 10 on *Another Side of Bob Dylan*.

I am still waiting for the transcriptions from the first six months of fieldwork. My research assistant kept on promising he had it ready, just misplaced: in his friend's laptop, his mother's USB, at home. 'I am walking to give it to you'. This is my last night. I am leaving tomorrow morning. This time I booked a flight to Nairobi.

Resilience and mobile identities

Notions of belonging, as reproduced and experienced by Turkana herders, can be a renewed site for the investigation of the meanings of resilience. Relying on ideas of performance by Turner (1987) and of relational identities by Brewer and Gardner (1996), I explored how Turkana herders present themselves in comparison to their urban counterparts, subverting dominant narratives of vulnerability, which most typically describe herders as vulnerable to hunger and food security. Conversely, *raiya* have built a sense of solidarity around their own hunger. Belonging is expressed in the form of toughness, endurance and ecological-situatedness, reproduced in the everyday through *gendered performances* around norms of aesthetics, epic qualities and ethics of being *raiya*.

Food was the opening analytical lens for this chapter because I was con-stantly reminded of my position among Turkana herders as the one in need of food. This positionality was at odds with the development discourse of pastoralists' vulnerability to food insecurity. The complex performances of hunger I observed in Turkana complicate the relationship between food insecurity, hunger and vulner-ability. Being accustomed to the place, *having gone through* and having learnt to *stay-without* are the primary elements in the creation of a collective identity which is a tool of *inner resilience*. However, in the lived everyday, the opposition between *raiya* and town dwellers is far less sharp. In common with other nomadic pastoralist groups, 'raiya continue to change, to adapt, and at times to spontaneously adopt techniques, technologies, and ideas they perceive to be their own interests' (Chatty 1996:190). The initial impression of a homogenous community of rural herders was countered by daily practices of imitation and appropriation of articles, attire, lifestyles found in urban centres. I have explained this observation by resorting to the notion of *ambivalence* proposed by Holtzman (2009) as a symptom of broader social, economic and political changes, and through the logic of *fuzzy epistemology* which explains the fluidity of one's own *being*. A mobility of being according to evolving situations is a mechanism employed to navigate socio-economic variabilities and different cultural environments. By navigating variability, through the *immediate* (see Chapter 4) and the *social imaginary* (this chapter), Turkana herders, r*aiya*, help broaden an understanding of resilience by incorporating its socio-cultural dimensions, and by disrupting categories, labels and identities. Mobility is the response I learnt with my host families to a mobile lifeworld, one that would never close its borders, imaginal, physical, perceived borders, because to be mobile in its many manifestations (quality of space, something people do and quality of identities) is to be resilient.

My research assistant is walking to my place to give me the USB with all his transcriptions, and I am waiting sitting on my doorsteps. The sand is colouring the wind red. I wonder if it is a spirit. I am still sitting when night falls. He switched off his phone. 'Stop being blind' says my hungry flatmate, dragging me to dinner. My farewell dinner. I keep on calling Eregae for the whole night. The phone is switched back on only at 4.00 a.m., but I hang-up: what is the point now? I wake up early, at 6.00 a.m. I am knocking loudly at my research assistant's door. He lives with his mother, his wife and his daughter. I wake everybody up. He slouches across the yard. 'I have not done it'.

～ Afterword. ～

Mobility, change, resilience

Ellos se llaman hijos de las nubes, porque desde siempre persiguen la lluvia.
Desde hace más de treinta años persiguen, también, la justicia,
que en el mundo de nuestro tiempo parece más esquiva
que el agua en el desierto.

They are known as the children of the clouds, for they have forever chased the rain.
For over thirty years, they have chased something else as well –
justice, more elusive in our time than water in the heart of the desert

GALEANO 2013, QUOTED IN VOLPATO (2025).

Walking back home with the herd. The other side of Lake Turkana, April 2016.

doi: 10.63308/63891908548751.after

Mobility, change, resilience

My host mother in Lorengelup, Akamaise, quite abruptly, as she used to, would say now: 'My story ends here'. She used to leave her stories semi-open, with food for the imagination of her listeners, and multiple possible endings. In the same way, through my attentive body, I listened to, saw, tasted, touched, experienced and tried to narrate a story of mobility, change, re-articulation and resilience. I did so by means of ethnographic exploration and writing, hoping to 'bring a people and a place to life in the eyes and hearts of those who have not been there' (Nordstrom 2004). I owe everything to my host families. It is thanks to them that I started seeing the world upside down, like a herder, from a different vantage point, as Gabriele Volpato writes through a 'relational ecology, a web of entanglements' (2025: 84), in which 'men, camels, insects, animals, plants, birds, sand, gravel, dust, even the rocks themselves had fused into a single harmonious whole' (Michael Asher cited in Volpato 2025: 84). The world of Turkana herders, like the world of all pastoralists I have met, is communally constructed and born out of direct lived experience. Their moving through the world results in weaving a fabric of desires, expectations, values, meanings and obligations as well as perception, knowledge and culture. In such a fabric, stories and agencies of the more-than-humans come to the foreground in a 'project of co-becoming' (Hustak and Myers 2012), which brings forth the landscape itself, in this case the drylands, in a process of continuous place-making.

Such emic understanding of an animate landscape contrasts with the 'detached ecology' (Großmann 2017) inscribed in the colonial and postcolonial language of crisis and disasters and associated attributions of wasteland and *terra nullius* to desert expanses, only functional for the appropriation of nature and resources (Volpato 2025). Today drylands are at best seen as 'places with potential' (food baskets, green energy hubs, carbon markets and so forth), but the other side of the coin, as my friend Tahira Mohamed and her colleagues maintain, is that these are seen as 'in need of urgent development and transformation' (2025: 10). Under such a lens, not only do we fail to truly unlock the potential of the drylands by understanding variability as a valuable resource rather than attempting to control it or manage it by means of uniformity and stability, but also pastoral livelihoods continue being undermined. Their work in forging and preserving territories is unrecognised, their ingenuity and skills are unnoticed and their sensitivities are disrespected. In these views, nomadic pastoralism remains a barrier to modernity and development, instead of a quite innovative heuristic to confront today's challenges, one above all: climate change (Krätli et al. 2022; Semplici and Campbell

2023). Nomadic pastoralism continues to be envisaged as driven by immutable knowledge passed down from generation to generation, rather than founded on 'dynamic learning, improvisation and creativity' (Derbyshire et al. 2024: 9). It is seen as working under sub-optimal conditions rather than 'working with nature' in responding to logics of variability and high reliability (FAO 2021; Roe 2020). In other words, we can fairly say that, despite decades of scientific revaluation of both drylands and pastoral populations, their struggle continues.

Despite pastoral systems having been around for about 9,000 years, they are recurrently under threat and perceived to be on the brink of collapse. It was in the 1990s that Khazanov wrote, 'Their past was unique, their present is transition … and as for the future, they have no future at all if present tendencies continue' (Khazanov 1990). Pastoral systems clearly still exist, and this is largely thanks to their distinct orientation towards uncertainty, their capacities to remain open and flexible, and their quite modern mindsets, forged on a collection of habits and institutions derived from both direct and inherited experience, established on the back of many generations of iterative change and adaptation. All these are part of what I call *resilience*. However, the sentiment and evidence of a sector in crisis persists, and indeed pastoralists across the world face numerous challenges, ranging from climate vulnerability to economic impoverishment and political marginalisation. According to an increasing number of scholars, such challenges are the outcome of ill-informed policies and interventions that undermine the adaptability of pastoralist systems. In other words, while generally the failure of development intervention is attributed, as Caravani and colleagues write, to a range of design and implementation errors including implementation flaws, poor governance, lack of coordination, lack of funds and so forth, 'it would be perhaps more honest to question the premises of the interventions themselves' (2022: 5). And so, more or less direct promotion of sedentarisation, provision of basic services to settled population, creation of permanent water sources, incentives for cash-crops and industrialisation, even commercialisation policies and livestock marketing can carry substantial risks as soon as they have the side effects of curtailing mobility, fragmenting rangelands, preventing access to grazing opportunities and water. By these means, pastoral populations are exposed and made vulnerable to the environment they specialise in using, while they see their core production strategies hampered. This leads to a vicious cycle, as Krätli and colleagues write: 'the more vulnerable pastoralists appear, the more they are prescribed the same old medicine: sedentarisation and exit from pastoralism' (2022: 1). Similar issues incur for technocratic management systems, such as early warnings, scientific forecasting and rangeland monitoring that, despite numerous cases of inaction or ineffective action, are gaining momentum across the world. An assessment by Samuel Derbyshire and colleagues shows how these have mainly served to centralise decision making, exclude local actors and institutions, and impose calculative control and reduction of uncertainty oriented toward a return to *normal* or *stable* conditions, thus lacking flexibility and the ability to experiment, improvise and fail that is so central to pastoral livelihoods (2024). There is, in other words, a substantial disconnect between programming and pastoralist practices on the ground (Mohamed et al. 2025).

Through the story of Turkana herders presented in this book I have tried to show how pastoral livelihoods more generally manage uncertainty while achieving relative stability of production. At the core of their livelihood there is *work with nature* rather than separation from it, which makes of pastoralism the innovation we are looking for to confront today's challenges, the best bet for a future of care for the environment, sustainable production and co-existence of men, animals and nature. By *seeing like the herder*, we regain a view of a space that moves through continuous reconfigurations across coexisting socio-ecological niches. I truly loved reading the pages by Gabriele Volpato in his recent book *Desert Entaglements* where he describes the desert coming to life.

> The sounds, smells, and sights that haunt refugees and against which they measure their present are the sounds of the wind blowing through the acacia trees, of the acute bleats of the goats and the low grunts of camels … They are the smells of the air when rain is approaching and of the flowers of the desert in the milk; they are the sights of a black galb, of a familiar well, of the flat horizon populated by camel silhouettes … westerlies cloud the sky, their patchy and almost accidental watery release triggers life to animate an otherwise barren landscape … Seeds, perhaps dormant for decades, absorb the water retained by the narrow layer of clay and silt particles descending from ancient rock weathering … Herbs and grasses shoot toward the sky, or creep over the gravel and the sand, greening the landscape and coloring it with short-living flowers … Plants dig down into the ground, where their root tips meet layers of ancient soils and their organic matter, which is mobilized from the past to reconstitute the present … Where larger stones, also outcome of past erosion by water, ice, and wind, congregate, the shaded ground may retain humidity that condenses during the cold desert nights, permitting the birth and growth of shrubs that will keep flashing green after annual herbs have dried up … Along the dry and sandy riverbeds, acacia trees and shrubs spread their roots wide to profit from light rains and push them deep down to intercept the water below … Animal life concurrently thrives. (2025:101)

With the same intention, I showed that resources are available even in apparently barren landscapes like the Turkana drylands, and these are co-produced by the joint action of biotic organisms (humans, livestock, wild animals, insects, bacteria and many more) and abiotic factors (rain, water, soil and the like) moving along with a mobile landscape. In this way, resources are more than mere *things* out there at people's disposal but are the product of a relationship. Important questions are when, where, for whom and for what purposes resources are available, namely relational questions of accessibility that do not only depend on physical dimensions of space (landforms, terrain, distances), but also climatic (rain), ecological (water and forage), territorial (rights) and social dimensions (human and more-than-human relationships). These questions are shared, discussed, contested, hidden and negotiated among herders through their wayfaring across the territory as a process of knowledge creation and transmission to new generations. My data bring evidence of how generated knowledge about the lived space is encoded in the environment which, in turn, becomes agentive and available also in symbolic terms, perceptually, through shared beliefs, use of amulets, and ritual life. In this way, Turkana herders mark their belonging to a territory which acquires a wider significance. Remoteness is used by Turkana herders as *grass-root resistance* against forces of modernisation, upon which they have built a *raiya* identity as expression of solidarity and belonging to a livelihood group (rural herders), but also entailing a lifestyle, certain codes of aesthetics and ethical behaviour: the model of a *hero*, a *survivor* in a fast deteriorating society corrupted by rising modern forces emanating from urban centres and a growing urban elite. During fieldwork with my host families, I could observe their toughness, inurement to *staying-without* and observance of customs but also the creativity and malleability of their identity by means of appropriation and imitation of elements from the urban world and adaptation to changes in society. Resilience rests in both: people's capacity to capitalise on their marginality, forming solidarity through a shared identity and its everyday performances (a component of *resistance* of the self is necessary for a theory of resilience), and in the ambivalences and contradictions managed in the everyday, symptomatic of the skill to incorporate new elements as situations evolve and change. Turkana pastoralism is characterised by high dynamism, intense mobility and livelihood flexibility. Under this logic, Turkana herders opportunistically build and unbuild *lolines* that pop up along improved roads and telecommunication infrastructure and contribute to the overall nomadism of the lived space. From these observations, I challenge dominant views about nomadism and sedentism and I show that settlements are not the end of mobility, far from it. They are a form of dynamic space-configuration that continuously takes new shapes out of multiple pathways followed by Turkana herders, in and out, demonstrating a longstanding orientation toward uncertainty. As Derbyshire and colleagues argue, the exploitation of a new resource such as relief aid (food or cash) or a road by which to sell charcoal is an 'interpretation of pastoralism that works best for the situation at hand', and there is no reason to believe that recent years of livelihood adaptation represent any form of rigidification (2021: 11). They are rather a manifestation of a habitude of change and opportunism. Along similar lines, livelihood making is based on intimate herding, breeding and training skills. It is based on detailed and perceptive knowledge of the territory, attentiveness and rootedness in place. It is based on a complex and articulated governance, established on accountable institutions and local culture. And it is based on the utilisation of expansive networks built on diverse social and economic relationships.

Building resilience is thus not a simple technical question. It implies bridging materialistic and constructivist accounts and incorporating in the analysis shifting subjective and collective cultural frameworks to achieve a meaningful comprehension of people's lives and choices. It requires drawing from local knowledges, as an alternative science that delves into a distinct *sense of place* emerging only from within, seeing, experiencing, perceiving. According to Pelling and colleagues, how 'expert analysis interacts with other knowledge traditions in developing more integrated understandings' is currently a central dilemma facing disaster studies' (2020: 120). Certainly, so far, both development and humanitarian aid are underpinned by linear principles and a prioritisation of single sources of knowledge and protocols. On the contrary, pastoralists' practices of disaster risk management are rooted in multiple forms of knowledge coupled with dynamic and agile decision making. Resilience thus emerges as a matter of perspective, and can only be understood locally, in this case by *seeing like the herder* as opposed to the bird's-eye view adopted by practitioners surveying the landscape. Additionally, resilience entails motion within motion, a way of navigation through a mobile social, ecological, economic and cultural terrain; it lies in the possibilities that movement opens. Following from this second point, we can say that resilience is probabilistic and not deterministic. In this, one cannot obtain the same output from given starting or initial conditions (deterministic approach), an uncertain truism alleged by development programmes that aim at enhancing resilience through, for example, the provision of certain productive assets (i.e. cash or livestock), or through the creation of *optimal* (for whom?) conditions (i.e. drilling of boreholes or building fixed social infrastructure). Rather, resilience entails a theory of probability in function of complex forms of variability, emerging from both the *immediate* (the contextual everyday) and the *social imaginary*, thus producing outputs that are themselves subject to or involving chance variation.

Resilience grows out of the *meshwork* of probabilities emerging through mobility. Theoretically, this book has sought to contribute to debates and discussions about resilience in drylands and pastoral settings through the lens of mobility, in its many manifestations (as a quality of space, as something people do and a question of identity). By this, I not only challenge the dominant negative characterisation of mobility as seen by outsiders (creating conditions of insecurity) but I go as far as proposing mobility as part of the solution, an inseparable part of life, an asset and source of strength, structurally part of the behaviour of and in drylands and beyond (see also Pappagallo 2023). Despite the link between mobility and resilience being little explored (or even resisted by imposing barriers to movement), there is a growing recognition that conditions of 'forced immobility' (Lubkemann 2008) can further deepen destitution, vulnerability and insecurity. This book contributes to these literatures, by arguing that resilience rests in the possibilities for mobility. Mobility is therefore not only a cultural narrative of nomadic lives, but a daily production practice, expression of alternative forms of sociality – including that with more-than-humans – enabling socio-economic opportunities and showing kaleidoscopic identities imbued in people's own motivations, aspirations and possibilities.

The challenge ahead of us is twofold. On the one hand, the support of international development and humanitarian aid will remain critical in the years to come, but this will require fundamental changes from design, to funding, implementation, monitoring and evaluation in order to be effective. Without adopting a critical understanding of resilience, the status quo in development operations will be maintained. Operationally, this implies turning resilience into a risk-management exercise (conventional DRR or DRM), characterised by a strong duality between the *insider* (whose problems need to be solved) and the *outsider* (proposing external solutions), continuing to deny agency to the local, thus negating the very meaning of resilience. Under these circumstances, the obvious question is: why resilience? Why bother with setting up a whole new language, without then following up with substantive changes in the architecture of the development sector? Indeed, resilience has been strongly criticised and many have suggested it should be abandoned. Nonetheless, it occurs to me that this still is way beyond the horizon. A *post-resilience era* is seemingly far ahead of us, as resilience continues to dominate policy discourses. Thus, we are left with three options:

1. Accept resilience dogmatically and apply it to various cases;

2. Criticise resilience entirely, in stark opposition to policymakers;

3. Recreate and reconceptualise resilience, as something more significant, poignant and adaptive to the lives of the people we are working with.

Through this book I have demonstrated the capacity of Turkana herders to appropriate elements from their urban counterparts' lives and transform them into something new which makes sense to them, for their needs and desires, as means of innovation and recreation. We should do the same for a new model of international cooperation and development. Many researchers are arguing for basing development efforts on the ways people are already managing uncertainty, and thus emphasising learning, collaboration, adaptation and flexibility (Caravani et al. 2022).

On the other hand, environmental, political and economic turbulence will affect us all, not only pastoral communities in drylands. But it is perhaps precisely from those pastoral communities in drylands that we can learn how to embrace uncertainty, confront ignorance and generate reliability. From them, we can learn about moving, allying with nature and saving fossil fuels. We can learn about multifunctionality as the expression of cooperation, collaboration and community building. We can learn about diversity, circularity and quality. But mostly we can learn about care. Pastoralism is the innovative choice we must make, a bet for the future. A future of care for the land, productive sustainability, and coexistence between humans, animals, and the environment. It is therefore an important choice in facing today's challenges, which require us to rethink the way we inhabit the world.

⁓ Some years later ⁓

May 2025. I've been away from Turkana for eight years. Thanks to one of my research assistants, Peter Ewoton, I managed to maintain connection, we kept on updating each other on our lives, and he gave me news about Turkana, rains and droughts, new government programmes, new research programs, people movements. I had planned to go back to Turkana but Covid struck, and that plan has yet to be realised. Life moves on. This can't be controlled. And that is the greatest teaching from Turkana herders. I followed the steps of south American herders, from Mexico to Argentina, and then I found my own herd. Life can be surprising and banal. I learnt, or better I am learning, that change is necessary but also painful, and that surely resilience nests in the capacity to embrace change instead of resisting it – but also how difficult that is.

I receive an email. I am on maternity leave, just about to give birth. I read it mainly because I am curious about the name of the sender: Acacia. Acacia is doing a Ph.D. at Oxford, like myself years ago. She is doing fieldwork in Turkana and is planning to go to Lorengelup. She is doing a study on water governance, especially intangible (for human senses) ground water, and how local ontologies can be mobilised for development practice. Throughout my study, water has been a critical vantage point. I preferred water coming up from hand dug wells, less salty and fresher than water from drilled boreholes. We walked longer distances to find water during the 2016 drought, but water was never really lacking, and the longer distances were due to security issues rather than scarcity. But I feared jumping down the wells as these were getting deeper and deeper. Time spent around wells was also very immersive. Time of sociality, information sharing, ceremonies and elders' meetings. The walks to water were never only about water but served multiple tasks, from grazing livestock to collecting wild fruit and herbs, locating dead trees for charcoal making, tracking footprints (of both humans and animals), assessing pasture, meeting someone … I was fascinated by the capacity to find hidden water, the intimate knowledge of the territory and the ability to speak more-than-human. And I learnt that water finishes as it flows, and it is better to follow it instead of imprisoning it, as every new borehole has socio-ecological consequences that go much beyond water availability, and frequently they dry up anyway.

I ask Acacia to look for Akamaise, one of my host mothers. In the intervening eight years we have lost track of each other. I hope she is still alive. I often remember the nights spent lying on a camel mat looking at the sky and listening

doi: 10.63308/63891908548751.conc

Some years later

Reconnecting, May 2025, Lorengelup, Turkana Central. Courtesy of Acacia Leakey.

to her stories, which I could understand only for the time my research assistant was awake, but I continued to listen till my eyes were closing too. Acacia finds her. She holds the picture I gave her of us under the Neem tree. How did she manage to conserve it? As a precious thing. She stands firmly under the same Neem tree, which has grown. I can imagine the rest of the homestead. Did they move during all these years? Yes, they did. They kept re-uniting and separating, breaking up in small units, on and off, rapidly and opportunistically responding to livestock and people's needs, and to how their terrain changed. Itiiri, the young girl they wanted me to take back to my home, whom they sent to school so that she could buy a car for her father, is now in form 2 (secondary school). Lopeyok has married. They ask me via Acacia: when will I be back?

I have also moved. Resiliently? We'll see. But I am now able to relate to the ambiguous feelings about mobility, in its broadest meaning, I found among Turkana herders. As my new life takes its course, I feel reassured about Acacia continuing our work of giving voice to hidden beings, both humans and waters.

Akamaise and me, January 2016, Lorengelup, Turkana Central.

～ Bibliography ～

Abbink, John, Kelly Askew, Feyissa Dori Dori, Elliot Fratkin, E.C. Gabbert, John Galaty, Shauna LaTosky, Jean Lydall, Hussein A. Mahmoud, John Markakis, Günther Schlee, Ivo Strecker, David Turton, and Afrika Studiecentrum. 2014. 'Lands of the Future: Transforming Pastoral Lands and Livelihoods in Eastern Africa'. *Max Planck Institute for Social Anthropology Working Papers* (154).

Abel, Nick. 1993. 'Reducing Cattle Numbers of Southern African Communal Range: Is It Worth It?' . In *Range Ecology at Disequilibrium: New Models of Natural Variability and Pastoral Adaptation in African Savannas*, ed. by R.H. Behnke, I. Scoones and C. Kerven. London: Overseas Development Institute.

Adam, Barbara. 1998. *Timescapes of Modernity: The Environment and Invisible Hazards*. London: Routledge.

Adey, Peter. 2006. 'If Mobility Is Everything Then It Is Nothing: Towards a Relational Politics of (Im)Mobilities'. *Mobilities* 1 (1): 75–94. https://doi.org/10.1080/17450100500489080.

Adger, W. Neil. 2000. 'Social and Ecological Resilience: Are They Related?' *Progress in Human Geography* 24 (3): 347–64. https://doi.org/10.1191/030913200701540465.

Ahearn-Ligham, Ariell. 2016. 'The Changing Meaning of Work, Herding and Social Relations in Rural Mongolia'. Ph.D. diss, School of Geography and the Environment, University of Oxford.

Alden Wily, Liz. 2018. 'The Community Land Act in Kenya Opportunities and Challenges for Communities'. *Land* 7 (1): 12. https://doi.org/10.3390/land7010012.

Alexander, David. 1997. 'The Study of Natural Disasters, 1977–97: Some Reflections on a Changing Field of Knowledge'. *Disasters* 21 (4): 284–304. https://doi.org/10.1111/1467-7717.00064.

Anderson, David and Vigdis Broch-Due. 1999. *The Poor Are Not Us: Poverty & Pastoralism in Eastern Africa*. Oxford: James Currey.

Anderson, David and Douglas H. Johnson. 1988. *The Ecology of Survival: Case Studies from Northeast African History*. London: Lester Crook.

Anderson, Ruben and Martin Saxer. 2016. 'Anthropological Takes on the "return of #remoteness" - Introduction'. *Allegra*. Retrieved 24 April 2019, http://allegralaboratory.net/introduction-to-the-week-remoteness-redux/

Aneesh, Aneesh. 2017. 'Relocating Global Assemblages: An Interview with Saskia Sassen'. *Science, Technology and Society* 22 (1): 128–34. https://doi.org/10.1177/0971721817694927.

AU. 2010. *Policy Framework for Pastoralism in Africa: Securing, Protecting and Improving the Lives, Livelihoods and Rights of Pastoralist Communities*. Addis Ababa, Ethiopia: Department of Rural Economy and Agriculture.

Aubreville, A. 1949. 'Climats, Forêts et Désertification de l'Afrique Tropicale'. *Société d'Editions Géographiques*.

Awuondo, Casper Odegi. 1990. *Life in the Balance: Ecological Sociology of Turkana Nomads*. Nairobi: ACTS Press.

Baker, Jonathan. 2001. 'Migration as a Positive Response to Opportunity and Context: The Case of Welo, Ethiopia'. In *Mobile Africa: Changing Patterns of Movement in Africa and Beyond*, ed. by M. de Bruijn, R. van Dijk and D. Foeken, pp. 107–25. Boston, Leiden: Brill.

Bakewell, Oliver. 2008a. '"Keeping Them in Their Place": The Ambivalent Relationship between Development and Migration in Africa'. *Third World Quarterly* **29** (7): 1341–58. https://doi.org/10.1080/01436590802386492.

Bakewell, Oliver. 2008b. 'Research Beyond the Categories: The Importance of Policy Irrelevant Research into Forced Migration'. *Journal of Refugee Studies* **21** (4): 432–53. https://doi.org/10.1093/jrs/fen042.

Bakewell, Oliver and Ayla Bonfiglio. 2013. 'Moving Beyond Conflict: Re-Framing Mobility in the African Great Lakes Region'. *IMI Working Paper Series* (71): 34.

Bakhtin, Mikhail Mikhailovich. 1981. *The Dialogic Imagination: Four Essays*. Austin: University of Texas Press.

Barfield, Thomas J. 1993. *Nomadic Alternative*. Englewood Cliffs, New Jersey: Prentice Hall.

Barrett, Antony. 1998. *Turkana Iconography, Deserts Nomads and Their Symbols*. Lodwar: Kijabe Printing Press.

Barrett, Christopher B. 2010. 'Measuring Food Insecurity'. *Science* 327: 825–28. https://doi.org/10.1126/science.1182768.

Barthes, Roland. 1961. 'Toward a Psychosociology of Contemporary Food Consumption'. In *Food and Culture: A Reader*, ed. by C. Counihan, P.V. Esterik and A. Julier. New York: Routledge.

Beck, Ulrich. 1992. *Risk Society: Towards a New Modernity*. London: Sage.

Behnke, Roy. 1985. 'Measuring the Benefits of Subsistence versus Commercial Livestock Production in Africa'. *Agricultural Systems* **16** (2): 109–35.

Behnke, Roy H. and Michael Mortimore (eds). 2016. *The End of Desertification? Disputing Environmental Change in the Drylands*. Heidelberg: Springer.

Behnke, Roy H. and Ian Scoones. 1992. 'Rethinking Range Ecology: Implications for Range Management in Africa'. *Dryland Network Programme* 3: 1–43.

Behnke, Roy H., Ian Scoones and Carol Kerven. 1993. *Range Ecology at Disequilibrium: New Models of Natural Variability and Pastoral Adaptation in African Savannas*. London: ODI.

Berkes, Fikret, Johan Colding and Carl Folke. 2003. *Navigating Social–Ecological Systems. Building Resilience for Complexity and Change*. Cambridge: Cambridge University Press.

Betti, Marianna. 2010. 'The Children of Eve. Change and Socialization Among Sedentarized Turkana Children and Youth'. Masters diss., Department of Social Anthropology, University of Bergen.

Betts, Alexander, Naohiko Omata, Cory Rodgers, Olivier Sterck and Maria Stierna. 2019. *The Kalobeyei Model: Towards Self-Reliance for Refugees?* Oxford: Refugee Study Centre (RSC), University of Oxford.

Bibliography

Bille, Mikkel, Frida Hastrup and Tim Flohr Sørensen. 2010. 'Introduction: An Anthropology of Absence'. In *An Anthropology of Absence, Materializations of Transcendence and Loss*, ed. by M. Bille, F. Hastrup and T.F. Sørensen. New York: Springer.

Bindi, Letizia (ed.) 2022. *Grazing Communities: Pastoralism on the Move and Biocultural Heritage Frictions*. New York: Berghahn Books.

Birch, Isobel. 1994. 'Emergency Food Distribution in Turkana: A Developmental Approach'. *Gender & Development* **2** (1): 30–33. https://doi.org/10.1080/09682869308519995.

Blaikie, Piers M. 1994. *At Risk: Natural Hazards, People's Vulnerability, and Disasters*. London: Routledge.

Blier, Suzanne Preston. 1987. *The Anatomy of Architecture: Ontology and Metaphor in Batammaliba Architectural Expression*. Cambridge: Cambridge University Press.

Bourdieu, Pierre. 1977. *Outline of a Theory of Practice*. Cambridge: Cambridge University Press.

Bouzarovski, Stefan. 2015. *Retrofitting the City. Residential Flexibility, Resilience and the Built Environment*. London: Bloomsbury Publishing.

Bovill, E. William. 1921. 'The Encroachment of the Sahara on the Sudan'. *Journal of the Royal African Society* **20** (80): 259–69.

Bracke, Sarah. 2016. 'Bouncing Back: Vulnerability and Resistance in Times of Resilience'. In *Vulnerability in Resistance*, ed. by J. Butler, Z. Gambetti and L. Sabsay. Durham, NC: Duke University Press.

Braidotti, Rosi. 1994. *Nomadic Subjects: Embodiment and Sexual Difference in Contemporary Feminist Theory*. New York: Columbia University Press.

Brand, Fridolin Simon and Kurt Jax. 2007. 'Focusing the Meaning(s) of Resilience: Resilience as a Descriptive Concept and a Boundary Object'. *Ecology and Society* **12** (1). https://doi.org/10.5751/ES-02029-120123.

Brassett, James, Stuart Croft and Nick Vaughan-Williams. 2013. 'Introduction: An Agenda for Resilience Research in Politics and International Relations'. *Politics* **33** (4): 221–28. https://doi.org/10.1111/1467-9256.12032.

Breman, H. and C.T. de Wit. 1983. 'Rangeland Productivity and Exploitation in the Sahel'. *Science* **221** (4618): 1341–47. https://doi.org/10.1126/science.221.4618.1341.

Brewer, Marilynn B. and Wendi Gardner. 1996. 'Who Is This "We"? Levels of Collective Identity and Self Representations'. *Journal of Personality and Social Psychology* **71** (1): 11.

Broch-Due, Vigdis. 1991. 'The Bodies within the Body: Journeys in Turkana Thought and Practice'. Ph.D. diss, Social Anthropology, Bergen University.

Broch-Due, Vigdis. 2000. 'The Fertility of House and Herds: Producing Kinship and Gender among Turkana Pastoralists'. In *Rethinking Pastoralism in Africa: Gender, Culture and the Myth of the Patriarchal Pastoralist*, ed. by D.L. Hodgson. Oxford: James Currey.

Broch-Due, Vigdis and Todd Sanders. 1999. 'Rich Man, Poor Man, Administrator, Beast: The Politics of Impoverishment in Turkana, Kenya, 1890–1990'. *Nomadic Peoples* **3** (2): 35–55. https://doi.org/10.3167/082279499782409389.

Broch-Due, Vigdis and Richard A. Schroeder. 2000. *Producing Nature and Poverty in Africa*. Stockholm: Elanders Gotab.

Brown, Katrina. 2011. 'Rethinking Progress in a Warming World: Interrogating Climate Resilience Development'. In *Rethinking Development in an Age of Scarcity and Uncertainty.* EADI/DSA Conference, York, September 2011.

Brown, Katrina. 2015. *Resilience, Development and Global Change.* London: Routledge.

Brown, Leslie H. 1971. 'The Biology of Pastoral Man as a Factor in Conservation'. *Biological Conservation* **3** (2): 93–100. https://doi.org/10.1016/0006-3207(71)90007-3.

Bruneau, Michel and Andrei Reinhorn. 2006. 'Overview of the Resilience Concept'. San Francisco, California, USA: Proceedings of the 8th US National Conference on Earthquake Engineering.

Campbell, Elizabeth and Luke Eric Lassiter. 2014. *Doing Ethnography Today: Theories, Methods, Exercises.* Chicester, UK: John Wiley & Sons.

Campbell, Thomas. 2021. 'Climate Change Policy Narratives and Pastoralism in the Horn of Africa: New Concerns, Old Arguments?' Ph.D. Thesis, Dublin City University, Dublin.

Carabine, Elizabeth, Marie-Agnes Jouanjean and Josephine Tsui. 2015. *Kenya Ending Drought Emergencies Policy Review: Scenarios for Building Resilience in the ASALs.* 1. Nairobi, Kenya: Report prepared by the Technical Consortium, a project of the CGIAR.

Caravani, Matteo, Jeremy Lind, Rachel Sabates-Wheeler and Ian Scoones. 2022. 'Providing Social Assistance and Humanitarian Relief: The Case for Embracing Uncertainty'. *Development Policy Review* **40** (5): e12613. https://doi.org/10.1111/dpr.12613.

Casciarri, Barbara and Abdel Ghaffar M. Ahmed. 2009. 'Pastoralists under Pressure in Present-Day Sudan: An Introduction'. *Nomadic Peoples* **13** (1): 10–22. https://doi.org/10.3167/np.2009.130102.

Casey, Edward S. 1996. 'How to Get from Space to Place in a Fairly Short Stretch of Time: Phenomenological Prolegomena'. In *Senses of Place*, ed. by S. Feld and K. Basso. Seattle: School of American Research Press.

Castells, Manuel. 1999. 'Grassrooting the Space of Flows'. *Urban Geography* **20** (4): 294–302. https://doi.org/10.2747/0272-3638.20.4.294.

Catley, Andy. 2017. *Pathways to Resilience in Pastoralist Areas: A Synthesis of Research in the Horn of Africa.* Boston: Feinstein International Center.

Catley, Andy, Jeremy Lind and Ian Scoones. 2013. *Pastoralism and Development in Africa: Dynamic Change at the Margins.* London: Routledge.

de Certeau, Michel. 1985. 'Practices of Space'. *On Signs* 129: 122–45.

de Certeau, Michel. 1988. *The Practice of Everyday Life.* Berkeley: University of California Press.

Cervigni, Raffaello and Michael Morris. 2016. *Confronting Drought in Africa's Drylands: Opportunities for Enhancing Resilience.* Washington, DC: World Bank.

Chandler, David. 2020. 'The End of Resilience?: Rethinking Adaptation in the Anthropocene'. In *Resilience in the Anthropocene. Governance and Politics at the End of the World,* ed. by D. Chandler, K. Grove and S. Wakefield. New York: Routledge.

Chandler, David and Jon Coaffee. 2015. *Routledge Handbook of International Resilience.* London: Routledge.

Chatty, Dawn. 1972. 'Pastoralism: Adaptation and Optimization'. *Folk* (14–15): 27–38.

Bibliography

Chatty, Dawn. 1996. *Mobile Pastoralists: Development Planning and Social Change in Oman.* New York: Columbia University Press.

Chatty, Dawn. 2006. *Nomadic Societies in the Middle East and North Africa: Entering the 21st Century.* Leiden: Brill.

Chatty, Dawn. 2007. 'Mobile Peoples: Pastoralists and Herders at the Beginning of the 21st Century'. *Reviews in Anthropology* 36 (1): 5–26. https://doi.org/10.1080/00938150601177538.

Chatty, Dawn. 2013. *From Camel to Truck: The Bedouin in the Modern World.* Revised second edition. Knapwell, Cambridge: White Horse Press.

CIDP. 2013–2017. *Turkana County Integrated Development Plan, 2013–2017.*

Clifford, James, George E. Marcus and Kim Fortun. 1986. *Writing Culture: The Poetics and Politics of Ethnography.* Berkeley: University of California Press.

Coates, Jennifer. 2013. 'Build It Back Better: Deconstructing Food Security for Improved Measurement and Action'. *Global Food Security* 2 (3): 188–94. https://doi.org/10.1016/j.gfs.2013.05.002.

Counihan, Carole and Penny Van Esterik (eds). 2013. *Food and Culture: A Reader.* 3rd ed. New York: Routledge.

Crang, Mike and Ian Cook. 1995. *Doing Ethnographies.* Norwich: Geobooks.

Cresswell, Tim. 2006. *On the Move: Mobility in the Modern Western World.* New York: Routledge.

Cuthbert, M.O., T. Gleeson, S.C. Reynolds, M.R. Bennett, A.C. Newton, C.J. McCormack and G.M. Ashley. 2017. 'Modelling the Role of Groundwater Hydro-Refugia in East African Hominin Evolution and Dispersal'. *Nature Communications* 8: 1–11. https://doi.org/10.1038/ncomms15696.

Czuba, Karol, Ana P. Ayala and Tyler J. O'Neill. 2017. *The Impact of In-Kind Food Assistance on Pastoralist Livelihoods in Humanitarian Crises.* Oxfam; Feinstein International Center; UKAID. https://doi.org/10.21201/2017.8760.

Da Ros, Achille. 1994. *Noi, i Turkana.* Bologna: Editrice Missionaria Italiana.

Dak, Elena. 2016. *Io Cammino Con i Nomadi. Una Straordinaria Esperienza Di Viaggio Insieme Ai Wodaabe Attraverso Il Sahel.* Milano: Corbaccio.

D'Andrea, Anthony, Luigina Ciolfi and Breda Gray. 2011. 'Methodological Challenges and Innovations in Mobilities Research'. *Mobilities* 6 (2): 149–60. https://doi.org/10.1080/17450101.2011.552769.

Darnhofer, Ika, Claire Lamine, Agnes Strauss and Mireille Navarrete. 2016. 'The Resilience of Family Farms: Towards a Relational Approach'. *Journal of Rural Studies* 44: 111–22. https://doi.org/10.1016/j.jrurstud.2016.01.013.

Davies, Jonathan Mark, Claire Ogali, Lydia Slobodian, Guyo Malicha Roba, and Razingrim Ouedraogo. 2018. *Crossing Boundaries: Legal and Policy Arrangements for Cross-Border Pastoralism.* Ed. by Gregorio Velasco-Gil and Natasha Maru. Rome: FAO and IUCN.

Davis, Diana K. 2016. *The Arid Lands: History, Power, Knowledge.* Cambridge, MA: MIT Press.

Bibliography

De Haen, Hartwig, Stephan Klasen and Matin Qaim. 2011. 'What Do We Really Know? Metrics for Food Insecurity and Undernutrition'. *Food Policy* 36 (6): 760–69. https://doi.org/10.1016/j.foodpol.2011.08.003.

De Jode, Helen. 2010. *Modern and Mobile: The Future of Livestock Production in Africa's Drylands.* London: International Institute for Environment and Development and SOS Sahel International UK.

De León, Jason. 2015. *The Land of Open Graves: Living and Dying on the Migrant Trail.* Oakland, California: University of California Press.

Derbyshire, Samuel F. 2020. *Remembering Turkana: Material Histories and Contemporary Livelihoods in North-Western Kenya.* London ; New York: Routledge.

Derbyshire, Samuel F. 2022. 'Embracing Uncertainty: What Kenyan Herders Can Teach Us about Living in a Volatile World'. *The Conversation.*

Derbyshire, Samuel F., Rupsha R. Banerjee, Tahira S. Mohamed and Guyo M. Roba. 2024. 'Uncertainty, Pastoral Knowledge and Early Warning: A Review of Drought Management in the Drylands, with Insights from Northern Kenya'. *Pastoralism: Research, Policy and Practice* 14: 13006. https://doi.org/10.3389/past.2024.13006.

Derbyshire, Samuel F., Joseph Ekidor Nami, Gregory Akall, and Lucas Lowasa. 2021. 'Divining the Future: Making Sense of Ecological Uncertainty in Turkana, Northern Kenya'. *Land* 10 (9):885. https://doi.org/10.3390/land10090885.

Diodato, Luciana. 2001. *Il Linguaggio Del Cibo.* Soveria Mannelli: Rubbettino.

Doel, Marcus A. 1999. *Poststructuralist Geographies: The Diabolical Art of Spatial Science.* Edinburgh: Edinburgh University Press.

Duffield, Mark. 2012. 'Challenging Environments: Danger, Resilience and the Aid Industry'. *Security Dialogue* 43 (5): 475–92. https://doi.org/10.1177/0967010612457975.

Dukhan, Haian. 2014. '"They Talk to Us but Never Listen to Us": Development-Induced Displacement among Syria's Bedouin'. *Nomadic Peoples* 18 (1): 61–79. https://doi.org/10.3197/np.2014.180105.

Dyson-Hudson, Neville. 1958. *The Present Position of the Karimojong: A Preliminary General Survey, with Recommendations, Produced for the Government of Uganda.* Oxford: Institute of Social Anthropology.

Dyson-Hudson, Neville. 1966. *Karimojong Politics.* Oxford: Clarendon Press.

Dyson-Hudson, Neville and Rada Dyson-Hudson. 1999. 'The Social Organization of Resources Exploitation'. In *Turkana Herders of the Dry Savanna. Ecology and Biobehavioural Response of Nomads to an Uncertain Environment,* ed. by M.A. Little and P.W. Leslie. Oxford: Oxford University Press.

Dyson-Hudson, Rada and Neville Dyson-Hudson. 1980. 'Nomadic Pastoralism'. *Annual Review of Anthropology* 9: 47.

Elam, Yitzchak. 1979. 'Nomadism in Ankole as a Substitute for Rebellion'. *Africa: Journal of the International African Institute* 49 (2): 147–58. https://doi.org/10.2307/1158671.

El-Baz, Farouk. 1988. 'Origin and Evolution of the Desert'. *Interdisciplinary Science Reviews* 13 (4): 331–47.

Bibliography

Ellis, James. 1995. 'Climate Variability and Complex Ecosystem Dynamics: Implications for Pastoral Development'. In *Living with Uncertainty: New Directions in Pastoral Development in Africa*. London: Institute of Development Studies.

Ellis, James and Kathleen A. Galvin. 1994. 'Climate Patterns and Land-Use Practices in the Dry Zones of Africa'. *Bio Science* **44** (5): 340–49. https://doi.org/10.2307/1312384.

Ellis, James and David M. Swift. 1988. 'Stability of African Pastoral Ecosystems: Alternate Paradigms and Implications for Development'. *Journal of Range Management* **41** (6): 450–59. https://doi.org/10.2307/3899515.

Evans-Pritchard, Edward E. 1940. *The Nuer: A Description of the Modes of Livelihood and Political Institutions of a Nilotic People*. Oxford: Clarendon Press.

Evans-Pritchard, Edward E. 1977. *Witchcraft, Oracles and Magic among the Azande*. Oxford: Clarendon Press.

Fabietti, Ugo. 1989. 'Nomadi, Santuari e Città in Medio Oriente' (Nomads, Sanctuaries and Cities in the Middle East)'. In *Centri, Ritualità, Potere: Significati Antropologici dello Spazio (Centres, Ritual, Power: Anthropological Meanings of Space)*, ed. by F. Remotti, pp. 169–240. Bologna: Il Mulino.

Fairhead, James, Melissa Leach and Ian Scoones. 2012. 'Green Grabbing: A New Appropriation of Nature?' *Journal of Peasant Studies* **39** (2): 237–61. https://doi.org/10.1080/03066150.2012.671770.

FAO. 2002. *Anti-Hunger Program: Reducing Hunger through Agricultural and Rural Development and Wider Access to Food*.

FAO. 2013. *Strengthening the Links between Resilience and Nutrition in Food and Agriculture*.

FAO. 2021. *Pastoralism - Making Variability Work*. 185. Roma: FAO. https://doi.org/10.4060/cb5855en.

FAO. 2022. *Making Way: Developing National Legal and Policy Frameworks for Pastoral Mobility*. 28. Roma: FAO. https://doi.org/10.4060/cb8461en.

Ferguson, James. 1999. *Expectations of Modernity: Myths and Meanings of Urban Life on the Zambian Copperbelt*. Berkeley ; Los Angeles; London: University of California Press.

Ferguson, James. 2005. 'Seeing Like an Oil Company: Space, Security, and Global Capital in Neoliberal Africa'. *American Anthropologist* **107** (3): 377–82. https://doi.org/10.1525/aa.2005.107.3.377.

Folke, Carl. 2006. 'Resilience: The Emergence of a Perspective for Social–Ecological Systems Analyses'. *Global Environmental Change* **16** (3): 253–67. https://doi.org/10.1016/j.gloenvcha.2006.04.002.

Folke, Carl, Stephen R. Carpenter, Brian Walker, Marten Scheffer, Terry Chapin and Johan Rockström. 2010. 'Resilience Thinking: Integrating Resilience, Adaptability and Transformability'. *Ecology and Society* **15** (4). https://doi.org/10.5751/ES-03610-150420.

Fortier, Jana. 2009. *Kings of the Forest: The Cultural Resilience of Himalayan Hunter-Gatherers*. Honolulu: University of Hawai'i Press.

Fratkin, Elliot M. and Eric Abella Roth. 2005. *As Pastoralists Settle: Social, Health, and Economic Consequences of the Pastoral Sedentarization in Marsabit District, Kenya*. New York: Kluwer Academic/Plenum Publishers.

Frost, Robert. 1923. 'Stopping by Woods on a Snowy Evening'. In *New Hampshire*. New York: Henry Holt & Company.

Galaty, John. 2013. 'The Indigenisation of Pastoral Modernity: Territoriality, Mobility and Poverty in Dryland Africa'. In *Pastoralism in Africa: Past Present and Future*, ed. by M. Bollig, M. Schnegg and H. Wotzka. New York: Berghahn.

Galvin, Kathleen A., Randall B. Boone, Nicole M. Smith and Stacy J. Lynn. 2001. 'Impacts of Climate Variability on East African Pastoralists: Linking Social Science and Remote Sensing'. *Climate Research* **19**: 161–72. https://doi.org/10.3354/cr019161.

Garcia, Angela Kronenburg, Tobias Haller, Cyrus Samimi, Han Van Dijk and Jeroen Warner. 2023. *Drylands Facing Change: Interventions, Investments and Identities*. 1st ed. London: Routledge.

Gernote, Bake. 1994. 'Water Resources'. In *Range Management Handbook of Kenya, Turkana District*, ed. by D. Herlocker, S. Shaabani and S. Wilkes. Nairobi, Kenya: Ministry of Agriculture, Livestock Development and Marketing (MALDM).

Glantz, Michael H. 1987. *Drought and Hunger in Africa: Denying Famine a Future*. Cambridge: Cambridge University Press.

GoK. 1965. *African Socialism and Its Application to Planning in Kenya. Sessional Paper N. 10*.

GoK. 2010. *Agricultural Sector Development Strategy 2010–2020*. Nairobi: Government of Kenya.

Graeber, David and David Wengrow. 2021. *The Dawn of Everything: A New History of Humanity*. Harmondsworth: Penguin.

Gross, Rainer, Hans Schoeneberger, Hans Pfeifer and Hans-Joachim A. Preuss. 2000. *The Four Dimensions of Food and Nutrition Security: Definitions and Concepts*.

Großmann, Kristina. 2017. 'The (Ir)relevance of Ethnicity among the Punan Murung and Bakumpai in Central Kalimantan'. In *Continuity under Change in Dayak Societies*, pp. 141–62. Cham: Springer.

Grove, Kevin. 2018. *Resilience*. New York: Routledge.

Gulliver, Phillip. 1951. *A Preliminary Survey of the Turkana: A Report Compiled for the Government of Kenya*. Cape Town: Cape Town.

Gulliver, Phillip. 1955. *The Family Herds: A Study of Two Pastoral Tribes in East Africa, the Jie and Turkana*. London: Routledge & Kegan Paul.

Gulliver, Phillip. 1968. 'The Turkana'. In *Man in Adaptation: The Cultural Present*. Chicago: Aldine PubCo.

Gulliver, Phillip. 1975. 'Nomadic Movements: Causes and Implications'. In *Pastoralism in Tropical Africa*, ed. by T. Monod. London: Routledge.

Guptill, Amy Elizabeth, Denise A. Copelton and Betsy Lucal. 2017. *Food & Society: Principles and Paradoxes*. Cambridge: Polity Press.

Habeck, Joachim Otto. 2006. 'Experience, Movement and Mobility: Komi Reindeer Herders' Perception of the Environment'. *Nomadic Peoples* **10** (2): 123–41. https://doi.org/10.3167/np.2006.100208.

Bibliography

Hammond, Laura. 2004. *This Place Will Become Home: Refugee Repatriation to Ethiopia*. Ithaca: Cornell University Press.

Hanrahan, Kelsey B. 2015. 'Living Care-Fully: The Potential for an Ethics of Care in Livelihoods Approaches'. *World Development* 72: 381–93. https://doi.org/10.1016/j.worlddev.2015.03.014.

Hardin, Garrett. 1968. 'The Tragedy of the Commons'. *Science* **162** (3859): 1243–48.

Harris, John and Michael Todaro. 1970. 'Migration, Unemployment and Development: A Two-Sector Analysis'. *The American Economic Review* **60** (1): 126–42.

Harvey, David. 1996. *Justice, Nature and the Geography of Difference*. Cambridge: Blackwell Publishing.

Hatcher, Jessica. 2014. *Exploiting Turkana: Robbing the Cradle of Mankind*. Newsweek Insights.

Hazan, Haim and Esther Hertzog (eds). 2011. *Serendipity in Anthropological Research: The Nomadic Turn*. Farnham, UK: Ashgate.

Headey, Derek and Adam Kennedy. 2012. *Enhancing Resilience in the Horn of Africa: Synthesis of an Evidence Based Workshop*. Washington, DC: International Food Policy Research Institute. https://doi.org/10.2499/9780896297975.

Headey, Derek, Alemayehu Seyoum Taffesse and Liangzhi You. 2014. 'Diversification and Development in Pastoralist Ethiopia'. *World Development* 56: 200–213. https://doi.org/10.1016/j.worlddev.2013.10.015.

Heidegger, Martin. 1971. 'Building Dwelling Thinking'. In *Poetry, Language, Thought*. New York: Harper Colophon Books.

Herlocker, Dennis, Salim Shaabani and Sybella Wilkes. 1994. *Range Management Handbook of Kenya, Turkana District*. Nairobi, Kenya: Ministry of Agriculture, Livestock Development and Marketing (MALDM).

Herrera, Pedro M., Jonathan Davies and Pablo Manzano. 2014. *The Governance of Rangelands: Collective Action for Sustainable Pastoralism*. London: Routledge. https://doi.org/10.4324/9781315768014.

Herrmann, Stefanie M. and Charles F. Hutchinson. 2006. 'The Scientific Basis: Linkages between Land Degradation, Drought and Desertification'. In *Governing Global Desertification: Linking Environmental Degradation, Poverty and Participation*, ed. by P. Johnson, K. Mayrand and M. Paquin, pp. 45–63. Farnham, UK: Ashgate Publishing.

Herskovits, Melville J. 1926. 'The Cattle Complex in East Africa'. *American Anthropologist* **28** (2): 361–88.

Hewitt, Kenneth. 1983. *Interpretations of Calamity from the Viewpoint of Human Ecology*. Boston ; London: Allen and Unwin.

Hobbs, Joseph J. 1989. *Bedouin Life in the Egyptian Wilderness*. Austin: University of Texas Press.

Hobsbawm, E.J. and T.O. Ranger. 1992. *The Invention of Tradition*. Cambridge: Cambridge University Press.

Hoddinott, John. 2014. 'Looking at Development through a Resilience Lens'. In *Resilience for Food and Nutrition Security*. Washington, D.C.: IFPRI.

Hogg, Richard. 1982. 'Destitution and Development: The Turkana of North West Kenya'. *Disasters* 6 (3): 164–68. https://doi.org/10.1111/j.1467-7717.1982.tb00531.x.

Hogg, Richard. 1987. 'Development in Kenya: Drought, Desertification and Food Scarcity'. *African Affairs* 86 (342): 47–58. https://doi.org/10.1093/oxfordjournals.afraf.a097878.

Holling, Crawford Stanley. 1961. 'Principles of Insect Predation'. *Annual Review of Entomology* 6 (1): 163–82. https://doi.org/10.1146/annurev.en.06.010161.001115.

Holling, Crawford Stanley. 1973. 'Resilience and Stability of Ecological System'. *Annual Review of Ecology and Systematics* 4: 1–23.

Holling, Crawford Stanley. 1986. 'Resilience of Terrestrial Ecosystems: Local Surprise and Global Change'. In *Sustainable Development of the Biosphere*, ed. by W. Clark and R. Munn. Cambridge: Cambridge University Press.

Holtzman, Jon. 2009. *Uncertain Tastes: Memory, Ambivalence, and the Politics of Eating in Samburu, Northern Kenya*. Berkeley: University of California Press.

Homer. 1924. *The Iliad*. Book XXII. Cambridge: Harvard University Press.

Homewood, Katherine. 2008. *Ecology of African Pastoralist Societies*. Oxford: James Currey.

HRW. 2015. *There Is No Time Left. Climate Change, Environmental Threats, and Human Rights in Turkana County, Kenya*.

Humphrey, Caroline. 2003. 'Chiefly and Shamanist Landscapes in Mongolia'. In *The Anthropology of Landscape. Perspectives on Place and Space*, ed. by E. Hirsch and M. O'Hanlon. Oxford: Oxford University Press.

Humphrey, Caroline and David Sneath. 1999. *The End of Nomadism?: Society, State and the Environment in Inner Asia*. Knapwell, Cambridge: The White Horse Press.

Hustak, Carla and Natasha Myers. 2012. 'Involutionary Momentum: Affective Ecologies and the Sciences of Plant/Insect Encounters'. *Differences* 23 (3): 74–118. https://doi.org/10.1215/10407391-1892907.

IFAD. 2018. *How to Do Engaging with Pastoralists – a Holistic Development Approach*.

IGAD. 2013. *The IDDRSI Strategy*. Intergovernmental Authority on Development.

Imamura, Masao. 2015. 'Rethinking Frontier and Frontier Studies'. *Political Geography* 45: 96–97. https://doi.org/10.1016/j.polgeo.2014.09.014.

Ingold, Tim. 2000. *The Perception of the Environment: Essays on Livelihood, Dwelling and Skill*. London: Routledge.

Ingold, Tim. 2007. *Lines: A Brief History*. London: Routledge.

Ingold, Tim. 2011. *Being Alive: Essays on Movement, Knowledge and Description*. London: Routledge.

Irons, William and Neville Dyson-Hudson. 1972. *Perspectives on Nomadism*. Leiden: Brill.

IUCN. 2012. *Supporting Sustainable Pastoral Livelihoods - A Global Perspective on Minimum Standards and Good Practices*.

IUCN. 2017. *Drylands and Land Degradation*. IUCN Policy Brief.

Jacobs, Alan H. 1965. 'The Traditional Political Organization of the Pastoral Masai'. Ph.D. diss, Anthropology and Geography, University of Oxford.

Jasanoff, Sheila. 2008. 'Survival of The Fittest'. In *Re-framing Resilience: a Symposium Report*, ed. by M. Leach. STEPS Centre.

Jedd, Theresa, Stephen Russell Fragaszy, Cody Knutson, Michael J. Hayes, Makram Belhaj Fraj, Nicole Wall, Mark Svoboda and Rachael McDonnell. 2021. 'Drought Management Norms: Is the Middle East and North Africa Region Managing Risks or Crises?' *The Journal of Environment & Development* **30** (1): 3–40. https://doi.org/10.1177/1070496520960204.

Jerneck, Anne and Lennart Olsson. 2008. 'Adaptation and the Poor: Development, Resilience and Transition'. *Climate Policy* 8 (2): 170–82. https://doi.org/10.3763/cpol.2007.0434.

Kahn, Miriam. 1986. *Always Hungry, Never Greedy: Food and the Expression of Gender in a Melanesian Society*. Cambridge: Cambridge University Press.

Kaika, Maria. 2017. '"Don't Call Me Resilient Again!": The New Urban Agenda as Immunology … or … What Happens When Communities Refuse to Be Vaccinated with "Smart Cities" and Indicators'. *Environment and Urbanization*. https://doi.org/10.1177/0956247816684763.

Kaufmann, Jeffrey C. 2009. 'The Sediment of Nomadism'. *History in Africa* 36: 235–64. https://doi.org/10.1353/hia.2010.0018.

Keightley, Emily. 2010. 'Remembering Research: Memory and Methodology in the Social Sciences'. *International Journal of Social Research Methodology* **13** (1): 55–70. https://doi.org/10.1080/13645570802605440.

Khazanov, Anatoly M. 1984. *Nomads and the Outside World*. Madison: University of Wisconsin Press.

Khazanov, Anatoly M. 1990. 'Pastoral Nomads in the Past, Present, and Future: A Comparative View'. In *The Struggle for the Land: Indigenous Insight and Industrial Empire in the Semiarid World*, ed. by P.A. Olson, pp. 81–98. Lincoln and London: University of Nebraska Press.

Klee, Paul. 1961. *Notebooks Vol.1 The Thinking Eye*. London: Lund Humphreys.

Köhler Rollefson, Ilse. 2023. *Hoofprints on the Land How Traditional Herding and Grazing Can Restore the Soil and Bring Animal Agriculture Back in Balance with the Earth*. London: Chelsea Green Publishing Co.

Krätli, Saverio. 2013. *Global Public Policy Narratives on the Drylands and Pastoralism*. London: IIED.

Krätli, Saverio. 2015. *Valuing Variability: New Perspectives on Climate Resilient Drylands Development*. Ed. by H. De Jode. London: IIED.

Krätli, Saverio. 2016. 'Discontinuity in Pastoral Development: Time to Update the Method'. *Revue Scientifique et Technique de l'OIE* **35** (2): 485–97. https://doi.org/10.20506/rst.35.2.2528.

Krätli, Saverio, Omer Hassan El Dirani and Helen Young. 2013. *Standing Wealth Pastoralist Livestock Production and Local Livelihoods in Sudan*. Nairobi, KENYA: United Nations Environment Programme.

Krätli, Saverio, Christian Huelsebusch, Sally Brooks and Brigitte Kaufmann. 2013. 'Pastoralism: A Critical Asset for Food Security under Global Climate Change'. *Animal Frontiers* **3** (1): 42–50. https://doi.org/10.2527/af.2013-0007.

Krätli, Saverio, Brigitte Kaufmann, Hassan Roba, Pierre Hiernaux, Wenjun Li, Marcos Easdale and Christian Hülsebusch. 2015. 'A House Full of Trap Doors: Identifying Barriers to Resilient Drylands in the Toolbox of Pastoral Development'. *IIED Discussion Paper* 48.

Krätli, Saverio, Christine Lottje, Friederike Mikulcak, Wiebke Foerch and Tobias Feldt. 2022. *Pastoralism and Resilience of Food Production in the Face of Climate Change Pastoralism and Resilience of Food Production in the Face of Climate Change 2*. Bonn and Eschborn, Germany: German International Cooperation Society (GIZ).

Krätli, Saverio and Nikolaus Schareika. 2010. 'Living Off Uncertainty: The Intelligent Animal Production of Dryland Pastoralists'. *The European Journal of Development Research* **22** (5): 605–22. https://doi.org/10.1057/ejdr.2010.41.

Krätli, Saverio and Jeremy Swift. 2014. '"Counting Pastoralists" in Kenya'. Nairobi: DLCI/ REGLAP.

La Cecla, Franco. 2011. *Perdersi*. Bari: Gius. Laterza & Figli Spa.

Lamphear, John. 1976. *The Traditional History of the Jie of Uganda*. Oxford: Clarendon Press.

Lamphear, John. 1988. 'The People of the Grey Bull: The Origin and Expansion of the Turkana'. *The Journal of African History* **29** (1): 27–39.

Lamprey, H. 1983. 'Pastoralism Yesterday and Today: The Overgrazing Problem'. In *Tropical Savannas, Ecosystems of the world,* v. 13, ed. by F. Bourlière. Amsterdam; Oxford: Elsevier.

Law, John. 2007. 'Making a Mess with Method'. In *The SAGE Handbook of Social Science Methodology*, pp. 595–606. London: SAGE Publications Ltd.

Le Houérou, Henry Noël. 1989. 'The Grazing Land Ecosystems of the African Sahel'. *Ecological Studies* 75: 99–109.

Leach, Melissa. 2008. 'Re-Framing Resilience a Symposium Report'. *STEPS Centre*.

Lee, Everett. 1966. 'A Theory of Migration'. *Demography* **3** (1): 47–57. https://doi.org/10.2307/2060063.

Lefebvre, Henri. 1991. *The Production of Space*. Oxford: Blackwell.

Leslie, Paul and J. Terrence McCabe. 2013. 'Response Diversity and Resilience in Social-Ecological Systems'. *Current Anthropology* **54** (2): 114–43. https://doi.org/10.1086/669563.

Lesorogol, Carolyn. 2008. *Contesting the Commons: Privatising Pastoral Lands in Kenya*. Ann Arbor, MI: The University of Michigan Press.

Lesorogol, Carolyn K. 2008. 'Setting Themselves Apart: Education, Capabilities, and Sexuality among Samburu Women in Kenya'. *Anthropological Quarterly* **81** (3): 551–77.

Levine, Simon. 2014. *Assessing Resilience: Why Quantification Misses the Point. HPG Working Paper*. Overseas Development Institute.

Levine, Simon, Adam Pain, Sarah Bailey and Lilianne Fan. 2012. 'The Relevance of "Resilience"?' *HPG Policy Brief 49*.

Lind, Jeremy. 2005. 'Relief Assistance at the Margins Meanings and Perceptions of Dependency in Northern Kenya'. *HPG Background Paper*.

Bibliography

Lind, Jeremy, Doris Okenwa and Ian Scoones (eds). 2020. *Land, Investment & Politics: Reconfiguring Eastern Africa's Pastoral Drylands*. Woodbridge, Suffolk; Rochester, NY: James Currey.

Lind, Jeremy and Daniel Salau Rogei. 2025. 'Contestation, Conflict and Claims-Making around the Lake Turkana Wind Power Windfarm, Northern Kenya'. *World Development* 188: 106913. https://doi.org/10.1016/j.worlddev.2024.106913.

Little, Michael A. and Paul Leslie. 1999. *Turkana Herders of the Dry Savanna: Ecology and Biobehavioral Response of Nomads to an Uncertain Environment*. Ed. by Michael A. Little and P. Leslie. Oxford: Oxford University Press.

Little, Peter D., Kevin Smith, Barbara A. Cellarius, D. Layne Coppock and Christopher Barrett. 2001. 'Avoiding Disaster: Diversification and Risk Management among East African Herders'. *Development and Change* 32 (3):401–33. https://doi.org/10.1111/1467-7660.00211.

Livingstone, David N. 1992. *The Geographical Tradition: Episodes in the History of a Contested Enterprise*. Oxford: Blackwell.

Lubkemann, Stephen C. 2008. 'Involuntary Immobility: On a Theoretical Invisibility in Forced Migration Studies'. *Journal of Refugee Studies* 21(4): 454–75. https://doi.org/10.1093/jrs/fen043.

Ludwig, D., D.D. Jones and C.S. Holling. 1978. 'Qualitative Analysis of Insect Outbreak Systems: The Spruce Budworm and Forest'. *The Journal of Animal Ecology* 47 (1): 315. https://doi.org/10.2307/3939.

Macfarlane, Robert. 2012. *The Old Ways*. London: Penguin Books.

MacKinnon, Danny and Kate Driscoll Derickson. 2013. 'From Resilience to Resourcefulness: A Critique of Resilience Policy and Activism'. *Progress in Human Geography* 37 (2): 253–70. https://doi.org/10.1177/0309132512454775.

Malinowski, Bronislaw. 1922. *Argonauts of the Western Pacific: An Account of Native Enterprise and Adventure in the Archipelagoes of Melanesian New Guinea*. London: Routledge.

Malkki, Liisa H. 1997. 'National Geographic: The Rooting of Peoples and the Territorialization of National Identity among Scholars and Refugees'. *Cultural Anthropology* 7 (1): 24–44.

Malkki, Liisa H. 2007. 'Improvising Theory. Process and Temporality in Ethnographic FIeldwork'. In *Improvising Theory: Process and Temporality in Ethnographic Fieldwork*, ed. by A. Cerwonka and L.H. Malkki. Chicago, US: University of Chicago Press

Mancilla García, María, Tilman Hertz, Maja Schlüter, Rika Preiser and Minka Woermann. 2020. 'Adopting Process-Relational Perspectives to Tackle the Challenges of Social-Ecological Systems Research'. *Ecology and Society* 25 (1): art29. https://doi.org/10.5751/ES-11425-250129.

Manyena, Bernard. 2009. 'Disaster Resilience in Development and Humanitarian Interventions'. Ph.D. diss, Northumbria University, Newcastle.

Manzano, Pablo, Agustín Del Prado and Guillermo Pardo. 2023. 'Comparable GHG Emissions from Animals in Wildlife and Livestock-Dominated Savannas'. *NPJ Climate and Atmospheric Science* 6 (1): 27. https://doi.org/10.1038/s41612-023-00349-8.

Bibliography

Manzano, Pablo, Guillermo Pardo, Moustapha A. Itani and Agustín del Prado. 2023. 'Underrated Past Herbivore Densities Could Lead to Misoriented Sustainability Policies'. *NPJ Biodiversity* 2 (1): 1–6. https://doi.org/10.1038/s44185-022-00005-z.

Manzano, Pablo and Concha Salguero. 2018. *Mobile Pastoralism in the Mediterranean: Arguments and Evidence for Policy Reform and to Combat Climate Change.* Ed. by Liza Zogib. Mediterranean Consortium for Nature and Culture.

Manzano, Pablo and Sr White. 2019. 'Intensifying Pastoralism May Not Reduce Greenhouse Gas Emissions: Wildlife-Dominated Landscape Scenarios as a Baseline in Life-Cycle Analysis'. *Climate Research* 77 (2): 91–97. https://doi.org/10.3354/cr01555.

Markakis, John, Günther Schlee and John Young. 2021. *The Nation State A Wrong Model for the Horn of Africa.* Berlin: Max Planck Institute for the History of Science.

Maru, Natasha. 2022. 'Haal Haal Ne Haal [Walk, Walk and Walk] Exploring the Pace of Pastoral Mobility among the Rabari Pastoralists of Western India'. Doctor of Philosophy in Development Studies (IDS), University of Sussex, Brighton.

Marx, Emmanuel. 1967. *Bedouin of the Negev.* Manchester: Manchester University Press.

Marx, Emmanuel. 2006. 'Tribal Pilgrimages to Saints' Tombs in South Sinai'. In *Archaeology, Anthropology and Cult: The Sanctuary at Gilat, Israel, Approaches to Anthropological Archaeology*, ed. by T.E. Levy. London: Equinox.

Massey, Doreen. 1991. 'A Global Sense of Place'. *Marxism Today.* 24–29.

Massey, Doreen. 1993. 'Power-Geometry and a Progressive Sense of Place'. In *Mapping the Futures*, ed. by J. Bird, G. Robertson and L. Tickner. London: Routledge.

Massey, Doreen. 2005. *For Space.* London: SAGE Publications.

Maxwell, Daniel, Nisar Majid, Heather Stobaugh, Jeeyon Janet Kim, Jacqueline Lauer and Eliza Paul. 2014. 'Lessons Learned from the Somalia Famine and the Greater Horn of Africa Crisis 2011–2012'. *Feinstein International Center. Desk Review.*

Maxwell, Simon and Marisol Smith. 1992. *Household Food Security: A Conceptual Review.* New York and Rome: UNICEF and IFAD.

Mbembe, Achille and Sarah Nuttal. 2004. 'Writing the World from an African Metropolis'. *Public Culture* 16 (3): 347–72. https://doi.org/10.1215/08992363-16-3-347.

McCabe, J. Terrence. 2004. *Cattle Bring Us to Our Enemies: Turkana Ecology, Politics, and Raiding in a Disequilibrium System.* Ann Arbor: University of Michigan Press.

McCabe, J. Terrence and James E. Ellis. 1987. 'Beating the Odds in Arid Africa'. *Natural History* 96 (1): 33–41.

McCabe, J. Terrence, Paul W. Leslie and Laura DeLuca. 2010. 'Adopting Cultivation to Remain Pastoralists: The Diversification of Maasai Livelihoods in Northern Tanzania'. *Human Ecology* 38 (3): 321–34.

McCabe, J. Terrence, Nicole M. Smith, Paul W. Leslie and Amy L. Telligman. 2014. 'Livelihood Diversification through Migration among a Pastoral People: Contrasting Case Studies of Masaai in Northern Tanzania'. *Human Organization* 73 (4): 389–400.

McDonell, Nick. 2016. *The Civilization of Perpetual Movement: Nomads in the Modern World.* London: Hurst & Company.

Mcmichael, Philip. 2009. 'Contemporary Contradictions of the Global Development Project: Geopolitics, Global Ecology and the "Development Climate"'. *Third World Quarterly* **30** (1): 247–62. https://doi.org/10.1080/01436590802622987.

Meier, Lars, Lars Frers and Erika Sigvardsdotter. 2013. 'The Importance of Absence in the Present: Practices of Remembrance and the Contestation of Absences'. *Cultural Geographies* **20** (4): 423–30. https://doi.org/10.1177/1474474013493889.

Meuret, Michel and Frederick Provenza. 2014. *The Art & Science of Shepherding: Tapping the Wisdom of French Herders*. Austin, TX: Acres USA.

Mitchell, Tom and Katie Harris. 2012. 'Resilience: A Risk Management Approach'. *ODI Background Note* 7.

Mohamed, Tahira Shariff. 2023. 'Responding to Uncertainties in Pastoral Northern Kenya: The Role of Moral Economies'. In *Pastoralism, Uncertainty and Development*, ed. by ian Scoones. Rugby: Practical Action Publishing.

Mohamed, Tahira Shariff, Todd Andrew Crane, Samuel Derbyshire and Guyo Roba. 2025. 'A Review of Approaches to the Integration of Humanitarian and Development Aid: The Case of Drought Management in the Horn of Africa'. *Pastoralism: Research, Policy and Practice* **15**: 14001. https://doi.org/10.3389/past.2025.14001.

Mol, Lisa and Troy Sternberg (eds). 2012. *Changing Deserts: Integrating People and Their Environment*. Knapwell, Cambridge: The White Horse Press.

Monod, Théodore. 1975. *Pastoralism in Tropical Africa*. 1st ed. London: Routledge.

Monsutti, Alessandro. 2010. 'Food and Identity among Young Afghans'. In *Deterritorialized Youth: Sahrawi and Afghan Refugees at the Margins of the Middle East*, ed. by D. Chatty. New York: Berghahn Books.

Morgan, W.T.W. 1974. 'The South Turkana Expedition: Scientific Papers X. Sorghum Gardens in South Turkana: Cultivation among a Nomadic Pastoral People'. *The Geographical Journal* **140** (1): 80. https://doi.org/10.2307/1797009.

Morgan, W.T.W. 1981. 'Ethnobotany of the Turkana: Use of Plants by a Pastoral People and Their Livestock in Kenya'. *Economic Botany* **35** (1): 96–130.

Mortimore, Michael. 2016. 'Changing Paradigms for People-Centred Development in the Sahel'. In *The End of Desertification? Disputing Environmental Change in the Drylands*, Springer earth system sciences, ed. by R.H. Behnke and Michael Mortimore. Heidelberg: Springer.

Mosel, Irina and Simon Levine. 2014. *Remaking the Case for Linking Relief, Rehabilitation and Development How LRRD Can Become a Practically Useful Concept for Assistance in Difficult Places*. London: Humanitarian policy group. HPG commissioned report.

Mosley, Jason and Elizabeth E. Watson. 2016. 'Frontier Transformations: Development Visions, Spaces and Processes in Northern Kenya and Southern Ethiopia'. *Journal of Eastern African Studies* **10** (3): 452–75. https://doi.org/10.1080/17531055.2016.1266199.

Mukherjee, Jenia, Kuntala Lahiri-Dutt and Raktima Ghosh. 2023. 'Beyond (Un)stable: Chars as Dynamic Destabilisers of Problematic Binaries'. *Social Anthropology/Anthropologie Sociale* **31**(4): 116–33. https://doi.org/10.3167/saas.2023.04132305.

Müller-Dempf, Harald. 1994. 'Turkana Traditional Land Uses'. In *Range Management Handbook of Kenya: Turkana District*, ed. by D. Herlocker, S. Shaabani and S. Wilkes. Nairobi, Kenya: Ministry of Agriculture, Livestock Development and Marketing (MALDM).

Müller-Dempf, Harald. 2014a. 'Hybrid Pastoralists – Development Interventions and New Turkana Identities'. *Max Planck Institute for Social Anthropology Working Paper* 156: 31.

Murdoch, Jonathan. 2006. *Post-Structuralist Geography: A Guide to Relational Space*. London ; Thousand Oaks, Calif.: SAGE.

Natarajan, Nithya, Andrew Newsham, Jonathan Rigg and Diana Suhardiman. 2022. 'A Sustainable Livelihoods Framework for the 21st Century'. *World Development* 155: 105898. https://doi.org/10.1016/j.worlddev.2022.105898.

NDMA. 2015. *Turkana County Hazard Atlas*. Lodwar: National Drought Management Agency.

Neely, Costance, Sally Bunning and Andreas Wilkes. 2009. *Review of Evidence on Drylands Pastoral Systems and Climate Change: Implications and Opportunities for Mitigation and Adaptation*. FAO.

Neocleous, Mark. 2013. 'Resisting Resilience'. *Radical Philosophy* 1 (178): 2–7.

Niamir-Fuller, Maryam. 1999. *Managing Mobility in African Rangelands: The Legitimization of Transhumance*. London: Intermediate Technology Publications.

Niamir-Fuller, Maryam. 2023. 'Concluding Commentary'. *Nomadic Peoples* 27 (2): 315–21. https://doi.org/10.3197/np.2023.270208.

Nordstrom, Carolyin. 2004. *Shadows of War: Violence, Power, and International Profiteering in the Twenty-First Century*. Berkeley: University of California Press.

Novelli, Bruno. 1988. *Aspects of Karimojong Ethnosociology*. Museum Com. Kampala: Comboni Missionaries.

NRC. 1994. *Rangeland Health: New Methods to Classify, Inventory, and Monitor Rangelands*. Washington, D.C.: National Academy Press.

Oba, Gufu. 1992. 'Ecological Factors in Land Use Conflicts, Land Administration and Food Insecurity in Turkana, Kenya'. *Pastoralist Development Network (ODI) Paper* 23.

Oba, Gufu, NIls Chr. Stenseth and Walter J. Lusigi. 2000. 'New Perspectives on Sustainable Grazing Management in Arid Zones of Sub-Saharan Africa'. *BioScience* 50 (1): 35–50.

Ocaido, O., R.T. Muwazi and J. Opuda-Asibo. 2009. *Financial Analysis of Livestock Production Systems around Lake Mburo National Park, in South Western Uganda*. 21(5). Livestock Research for Rural Development.

Odhiambo, Michael Ochieng. 2014. *The Unrelenting Persistence of Certain Narratives*. London: IIED.

Ohta, Itaru. 2007. 'Marriage and Bridewealth Negotiations among the Turkana in Northwestern Kenya'. *African Study Monographs* 37: 24.

Okenwa, Doris. 2020. 'Contentious Benefits & Subversive Oil Politics in Kenya'. In *Land, Investment and Politics: Reconfiguring Eastern Africa's Pastoral Drylands*, ed. by J. Lind, D. Okenwa and I. Scoones, pp. 55–65. New York: Boydell and Brewer.

Bibliography

Oliveira, Thierry, Anantha Duraiappah and Gemma Shepherd. 2003. *The Global Drylands Imperative: Increasing Capabilities through an Ecosystem Approach for the Drylands*. UNEP.

Olsson, L., L. Eklundh and J. Ardö. 2005. 'A Recent Greening of the Sahel – Trends, Patterns and Potential Causes'. *Journal of Arid Environments* **63** (3): 556–66. https://doi.org/10.1016/j.jaridenv.2005.03.008.

Olwig, Kenneth. 2002. 'Landscape, Place, and the State of Progress'. In *Progress: Geographical Essays*, ed. by R.D. Stack. Baltimore: Johns Hopkins University Press.

Pain, Adam and Simon Levine. 2012. *A Conceptual Analysis of Livelihoods and Resilience*. HPG Commissioned Report.

Pappagallo, Linda. 2023. 'Confronting Uncertainties in Souther Turnisia: The Role of Migration and Collective Resource Management'. In *Pastoralism, Uncertainty and Development*, ed. by I. Scoones. Rugby: Practical Action Publishing.

Pascal, Blaise and A.J. Krailsheimer. 1966 [1678]. *Pensées*. Harmondsworth: Penguin.

Pelling, Mark, Detlef Müller-Mahn and John McCloskey. 2020. 'Disasters, Humanitarianism and Emergencies'. In *The Politics of Uncertainty*, pp. 127–40. London: Routledge.

Phillips, Kristin. 2018. *An Ethnography of Hunger: Politics, Subsistence, and the Unpredictable Grace of the Sun*. Bloomington: Indiana University Press.

Piasere, Leonardo. 2009. *I rom d'Europa. Una storia moderna*. 10 edizione. Roma: Laterza.

Pickett, Steward T.A., Mary L. Cadenasso and Morgan Grove. 2004. 'Resilient Cities: Meaning, Models, and Metaphor for Integrating the Ecological, Socio-Economic, and Planning Realms'. *Landscape and Urban Planning* **69** (4): 369–84. https://doi.org/10.1016/j.landurbplan.2003.10.035.

Pimm, Stuart. 1984. 'The Complexity and Stability of Ecosystems'. *Nature* 307 (5949): 321.

Pratt, D.J. and M.D. Gwynne. 1977. *Rangeland Management and Ecology in East Africa*. London: Hodder and Stoughton.

Procter, Caitlin. 2019. 'Claiming the State: The Everyday Lives of Palestinian Refugee Youth in East Jerusalem'. D.Phil. in Development Studies, University of Oxford.

Quarantelli, E.L. 1998. *What Is a Disaster?: Perspectives on the Question*. London: Routledge.

Reidy, Eugenie. 2012. 'You Will Not Die When Your Animals Are Shining: "Aid-Waiting" in Turkana'. *Development* 55 (4): 526–34. https://doi.org/10.1057/dev.2012.81.

Retaillé, Denis. 2013. 'From Nomadic to Mobile Space: A Theoretical Experiment (1976–2012)'. In *Nomadic and Indigenous Spaces: Productions and Cognitions*, ed. by J. Miggelbrink, J.O. Habeck, N. Mazzull and P. Koch. Farnham, Surrey, England; Burlington, VT: Ashgate.

Riesman, Paul. 1977. *Freedom in Fulani Social Life: An Introspective Ethnography*. Chicago: University of Chicago Press.

Rigg, Jonathan and Katie Oven. 2015. 'Building Liberal Resilience? A Critical Review from Developing Rural Asia'. *Global Environmental Change* 32: 175–86. https://doi.org/10.1016/j.gloenvcha.2015.03.007.

Robben, Antonius and Jeffrey Sluka. 2007. *Ethnographic Fieldwork: An Anthropological Reader*. Malden, MA ; Oxford: Blackwell.

Robbins, Michael. 2022. 'Look Back in Anger. A Radical Reading of Early Human Societies'. *Bookforum*.

Rodgers, Cory. 2018. 'Rural, Remote, Raiya: Social Differentiation on the Pastoralist Periphery in Turkana, Kenya'. Ph.D. diss, Anthropology, University of Oxford.

Rodgers, Cory and Greta Semplici. 2023. 'Special Issue: Sedentist Biases in Law, Policy and Practice'. *Nomadic Peoples* 27 (2): 155–329.

Roe, Emery. 1998. *Reading Policy Analysis and Formulation for Sustainable Livelihoods*. Sustainable Livelihoods Unit of United Nations Development Programme.

Roe, Emery. 2013. *Making the Most of Mess: Reliability and Policy in Today's Management Challenges*. Durham, NC; London: Duke University Press.

Roe, Emery. 2020. 'A New Policy Narrative for Pastoralism? Pastoralists as Reliability Professionals and Pastoralist Systems as Infrastructure'. *STEPS Working Paper* 113: 33.

Roe, Emery, Lynn Huntsinger and Keith Labnow. 1998. 'High-Reliability Pastoralism Versus Risk-Averse Pastoralism'. *The Journal of Environment & Development* 7 (4): 387–421. https://doi.org/10.1177/107049659800700404.

Rotarangi, Stephanie and Darryn Russell. 2009. 'Social-ecological Resilience Thinking: Can Indigenous Culture Guide Environmental Management?' *Journal of the Royal Society of New Zealand* 39 (4): 209–13. https://doi.org/10.1080/03014220909510582.

de Saint-Exupéry, Antoine. 1944. *The Little Prince*. London: Wheinemann.

Salza, Alberto. 1997. *Atlante Delle Popolazioni*. Torino: Unione Tipografica-Editrice Torinese.

Salza, Alberto. 2000. 'Cambiare per Vivere'. *La Stampa* 945.

Salza, Alberto. 2010. *Bambini perduti. Quando i piccoli non hanno bisogno dei grandi: storie della parte migliore del genere umano*. Milano: Sperling & Kupfer.

Salza, Alberto. 2014. Lecture 'Il Quinto Punto Cardinale: Orizzonti Monili in Africa'. COLLOQUIA. Festival delle idee, Foggia. 22 March.

Salza, Alberto. 2018. 'The African Triangle. Image Making and the Imagnal World in the Sub-Saharan Region'. In *Nuances africaines*, ed. by F. Janot. Nancy: Presses Universitaires de Lorraine.

Salza, Alberto. 2023. 'Drought and Floods at Lake Turkana: an Anomaly for Pastoralists?' Nomadic Peoples 27 (1): 95–99

Salza, Alberto. 2025. 'Quantum Table'. In Cyntia Concari and Roberto Marcatti (eds), *The Table Changes Course*, pp. 86–97. Bari: Sfera Edizioni.

Salzman, Philip Carl. 1980. *When Nomads Settle: Processes of Sedentarization as Adaptation and Response*. New York: Praeger.

Sandford, Stephen. 1983. *Management of Pastoral Development in the Third World*. Chichester: Wiley.

Santopietro, Ginevra. 2015. 'Fish As Food, Fish For Food. Produzione e Cultura Alimentare Di Una Piccola Comunità Di Pescatori Sul Lago Turkana, Kenya'. Master's diss., Antropologia culturale, Università di Torino.

Schilling, Janpeter, Moses Akuno, Jürgen Scheffran and Thomas Weinzierl. 2014. 'On Raids and Relations: Climate Change and Pastoral Conflict in Northern Kenya'. In *Climate Change and Conflict: Where to for Conflict Sensitive Climate Adaptation in Africa?*, ed. by S. Bronkhorst and U. Bob. Berlino: Berliner Wissenschaftsverlag.

Schipper, Lisa and Lara Langston. 2015. 'A Comparative Overview of Resilience Measurement Frameworks: Analyzing Indicators and Approaches'. *ODI Working Paper* 422. https://doi.org/10.13140/rg.2.1.2430.0882.

Scoones, Ian. 1995a. *Living with Uncertainty: New Directions in Pastoral Development in Africa*. London: Institute of Development Studies.

Scoones, Ian. 1995b. 'New Directions on Pastoral Development in Africa'. In *Living with Uncertainty: New Directions in Pastoral Development in Africa*. London: Institute of Development Studies.

Scoones, Ian. 1998. 'Sustainable Rural Livelihoods. A Framework For Analysis'. *IDS Working Papers* 72:22.

Scoones, Ian. 2009. 'Livelihoods Perspectives and Rural Development'. *The Journal of Peasant Studies* 36 (1): 171–96. https://doi.org/10.1080/03066150902820503.

Scoones, Ian. 2018. 'Review of The End of Desertification? Disputing Environmental Change in the Drylands by Roy H. Behnke and Michael Mortimore'. *Pastoralism* 8 (1): 26. https://doi.org/10.1186/s13570-018-0133-5.

Scoones, Ian. 2021. *Sustainable Livelihoods and Rural Development*. Rugby: Practical Action Publishing.

Scoones, Ian. 2023. 'Confronting Uncertainties in Pastoral Areas: Transforming Development from Control to Care'. *Social Anthropology/Anthropologie Sociale* 31 (4): 57–75. https://doi.org/10.3167/saas.2023.04132303.

Scott, James. 1998. *Seeing like a State: How Certain Schemes to Improve the Human Condition Have Failed*. New Haven: Yale University Press.

Scott, James. 2020. 'In the Praise of Floods – Luce Lecture with James Scott', Duke University.

Scott-Smith, Tom. 2018. 'Paradoxes of Resilience: A Review of the World Disasters Report 2016'. *Development and Change* 49 (2): 662–77. https://doi.org/10.1111/dech.12384.

Semplici, Greta. 2020. *Resilience in Action. Local Practices and Development/Humanitarian Policies. A Review of Resilience in the Drylands of Turkana*. London: Research and Evidence Facility (REF).

Semplici, Greta and Tom Campbell. 2023. 'The Revival of the Drylands: Re-Learning Resilience to Climate Change from Pastoral Livelihoods in East Africa'. *Climate and Development* 0 (0): 1–14. https://doi.org/10.1080/17565529.2022.2160197.

Semplici, Greta and Cory Rodgers. 2023. 'Sedentism as Doxa: Biases against Mobile Peoples in Law, Policy and Practice'. *Nomadic Peoples* 27 (2): 155–70. https://doi.org/10.3197/np.2023.270201.

Sen, Amartya. 1981. *Poverty and Famines: An Essay on Entitlement and Deprivation*. Oxford: Clarendon Press.

Shanahan, Mike. 2016. 'Media Perceptions and Portrayals of Pastoralists in Kenya, India and China'. In *The End of Desertification? Disputing Environmental Change in the Drylands*, ed. by R.H. Behnke and M. Mortimore, pp. 407–25. Heidelberg: Springer.

Shaw, Brent D. 1983. 'Eaters of Flesh, Drinkers of Milk': The Ancient Mediterranean Ideology of the Pastoral Nomad'. *Ancient Society* 13/14: VI-5-VI-315–31. https://doi.org/10.4324/9781003556909-8.

Simula, Giulia, Tsering Bum, Domenica Farinella, Natasha Maru, Tahira Shariff Mohamed, Masresha Taye and Palden Tsering. 2021. 'COVID-19 and Pastoralism: Reflections from Three Continents'. *The Journal of Peasant Studies* **48** (1): 48–72. https://doi.org/10.1080/03066150.2020.1808969.

Solnit, Rebecca. 2001. *Wanderlust: A History of Walking*. London: Penguin Books.

Soper, Robert. 1985. 'A Socio-Cultural Profile of Turkana District'. *Azania* 20: 181.

Spencer, Paul. 1965. *The Samburu: A Study of Gerontocracy in a Nomadic Tribe*. London: Routledge & Kegan Paul.

Stafford Smith, Mark. 2016. 'Desertification: Reflections on the Mirage'. In *The End of Desertification? Disputing Environmental Change in the Drylands, Springer earth system sciences*, ed. by R.H. Behnke and M. Mortimore. Heidelberg: Springer.

Stebbing, E.P. 1935. 'The Encroaching Sahara: The Threat to the West African Colonies'. *The Geographical Journal* **85** (6): 506. https://doi.org/10.2307/1785870.

Stenning, Derrick. 1959. *Savanna Nomads: A Study of the WoDaabe Pastoral Fulani of Western Bornu Province, Northern Region, Nigeria*. Oxford: Oxford University Press.

Sutton, David E. 2001. *Remembrance of Repasts: An Anthropology of Food and Memory*. Oxford: Berg.

Swift, Jeremy. 1996. 'Desertification: Narratives, Winners and Losers'. In *The Lie Of The Land: Challenging Received Wisdom On The African Environment*, African issues, ed. by M. Leach. Oxford; Portsmouth, NH: International African Institute in association with James Currey ; Heinemann.

Taiye, Selasi. 2014. *Ghana Must Go*. Penguin Book.

Testa, Gianmaria. 2006. *Seminatori Di Grano. Dall'altra Parte Del Mare*.

Thompson, Logan, Jason Rowntree, Wilhelm Windisch, Sinéad M. Waters, Laurence Shalloo and Pablo Manzano. 2023. 'Ecosystem Management Using Livestock: Embracing Diversity and Respecting Ecological Principles'. *Animal Frontiers* 13: 28–34. https://doi.org/10.1093/af/vfac094.

Thrift, Nigel. 2006. 'Space'. *Theory, Culture & Society* **23** (2–3): 139–46. https://doi.org/10.1177/0263276406063780.

Touber, Luc. 1994. 'Landforms and Soils'. In *Range Management Handbook of Kenya, Turkana District*, ed. by D. Herlocker, S. Shaabani and S. Wilkes. Nairobi, Kenya: Ministry of Agriculture, Livestock Development and Marketing (MALDM).

Tozzi, Arianna. 2021. 'An Approach to Pluralizing Socionatural Resilience through Assemblages'. *Progress in Human Geography* **45** (5): 1083–1104. https://doi.org/10.1177/0309132520983471.

Tsering, Palden and Ryan R. Unks. 2024. 'Navigating Rules of "the Range" beyond the Commons'. In *Researching Institutions in Natural Resource Governance*, ed. by F. Nunan, pp. 189–210. London: Routledge.

Turkana County. 2018. *County Integrated Development Plan (2018-202)*. Lodwar: Turkana County Government.

Turkana County. 2023. *Third County Integrated Development Plan 2023–2027*. Department of Finance and Economic Planning.

Turner, John C., Penelope J. Oakes, S. Alexander Haslam and Craig McGarty. 1994. 'Self and Collective: Cognition and Social Context'. *Personality and Social Psychology Bulletin* **20** (5): 454–63. https://doi.org/10.1177/0146167294205002.

Turner, Matthew D. and Eva Schlecht. 2019. 'Livestock Mobility in Sub-Saharan Africa: A Critical Review'. *Pastoralism* **9** (1): 1–15. https://doi.org/10.1186/s13570-019-0150-z.

Turner, Victor. 1987. *The Anthropology of Performance*. Baltimore: Johns Hopkins University Press.

Uexküll, J. von. 1957. 'A Stroll through the Worlds of Animals and Men: A Picture Book of Invisible Worlds'. In *Instinctive Behavior: The Development of a Modern Concept*. New York: International Universities Press.

UNDP. 2011. *The Forgotten Billion: MDG Achievement in the Drylands*.

UNDP and GoK. 2021. Rising Water Levels in Kenya's Rift Valley Lakes, Turkwel Gorge Dam and Lake Victoria. A Scoping Report. Nairobi. https://ir-library.ku.ac. ke/handle/123456789/22851

UNESCO. 2019. *Recognition of Transhumance as Intangible Heritage in the Mediterranean and the Alps*.

Unks, Ryan. 2023. 'Reframing Rangeland Systems Science Research in Kenya: A Synthesis of Social-Science Mixed Methods to Inform Integrative Analysis of Landscape Pattern and Process'. *Landscape Ecology* **38** (12): 4343–64. https://doi.org/10.1007/s10980-023-01723-w.

Valdés, Alberto. 1981. *Food Security for Developing Countries*. Boulder: Westview.

Vigh, Henrik. 2006. *Navigating Terrains of War: Youth and Soldiering in Guinea-Bissau*. New York: Berghahn.

Vigh, Henrik. 2009. 'Motion Squared: A Second Look at the Concept of Social Navigation'. *Anthropological Theory* **9** (4): 419–38. https://doi.org/10.1177/1463499609356044.

Volpato, Gabriele. 2025. *Desert Entanglements The Making of the Badiya by Sahrawi Refugees of Western Sahara*. New York; Oxford: Berghahn Books.

Von Grebmer, Klaus, Derek Headey, Tolulope Olofinbiyi, Doris Wiesmann, Heidi Fritschel, Sandra Yin and Yisehac Yohannes. 2013. *Global Hunger Index. The Challenge of Hunger: Building Resilience to Achieve Fod and Nutrition Security*. International Food Policy Research Institute.

Vrålstad, Kari. 2010. 'Sedentarization in Filtu Woreda, Ethiopia: Impacts on Health, Ecology and Society'. M.Sc. in International Environment and Development Studies, Norwegian University of Life Sciences.

Waiswa, C.D., B. Mugonola, R.S. Kalyango, S.J. Opolot, E. Tebanyang and V. Lomuria. 2019. *Pastoralism in Uganda. Theory, Practice, and Policy*. London: IIED.

Walker, B.H., J.L. Langridge and F. McFarlane. 1997. 'Resilience of an Australian Savanna Grassland to Selective and Non-Selective Perturbations'. *Australian Journal of Ecology* (22): 125–35.

Walker, Brian, C.S. Holling, Stephen Carpenter and Ann Kinzig. 2004. 'Resilience, Adaptability and Transformability in Social–Ecological Systems'. *Ecology and Society* **9** (2). https://doi.org/10.5751/ES-00650-090205.

Walker, Brian, D. Ludwig, C.S. Holling and R.M. Peterman. 1981. 'Stability of Semi-Arid Savanna Grazing Systems'. *The Journal of Ecology* **69** (2): 473. https://doi.org/10.2307/2259679.

Walker, Jeremy and Melinda Cooper. 2011. 'Genealogies of Resilience: From Systems Ecology to the Political Economy of Crisis Adaptation'. *Security Dialogue* **42** (2): 143–60. https://doi.org/10.1177/0967010611399616.

Walther, Olivier J., Allen M. Howard and Denis Retaillé. 2015. 'West African Spatial Patterns of Economic Activities: Combining the "Spatial Factor" and "Mobile Space" Approaches'. *African Studies* **74** (3): 346–65. https://doi.org/10.1080/00020184.2015.1041286.

Western, David. 1982. 'The Environment and Ecology of Pastoralists in Arid Savannas'. *Development and Change* **13** (2):183–211. https://doi.org/10.1111/j.1467-7660.1982.tb00117.x.

Westoby, Mark, Brian Walker and Imanuel Noy-Meir. 1989. 'Opportunistic Management for Rangelands Not at Equilibrium'. *Journal of Range Management* **42** (4): 266–74.

WFC. 1974. *Communication from the Commission to the Council World Food Conference*. Commission of the European Communities.

WFS. 1996. *Report of the World Food Summit: Part One*. Food and Agriculture Organization of the United Nations.

Winderl, Thomas. 2014. *Disaster Resilience Measurements. Stocktaking of Ongoing Efforts in Developing Systems for Measuring Resilience*. UNDP.

~ Annexes ~

Annex 1. Physical map

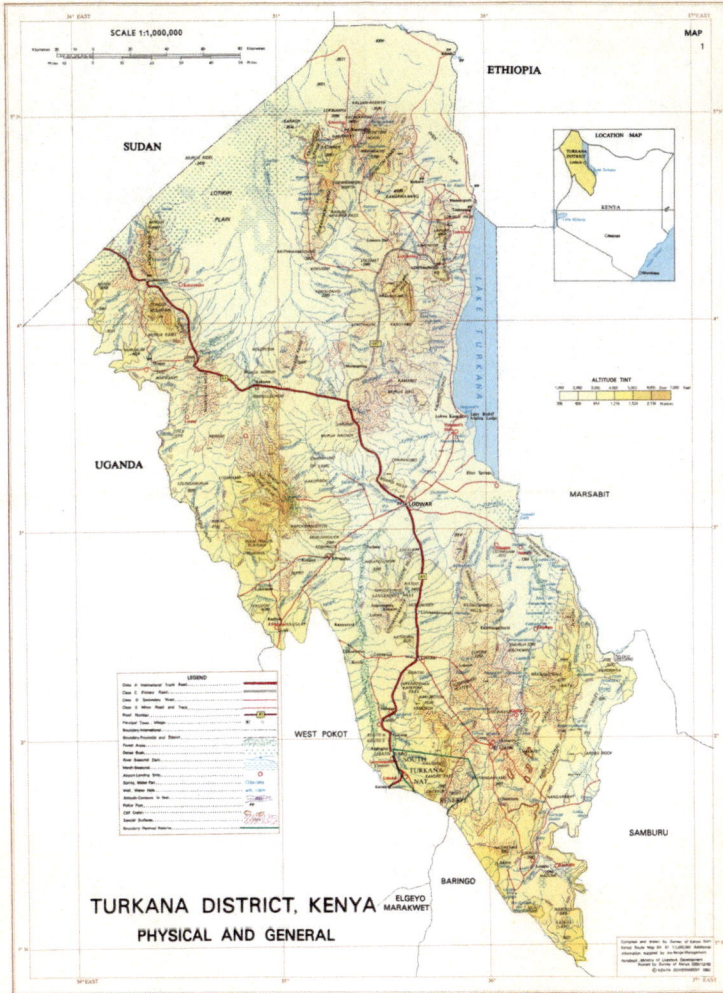

Annex 2. Landforms and soils map

Source: Ministry Of Agriculture, Livestock Development and Marketing; and GTZ, Fed. Rep. Germany. *Kenya Range Management Handbook* (Volume II, 9).

Satellite Image Interpretation, Field Survey and Map Compilation: L. Touber, September–October 1990. Base map: Survey of Kenya. Cartography: G. de Souza, Dept. Geography, Univ. Nairobi. This map is excluded from the book's CC BY licence.

Annexes

Annex 3. Geology map

Source: Ministry Of Agriculture, Livestock Development and Marketing; and GTZ, Fed. Rep. Germany. *Kenya Range Management Handbook* (Volume II, 9).

Map Compilation (left hand map): L. Touber. Data (right hand map): Norconsult, 1983. This map is excluded from the book's CC BY licence.

Annex 4. Restriction on livestock movements

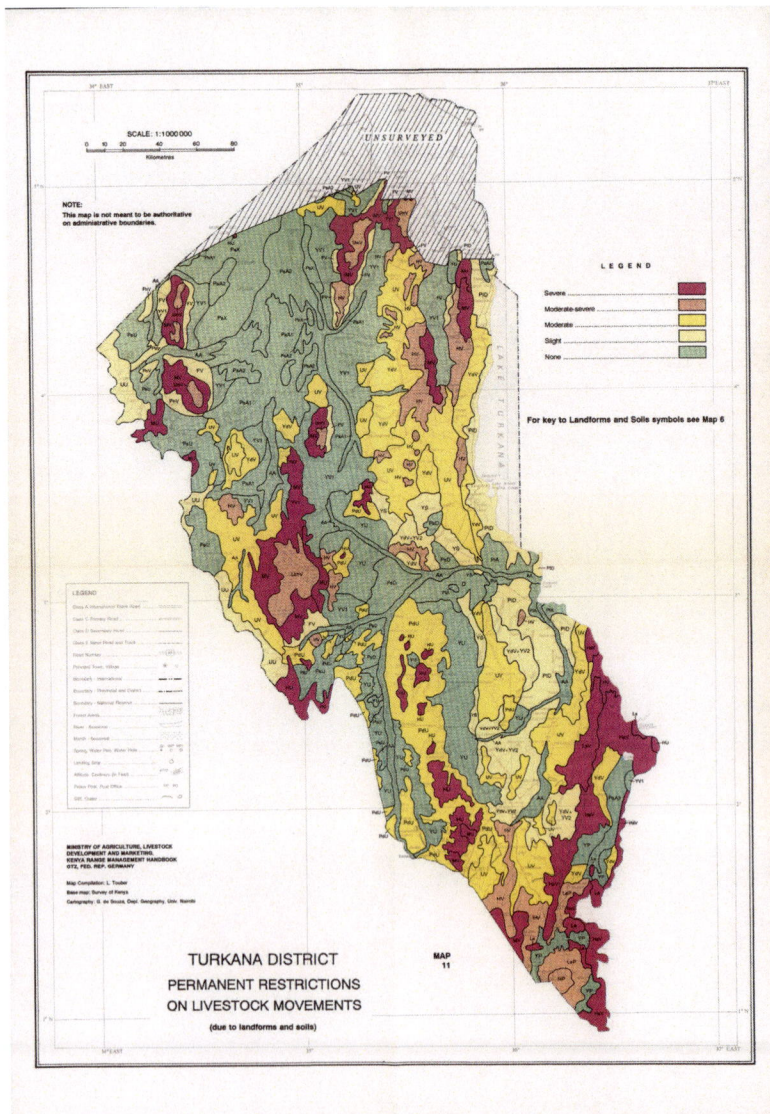

Source: Ministry Of Agriculture, Livestock Development and Marketing; and GTZ, Fed. Rep. Germany. *Kenya Range Management Handbook* (Volume II, 9).

Satellite Image Interpretation, Field Survey and Map Compilation: L. Touber. Base map: Survey of Kenya. Cartography: G. de Souza, Dept. Geography, Univ. Nairobi. This map is excluded from the book's CC BY licence.

Annexes

Annex 5. Vegetation map

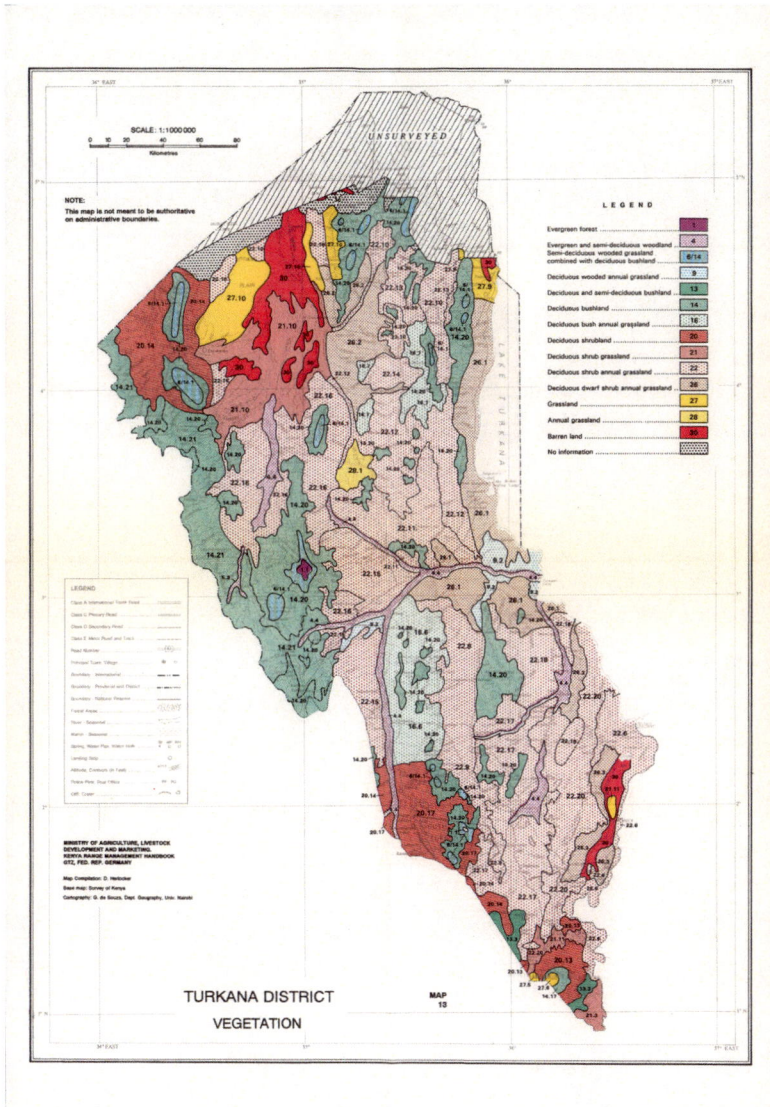

Source: Ministry Of Agriculture, Livestock Development and Marketing; and GTZ, Fed. Rep. Germany. *Kenya Range Management Handbook* (Volume II, 9).

Satellite Image Interpretation, Field Survey and Map Compilation: D. Herlocker. Base map: Survey of Kenya. Cartography: G. de Souza, Dept. Geography, Univ. Nairobi. This map is excluded from the book's CC BY licence.

Annex 6. Selected list of laws, declarations reports and policies

As discussed, a positive reframing of mobility and pastoralism is increasingly gaining purchase in some international organisations and policy circles. Below follows a non-exhaustive list of relevant laws, declarations, reports and policies that go in the direction of supporting pastoralism. However, despite good intentions, these often remain nice words from which little action follows: see a good discussion in the book *Crossing Boundaries: Legal and Policy Arrangements for Cross-border Pastoralism* by Davies and colleagues (2018). In addition, they are often more or less inadvertently imbued with old mind sets and assumptions that reduce the effectiveness of the interventions. In a special issue I edited with Cory Rodgers, we referred to these legacies as sedentist biases (Rodgers and Semplici 2023). Generally policies that support pastoral mobility are lacking. In the absence of legislation that protects and regulates mobility, pastoralists enter into conflict with other resource users and the state. Prohibitive legislation that excludes pastoralists from certain resource areas also causes increasing grazing pressure in other areas, leading to rangeland degradation and reducing the environmental benefits of pastoralism, as well as impoverishing and making vulnerable entire communities with the danger of losing cultures and knowledges.

The Dana Declaration (2002, 2022)

The Dana Declaration on Mobile Peoples and Conservation is the outcome of the Dana Conference, an international meeting of social and natural scientists and NGOs that first took place in Wadi Dana Nature Reserve in Jordan in early April 2002, and again twenty years after in September 2022. The Dana Declaration is an attempt to forge a new partnership between conservationists and mobile peoples in order to ensure future conservation policies help maintain the earth's ecosystems, species and genetic diversity while respecting the rights of indigenous and traditional communities which have been disregarded in the past.

Framework Convention on the protection and sustainable development of the Carpathians (2003)

For Eastern Europe, it provides that parties should take appropriate measures 'to ensure a high level of protection and sustainable use of natural and semi-natural habitats, their continuity and connectivity' (Art. 4) and should aim at 'preserving the traditional architecture, land-use patterns, local breeds and domestic animals and cultivated plant varieties' (Art. 11).

The Framework Convention on environmental protection for sustainable development in Central Asia (2006)

It lays down general obligations for cooperation in the management of transboundary resources. It provides for the use of regional projects and other bilateral and multilateral schemes and mechanisms for cooperation to combat land degradation.

The Segovia Declaration of Nomadic and Transhumant Pastoralism (2007)

This declaration was made at the world gathering of nomadic and transhumant pastoralists in Segovia, Spain in September 2007. Two hundred nomadic and transhumant pastoralists urged governments and international organisations to recognise the importance of pastoralism and to support pastoralist communities worldwide.

AU Border Programme (2007)

The African Union Border Programme has also sought to facilitate cross-border integration of African states and the development of local cross-border cooperation initiatives within the framework of the Regional Economic Communities (RECs), such as COMESA, IGAD and ECOWAS.

COMESA Green Pass (2008)

The Common Market for Eastern and Southern Africa has since 2008 developed a *Green Pass* system, a commodity-based health certification that offers opportunities to formalise and facilitate transnational movements and trade of livestock in the region.

AU Policy Framework for Pastoralism in Africa (2010)

Approved in 2011, the African Union Policy Framework for Pastoralism in Africa provides guidance on, and promotes the development and implementation of, pro-pastoral policies by African Union Member States. Among the eight principles articulated in the framework is the importance of strategic mobility for efficient use and protection of rangelands. It was adopted in part to facilitate policy coordination and harmonisation and provide a platform to address 'in a holistic manner, the many challenges confronting pastoral communities' including challenges associated with its transnational character.

The N'djamena Declaration and The Nouakchott Declaration (2013)

In 2013, two regional forums brought together policymakers from countries in the Sahara–Sahel region to discuss the strengthening of policies related to pastoralism. In May, a meeting of ministers from North and West Africa in N'djamena, Chad, resulted in the N'djamena Declaration concerning the contribution of pastoral livestock to the security and development of the Saharo–Sahelian areas. The N'djamena declaration affirms that pastoral practices help promote security in the region, and that mobility requires unhindered free movement of herds and animal products across national borders. The Declaration includes recommendations to adopt decentralisation policies which 'fully involve nomadic and sedentary communities', to consider livestock in spatial planning and to 'reinforce interstate co-operation with a view to facilitating cross-border movements and regional trade'. Representatives of six West African countries met in Nouakchott, Mauritania, and adopted the Nouakchott Declaration on Pastoralism. The Nouakchott Declaration recognises pastoralism as an 'effective practice and lifestyle suited to the Sahelo–Saharan conditions and adopts an objective of securing the lifestyle and means of production of pastoral populations, and increasing the gross output of livestock production by at least 30% in the 6 concerned countries over the next 5 years'.

FAO Technical Guide on Improving Governance of Pastoral Lands (2016)

In 2016 FAO launched a technical guide on improving governance of pastoral lands to support implementation of the 2012 Voluntary guidelines on the governance of responsible tenure of land, fisheries and forests in the context of national food security, which shows shared resource use and mobility as the twin pillars supporting pastoral production systems.

FAO and IUCN Crossing Boundaries: Legal and Policy Arrangements for Cross-Border Pastoralism (2018)

FAO and IUCN commissioned a review of legal and policy arrangements for cross-border mobility with the aim to inspire and inform action by governments and civil society actors in developing legislation and other legal instruments and cooperative agreements for transboundary pastoralism.

IFAD How to do: engaging with pastoralists – a holistic development approach (2018).

The How to Do Note first outlines the problems developers need to be aware of in pastoral development. It also indicates which IFAD policies are relevant for the key issues of pastoral development and provides guidelines for engaging in pastoral development in IFAD-supported projects and programmes. It describes how to balance and apply IFAD's procedures, instruments and practical guidance. Building on the Lesson Learned part of the pastoral development toolkit and on the key issues, a general framework for pastoral development is set out and additional guidance is provided for designing and implementing projects in pastoral areas.

FAO Making way: Developing frameworks for Pastoral Mobility (2022)

The handbook sponsored by FAO in 2022 aims to provide guidance on the development of legal and policy frameworks for securing mobility for various pastoral production systems and practices. It addresses a gap between policies and scholarship by providing the key elements for the development of legal and policy frameworks for pastoral mobility. It calls for the legal recognition and securing of pastoral mobility as a way of safeguarding and facilitating a continuous stream of economic and social benefits for pastoralists, countries and the environment.

UNESCO's Intergovernmental Committee for the Safeguarding of the Intangible Cultural Heritage (2022)

The multinational file *Transhumance, the seasonal driving of livestock* was submitted to UNESCO in March 2022 by ten European countries (Albania, Andorra, Austria, Croatia, France, Greece, Italy, Luxembourg, Romania, and Spain) after transhumance was recognised as a national heritage in each of the country. This submission was an extension of a similar element registered in 2019 in the Representative List of the Intangible Cultural Heritage of Humanity, *Transhumance, the seasonal migration of herds along the migratory routes in the Mediterranean area and in the Alps*, proposed by Austria, Greece and Italy.

The European Union's Common Agricultural Policy (CAP)

The CAP articulates guidelines for supporting and improving agriculture. The CAP's detailed implementation framework is set at the country level in line with the principle of subsidiarity. Regulation number 1307/2013 of the European Parliament and the Council establishes rules for direct payments made to farmers and pastoralists under support schemes within the framework of the CAP. Commission Decision number 2010/300/EU amended Decision number 2001/672/EC as regards time periods for the movement of bovine animals to summer grazing areas.

IYRP (2026)

The UN General Assembly's declaration of 2026 as the International Year of Rangelands and Pastoralists highlights the global significance of rangelands and pastoralists. The initiative seeks to increase awareness of the value of rangelands and pastoralism for food security, the economy, the environment and cultural heritage, fill knowledge gaps through participatory research and strategic communication, advocate for policies supporting sustainable land use, livelihoods and biodiversity conservation through pastoralism, promote investment in rangelands and pastoralists as a climate solution.

Transhumance Protocols

The East African Community Protocol on environment and natural resource management includes a section on rangelands, which calls for the 'development of common policies, law and strategies for ensuring sustainable development of rangelands' (Art. 22). It also includes a section on managing 'transboundary resources that calls on states to jointly develop and adopt harmonized common policies and strategies for the sustainable management of transboundary natural resources' (Art. 9). However, the Protocol, which was signed in 2006, has not yet entered into force (Davies et al. 2018: 52).

The Economic Commission of West African States (ECOWAS) and the Intergovernmental Authority on Development (IGAD) have developed transhumance protocols and committed Member States to collaborating in the facilitation of pastoral mobility.

ECOWAS decision on the regulation of transhumance between Member States provides for the free passage of all animals across the borders of all Member States. Transhumance is conditional on issuance of an ECOWAS International Transhumance Certificate, which contains details on the 'composition of the herd, the vaccinations given, the itinerary of the herds, the border posts to be crossed, and the final destination' (Article 5). The certificate enables authorities to monitor herds before they leave the country of origin, protect the health of local herds and inform host communities of the arrival of transhumance animals. The primary mechanism of this system is the International Transhumance Certificate (ITC), which functions as a herd passport to help monitor cross-border movement. The certificate must include information on the herd, vaccinations, itinerary and border posts to be used. The Decision also provides for pastoral rights and obligations and conflict resolution. Despite its comprehensiveness and regional coverage, the ECOWAS ITC system has faced implementation challenges (Davies et al. 2018: 57). Herders object to the bureaucracy and administrative harassment involved in obtaining the necessary paperwork to support transboundary movement and complain that, when they do arrive in the host country, livestock corridors are blocked and reception zones are occupied; on the other hand, local populations complain that pastoralists damage crops and protected areas and commit violence against locals. In addition, authorities claim that many pastoralists are crossing the border on traditional livestock routes rather than at designated crossings, and without using an ITC (Davies et al. 2018).

The Intergovernmental Authority on Development (IGAD) Transhumance Protocol was approved in early 2020 by IGAD for its eight Member States in eastern Africa along the lines of the ECOWAS International Transhumance Certificate. It commits Member States to harmonising legislation and policies on livestock and pastoral practices, animal health and land use in order to facilitate its implementation (FAO, 2022: 9, 29)

Bilateral Agreements

There are numerous bilateral agreements for the regulation of transboundary livestock migration. In West Africa, there are several examples of bilateral treaties on transhumance. In the late 1980s, Mali began negotiating treaties with its neighbours: Burkina Faso (1988), the Niger (1988), Mauritania (1989), Senegal (1993) and Côte d'Ivoire (1994). They provide for vaccination and health certificates, border documents, seasons and duration of transhumance, entry and exit points, geographical limits on pastoralism, and dispute resolution between pastoralists and farmers (Davies et al. 2018: 55). In 2013, a cross-border animal health agreement was signed between Uganda and Kenya. The Italy–Switzerland Convention concerning frontier traffic and grazing (1953) provides rights, customs procedures and tax exemptions for frontier inhabitants grazing their herds in the frontier zone. The Belgium–France Arrangement concerning frontier pastures (1982) sets conditions and a permitting process for transboundary use of both daily and seasonal pastures in the frontier zones. The China–Nepal Agreement on cross-border grazing of inhabitants of border areas (2012) regulates grazing zones and activities that may be undertaken by herders who cross the border, and sets up a process for annual meetings of local governments to agree on livestock quotas, time frames and disease prevention (Davies et al. 2018: 56). The Iran–Iraq Agreement concerning transhumance (1975) provides for use of the grazing land within the countries' frontier zones, in accordance with stipulated conditions. The Agreement is no longer in force (Davies et al. 2018: 56).

Country Legislation

Several countries have legislated on pastoral mobility (see more from Davies et al. 2018; FAO 2022):

- Spain's law on cattle trails (1995) emphasises the social and environmental importance of seasonal livestock migration.

- The Stock Route Management Act of Queensland, Australia (2002) is the legal framework for managing the network of stock routes and reserves for travelling stock in the State.

- Morocco's law on transhumance and rangeland management (2016) articulates the principles and establishes the institutional framework for management of rangelands and pastoral mobility, guarantees pastoralists' rights of access to and use of rangelands and their resources, and provides for the settlement of disputes that may arise in the course of transhumance.

- The Pastoral Code of the Niger (2010) states that mobility is a fundamental right of pastoralists that is recognised and guaranteed by the state and local government authorities, noting that it constitutes a rational and sustainable mode of exploitation of pastoral resources.

- Law number 3016 of the Province of Neuquén in Argentina (2016) guarantees mobility between summer and winter grazing areas for pastoralist families and their livestock, recognising this as integral to environmental conservation and respecting the natural and cultural heritage of the region. The law affirms that livestock migration corridors be used primarily for pastoral mobility, and prohibits their use for non-complementary or incompatible purposes.

- The pastoral code of Mauritania declares illegal 'any form of exclusive appropriation of pastoral space' (Article 14) and prohibits any development that may harm the interests of pastoralists or limit their access to pastoral resources.

- The Pastoral Charter of Mali mandates local authorities, in collaboration with the competent traditional authorities, crop farmer organisations and local technical services to establish the transhumance calendar 'in a concerted manner, each year if necessary'. The calendar specifies the maximum periods that the livestock will spend in each locality and must be communicated to pastoralists in an appropriate form (Article 22).

- Kyrgyzstan Law on Pastures, 2009: provides that pastures may be allocated to foreign users in accordance with interstate and intergovernmental agreements (Art. 13), though no such agreements currently exist.

- Mali Pastoral Charter, 2001: allows entry of herds from neighbouring countries into Mali on condition that those countries also allow entry of Malian livestock (Art. 23).

- Burkina Faso, Guinea and Mali have adopted laws that provide pastoralists the right to move animals across national borders. In the Côte d'Ivoire, Decree No. 96-431 (June 1996) regulates external transhumance, establishes a calendar and governs movements within the country. Subsequently adopted decrees and orders establish dispute-resolution mechanisms, compensation measures for damage caused to livestock or crops, and other appropriate measures.

- The South African Animal Improvement Act (1998) provides for the issuing of permits for citizens of Lesotho to graze cattle in South Africa. A few years ago, this system came under criticism when South African residents alleged that the South African Department of Agriculture, Forestry and Fisheries lacked capacity to effectively enforce the permit system, with the result that Lesotho farmers were grazing animals in South Africa illegally, leading to overgrazing and spread of disease.

- Cameroon adopted legislation to identify corridors used by herders from Nigeria and the Niger; the legislation has been criticised as fundamentally inflexible, because it does not allow for transhumance routes to change as necessary depending on conditions.